A HISTORY OF

MODERN CRITICISM

1750-1950

IN FIVE VOLUMES

OTHER BOOKS BY RENÉ WELLEK

Immanuel Kant in England

The Rise of English Literary History

Theory of Literature (*with Austin Warren*)

Concepts of Criticism

Essays on Czech Literature

Confrontations

A HISTORY OF MODERN

Criticism: 1750-1950

BY RENÉ WELLEK

The Age of Transition

New Haven and London
YALE UNIVERSITY PRESS

THE THIRD and fourth volumes of this *History of Modern Criticism* have turned out much longer and have taken much more time than I originally thought possible. The incredible bulk of critical writing in the 19th century, the pattern of documentation established and imposed by the first two volumes, the long temporal span of these next two, and the need of expansion to two new countries, the United States and Russia, are, I trust, sufficient explanations for the delay in the execution and the size of the volumes. I postpone consideration of Spain, as Spanish criticism before the so-called generation of '98 seems largely a reflection of French and German developments. A backward glance at the 19th century in Volume 5 will hopefully suffice.

Still, something should be said in definition of the aim, theme, and method of the work, which in part reasserts the Preface of the first volume and in part takes some account of the objections raised against it. I am mainly concerned with tracing the history of literary theory, i.e. poetics of all imaginative writing, whether in verse or prose. I try to keep a middle course between general aesthetics on the one extreme and literary history and mere literary opinion on the other. I am convinced that literary theory cannot be divorced from aesthetics and from practical criticism in the sense of judgment and analysis of single works of art. The attempts made, e.g. by Northrop Frye in the "Polemical Introduction" to his *Anatomy of Criticism* (1957) to divorce theory (which he calls criticism) from the history of taste and to argue that "the study of literature can never be founded on value-judgments" (p. 20) are surely doomed to failure. Literary theories, principles, criteria cannot be arrived at *in vacuo:* every critic in history has developed his theory in contact with concrete works of art which he had to select, interpret, analyze, and, after all, judge. The literary opinions, rankings, and judgments of a critic are buttressed, confirmed, and developed by his theories, and theories are drawn from and supported, illustrated, made concrete, and plausible by an inspection of works of art. The subject forms a totality from which we cannot abstract single strands without serious damage to its understanding and meaning.

There may be some doubt whether I have always preserved the right proportions of aesthetics, theory, literary history, and practical criticism but this, I believe, is not a theoretical question that can be settled *a priori* but an empirical decision that has to be made case by case. As long as I keep my general object steadily in mind, I must judge how much of general aesthetics, literary history, and the history of taste enters the argument. I am convinced that these subjects will enter differently in different ages, countries, and contexts. Thus in the 19th century more attention must be given to literary historiography than in earlier times; and in the later 19th century less attention may be devoted to abstract aesthetics than was necessary when discussing the early part of the century.

An author has the right to define for himself the nature and scope of his book. I cannot see that the divorce between theory and practical criticism is possible, nor did I want to write the kind of book Saintsbury provided when he deliberately rejected interest in theory and aesthetics. Nor can I be convinced by the objection that "criticism" does not constitute a unified subject at all. Erich Auerbach has argued in *Romanische Forschungen, 62* (1956), 387–97, that literary criticism is not a unified subject because of the number of possible problems and crossings of problems, the extreme diversity of its presuppositions, aims, and accents. But this diversity (still aimed at a single subject—literature) is precisely the topic of the book: one of its basic motifs is the sorting out of the different emphases, approaches, methods, concerns, and interests. But these discriminations, judgments, and rankings do not require an Alexandrian eclecticism, an anarchical relativism; nor can they, on the other hand, imply a denial of a spirit of tolerance, of historical empathy, and of scrupulous accuracy. Complete relativism, as advocated by some scholars, leads to skepticism and finally to a paralysis of judgment: to a surrender of the very reasons for the existence of criticism. I keep, and want to keep, a point of view and am convinced of the truths of several doctrines and the error of others, though I know that some doctrines may be acceptable with careful reservations, in special contexts. But this core of convictions (expounded elsewhere, in *Theory of Literature* and in many scattered writings now collected as *Concepts of Criticism*) is, I hope, never obtruded or imposed as a fixed, preconceived pattern. It is to emerge from the history, just as the history itself, in its turn, can be understood only with a net of questions and answers in mind. Neither relativism nor absolutism is my guiding standard, but a "perspectivism" that tries to see the object from all possible sides and is convinced that there *is* an object: the elephant in spite of all the diverse opinions of the blind men. How can the claim be justified that I or any other historian is not another of the blind men—seizing the trunk, the tusk, the tail, or the foot of the elephant alone? The only answer is precisely that which grows out of history itself: a body of doctrines and insights, judgments and theories which are the accumulated wisdom of mankind. Thus, I hope, the book does not simply leave its reader floundering among a welter of opinions, nor does it, look down at history as a series of failures, as doomed attempts to scramble to the heights of our present-day glories. On the contrary, this book is written with the conviction that history and theory explain each other, that there is a profound unity of fact and idea, past and present.

Such a book could not have been written without the encouragement and help of institutions and friends. I owe a heavy debt of gratitude to the Guggenheim Foundation, which made possible an instructive trip to Europe in 1957, and to the American Council of Learned Societies and the Fulbright Commission, which allowed me to spend a year (1959–60) mainly in Italy and England. The Rockefeller and the Bollingen Foundations have allowed me to take another leave of absence from academic duties in 1963–64. Friends have read parts of the manuscript and made valuable suggestions. I in particular recall gratefully Edith Kern, Lowry Nelson, Jr., Stephen G. Nichols, Jr., Blanche A. Price, Mr. and Mrs. R. W. Riddle, Nonna D. Shaw, Alexander Welsh, and William K. Wimsatt. Nils Sahlin helped with the proofs. David Horne has been a careful editor. It seems not the habit nowadays to acknowledge the simple fact that such a book would be impossible without liberal access to great libraries. The Yale University Library comes first on my list, but in Europe I used the Biblioteca Nazionale in Florence, the Alessandrina in Rome, the British Museum in London, the Bodleian and the Library of the Tailorian Institute at Oxford. They all deserve thanks for their hospitality.

R. W.

New Haven, Connecticut
June 1964

CONTENTS

INTRODUCTION TO VOLUMES 3 AND 4

THIRTY OR FORTY years ago the later 19th century would have inevitably appeared as the golden age of criticism. This was true especially in France; the reputation of Sainte-Beuve and Taine stood high, higher than that of any other critics in the whole history of literature whose reputations were established almost entirely by criticism. But in other countries also, criticism became a central preoccupation, a favored genre, and the critic a great public and national figure: Belinsky in Russia, De Sanctis in Italy, Brandes in Denmark, Menéndez y Pelayo in Spain, Matthew Arnold in England. Significantly, only Germany and the United States appeared to have lacked comparable figures, though in retrospect Henry James seems a great critic indeed, and Heine, Nietzsche, and Dilthey can hardly be overlooked as critics, though their reputations were established on different grounds.

The enormous public role of criticism in the century was supported and paralleled by an unprecedented development of the study and discussion of literature in general. The number of critics reflects the number of literary magazines and manifestos, and the growth of academic concern for literature. The role of the *Edinburgh Review,* the *Quarterly Review,* and *Blackwood's Magazine* in the early decades of the 19th century is matched by that of the *Fortnightly Review* or the *Saturday Review* in later years. In France hardly anything can compare with the role of the *Revue des Deux Mondes,* in Italy with that of the *Nuova antologia,* in the United States with that of the *North American Review,* in Germany with that of the *Grenzboten* and *Preussische Jahrbücher,* and in Russia with that of *Sovremmenik* and *Otechestvennye Zapiski.* Monographs have been written and many more could be written about the role of the large 19th-century reviews in molding public opinion and particularly in determining literary taste and discussing literary ideas.

The role of the universities was hardly less important. The French speak of a "critique universitaire" which had its beginnings in the eloquent courses given to large audiences at the Sorbonne soon after the Restoration by Abel François Villemain. Brunetière was a professor at the École Normale for many years. Even Sainte-Beuve and Taine appeared on academic rostrums. Matthew Arnold was Professor of Poetry at Oxford for ten years. De Sanctis became Professor of Comparative Literature at the University of Naples in 1870, and Carducci was a professor at Bologna for more than four decades. In Germany much serious literary study passed into the hands of university teachers: Nietzsche was in his youth Professor of Classics at Basel; Dilthey was Professor of Philosophy all through his long adult life (from 1866 to 1911). In the United States only Lowell was a critic with academic associations, while in Russia criticism remained largely in the hands of journalists and free-lance writers.

Academic literary study was not, of course, necessarily critical. In general it rather encouraged the development of literary history. The expansion of literary history into practically all ages and nations is largely the work of the 19th century. Literary historiography was founded in the 18th century as a subject, but it floundered then between the brilliant speculations of a Herder and the laborious, antiquarian compilations of a Tiraboschi or a Thomas Warton. Narrative literary history did not exist before the romantic movement. The Schlegels were the first modern literary historians, and in their wake Sismondi, Fauriel, Ampère, and Villemain created French literary historiography. At first Italy and England, which had no successor to Warton, lagged strangely behind. Still, the seeds sown in the early decades sprouted much later in the great works of Gervinus and Hettner, Taine and Brunetière, De Sanctis and Brandes, and their innumerable followers. Literary history supplied criticism with a new, unlimited mass of materials and problems—a challenge that proved by its very enormity paralyzing.

Nobody can deny the incredible bulk of the criticism of the time, or the expansion of its claims, the proliferation of its methods and materials, the increase of its prestige. But from a present-day point of view we might arrive at a more sober and less favorable judgment of the achievements of criticism proper during the seventy years under consideration. One could even argue that the second half of the 19th century constitutes in some respects a decline or even an aberration in the history of criticism.

If we consider the central task of criticism to be the definition and description of the nature of poetry and literature—poetics, literary theory—we might come to the disconcerting conclusion that the later 19th century did not advance and often rather retreated from the systematic achievements of the great romantic critics. If we ignore the extravagant and erratic E. S. Dallas, no poetic theory was produced in England that could claim novelty and systematic coherence. Even in Germany, the home of romantic theories, little was written after Vischer's eclectic *Ästhetik* that is more than a restatement of the doctrines of Goethe and Schiller, Humboldt and Hegel, if we except the highly original though hardly noticed young Nietzsche. The main new enterprise of the time—pursued particularly in France by Taine, Hennequin, Brunetière, and Zola, but also in Germany by Dilthey and Wilhelm Scherer and in Russia by Alexander Veselovsky—was the attempt to set up a science of poetics on the analogy of the natural sciences. I believe we would agree today that this enterprise failed dismally. The related aesthetics of realism and naturalism—whatever their historical justification as an antiromantic weapon of polemics may have been—must appear today extremely inadequate as aesthetics, at least on this side of the Iron Curtain. They led to a confusion of life and art, to a denial of the imagination, to a misunderstanding of the nature of art as making, as creating, a world of symbols. Historicism, the other great achievement of the 19th century, which immensely widened the horizons in time and space and increased the sense of the variety of art and its forms, also had its adverse effects on criticism: it led to a crippling relativism and an anarchy of values that became more and more conspicuous as the century advanced.

Sheer subjectivism, "impressionism" in criticism, was only the reverse side of the same coin. "The adventures of the soul among masterpieces" is only another formula for the loss of a sense of values, for relativism and anarchy. The well-defined position of the art-for-art's-sake movement, which was valuable as a reaction against Philistinism and crude didacticism, also led to dehumanizing results as it surrendered every claim to a social and philosophical significance of art. Nor can we deny the dessicating narrowness of the new French classicism of Désiré Nisard and Brunetière, or the Victorian limits of the "culture" propounded by Arnold, or the obtuse fierceness of the moralism of Tolstoy.

It seems not too rash a generalization about 19th-century criticism to say that it lost its grasp on the unity of content and form: that it went either to the extremes of didacticism or to the extremes of art-for-art's-sake formalism—or, to vary this dichotomy, to the extremes of claiming mystical insight into the supernatural on behalf of art or to reducing it to a mere technicality, a game or craft. Poe, who combines both views, illustrates the dilemma early in the century. Mallarmé, who dreamed of a "negative aesthetics of silence," of a single book that would supersede all other books, faced it at the threshold of the 20th century. We could even argue that so deft and competent a writer as Sainte-Beuve—wide-ranging, subtle, learned, and sensitive—led criticism astray into biography and even, on occasion, into anecdotage and gossip-mongering.

But if we look at this indictment we must ultimately be struck by its injustice or, at least, its inadequacy. The 19th century precisely by its divergent efforts in all directions presents us rather with a laboratory of criticism, with an enormous, ceaseless debate in which every possible position was pushed to its extreme. We can observe the working out (and sometimes the reduction to absurdity) of almost all the theories that are still with us: scientism, historicism, realism, naturalism, didacticism, aestheticism, symbolism, etc. But most important, from the discussions of these issues critical personalities emerge, not just persons but personalities with their individual mental physiognomies, their contradictions, their patterns of tensions, their triumphs and defeats. That is why a history of criticism cannot be merely a history of ideas *in vacuo*, a mere tracing of concepts and arguments. Happily, concepts, arguments, and doctrines come alive in the work of a great critic in a configuration that is not repeated anywhere else, that is unique and therefore valuable if we value personality and man.

Among these critics were a few who built, as it were, a bridge between the early 19th century and our time and who preserved the essence of the great tradition and transmitted it to us. They are, as I hope to show, the greatest critics of the time: Taine and Baudelaire in France; De Sanctis in Italy; Nietzsche and Dilthey in Germany; Henry James in the United States. These critics can best be understood in terms of a continuity that is still obvious in such early figures as Belinsky, Heine, Carlyle, or Emerson. Taine is basically a Hegelian; Baudelaire summarized motifs of the German romantics that filtered through to him by devious ways, via Carlyle, Poe, and even Coleridge (second-hand); De Sanctis is, as is Dilthey, in the direct line of succession from the Schlegels and Hegel. Nietzsche is nourished by Schopenhauer and the romantic classical philologists. Henry James is saturated with an almost Goethean sense of the organicity of art. These critics prepared the way for the regeneration that came in the 20th century with Croce, Valéry, T. S. Eliot, and many others. Croce goes back to De Sanctis and further, to the Germans. Valéry knows Mallarmé and Poe. Eliot draws on the immediate French sources and on Coleridge. But whatever the exact contacts and channels to the past may be, something has been reconstituted in the 20th century that had fallen apart in the 19th: a sense of the unity of content and form, a grasp of the nature of art.

There is one feature of 19th-century criticism which we must not minimize: nationalism. Clearly criticism is not an affair of a single nation: ideas wander, migrate, blow about, are carried by winds of doctrine. It is impossible to think of the history of French or English or German criticism in isolation. Still, linguistic traditions and local nationalisms importantly contributed to the growth of criticism. The enormous diversification of the national traditions, the rise of criticism in nations which before had hardly taken part in the critical debate—in the United States, Russia, the other Slavic countries, Spain, and Scandinavia—is the bright side of the matter. But there is also a dark side to literary nationalism: not only in the obvious exaggerations of national claims and the long and repetitious debates about the same questions of nationality in literature but also in the fragmentation of criticism. We must take into account the astonishingly decreased sense of community (even compared with the Romantic Age) among the European nations in the later 19th century and the increased differences among their developments. France and England had the liveliest interchange, and the United States naturally emancipated itself slowly from British dominance, partly with the help of the French. But Germany, which led aesthetic speculation in the early 19th century, drifted into a curious isolation, which only such a lonely spirit as Nietzsche could overcome by singlehanded effort. Problems of its national *Risorgimento* absorbed Italy even in criticism, and Russia was faced with quite specific local issues, which permeated all literary debates. Though the central problems of criticism are perennial and the greatest critics rise above their local horizon, criticism is written in a historical context, often with a specific audience in mind, in a temporal social situation. We must not reduce it to a mirror of that situation: we must see how it transcends it everywhere, to rise to the issues debated since Aristotle and still discussed today in totally different social and political conditions. Yet we cannot ignore the setting, the persons, and the nations if our history is to assume flesh and blood and is not to remain a shadowy play of ideas. A procedure by nationality is unavoidable. France must be discussed first, as it is the most important country for the development of Western criticism in our age.

OSSIFIED NEOCLASSICISM died slowly in France, and the emotional romanticism which took its place had little to offer for criticism except a standard of feeling and freedom from the rules. But even before the Restoration (1815) new ideas were stirring everywhere. There was a sudden proliferation of the varieties of criticism: not a leaping ahead in one direction but almost a flying apart to all corners of the intellectual universe. The man who eventually arises from the chaos, Sainte-Beuve, wears the traces of the conflicts of his youth. We shall understand him better if we know his immediate predecessors and contemporaries. But they deserve attention also for their own sake: they laid the foundations of French literary history, formulated a symbolist theory of poetry, demanded a literature in the service of humanity, and started the art-for-art's-sake movement.

France inherited a great tradition of cultural historiography from the 18th century. Transferred to literature, the tradition was summed up in De Bonald's famous formula: "literature is the expression of society." [1] As early as 1800 in *De la Littérature* Madame de Staël had drawn up a rather vague scheme of a history of literature determined by society. The influence of letters on society was then examined much more concretely by Prosper de Barante (1782–1866) in his *De la Littérature française au XVIIIe siècle* (1809). Barante, who knew Madame de Staël but was a Napoleonic official at the time of writing his book, tries to put the controversy about the causes of the Revolution in a new perspective. He deplores the destructive radicalism of the *philosophes* and argues from a vaguely Kantian point of view against the premises of sensualist philosophy; but he sees that the Revolution was not caused by Voltaire or Rousseau. French writings of the 18th century were rather "symptoms of the general illness." Men of letters became spokesmen of the discontent and unrest caused by the

despotism and obscurantism of the *ancien régime*. The philosophy
of the 18th century was "a universal spirit of the nation which we
meet again in the writers." Their books were, so to speak, "not only
influenced by the public; they were written as if dictated by it." [2]
In a preface added in 1824 Barante found the striking formula that
literature in the 18th century "had become an organ of opinion,
an element of the political constitution. In the absence of regular
institutions, literature provided one." [3] But this insight into the
role of literature as a social institution remains only an argument
in a thesis and does not animate a real history. In the body of the
book Barante surveys the main writers, characterizing each in very
general terms. One recognizes his sympathies from the generous
praise of Montesquieu, the cool appraisal of Voltaire and Rousseau,
and the curt abuse of Diderot. Commenting on criticism, Barante
shows his acute awareness of the new creed: he rejects the imitation
theory, the concept of language as a system of fixed signs, and the
distinction between thought and style. He rebukes La Harpe for
ignoring the "circumstances" of authors.[4] But in tone and style
nothing anticipates Barante's later *Histoire des Ducs de Bourgogne*
(1824–27), an evocation of the late Middle Ages which reproduces
the texts of the chronicles of Froissart and Commynes almost
literally for narrative and picturesque effect, without analysis, without the overt "ideology" that is the main concern of the book on
the 18th century.

François Guizot (1787–1874) also argued concretely for the
influence of society on literature. Guizot began with literary
studies: reports on German scholarship, a life and times of Corneille
(1813) with emphasis on the times,[5] and a preface to a revision of
Le Tourneur's translation of Shakespeare (1821). In the last he
asserts that "literature cannot escape the revolutions of the human
mind; rather it is compelled to follow it in its progress." "The
classical system was born from the life and manners of its age. That
age has passed." In France the genres separated sharply with the
rise of the rigid class-system; in England, "the refuge of Germanic
manners and liberties," the confusion of genres survived from the
Middle Ages. The new drama will be "large and free, but not without principles and laws." [6] It will, apparently, follow the analogy
of constitutional monarchy, the proper balance between despotism

and anarchy that Guizot defended all his life as a statesman and historian of civilization.

For Madame de Staël, Barante, Guizot, Stendhal, and even the Hugo of the preface to *Cromwell* (1827), the general concept of history is a scheme of progress and perfectibility within a rigid causal sequence of psychological states. This idea anticipates later deterministic, positivistic, sociological concepts of historical development that must be sharply distinguished from the new historicism imported from Germany. German historicism combined an insight into individuality, national tradition, and period with the ideal of universal toleration and a concept of development as free-flowing continuity and slow organic growth. German historicism was less concerned with society than with the national mind, less with causal explanation or general laws than with tracing living traditions to their origins in dim antiquity. The process of the importation of these ideas into France is, in its details, still obscure. As we have seen, Madame de Staël herself cannot be described as a convert to the German doctrines. Still, her circle was the decisive intermediary. The translations of actual German literary histories—Bouterwek's volume on Spanish literature with a preface by Phillipe-Albert Stapfer in 1812; August Wilhelm Schlegel's *Dramatic Lectures,* in the translation by a cousin of Madame de Staël, Madame Necker de Saussure, in 1814; and Friedrich Schlegel's *History of Ancient and Modern Literature* in 1829—were widely noticed.[7] But it was rather the general assimilation of the central ideas of German historicism that made the difference. These ideas came also from many sources not directly concerned with literature: from political historiography, aesthetic speculation, and the new sciences of comparative philology and religion. However, these routes were so varied that for our purposes it seems best to observe only the consequences for literary history and criticism.

The first French literary history informed by the new spirit is *De la Littérature du Midi de l'Europe* (4 volumes, 1813) by Jean Charles Léonard Simonde de Sismondi (1773–1842). Sismondi, a Genevan who adopted an Italian title, still well-known as an economist and historian of the medieval Italian republics, has also the indisputable merit of being the first modern literary historian in French. Sismondi knew Madame de Staël; he traveled with her to

Italy (1804–05) and to Vienna (1808), where he heard A. W. Schlegel deliver his *Dramatic Lectures*. He did not care for Schlegel as a person, but listened somewhat incredulously to his ideas. He read Bouterwek, whose many-volumed *History* became the primary source, especially in its Spanish and Portuguese sections, for his own book.[8] *Littérature du Midi* is the first attempt to treat medieval literature as a totality. Beginning with the Arabs, it surveys Provençal, Old French, and Italian literature—the latter from its origins to Alfieri; treats Spanish literature up to the 18th century; and concludes with Portuguese. Further volumes on Nordic literatures—English and German, with remarks on Dutch, Danish, Swedish, and even Slavic literatures [9]—were projected, but remained unwritten for reasons not difficult to guess: Sismondi lacked the linguistic competence, and his interests shifted away from literature. The title of the book, "Literature of the South," derives from Madame de Staël's main contrast of Southern with Northern literatures; but, unlike her, Sismondi makes nothing of climate. The program instead calls for a study of the "reciprocal influence of the political and religious history of the people on their literature and of their literature on their character." [10] In practice, the book mainly expounds the German "romantic" thesis. The literatures of the South are romantic literatures, among which the French forms the only exception: it alone "reproduced the classical literature of the Greeks and Romans." French literature after the Middle Ages is thus excluded from Sismondi's *History*, since it broke with what he conceives to have been the unity of the Romance world of the Middle Ages. It remained "far behind in regard to sensibility, enthusiasm, warmth, depth and truth of sentiments." It deviated from the original romantic tradition of "love, chivalry and religion." [11]

Sismondi's knowledge is often secondhand, derivative, defective; his method often purely descriptive and compilatory; and his taste timidly romantic. As a critic he comes to life mainly in the discussion of Italian literature, for he knows and loves the poets and has access to a tradition of erudite literary history (Tiraboschi, Andrés, Ginguené). Dante is seen in romantic terms: as the author of the *Inferno,* the portrayer of Farinata and Ugolino. The *Paradiso* is condemned as rhymed theology. Ariosto is praised almost in terms of a celebration of art for art's sake: "Revery without purpose agrees with the essence of poetry, which must never be a means, but is its own proper aim." Tasso is, in Sismondi's mind, the greatest of all modern poets, for he combines the romantic and the classic: he knows how to be classical in the whole, in the structure, and romantic in painting manners and situations. His poem is conceived in the spirit of antiquity but executed in the spirit of the Middle Ages. Not surprisingly, the lover of Ariosto enjoys Metastasio, and the fervent liberal admires Alfieri, whom he defends against the strictures of August Wilhelm Schlegel.[12] The Spanish chapters, compared with the Italian, show their dependence on Bouterwek. The discussion of Cervantes presents for the first time in French the German romantic view of *Don Quixote* as a melancholy, tragic book. But Bouterwek could not agree with Schlegel's extravagant praise of Calderón. Spanish literature, Sismondi argues, is distorted by the sinister influence of the Inquisition, and Calderón deviates too widely from the standard of probability to be palatable to Sismondi's basically conservative taste.[13] Theoretically, however, Sismondi constantly rehearses the historistic argument that each nation has its own kind of literature with its particular rules, especially in the drama, and that the three unities, derived from a "very obscure treatise by Aristotle," cannot be and were never prescriptive for other dramatic systems.[14] Sismondi's point of view is still ambiguous: one feels that he has embraced a theory in which he did not quite believe, which even ran counter to his own conservative tastes. Stendhal could ask whether "Sismondi is obsessed by two opposite systems. Will he admire Racine or Shakespeare? In these perplexities he does not tell us where his heart is; probably he is of no party." [15] Yet in France, in its time, the book was understood and attacked as a romantic manifesto, as part of the German invasion and the medieval revival.[16]

The scholarly foundation for a history of medieval literature was laid by two men: Claude Fauriel (1772–1844) and his pupil Jean-Jacques Ampère (1800–64). Fauriel was an almost legendary figure: he published hardly anything during his lifetime that could justify his enormous reputation. His relations with Madame de Staël, Manzoni, and, more distantly, with the Schlegel brothers put him at the crossroads of cultural influences. His translation of modern Greek popular songs, *Chants populaires de la Grèce moderne* (2 volumes, 1823), was not only a timely contribution to the cause of

Greek independence but, with its preface, a declaration of the creed of universal folk poetry. As in Herder, popular and artificial poetry are sharply contrasted. Popular poetry is "the direct and true expression of the national character and mind" which lives "in the people itself, and of the whole life of the people." Greek poetry is "at the same time the genuine national history of modern Greece and the most faithful picture of the manners of its inhabitants." Though Fauriel recognizes that none of the songs he prints and translates can be dated before 1600, he assumes that they are "a continuation, a slow and gradual alteration of the ancient poetry and particularly of the ancient popular poetry of Greece." There could not have been any interruption in the tradition. While the other arts need cultivation, untutored genius achieves perfection in poetry. "The very defect or imperfect use of art, that species of contrast or of disproportion between the simplicity of means and the fullness of effect, makes the principal charm of such a composition." Thus popular poetry "participates in the character and privilege of works of nature." [17] Fauriel sees that the Greek songs should be compared to Spanish romances, Scottish and Danish ballads. He later reported on the Russian folk epics and the forged Czech manuscripts; he even sketched a general history of the epic, in which he draws on his knowledge of Sanscrit epics, Homer, and other heroic poetry to define three universal stages: spontaneous popular inspiration, recitation by singers, and written reflective editing.[18] Universal literary history is envisaged as an ideal and is buttressed by wide-ranging learning. Still, the assumptions are always those of the German romantics, except that Fauriel posited a different radiating point in the early Middle Ages: Provence rather than the Teutonic *Urwelt* of the Grimms.

Fauriel's main research was devoted to the rise of vernacular medieval literature, to the Provençal poets and the beginnings of Italian literature. But the lectures he gave as Professor of Foreign Literature at the Sorbonne in the thirties were published only after his death, and somewhat fragmentarily, as *Histoire de la poésie provençale* (3 volumes, 1846) and *Dante et les origines de la langue et de la littérature italiennes* (2 volumes, 1854). The inaugural lesson of the first course (1831) emphasizes that "all literatures participate in the general movement by which humanity lifts itself progressively from one condition to another, from childhood to youth, from youth to maturity." "This general tendency is crossed by and combined with other particular tendencies of the climate, soil, social condition, religious creed, commercial relations, and the results of wars and conquests," which modify the common core and give to each literature "a local physiognomy, a character of individuality." [19] *The History of Provençal Poetry* propounds an extravagant thesis: Provence was the center of the new Christian secular civilization and literature. Teutonic influence was small or detrimental. Breton and Welsh sources were confined to the borrowing of a few names and floating traditions. Arabic influence was real but peripheral, affecting manners rather than writing. The Provençals were the initiators not only of troubadour poetry but also of the medieval epic, even though the epic is preserved only in Northern French versions by the *trouvères* or in German translations (like Wolfram's *Parzival* translated, by the poet's admission, from the lost epic of the Provençal Kyot). Provençal love poetry itself must be "an extension, modification and systematic refinement of cruder, more natural, and more popular literature." Provençal influence (in Fauriel's wide sense) was decisive not only for Italian literature but also for Spanish, German, and English. The whole scheme is apparently based on the analogue of comparative philology searching for the Proto-Indo-European ancestor of French or Italian: an original folk poetry is postulated which must, for instance, have contained epic poetry because its absence would be "a hypothesis contrary to the usual working of the human mind." Thus Fauriel looks everywhere for the hidden traces of original folk poetry: even the monkish Virgilian *Waltharius* from the monastery of St. Gall becomes an argument for the Provençal origin of the heroic epic, and a 9th-century "Song of the Guards of Modena," a Latin clerical hymn, attests the survival of popular traditions. *Alba, ballata,* and *pastorella* are popular forms. Latin and Teutonic traditions are persistently minimized.[20] Modern scholarship has reacted against Fauriel's assumptions but has not, it seems, solved the issues convincingly. There is a basic core of truth in the romantic theories of folk poetry that cannot be refuted merely by challenging Fauriel's passion for localizing all important developments in the South of France.

The course on Dante (given 1833–35) pursues the theme of the spread of Provençal poetry to Italian literature. Fauriel lingers on the state of politics in Italy, the constitution of the Italian republics and of Florence in particular, before he gives an account of Dante's life, of Provençal poetry in Italy, and early Italian courtly love poetry. His treatment of the *Divine Comedy* is preserved only in fragments. Fauriel emphasizes Dante's intellectual aspirations, the fact that he did not feel the modern conflict between science and poetry. On the other hand, Fauriel sharply rejects the attempt to reduce the *Divine Comedy* to an allegory, "the coldest, most artificial, and falsest of all poetic forms." The central figure of the *Comedy* is Beatrice, its main motif "a noble confession of his wrongs against her memory." Other chapters give an excellent interpretation of the way in which Dante transformed the figures of classical mythology (Charon, Cerberus, etc.) to fit them into his Christian scheme. Fauriel also argues that the crucial events in such stories as those of Francesca da Rimini, Ugolino, and Sordello are the unverifiable workings of Dante's free imagination.[21] The long description of historical setting and circumstance is modified by Fauriel's recognition of Dante's personal experience and inventive power. Unfortunately, the second volume of the Dante book is taken up by an obsolete history of the Italian language. All the lectures leave an apparently inadequate picture of the scholar whom Sainte-Beuve, Renan, Ampère, Ozanam, and others acknowledged as the *magnus parens* of French literary scholarship. Renan said that Fauriel "really created comparative literature in France, and the science of literary origins, the point of view of envisaging literature as a historical science, undoubtedly very superior to the shallow and trivial literary criticism of La Harpe, Geoffroy, Petitot, and even Marmontel and Voltaire."[22]

Ampère is closely related in attitude and preoccupations to Fauriel. As with Fauriel, we feel a certain lack of fulfillment considering his gifts and the promise of his early years. Ampère went to Bonn in 1826, where he heard A. W. Schlegel and B. G. Niebuhr lecture. He had published an article on Goethe previous to his stay in Germany which makes much of Goethe's originality and nationality, the diversity of his works, and their sources in Goethe's mental evolution. "Each of these works corresponds to some disposition of his soul or mind: one must look there for the history of the sentiments and events that filled his existence." Ampère notices the continuity between Werther and Tasso. There is Christian delicacy

and modern refinement in Goethe's Iphigenia, and Egmont is close
to Goethe's heart. Ampère defines his method as "the historical
point of view, searching for nothing but Goethe in his works." [23]
No wonder that Goethe translated the article, dined the young man
in Weimar, and praised him in talking to Eckermann.[24] During his
German stay Ampère wrote appreciative accounts of Tieck, E. T. A.
Hoffmann, and Chamisso. But Ampère did not merely want to
follow in the footsteps of Madame de Staël: he wanted to become a
scholar, a philologist like the Grimms (whom he visited at Kassel).
The German stay culminated in a tour of Scandinavia, which
yielded articles on Holberg, Oehlenschläger, and the Swedish
romantic group, and later accounts of the Eddas and sagas as well as
of the Danish ballads. Inspired by a brief visit to Prague, Ampère
even glanced at ancient Czech history and poetry.[25]

Thus fortified, he propounded an ambitious program in a
Discours sur l'histoire de la poésie (1830). Philosophy of literature
and literary history are the two parts of literary science. A philosophy
of literature and the arts must grow out of a comparative history of
the arts and literature. Literary history is thus next on the program,
and a history of the Northern literatures the most urgent task. We
shall learn the different stages through which the human soul and
imagination have passed. We shall thus fulfill the great work of our
time: to understand and to remake the ages. The ultimate goal is a
complete history of humanity. Ampère describes the steps of the
critical process: philological criticism comes first, but only a higher
understanding of the intimate meaning of a work gives us the right
to judge. One needs then to know the society in which the artist
lived: the race, the country, the language, the manners, the arts,
the philosophy, the religion, the government. In order to appreciate
the artist, one must expatriate oneself completely, establish oneself
in imagination in the circle of habits in which he lived. Filiations,
causes, and effects must be traced. As in botany and zoology, we
must look not for arbitrary divisions but for chronological series
and natural families. As in geology, each of the great epochs of
poetic history corresponds to one of the great phases of civilization.
Originally poetry was everywhere: the poet expressed the general
thought. "The real individual was the race, the tribe. The poet was
the voice of this collective individual and nothing more." But in
modern times the individual stands out of the crowd: his tempera-

ment and education become decisive. We must sympathize with the poet, but also judge him, employing "a large, fertile criticism which, full of respect for genius and severity for error, admires freely and condemns with independence." The critic has to rank poets, and he does so by selecting the poet who best incarnates the time in its proper substance, creates its type, presents its image. Good criticism is rare. Ampère even believes that there are more great artists in the world than great critics. They are faced with the task of assembling a magnificent museum of monuments.[26] We understand from this lecture alone why Sainte-Beuve, who met Ampère that very year (1830), could call himself "in some respects his pupil," assiduously attend his lectures, and testify that Ampère freed him from purely biographical and anecdotal criticism.[27] The balance of history and psychology, of sympathy and criticism is both Ampère's and Sainte-Beuve's.

Ampère, however, earned the title "Fauriel II" by his later work. He gave up his early Nordic and universalist plans and, on the basis of original research, attempted to write the first continuous history of French literature from its obscure beginnings. His *Histoire littéraire de la France avant le douzième siècle* (2 volumes, 1839–40) begins, as he himself recognized, with the antediluvian age: with the Iberians, the Celts, Phoenicians, and Greeks on French soil. "We must plunge into this creative darkness . . . into this chaos which will give birth to a world." He leads us slowly up to the Roman literature on Gallic soil (Lactantius, Ausonius), to the Christianization of Gaul, to the struggle with the Teutonic invaders, and to the emergence of a new civilization, which always reveals "the Roman road, the Roman soil" underneath. A sense of the continuity of the Latin tradition and a devotion to the local unity of France have replaced Ampère's original conception of folk poetry. Thus the two volumes are almost entirely devoted to literature in Latin. A thesis of three renaissances is propounded: the Carolingian renaissance in the 9th century, the flowering at the end of the 11th century, and the renaissance that came from Italy in the 16th century.[28] In all this welter of almost anonymous writings on history and theology, Ampère never loses sight of individuality. Reflecting on Sidonius Apollinarius, he expresses his surprise at finding such a man in such a century and society and corrects the saying "Literature is the expression of society." Literature rather "expresses what is hidden: it is a confident who reveals to us what has been thought and felt in secret, what had been latent, suppressed. It is like echoes that repeat from afar words pronounced in a whisper. It often shows not the dominance of a fact but the reaction against it. It expresses the desires, the vows, a certain ideal in the depths of the soul. Moreover, it is not always the voice of the moment in which it is produced; it is often the reverberation of what has been, the last sigh of what is dying, the first cry of what will live." [29]

Ampère lingered too long in this obscure period: his next book, *Histoire de la littérature française au moyen âge comparée aux littératures étrangères* (1841), does not fulfill the high promise of the title. It contains an "Histoire de la formation de la langue française," which was planned as the first volume of a new series. The body of the volume, an inevitably obsolete treatise in philology, has a long preface that surveys French medieval literature. The 12th, 13th, and 14th centuries are distinguished in terms of an ascent, climax, and decline. The parallel to developments in other countries and to the stages of Gothic architecture is suggested. Ampère surveys the genres of French literature and their influence abroad. But he accepts too docilely Fauriel's thesis of Provençal dominance and seems uncertain on such issues as the Arab influence or the distinction between *chanson de geste* and chivalrous romance.

The projected continuation of Ampère's work must be reconstructed from his articles on the *Roman de la Rose,* on Joinville, and on Amyot.[30] The whole ambitious project remained a fragment, because Ampère became discouraged by the poor reception of the first volumes (not surprising in view of their antiquarian and philological character) and moved into other subjects, Roman history in particular.

Out of Ampère's later interests grew an attractive book, *La Grèce, Rome et Dante: Études littéraires d'après nature* (1848), constructed as a "critique en voyage." Its motto is "Compare art with the reality that inspired it and explain it by the reality." Greek poets are studied in their landscape; Dante is followed in a "Dantesque journey" from Florence to Ravenna, in the belief that "it is good to see what he saw and to live where he lived." [31]

Ampère's great *History* bogged down in the dark ages. His clear theoretical insight and historical vision did not succeed in breathing life into his materials. His fine programmatic statements, the early promise as a critic demonstrated in the German essays, were not fulfilled. His work has not survived, but it was historically effective as a stimulus for Sainte-Beuve and for the long line of students of Old French literature.

In their time, both Fauriel and Ampère were overshadowed by the success of Abel François Villemain (1790–1870). Brunetière, Chasles, and others proclaimed him the founder of literary history, forgetting about Sismondi and all the English, Germans, and Italians before.[32] Most of his work is drearily academic: the pompous eulogies of Montaigne and Montesquieu that began his career; the dull and ill-informed lives of Shakespeare, Milton, Pope, Thomson, and Byron; the dissertations on the Greek novels, on Christian eloquence, on the funeral oration; and so on.[33] Whenever Villemain writes formally, he becomes stuffy, conventional, vague, bombastic, and hypercautious. Only the early *Tableau de la littérature française au XVIIIe siècle* (4 volumes, 1828–29), revised transcripts of immensely successful lectures at the Sorbonne, comes to life. There he indulges in free oratorical flights and political allusions and can print the audience reaction ("Vifs applaudissements," "on rit"). In discussing the French 18th century, Villemain drew on an immediate knowledge of the main texts. But like almost every Frenchman of the time, he had a cautious antirevolutionary attitude toward the ideological issues. Thus Villemain has little new to say about ideas and often seems to distort proportions and caricature men. He neglects the *Encyclopédie* and roughly dismisses Diderot. He is primarily concerned with the contrast between the 17th century, dominated by religion, antiquity, and the monarchy, and the 18th century, dominated by skepticism, the imitation of modern literatures, and the advocacy of political reform.[34] In a later essay Villemain asked that literary criticism and questions of taste be made "an appendix of social history" and argued that all great literature is involved in the broad moral interests of its society.[35] But in the *Tableau* the actual dependence of literature on society remains vague: the prosaic tone of *Gil Blas* could be ascribed to "the stamp of the time, the spirit of the last years of the reign of Louis XIV." Most of the time Villemain is content to mingle biography, criticism of a rather liberal but still definitely classicist taste, and political history. What is new and meritorious in his lectures is the attempt to bring in the other European literatures, to show "the counterstroke of the French genius abroad in several famous works of England and Italy." Villemain attempts a "comparative picture of what the French mind has received from foreign literatures and what it has returned to them." He wants to describe "the crossfire" between France and England.[36] The performance remains, however, far behind the promise. We get unrelated accounts of English writers and hear very little of Italy or Germany. But it was new to emphasize so strongly Voltaire's visit to England, to describe Pope, Addison, Bolingbroke, Swift, and others, and to give an account of British Parliamentary oratory, of Pitt, Sheridan, Fox, and Burke, in a French context.

Compared with the lectures on the 18th century, *Tableau de la littérature au moyen âge en France, en Espagne et en Angleterre* (2 volumes, 1830) suffers from defects of knowledge and sympathy. The lectures preceded, one must realize, the published work of Fauriel and Ampère. They are more articulate than the 18th-century series in their defense of the new historicism. Villemain declares himself an "eclectic" in the sense that "we love everything that is beautiful, ingenious, new, of whatever school. We believe even that one need not want to be of any school, even of the school of genius." Modern criticism is distinguished by its search for first origins, for the discovery of borrowings of one literature from another, for its interest in "the most expressive" and the most successful type of every age. Thus the *Divine Comedy* is "the most complete monument of the imagination and the beliefs of a people." Villemain is wary of rigid schemes of evolution, and of any psychological history of the race, whether derived from Vico or the Germans. The idea of a close parallelism between antiquity and the Middle Ages in their decline and fall seems to him false. He asserts antiromantically that medieval writers are the heirs of the Greeks and the Romans. In his critical judgments he refuses to be carried away by the new enthusiasm: "even though one can discuss, with the justice of a scholar, what suits an age, one is not therefore oneself seduced by one's own words: one is not duped, one does not dupe others." Not being duped means to Villemain holding firmly to his neoclassical taste. "Whatever the lucky genius of a writer of the old time, there remains always something Gothic and strange in him."

"True poetry, in France at least, was always contemporaneous with good taste." Villemain deplores the attempts to disparage the great French poets in favor of the poets of Germany and England. Goethe is artificial, Alexandrian, "subtly natural, laboriously bold"; Byron cultivates "a sophisticated disgust" for life.[37] Shakespeare is great but he belongs to the English and should remain their poet. Shakespeare appeals to Villemain most when he can show that he is "eminently classical," when he agrees with Euripides.[38] In a general history of criticism Villemain's position can be compared to Thomas Warton's: a basically neoclassical taste that allows, in a subordinate position, an erudite interest in other tastes and traditions. It seems only right that Villemain became the Perpetual Secretary of the French Academy and for eleven years (1846–56) composed the solemn discourses at the annual distribution of prizes.[39]

The first frankly cosmopolitan French critic was Philarète Chasles (1798–1873). Chasles spent several years (1817–23) as a compositor in London, had a long career as literary journalist with the *Revue britannique,* which abstracted English reviews, and with the *Journal des débats,* and was a Professor of Germanic Languages and Literatures (including English) at the Collège de France from 1841. The books collecting his articles run to some thirty volumes not counting prefaces, collaborations, or the innumerable articles buried in periodical files. His work on French literature, mainly of the 16th and 19th centuries, begins with *Tableau de la marche et des progrès de la littérature française au XVIe siècle* (1828), which won the prize of the Academy in the competition for which Sainte-Beuve had originally planned his book on the same topic. But Chasles' essays cover all literature and all subjects: classical literature, English literature since the Renaissance, American literature and life, German literature, and excursions into Spanish and Italian topics.[40] A vast map of Western literature is spread out; the emphasis is on literary influences and affinities which, Chasles recognizes, can bridge centuries. "Bayle the Protestant touches Montaigne the Catholic; the Ghibelline Dante, the servants of Provençal love; Molière reaches across toward Terence." In order to study literature deeply, we must study politics, religion, society itself; otherwise, literary criticism would be "a labyrinth without light." [41]

The ideal aim is a general intellectual history. Literature as an art dissolves into history.

Chasles' inspiration is sympathy, not exclusion: "a harmony of the varieties in the works of the mind; the *Weltliteratur* of which Goethe spoke, that is, the conciliation of opposite points of view." France has the role of the "grand-sympathique," [42] the mission of diffusing ideas as well as of receiving and transforming them. But Chasles recognizes the initiatory role of German criticism and knows the English romantic critics as well. Germany "is the only country where criticism has rested on broad foundations; taking into account national genius, appreciating the immense variety of human nature and the influence of this variety on the arts, accepting the thought of each people as dependent on political and social changes, and admiring one after another the thousand forms which the beautiful and the ideal may assume in their passage through history." [43] In a list of great critics appear Coleridge (whom Chasles had visited at Highgate), Hazlitt, Villemain, A. W. Schlegel, and Sainte-Beuve; Chasles elsewhere praises Lamb as "the first modern critic who has penetrated most deeply into the study of the old language and the English authors of the 16th century." Chasles looked for "the vastest spirit, who would conciliate everything." [44]

Chasles' range is enormous, his information is plentiful (though often inaccurate or obsolete), and his observations and perceptions are frequently acute and new in their time. He has a great facility for making connections, confrontations, and sweeping comparisons. But it is rather difficult to find a satisfactory essay; most of his pieces are too prolix, too overloaded with long quotations, too purely descriptive or informative to rise above the transient function of literary journalism and cultural interpreting. There are exceptions, but they are, I believe, very few. The brilliant review of *Hernani* (1830) might be singled out. It recognizes that Hugo did not emancipate himself from the French dramatic system: "he merely condensed the devices hitherto used; he has not changed them but rather multiplied them." [45] We should add the obituary of Balzac (with whom Chasles had been associated and whom he helped with the fake Rabelaisian language of *Contes drolatiques*). There Chasles coined the phrase that Balzac was a visionary (*voyant*), a phrase picked up by Sainte-Beuve and developed in recent decades.[46] There is also the skillful defense of Racine's *Phèdre* against the strictures of August Wilhelm Schlegel, correcting Schlegel's comparison of the play with Euripides' *Hippolitos*.[47] There was merit for his day in the comparison between Shakespeare and Montaigne: Shakespeare seems to Chasles "a skeptical poet, a calm and often cruel observer, a brother of Montaigne, moved by a slightly ironical pity for men." [48] Chasles was one of the first in France to praise Jean Paul and Heine. The accounts of Melville's early books and a glimpse of the mad Hölderlin in Tübingen in 1840 are interesting curiosities.[49]

But though a judicious anthology may help to revive Chasles' reputation, he can never be considered a great critic. He fails in some final tests: he lacks edge, personality, and does not compensate by profundity of learning or acuteness of theory. His literary theory is quite loose and vague: he rejects the distinction between literature and social history and thus cannot focus on the literary object, nor is he prepared to face the isues of a sociology of literature. He complains, for instance, about Sainte-Beuve's skepticism and asserts his "own firm belief in causality"; but, on the other hand, he recoils before Taine's determinism because "the essence of the soul is liberty and liberty is life." [50] The in-between solution may be defensible and even right, but it is not elaborated or analyzed. Similarly, Chasles' taste disconcertingly wavers between an unbounded enthusiasm for the great French classics and an appreciation not only of Shakespeare but also of Calderón, Rabelais, and even of Jean Paul (whose *Titan* he translated) and Carlo Gozzi. In his work, historistic sympathy has led to an indiscriminate relativism, to an abandonment of standards, and hence to a dissolution of criticism. Chasles lacks center, lacks conviction. He was more and more overshadowed by his rival Sainte-Beuve, who was so much more personal, sensitive, and accurate. They were friends at first, but later Chasles came to dislike Sainte-Beuve for his extreme mobility, as a "traitor on principle" and a "dazzling Don Juan in the intellectual harem." [51] Chasles felt that he, on the other hand, had been faithful to himself—but he could feel so only because he had no cause to betray except cultural cosmopolitanism, a generous, tolerant relativism which could be held indefinitely, under any circumstances.

The new historicism, with its widened international perspective

and its tolerant attitude toward other art forms, was far from victorious in its own time. When the actual classic-romantic debate
had died down—after its comic epitaph had been written in
Musset's witty *Lettres de Dupuis et Cotonet* (1836)—a reaction in
favor of classicism set in. Rachel, in roles of the classical repertory,
and Ponsard's "classical" tragedy *Lucrèce* (1838) made a strong
impression; and Hugo's *Les Burgraves* (1843) failed on the stage. In
criticism this reaction was represented mainly by the polemical
journalist Gustave Planche (1808–57) and more formidably by the
literary historians Saint-Marc Girardin and Désiré Nisard. Planche
in his time appeared as a serious rival of Sainte-Beuve. Defiantly he
published a collection of essays under the same title, *Portraits littéraires* (1836); but today he is remembered only as an inveterate
enemy of the romantic drama. Planche attacks Hugo's plays for
violating history and human nature. Also *Notre Dame de Paris*
replaces emotion with mere "surprise." "Stone and cloth are the
principal and, I should rather say, the only actors in the book." *Ruy
Blas* is "a puerile string of impossible scenes," "an act of madness." [52]
Planche likewise trounces Chateaubriand. Boredom oozes from *Les
Martyres*, the *Essay on English Literature* is incoherent and poorly
informed, the translation of *Paradise Lost* is a schoolboy's trot full
of gross boners. Chateaubriand "hides behind Shakespeare and
Milton in order to breathe more comfortably the incense he has
lighted for himself." [53] And so it goes for Lamartine, Vigny, and the
others. Planche always asks simple questions: does the work reflect
reality? Is it probable? Is it moral? Does it hang together? He is not
a classicist in the sense of idolizing the 17th century or defending
the rules. He is rather a fiercely independent upholder of "good
sense," which in practice turns out to be a denial of imagination
and poetry.

Planche, in his theory of criticism, reiterates the need for severity,
impartiality, and vigilance; he complains about other kinds of
criticism—commercial, erudite, the merely amusing, witty and
paradoxical, the uncritically admiring—in order to set up, in contrast, his own kind of severe judicial criticism.[54] The conflict with
Sainte-Beuve, which had been slowly simmering for a long time,
comes to a boil in Planche's review of *Causeries du Lundi* (1851).
The way Sainte-Beuve had turned against his early admirations
seems to Planche an expiation for the excessive eulogies he had

lavished on the romantic poets. "I admit the sincerity both in the blame and the praise but see, in this mobility of judgment, simply a moral disease." [55]

But Planche's rigidity or firmness, which may be an admirable trait of character, is not, unfortunately, matched by real critical discernment. The high standards proclaimed are continually relaxed, not only for George Sand, whom he greatly admired, partly on personal grounds, but also for Béranger and such mediocrities as Barbier and Jules Sandeau. Planche spent some time in England (1835), but what he wrote on English literature is mere reporting. An article on Fielding is, without acknowledgment, copied from the French translation of Walter Scott's article. The praise of Bulwer's *Eugene Aram* as comparable to Euripides and Shakespeare, and the attention to Henry Mackenzie prove rather lack of critical sense than neoclassical narrowness.[56] Planche admired many good things (e.g. *Manon Lescaut,* Chénier, and *Adolphe* [57]), but his essays do little more than comment on the stories in terms of character and plot, or rank poems by genre and presumed excellence. In spite of all his show of logic, he has little analytical skill, little power of characterization, and hardly any sensibility. He will be remembered as the type of the cantankerous critic—a type often unjustly satirized, no doubt. He fulfilled a useful function in combating the extravagances of the romantic poets.

The success of Saint-Marc Girardin (1801–73) was much greater than that of the lonely Bohemian Planche. Saint-Marc Girardin lectured for thirty years to crowds of students (sometimes more than a thousand) at the Sorbonne, hammering home one single thesis: modern literature is morally bad and socially dangerous; it encourages disgust with life and leads ultimately to suicide. Classical and French literature are good and great, good for morals and society. Saint-Marc Girardin obviously learned his method from Chateaubriand's *Génie du Christianisme,* though, unlike Chateaubriand, he always compares the ancients with the moderns to the detriment of the latter. The widely read *Cours de littérature dramatique* (5 volumes, 1843, 1849, 1855, 1860, 1868) starts with the excellent idea that "every sentiment has its history, and that history is interesting, for it is, so to speak, an abridgment of the history of humanity. Though the sentiments of the human heart do not change, nevertheless they do show the effect of religious and political revolutions."[58] Unhappily, Saint-Marc Girardin is no historian: he is merely a moralist who juxtaposes the suicide of Dido to that of Chatterton (in Vigny's play), or compares the paternal love of the old Horace in Corneille's tragedy with that of Triboulet in Hugo's *Le Roi s'amuse,* or contrasts the ingratitude of children in *Oedipus at Colonus* with the ingratitude of Regan and Goneril. Girardin never recognizes that abstractions such as "paternal love" and "jealousy" are critically meaningless outside of the context of a play, that nothing whatever is proved for criticism by preferring Horace to Triboulet or chiding his daughter Blanche for her unreasonable love.[59] The morality preached is narrowly middle-class—a recommendation of domesticity, good humor, and moderation, of such blatant complacency that Girardin was proclaimed the model bourgeois of the *juste milieu* and served as a warning example to Sainte-Beuve and De Sanctis.[60] But one should recognize that Saint-Marc's *History,* especially in the later volumes published under Napoleon III when the social dangers of romanticism had passed, contains much shrewd, witty, and agreeable comment of a psychological and moralistic kind, arranged according to themes or topics: "Conjugal love in Shakespeare," "Jealousy in Molière," "The repentant adulteress," and so on.

Like Planche and Saint-Marc Girardin, Désiré Nisard (1806–88) began with a protest against the literature of his time. A pamphlet, *Contre la littérature facile* (1833), casts its darts against the sensational novel, the spurious medievalism of the historical novel, and the gory and tawdry romantic drama.[61] But this slight piece was merely the forerunner of the formidable *Études de mœurs et de critique sur les poètes latins de la décadence* (2 volumes, 1834). There a harshly critical discussion of the writers of Silver Latinity— of Phaedrus, Seneca, Persius, Statius, Martial, Juvenal, and Lucan— leads to an explicit indictment of the literature of Nisard's own age.[62] Nisard distinguishes three stages in the history of poetry: that of the primitive poets, Homer, Dante, Shakespeare; that of men of letters, with Virgil as their representative; and that of the erudite versifiers described in his book. Modern French poetry is in a parallel stage of decadence; it shows the same symptoms as late antiquity: moral debility, indulgence in mere external description, violence, baroque style, obscurity, and vagueness.[63] The book has considerable historical importance, since it gave rise to the whole discussion of decadence in French literature (soon to be used as a term of praise by Gautier and Baudelaire).

In the book on Roman literature, Nisard's indictment of recent French literature is quite general; he explicitly focuses on the great names of French romanticism only in two later essays on Hugo and Lamartine (1836–37). Hugo is attacked for "substituting images for reality, colors for thought," for his "piebald, dazzling language which one sees with the eyes of the body; a painter's palette thrown on a canvas, but not a picture." Hugo is all material description, glare and glitter, but suffers from sterility of the heart and sensuality of the imagination. There is no place for reason, no design, no taste, no critical sense, only imagination rampaging without restraint or control. Lamartine is a poet of nebulous generalities, incapable of self-criticism, hazily pantheistic, expansively, sentimentally humanitarian.[64]

These powerful essays imply the basic concept of poetry and history that animates Nisard's largest work, *Histoire de la littérature française* (Volumes 1 and 2, 1844; Volume 3, 1849, Volume 4, 1861). Nisard's book was the first complete history of French literature conceived in a unitary spirit, clearly articulated and firmly carried out. In the *History* and in a favorable review of Saint-Marc Girardin (1849) Nisard defined his own concept of criticism and literary history in opposition to the two other trends of the time: the new form of general history that describes the influence of society on authors and of authors on society, represented by Villemain; the criticism in biographical portraits which is inspired by a sentiment for the varieties of individual life (Nisard must have been thinking of Sainte-Beuve). Nisard's own type of criticism aims at freeing works from the tyranny of "each according to his taste," and at making criticism an "exact science." [65] He propounds an ideal of the universal human spirit in books, another ideal of the particular genius of France, and another of its language, and he places every author and every book in relation to this triple ideal. What lives up to this ideal is praised; what deviates from it is condemned. The ideal type finds its synthesis only in 17th-century France. French literature of the great age has the proper balance of the human faculties, of sentiment and imagination dominated by reason, while the Nordic literatures are more individual but also more local and less universal. Thus a concept of a universal ideal man, harmonious, reasonable, capable of taming his emotions and imagination, underlies all of Nisard's criticism. Universality as an ideal is enforced even in style and language. "The necessary resemblance of styles within the difference of subject matters or the special genius of the great writers makes the beauty of our literature: it is the unity of language in the diversity of the writings. I defy the most experienced critic to recognize the author of a perfectly expressed idea (unless he knows the passage by heart)." [66] Our contemporary standards of the characteristic, the individual, and the concrete could hardly be denied more explicitly.

With such universals in mind, history can be conceived only as a series of approximations and deviations from this ideal. The effect of Nisard's book is something like that of a novel without suspense, a novel written from a flagrantly omniscient point of view. Everything up to the classical age appears as preparation; everything after it as decadence. Nisard's last volume on the 18th century displays the scheme in all its nakedness. A balance sheet of gains and losses is drawn up, always comparing the 18th century with the 17th, to the disadvantage of the former. The book follows an order of genres beginning with lyrical poetry. The history of "losses" in poetry is demonstrated by the poverty of Jean-Baptiste Rousseau's and Voltaire's verse. Poetry was rediscovered only by Chénier. "Gains" can be registered in the prose of Montesquieu, Voltaire, and Buffon, but only indignation is reserved for Rousseau and his chimerical Utopianism. [67] The 120 pages allotted to Bossuet in contrast to 30 for La Fontaine or 50 for Molière in the third volume indicate the bias: Nisard is a militant conservative who condemns "imagination" as a lower faculty, an anarchic element. Imagination sways the crowd and keeps it from perceiving the eternal verities. Ronsard's popularity is thus accounted for; even Racine appeals through these inferior traits in his work; the success of the modern romantic poet is due to the exploitation of sensual imagination. [68] Nisard does not see that, implicitly, he condemns all poetry and art; that his standards are simply religious, moralistic, intellectual, political in a wide sense; and that his judicial criticism, which he defends against the criticism of beauties, has, in practice, completely abandoned the sphere of literature. Imagination is disruptive, shiftless, innovating, and revolutionary; art is a social menace. Nisard gave to his time a formula for a revived classicism, for the exaltation of the 17th century, for the permanence of the French spirit and taste—a formula that substantially survives in Brunetière and even in Lasserre and Irving Babbitt.

With Nisard, Planche, and Saint-Marc Girardin, literary conservatism and classicism have political and moral motives. Alexandre Vinet (1797–1847) draws from deep religious sources. Nisard is a Catholic: Bossuet is his hero. Vinet is a Calvinist pastor from Lausanne who spent twenty years in Basel teaching French and died as Professor of the Academy of Lausanne. His heroes are Pascal and Port Royal; his standards are definitely and clearly religious. His writings, mainly lectures published posthumously, cover all of French literature since the early 17th century. The lectures are often purely expository; they are interspersed with long extracts, diffuse, sermonic, occasionally even unctuous in tone, and might easily be dismissed as old-fashioned, earnest pedagogy. Even the high praise by Sainte-Beuve, who knew Vinet when he lectured on Port Royal at Lausanne, or the recent attempts in Switzerland to revive Vinet as a moralist and theologian, a "Protestant Pascal," would not suffice to give him a place among literary critics. But Études sur la littérature française au XIXe siècle (3 volumes, 1848) does not only confront the main French romantics (Madame de Staël, Chateaubriand, Lamartine, Hugo, Michelet, Quinet, Sainte-Beuve) with the standards of a firmly held and deeply felt Protestant Christianity; it also incorporates a view of poetry as symbol and revelation which was almost unique in the French-speaking world of the time.

Vinet must have learned something of German thought during his stay at Basel, though he rarely quotes German writers (Jean Paul, Friedrich Schlegel) and criticizes Goethe for his excessive objectivity and aloofness.[69] He understood (whatever his exact source) the central doctrines of German idealist aesthetics: the concrete universal, the incarnation of the general in the particular, the materialization of the spiritual, the organic unity of the perfect work of art. Vinet, who is usually described as a "spiritualist," knew that in literature the doctrine of idea for idea's sake was as false as the doctrine of art for art's sake, that a contempt for the particular and concrete runs counter to the nature of art.[70] "The poet's calling is not to know, but to see. Intuition is his special faculty." He sees and understands with the soul.[71] Vinet takes seriously the knowing heart and therefore defends Pascal against Cousin's accusation of radical skepticism.[72] The heart has its *reasons*. Hence poetry is the "incessantly new and surprising reproduction of the unchanging mystery," "the most complete and most profound revelation that can be given to man" next to Revelation itself.[73] Poetry is the Word, *le verbe,* of fallen nature. The poet is here to remake the universe in order to restore it to its pristine glory.[74] But this revelation through the heart, this intuitive insight is achieved in poetry only in the concrete world of characters or in images and metaphors. "Poetry, in general, does not define objects; it shows them, gives them form; what we ask of the poet is not the idea of an object, but the object itself, concrete, complex, alive." [75] "Poetry," he repeats insistently, "will never live by pure ideas and generalities. The reader always will look for an individual in order to identify with him." [76] Thus metaphor is not invented arbitrarily but is found "in the depths of the soul. It colors diction not from the outside but from the inside. It is not a varnish but an incarnation." [77] In a rapturous praise of Milton, Vinet plays variations on this concept of metaphor that makes the invisible visible, the abstract palpable. "Poetry materializes everything," individualizes, incarnates ideas. The parallel to the incarnation of Jesus Christ is drawn explicitly.[78] Hence myth is defended, even classical myth. "The fables of Orpheus and Amphion are truth; they bring us to the point of junction between the good and the beautiful, the real and the ideal and, one might say, to the true ground of poetry." [79]

Vinet's concept of the concrete universal, his incarnationism, is closely linked with his grasp of organicity. Content and form are one. Their unity depends on personality. The stronger the individuality, the stronger will be the internal unity. "Everything which is assembled from the outside, everything which, instead of growing like a plant, is constructed like a building, cannot have any truth poetically." [80] Vinet, alone among the French critics of his time, has, at least in his theory, overcome the divorce of content and form, of didacticism and formalism—the division that was to plague French criticism (and not only French) throughout the century. Vinet's grasp of the symbolic and dialectical point of view still allows him a surprising sympathy with his sentimental romantic contemporaries. But he can criticize them on the basis of moral and religious standards: Lamartine for his pantheism, Madame de Staël for her vague idealism. He can also judge them aesthetically for false concreteness, as he did Hugo, or false abstraction, as he did Lamartine. "Lamartine," he wittily ends a review, "still remembers a first vision, and he will remember some day that he remembered." [81]

The further Vinet moves into the past, the more conventionally classical and moralistic his criticism becomes. The 18th-century lectures are a running polemic against the *philosophes*. The 17th-century lectures are stodgy classroom expositions and moralizing oratory. Only the book on Pascal, *Études sur Blaise Pascal* (1848), has any value. Vinet emphasizes Pascal's psychology and ethics rather than the theology and metaphysics. He tries to make Pascal less sharply dualistic than Cousin does. Pascal expounds a knowledge of the divine truth, a knowledge by the heart that is real knowledge and not the desperate *salto mortale* from total skepticism into faith which Cousin found in Pascal. Vinet's reasonable, warmly emotional Christianity inspires this interpretation (the rights and wrongs of which we do not have to decide here) as it inspires all his work. His grasp of the symbolic and organic view preserved him from mere didacticism.

Charles Magnin (1793–1862) shows, on occasion, a similar grasp of the symbolic nature of poetry. The bulk of his writings—*Les Origines du théâtre moderne* (1838), a translation of the plays of Hroswitha (1845), and *L'Histoire des marionettes en Europe* (1852)—constitute an important contribution to literary history. The book on the origins of the theater, dedicated to Fauriel, learnedly argues the thesis of a threefold origin of the modern stage. The opera, the official drama, the popular theater have their origins in the liturgical drama, the court spectacles, and the street entertainments respectively. The insistence that drama grew out of lower forms, that there is an uninterrupted continuity of dramatic art since antiquity, that an understanding of these "dark ages" is necessary for an appreciation of Lope de Vega, Calderón, and Shakespeare, was a valuable (though today superseded) demonstration of the principles of historicism: its search for origins, the concern for popular art, the dogma of continuity. The historian, Magnin argues, must "re-establish one of the broken links of human perfectibility."[82] But as in the case of Ampère and Fauriel, the ambitious project remained a fragment: the published volume is largely devoted to antiquity, to rituals, mysteries, circus plays, and so on, as pre-forms of dramatic art; and the later books and scattered articles are only partial demonstrations of the underground survival of dramatic art through the Middle Ages.[83]

Magnin's sympathetic reports about the performances of the English players in Paris[34]—judging the plays and the acting of Kemble, Kean, Macready, Miss Smithson, and others, criticizing the adaptations of Shakespeare then used for their deviation from Shakespeare's text—were important empirical demonstrations of the effect and success of the English form of drama, sallies for the romantic side in the great debate. Magnin is also an excellent theorist, though unfortunately he formulated his views only briefly and occasionally, never elaborating them to a coherent position. He sharply proclaims the end of the old poetics and the need of a new "aesthetic" concerned with the "poetic state." He just as clearly rejects the theory of imitation and proclaims "imagination" as the central poetic faculty that combines image and music in one. He also rejects the usual genre theories, including Hugo's rigid evolutionary scheme, realizing that genres mingled and interpenetrated in older times.[85] While he recognizes the distinctions of narrative, song, and dialogue, he would want genres to be established not on the "artificial differences of form, but according to the natures of the internal chords which each of them sets vibrating in the brain of the poet and in the soul of the auditors."[86] The aim of the poet is to "decipher the grand characters which the finger of the Eternal has imprinted on all things, to translate into poetic vibrations the secret music which the world exhales from deep within all its elements and all creatures."[87] "Poetry, which could be called a demiscience, or rather a prescience, calls up through the effulgence of its symbols and the flashing of its metaphors a throng of anticipated truths for which science will later find a demonstration." This is so because "all truly poetic expression is the revelation of a newly discovered relation between the physical and the moral world."[88] The poet cannot be content with the current language, since he seeks to express the ineffable, the indefinable in the soul of man, and "ought to open, at any moment, a vista into the infinite." Thus poets are the creators of language; they incessantly make and unmake it.[89]

It is surprising to find Magnin, in his time and place, defending even obscurity, extravagance, the fantastic—of which Hoffmann's Kreisler is an example—and the magic of distance. Like Diderot and Wordsworth, he excludes violent sensation from poetry: it must be the memory of sensation, not sensation itself. Eloquence is the voice of sensation, but not poetry. Poetry "not only reflects the images and sensations it receives: it creates the relations which it discovers between two images or two ideas, from which it draws a third image or a third idea, an expression of that relation which is its own particular accomplishment. In this sense, poetry is creative." [90] With this exalted view of poetry as creative imagination, as the interpreter of the tangled web of the universe, as prescience, Magnin nevertheless maintains a sound skepticism about the social role of poetry. He objects to Hugo's grandiose pretensions. "Does it follow that social and religious initiative in our age should belong to the poets and that they should make a frontal assault on metaphysical and social problems?" Magnin cannot see how a poet can discover social truth. There is "more invention, creation, real originality" in some of Hugo's poems written "with the promptings of the heart and the imagination" than "in the vague commonplaces about the future with which the poet frequently felt obliged to hide the emptiness of his thought." [91] The very moderation of Magnin's claims, as well as the casualness with which he stated them, obscured his position, which successfully combined the insights of symbolic poetics with the new historicism.

Magnin and many others shied away from the exaltation of the poet as inspired prophet and social leader. This exaltation of the poet was, surprisingly enough, the strange position into which poets were forced by the early forms of socialism representing the most rationalistic utilitarian, didactic movements of the time. In the writings of Saint-Simon (1760–1825) literature still plays a very minor role. But Saint-Simon established one feature of the theory of literature descending from his movement: the sharp distinction between reason and sentiment, between the philosopher and the scientist on the one hand, and the artists, poets, and painters, whose function it is, in Comte's words, "passionner les masses." [92] Saint-Simon's own outlook is rationalistic, but his disciples felt the contagion of the romantic atmosphere and proclaimed themselves the founders of a new religion. Just before the July revolution, Émile Barrault, a minor Saint-Simonian, appealed to artists to join the movement and promised them a leading role in the new society. "The artist alone, by virtue of that sympathy with which he embraces God and society, is worthy of directing humanity." [93] *Poeta vates* returns in a new disguise. But the actual leaders of the Saint-Simonian movement thought of the poets only as servants of their creed. Enfantin, as Father of the Church, declared the artist to be the "Word of the Priest"—the Priest being himself.[94] No wonder that poets and writers who at first were carried away by the movement were soon disillusioned. Almost the same can be said of the utopian socialism of Charles Fourier (1772–1837). He and his adherents likewise considered the poet as a valuable potential ally, but the Fourierists, more clearly than the Saint-Simonians, made definite demands for a popular, democratic art. In the forties they had closer contact with the rising realism, in spite of the mystical and sentimental dreams of Fourier himself.

The one real literary critic among the prominent Utopian socialists, Pierre Leroux (1797–1871), had close contacts with the romantic groups and formulated a theory that combined a demand for social art with a symbolism not far removed from that of Magnin or Vinet. Leroux admired Jean Paul and knew something of Creuzer's work on symbolism. In an article, "Du style symbolique" (1829), he recognizes that modern poetry continually substitutes images for abstract terms, "vague and indeterminate expressions for proper expressions, metaphors and allegories for comparisons of ideas." "To speak in symbols, to allegorize," seems to him the "great innovation, in point of style, of the last fifty years." [95] Symbol, of course, here means little more than any kind of trope, imagery, or substitution.

But in a series of remarkable articles in the *Revue encyclopédique* (1831), the symbolic principle is defined far more closely. The unique principle of art is the symbol in the sense that the artist cannot but incarnate his inner life in something that already exists in nature. There is, on the one hand, abstract language, which does not exclude eloquence or even sublimity; and there is, on the other hand, poetry, the language of symbols, a system of correspondences, a network of "vibrations":

Poetry is that mysterious wing which soars at will in the world of the soul, in that infinite sphere of which one part is color, another sound, another movement, another judgment, etc., yet all vibrate together according to certain laws, so that a vibration in one region is communicated to another region, and the privilege of art is to perceive and to express these relationships, hidden deep in the very unity of life. For from these harmonic vibrations of the different regions of the soul a *chord* results, and this chord is life; and when this chord is expressed, it is art; now the expression of this chord is the symbol; and the form the expression takes is rhythm which is part of the symbol; that is why art is the expression of life, the reverberation of life, and life itself.[96]

Elsewhere Leroux recognizes that in his sense "metaphor, symbol, myth are but different degrees of allegory" [97] and sees in symbol "an intermediary form between comparison and allegory properly speaking, swifter than comparison and less obscure than allegory. It is truly an emblem, the metaphor of an idea." [98] The term "symbol" shifts rather disconcertingly from a rhetorical category to an element in a mystical view of nature. The whole theory is then animated by a fervent belief that art must not only symbolize the life within the poet but appeal to new life and anticipate the future destiny of humanity.

Still, in these articles and in an introduction to a translation of *Werther* (1845), Leroux accepts the view that the poet cannot but faithfully reflect his society. While he chides the poet for not knowing where humanity is going (that is, for not being an adherent of his creed), he at the same time offers a defense of romantic pessimism, of the Byronic poetry of his time. Lamartine and Hugo, he argues, are not really Christians: they float indecisively between the past and the future without having any other social religion than the cult of art. Nevertheless, they express the real state of humanity, "the dark and profound depths of the human heart in our age." [99] The objection that there are conservative or optimistic writers such as Scott, J. F. Cooper, and Béranger is explained away by the different society to which they belong or by special temperament. The literature of our age is "the symbol of the chaos in which we flounder and from which a world will arise." *Werther* is interpreted

not in what Leroux considers the trivial biographical terms of
Goethe's own account in *Dichtung und Wahrheit* but as a conflict
between Goethe's native German Protestantism and the new French
atheism. Werther has the sense of nature, of pure love, and of
human equality; but he lacks the vivid sense of the destinies of
humanity. Nature, humanity, family are felt strongly in *Werther*,
but each is felt in isolation. Leroux wants the poet to show us
"the salvation of individual destiny linked to that of universal
destiny." [100] A shrewd analysis of the *mal du siècle* goes hand in hand
with a symbolist theory of poetry and a concept of the poet as a
prophet and upholder of the new society of the future. A critic of
the time could thus declare that "symbolic poetry has no future in
France, and socialism, by taking possession of it, has dealt it a hard
blow." [101] Sainte-Beuve, who for a time shared Leroux's views,
turned against his prophetic pretensions and complained that in becoming "a god and a revealer," Leroux had become a charlatan.[102]

The social enthusiasm of the time—the old-style didacticism that
asked literature to instruct by pleasing, the many official and
unofficial attempts at government control and direction of literature
since the Revolution,[103] and the new liberal or socialist demand of
an art in the service of progress or Utopia—caused a reaction that
is usually described as the art-for-art's-sake movement. Its spokesman was Théophile Gautier (1811–72) and the central text the
preface to his novel, *Mademoiselle de Maupin* (1834). One cannot,
however, speak of an art-for-art's-sake movement in any strict sense:
there was only a Bohemia that felt very keenly its divorce from the
bourgeois society of the time. Gautier's manifesto can hardly be
taken seriously. It is a diatribe against critics and journalists as
impotent, envious fools who confuse author and work, who call a
man a drunkard because he describes an orgy, or a rake because he
tells of a debauch. Literature and the arts do *not* influence society:
the beautiful is utterly superfluous. "What is the use of beauty in
woman?" Gautier derides the Utilitarians. "Provided she is capable
of receiving a man and of bearing children she is always good
enough for the economists. What is the good of music? or of painting?" "Nothing truly beautiful serves a purpose: everything useful
is ugly." The most useful part of the house is the privy. Gautier
prefers a useless Chinese pot, covered with dragons and mandarins,

to his chamber pot. He would joyfully "renounce his rights as a Frenchman and citizen, to see an authentic picture of Raphael or a beautiful woman in the nude." He would rather have torn shoes than verse badly rhymed, and would rather get along without boots than without poems. Gautier laughs also at the Utopians, at Fourier, and the foolish belief in progress. Progress has not achieved anything humanly important. "Has anyone invented a single new mortal sin?" [104]

In his preface Gautier sticks out his tongue at the Philistines but does not formulate a theory beyond asserting the independence of beauty. This idea in itself was of course far from new. Usually it has been traced back to the Germans, to Kant and Schiller, who defined and defended the autonomy of art. The phrase "art for art, and without purpose" can be found in Benjamin Constant's diary, in 1804, when he reported on a conversation in Weimar with Henry Crabb Robinson, who was telling him about the aesthetics of Kant.[105] But the Germans never dreamed, of course, of surrendering the social and metaphysical claims of art; autonomy of art with them could not mean anything like the "uselessness" flaunted by Gautier. Gautier, no doubt, had heard of these aesthetic theories in general terms, since they were expounded in France in different versions by Victor Cousin (1792–1867) and Théodore Jouffroy (1796–1842). In a lecture course first given in 1818 (printed only in 1836) Cousin apparently spoke of the need of "religion for the sake of religion, of morals for the sake of morals, and art-for-art's-sake."[106] Jouffroy, in his course on aesthetics given privately before a small group that included Sainte-Beuve, in 1828 (but printed only in 1843), devoted a whole lesson to the distinction between the beautiful and the useful.[107] Cousin's aesthetics is a Platonizing celebration of intelligible, ideal beauty. In Du Vrai, du Beau, et du Bien (1836)—a revision of his lectures at the Sorbonne—he argues for the final unity of the old triad. Ideal beauty is Truth "under sensible forms"; it is beauty infused with an idea or with the highest kind of intelligibility.[108] Jouffroy's aesthetics is a development of the British 18th-century aesthetics that considers beauty an effect of sympathy, of a process of association of ideas conveyed by signs or symbols. Nothing could be further from Gautier's sense of sensual, corporeal, even sexual beauty than the abstract ideal of Cousin, which harks back to Plato and Winckelmann, or the humanitarian feeling of Jouffroy, which comes from the Scottish common-sense school.

Rather, Gautier asserts the autonomy of art because he loves the aesthetic surface, the color, the outward form of pictures and painting, even to the confusion of sexual attraction or mere luxury with aesthetic enjoyment. He himself recognizes that "the lust of the eyes, *concupiscentia oculorum* is my sin."[109] "Art is liberty, luxury, extravagance—it is the flowering of the soul in idleness," said Gautier in 1832, and meant by soul rather the senses or, at best, the sensibility of the artist.[110] He consistently defends the primacy of form and feels strongly its difficulties: the need of labor, of craft. Art is "exquisite care of execution; the word *poet* means literally maker; anything that is not well made does not exist." Gautier, who wanted himself to become a painter, conceives of language as the medium the artist has to subdue: "Verse is a gleaming and hard material like Carrara marble." [111] In many of his poems he tried to evoke pictures, to rival in words the colors of the painter. This transposition of the arts supplies also the best-known technique of his criticism. Metaphorical characterizations by pictorial similes are scattered all over Gautier's practical criticism. There are anticipations of the method in Lamb and in Hazlitt, but in Gautier it becomes an elaborate mannerism, a virtuoso indulgence. Thus, for instance, Chapelain's epic poem, *La Pucelle*, is described as "stony." "The air is also of stone . . . the little streams that fall from the rocks have an air of stalactites rather than of soft and penetrable water, the leafage of the trees seems to be made of white iron" and so on for a whole page, in constant variation on the elementary perception that *La Pucelle* is dull, lifeless, hence like a stony world.[112] It is not at all "impressionistic criticism" in the sense of being personal or subjective. It is pictorial fantasy on the occasion of a work of literature.

But it would be unjust not to recognize that Gautier was also a critic with a definite taste who helped reinterpret the history of French poetry. His most important book is *Les Grotesques* (1844), a series of uneven essays on French poets beginning with Villon, through Théophile de Viau, Saint-Amant, Cyrano de Bergerac, and Georges Scudéry, to Scarron. The first essay on Villon today appears lukewarm and out of place. But Gautier does sketch an anticlassicist history of French poetry and shows a real appreciation for what we have come to call the baroque. The term "grotesque" comes from

Hugo's preface to *Cromwell*, but it here means little more than something irregular, bizarre, exuberant—the same as the "arabesque," or the fantastic. The term is neither clearly kept in mind nor consistently advocated. But the hostility to the accepted dogma of French classicism comes through. Gautier is one of those who regret Malherbe's influence. Malherbe seems to him the least poetic spirit that ever was. He founded the "school of versifier-grammarians" continued by Boileau, "a just, but narrow mind, a passionate and ignorant critic." At that time the French acquired their deplorable taste in poetry for "glassy clarity, for the limpidity of filtered water, for geometrical exactness," for mere fable and subject. For Gautier, of course, metaphors, figures, and passion are poetry. He finds them in Théophile de Viau, a "truly great poet with whom the romantic movement begins," and in Saint-Amant, who, great and original as he is, "lacks the elevation and melancholy" of Théophile.[113] Gautier can then afford to treat his other "grotesques" as curiosities. Cyrano and Scarron were comic monsters battling against their time; Chapelain and Scudéry, monuments of majestic dullness.

Gautier's other writings show how his history of French poetry would have proceeded. He wrote, late in life, an unfinished *Histoire du romantisme* (1872), a series of reminiscences proudly recalling, among other things, the red waistcoat he wore at the first night of *Hernani*. Romantic poetry, he asserts, began anew with Chénier; Chateaubriand was its father, Hugo the great master. Nostalgically, Gautier evokes the figures of his Bohemian friends, Pétrus Borel, Philothée O'Neddy and Gérard de Nerval.[114] All through his writing life he encouraged the young, the Parnassians. Banville's and Leconte de Lisle's visual art and respect for craft struck sympathetic chords in him, though he could not share their objectivity and never felt *impassibilité* himself.

Among his young admirers Gautier singled out Baudelaire, to whom he devoted an essay (1862), a passage in the survey "Les Progrès de la poésie française depuis 1830" (1868), and one of the *Portraits et souvenirs* (1875). The first essay contains a defense of "decadence," which to Gautier means "complete maturity, extreme civilization, the crowning of matters." Needless to say, Gautier sides with Baudelaire against the didactic heresy. Baudelaire's work must not be used against the man: he is perfectly innocuous. Every one of his poems is an essence. He has, as Hugo said, "created a new shudder." [115] In the "Progress" essay, which is frequently over-generous to very minor poets, Gautier treats Baudelaire a little as Sainte-Beuve had treated him—as a strange man "at the extreme confines of romanticism," as a poet lacking "ingenuousness and candor." Gautier characterizes Baudelaire by quoting, at length, the description of the garden of poisonous flowers from Hawthorne's story "Rappacini's Daughter." But he realizes that Baudelaire does not approve of "the vices, depravities, and monstrosities that he traces as cold-bloodedly as a painter in a museum of anatomy. He rejects them as infractions of the universal rhythm; for, in spite of these eccentricities he loves order and the norm. He is without pity for others, but he judges himself no less severely." [116] This is also the theme of the far more sympathetic later portrait. Baudelaire is mannered but "naturally mannered," decadent, or Byzantine. He believed in the metamorphosis of everything natural into art: he transfigured even the ugliest theme into a serenity achieved by sheer will power. Though Gautier knows of Baudelaire's system of correspondences and senses his spirituality,[117] he sees him finally as a disciple who has gone far—a little too far for Gautier's taste—in the worship of strange and severe beauty.

In Gautier's patronage of Baudelaire and in Baudelaire's tribute to Gautier the beginning and the end of the century seem to be linked. Yet the gulf between the two men remains: the sensual, expansive, indulgent, jovial Gautier knows nothing of the tragic depth, the despairing intensity of the younger man. Gautier well represents—in spite of his seeming isolation—the first half of the century: the ardent expansion in history and aesthetics, the trust in the greatness of literature and humanity in spite of the superficial, romantic melancholy of the time. Sainte-Beuve, who absorbs and synthesizes all the main motifs of his predecessors, who rivals and passes through all stages, belongs, in spirit and temperament, to the later, harsher, disillusioned age.

2 : SAINTE-BEUVE

CHARLES AUGUSTIN SAINTE-BEUVE (1804–69) did more than any other critic to re-establish the supremacy of French criticism. He became *the* critic, the master not only in France but all over Europe and the Americas. The enormous scope of his work extends to some sixty volumes of criticism in a wide sense of the term. The readability and deft charm of his writings, the authoritative voice of his pronouncements, the impressive erudition and substantial knowledge he conveys, the basic sanity, good sense and good taste, a certain centrality, suspicion of the eccentric and extravagant—all these qualities have made Sainte-Beuve a major figure in European intellectual history. Just because of this pre-eminence, it is not surprising that a reaction has set in, mainly during the last thirty years. Increasingly, the limitations of Sainte-Beuve's taste are being stressed: in an age that has exalted Stendhal, Balzac, and Baudelaire as the greatest figures of the French 19th century, Sainte-Beuve's attitude toward them—grudging, hostile, and patronizing—seems a major test in which he failed. The argument against him runs that he did not rank his contemporaries and followers rightly; that he overrated mediocrities and ephemeral successes, and that he was blind or almost blind to much that was to prove fertile in the future. Even in his judgments of the more remote past, Sainte-Beuve showed the narrow limits of his taste: his preference for the mediocre, the safe, the harmless, his distaste for the baroque and the grotesque, his fear of the grand and sublime.

The attack against him also has moral overtones. The impression of judicious equanimity and urbanity, we hear, is deceptive. His envy or even downright malice is fully revealed in the notebooks published under the title *Mes Poisons* (1926). Sainte-Beuve, while nourishing his bitter hatreds and petty grudges, flattered his middle-class audience, changing his opinions on men and books like a weathercock before the winds of fashion. He was not primarily a literary critic at all but was mainly interested in biography, the

34

psychology of the author, and social history. He constantly confused life and art, man and work. Proust, in three sharply worded essays not published until 1954, accused Sainte-Beuve of not understanding "the unique closed world, without communication with the outside, which is the soul of the poet," of not seeing "the abyss that separates the writer from the man of the world," of not knowing that "the self of the writer appears only in his books." [1] Moreover, with the growing theoretical and analytical preoccupations of the 20th century, it has become obvious that Sainte-Beuve is not centrally concerned with literary theory and textual analysis, that his theory, as far as it can be discovered, is extremely elusive and often contradictory and his analysis of texts perfunctory and hurried. An admirer, Logan Pearsall Smith, has approvingly described Sainte-Beuve as "an enemy of all systems." "To confront his subtle, irritable, and not unmalicious ghost with anything so crude as a demand for theory, would seem to be offering it almost a show of violence." [2] But this violence has been offered before, and, according to our plan, we shall have to offer it again.

Is it quite true that Sainte-Beuve has no theory, no system of questions and presuppositions? In a late essay on Chateaubriand (1862) Sainte-Beuve protests against the accusation of having no theory, of being purely historical, all individual, of being the most skeptical and indecisive of critics. He formulates here a theory of psychological types of men which he calls "families of the mind." Convinced of the close relation between work and man, of the proverb "as the tree, so the fruit," he argues that literary study leads to a typology of character.[3] This typology is assumed to be simply given: there are innate antagonisms among men, "hatreds of the race." "How can you force Boileau to enjoy Quinault, or Fontenelle to have a high regard for Boileau? Or Joseph de Maistre or Montalembert to love Voltaire?" [4] Sainte-Beuve conceives these families of the mind as groupings of some spiritual affinity and even in historical continuity. Virgil is surrounded by Menander, Tibullus, Terence, and Fénelon; Horace presides over a group of poets of civic life and "those who know how to talk in verse": Pope, Boileau, La Fontaine, Voltaire.[5] Sainte-Beuve expects some future great advances in this field. Hitherto critics have written simple monographs and accumulated detailed observations: but he "can see links and connections; and a broader, more luminous, and yet refined spirit may someday discover the great natural divisions which correspond to the families of the mind." [6] Sainte-Beuve seems to envisage the characterology cultivated since his day in France by Le Senne and others, or the types of world-view defined by Dilthey, Jaspers, Spranger, and even Jung, as a dim ideal of the future to which literary study would supply empirical evidence.

But Sainte-Beuve could hardly have thought of literary criticism as merely providing documents for the study of psychological types. Although he cherished this idea early as a guiding principle for the writing of *Port Royal*, for arranging its portrait gallery of monks and nuns,[7] he gave prominence to typology only in the atmosphere of the systematic naturalism of the sixties. Sainte-Beuve was then on the defensive, trying to show that he was not inimical to these younger men, though he could not embrace their doctrines unreservedly. Reviewing a rather shoddy book by Émile Deschanel, *Essai de critique naturelle* (1864), Sainte-Beuve accepts "natural" or "physiological" criticism as the new movement which will supplement the earlier criticism of taste and historical criticism. But he strongly urges a reservation. "There will always be a certain unexplained, inexplicable side, of which the individual gift of genius consists . . . there is always a place for the unknown mover, the center and focus of higher inspiration or the will, the inexpressible monad." [8] In his highly laudatory review of Taine's *History of English Literature* Sainte-Beuve raises the objection that the "spark of genius," "what is essential in a poet," cannot be reached by Taine's analysis. "There is only one soul, one particular form of the mind to make this or that masterpiece," and "there will always remain a last point and a last irreducible citadel." The poet is not something simple, he is not a resultant or a simple focusing lens. He has a mirror of his own, his "individual unique monad." [9] The defense of individuality by means of the Leibnizian term runs throughout these articles. Sainte-Beuve refuses to surrender to a positivistic determinism, even though he is impressed by it, feels that he himself has moved in this direction, and vaguely anticipates a great future for it.

These late pronouncements, made in a changed intellectual atmosphere, do not define Sainte-Beuve's theories as they actually enter into his practice as a critic. Sainte-Beuve is not a naturalist of the new kind. Rather, he should be described as the greatest representative of the historical spirit in France in the sense in which this spirit is understood by modern German theoreticians such as Meinecke. True historicism is not simply a recognition of historical conditioning, but a recognition of individuality along with and even through historical change. Sainte-Beuve recognizes both things, and at his best he preserves the delicate balance needed to save himself from relativism or overemphasis on external conditions.

Sainte-Beuve's greatest strength is this sense of individuality, his ceaseless striving to define the special tone, the elusive kernel of a personality, whether of a person in real life or the personality emerging from an author's writings. Clearly he is not always a *literary* critic. Frequently—too frequently from our point of view— he is a historian of manners, a psychologist, or a moralist. He has written much on figures who are hardly literary at all—statesmen, generals, monks, nuns, society women—and even more on writers who are only on the fringes of imaginative literature—memoir-writers, letter-writers, diarists, historians, critics, etc. Much of his interest is frankly biographical and much of Sainte-Beuve's theorizing is concerned with a systematic approach to biography in terms of heredity, physique, environment, early education, or important experiences. Sainte-Beuve often finds occasion to remark on the ancestry of his subject; he discusses the father of Saint-Simon, the sisters of Pascal and Chateaubriand, the brothers of Boileau. He advises us to study the childhood, the place and landscape in which the author grew up.[10] Taine, for instance, mysteriously bears the imprint of the gloomy Ardennes.[11] We should study the first group with which a writer associated, the first book that made him famous, and then again the hour of his decline, the turning point that led to his fall. Sainte-Beuve wants us to ask: "What has he thought of religion? How has he been affected by nature? How did he behave toward women? Was he rich or poor? What was his way of life? What was his vice or weakness?" [12] And of a woman he wants to hear, "Was she pretty? Did she fall in love? What was the determining factor in her conversion?" [13] Such questions are not only asked but are frequently answered from details of an author's childhood, of his love life, of his religion, or simply by anecdotes and even gossip on his daily routine. Yet we can hardly say that Sainte-Beuve coordinates all this information. He merely assumes that it will contribute to a final concrete image. Though he often conceives himself in the role of a Bacon, a botanizer, a "naturalist of minds,"[14] Sainte-Beuve never fully embraces a causal view of literary production.

In many cases the information serves to document Sainte-Beuve's persistent moral theme: the contrast between reality and appearance, the man and his mask. The free examination that no longer spares even gods and religions cannot spare the poets.[15] This need of "looking below and behind the hearts"[16] Sainte-Beuve sometimes conceives as a serious process of debunking: the critic, like a Shakespearean fool, is to "tell the king that he is a man";[17] he has "to provide a little appendix in support of La Rochefoucauld."[18] Thus Sainte-Beuve denounces Vigny's self-apotheosis, as an "attempt to impose something sculptured, fashioned by his own hands."[19] The book on Chateaubriand has been interpreted as Sainte-Beuve's unmasking of an insincere *poseur* and even a liar. Chateaubriand's pilgrimage to Jerusalem led to a tryst with a woman in Granada; there is "affectation and posing until death" in Chateaubriand's mausoleum obsession.[20] Sainte-Beuve wants to "draw as true portraits as possible, put the warts and marks on the face, everything that characterizes a physiognomy or temperament, and make us feel the nude flesh under the robes, under the fold and pomp of the mantle."[21] At times he likes "to insert the scalpel and to point to the crack in the armor," as with Villemain, whom he came to detest as the "most sordid soul, the most spiteful ape that exists."[22] At other moments he is somewhat saddened to discover the disagreement between life and work, as in the case of Bernardin de Saint-Pierre, who wrote the gentle and chaste idyll of *Paul et Virginie* but was a hard and quarrelsome man.[23] Sometimes Sainte-Beuve feels taken in personally: he enters in his private notebook that he cannot expose Hugo as a charlatan without accusing himself of being naive. "Molé told me: this is a man who calculates everything, even saying 'good morning.' He was that way since he was 16; but I believed in his words for a long time. I don't believe that there is another man to whom lying costs so little."[24] The whole 19th century appears to Sainte-Beuve as, in great part, "the century of charlatanism—literary, humanitarian, eclectic, neocatholic and what have you."[25] The unity of the human person, "sincerity," is Sainte-Beuve's moral imperative and also a literary ideal. It is high praise for him to say of a forgotten poet, Veyrat, that "his lyre and his soul, his life and his work are one and the same thing." [26] Biography, with such an assumption, becomes identical with criticism.

The center of gravity appears to lie in biography. "Biographers have imagined, I don't know why, that the history of a writer is entirely in his writings, and their superficial criticism never penetrates to the man at the bottom of the poet." [27] Sainte-Beuve even thinks that "it is always easy to judge a writer, but not so easy to judge a man." "The man is hard to know and when one looks for the man in the writer, the link between character and talent, one must study the man closely as a living being." [28] In such pronouncements and in much of Sainte-Beuve's practical criticism, literary study becomes subordinate to biography; the poet has to be penetrated, unmasked, discarded in order to reach the man at the bottom. The method, we would feel today, is entirely mistaken. For our literary critic there is no mask to be torn off; there is no "bottom" in the man rather than the work, no question of "sincerity" that can be answered by comparisons with documents from biography. We can merely plead in Sainte-Beuve's behalf that he grew up in the romantic atmosphere in which poets exalted and exhibited their ego and their private lives without apparent disguise. Sainte-Beuve was a romantic poet himself: his novel *Volupté* is thinly disguised autobiography, and his *Livre d'Amour* is an indiscreet versification of his dismal love affair with Madame Hugo. Sainte-Beuve observed the transformation of experience into the stuff of poetry and fiction in himself and could not help observing it all around him. He knew many prominent writers intimately, or lived at least in a circle in which biographical information, conjecture, gossip, and slander were easy to come by. The writers who loomed largest on the literary horizon of his youth—Chateaubriand, Madame de Staël, Lamartine, Hugo, and somewhat later George Sand and Musset—were subjective to a degree hardly known before in literary history. The relation between their life and work offered itself as a matter of course. Sainte-Beuve's slow abandonment of romanticism must be interpreted as a process, at least in part, of moral disillusionment with his early associates. It is scarcely unfair to turn Sainte-Beuve's instrument against himself and to suggest that the relation between his own public words and private feelings worried him morally and puzzled him intellectually.

But Sainte-Beuve is always a jump ahead of his critics. While he is frankly preoccupied with biography, with the psychology of the writer, and the moral problem of sincerity, he knows very well the difference between art and life, the separateness of the world of imagination, and the obliqueness of the relationships between work and man. Especially around 1830 Sainte-Beuve upholds (in company with Leroux) a symbolic view of poetry: "The artist, as if he were endowed with an extra sense, is peacefully occupied with perceiving beneath the outer world that inner world of which most men are ignorant . . . he observes the invisible interplay of natural forces, and sympathizes with them as though they were souls; at his birth he was given the key to symbols and the understanding of images." [29] As late as 1863 Sainte-Beuve recognizes that "art is also a world," that there is a conflict between man's life of feeling and the inventive and creative faculty, which suffers if the poet is too much at the mercy of natural feelings. "The philosopher, the moralist, the sage, the Christian may profit by them, but the poet who, by his powerful conceptions, sets up as rival of the world and whose secret is to reflect it in an immense magic mirror, feels disconcerted, discouraged; he stops in despair midway, if he has found his calvary." [30] Sainte-Beuve knows that art is not life, that the imaginative life is not the life of feeling, that personal refinement and moral delicacy may even hinder the achievement of great works of the imagination.

The book on Chateaubriand, which expresses harshly Sainte-Beuve's disillusionment with acting and posing, acknowledges that "the true reason why no one has ever torn off the mask of Chateaubriand is simply that he had his own sincerity, and that he never much disguised the fact that it was anything but a mask, a noble mask." [31] Even at the moment of conversion, which seems suspect to Sainte-Beuve, Chateaubriand "had his sincerity, not necessarily that of a believer (that superior and intimate order eludes us), but the sincerity of an artist and writer." [32] Sainte-Beuve also liked Gautier's preference for seeing "nature through a transparent disguise." He approves of Gautier's motto: "The mask has made us true." [33]

Even in the much debated case of his judgment of Stendhal, Sainte-Beuve was aware of the issue. Admittedly, he appeals first to a personal impression of the man. Though Stendhal was "witty, keen, refined, perceptive, and provocative," [34] Sainte-Beuve cannot believe that he deserves the praise that Taine and others were beginning to heap upon him. "I cannot agree with such a judgment, and I do not think that anyone who knew him personally would subscribe to this opinion." Sainte-Beuve seeks corroboration in the memories of men who knew Stendhal early in life—Mérimée, Ampère, and Jacquemont. Sainte-Beuve, however, does not rely on these personal impressions alone. He grants the possibility that "a man may leave finished works, monuments little understood by his contemporaries," even though during his lifetime he may have been merely a distinguished original [35]—as he himself obviously sees Stendhal. Sainte-Beuve believes that Stendhal left incoherent books. They have remarkable passages but are without totality; they do not resemble monuments. Sainte-Beuve sees that the final appeal lies with a judgment of the works themselves, although his own judgment, which may seem to us obtuse in its application of a narrow standard of classical composition, is clearly colored by his impression of the personality.

To the objection that only the work of art survives, which he knows well, Sainte-Beuve answers that he cares for more than great works: "Secondary men and works interest me much in many circumstances. It is for me really a matter of justice." [36] He protests often against the idolatry of the very great and the oblivion into which minor writers fall. He suggests that the inequality between works does not correspond to the real inequality among men. He does not recognize that by ranking men and women ethically and intellectually, as personalities and characters, he will arrive at a very different scale from that at which he would arrive by judging them in terms of accomplishments. The lack of direct correspondence between human worth in a social sense and creative accomplishment is a fact of history that Sainte-Beuve would not admit. Furthermore, he is unwilling to see that the weeding-out process, the struggle for survival in history, is necessarily a cruel one, since mankind cannot remember as much as Sainte-Beuve and other historians would like it to remember. Sainte-Beuve obviously felt that his own poetry and novel had not deserved their ill-reception and could feel, rightly, that intellectually he was above many contemporaries who had received far more public attention. One can speak of his envy of the demigods and idols of his time, but one must also recognize his genuine solicitude for the unacknowledged merits of the humble, the modest, the retiring, and often, to our taste, the merely sweet and appealing, the curious and the average.

It would be a mistake to reduce a discussion of Sainte-Beuve to the question of biography and to contrast him with the historian Taine. Sainte-Beuve cares for both individuality and history. He wrote prolifically not only on the history of thought, the history of sentiment, and social history but also on literary history in a narrow sense. The attention to minor and sometimes minimal writers follows from the whole concept of historical representativeness. Almost all his books, as distinct from collections of essays, are literary histories. The earliest, *Tableau de la poésie française au seizième siècle* (1828), is closest to pure literary history. Sainte-Beuve treats Renaissance literature largely in terms of its poetic and dramatic techniques. He is primarily interested in questions of diction, style, and prosody, and in the differences between the groups and schools of poets. Though the book was understood in its time as a romantic manifesto, Sainte-Beuve was not the "discoverer" of Ronsard and the Pléiade. Particularly in the earlier version of the essays in the *Globe*, he harshly criticized Ronsard for producing only pale copies of the ancients in a dead language, and he praised Malherbe for prohibiting run-on lines.[37] The *Tableau* is an unenthusiastic, cool, and often unperceptive, descriptive account of the Pléiade, fortified with ample quotations. In the revised form, Sainte-Beuve does suggest a genealogy for romanticism in the 16th century and even speculates that the French theater would have developed more freely if Alexandre Hardy had been a genius like Shakespeare.[38]

Sainte-Beuve's longest work, *Port Royal*, which grew out of lectures given at the Academy of Lausanne in 1837–38 and comprised eventually five volumes (1840–59), does not pretend to be literary history. It is primarily the history of the monastery, of the men and women who inhabited it, and of what Sainte-Beuve calls the spirit of Port Royal. Sainte-Beuve is neither expert in theological arguments nor interested in theology, though he obviously sides with the Jansenists against the Jesuits. He is more concerned with a history of religious sentiments, with the depiction of a spiritual type, of a way of life and a form of feeling and thinking. Clearly his own attitude toward his subject changed in the course of the years. In the thirties, when Sainte-Beuve prepared the lectures, he was still enveloped in the atmosphere of romantic

religiosity, deeply impressed by his encounter with Lamennais. At
Lausanne he felt a need for some regard for his Calvinist audience
and such friends as Alexandre Vinet. Later he reverts to the skepticism of his early training under the *idéologues* and felt more
strongly his distance from the mentality of Port Royal. He then
realizes the weaknesses and limitations of his subject; he is shocked
by the "odious point" of their monkish "uncleanliness," the credulity of their beliefs in miracles, their glorification of disease, suffering, and poverty, and their preoccupation with death as the sole
aim of life.[39] In the conclusion of *Port Royal* (1857) he expresses
his disillusionment and retreats to a position of scientific objectivity. He is "an investigator, a sincere, attentive and scrupulous
observer." He wants to "see the things and the men as they are, and
to express them as he sees them, describe in the round, as a servant
of science, the varieties of the species, the diverse forms of human
organization, strangely modified morally in society and in the
artificial labyrinth of doctrines." The idea of a typology of men and
of a collective psychology has won out over the early personal
sympathy for the "mystery of these pious souls, of their interior
existences, and the intimate and profound poetry it exhaled." [40]

Port Royal discusses incidentally many literary figures and some
literary texts. The book has been criticized for artificially dragging
in literary subjects that are only remotely connected with Port
Royal and for overrating the literary influence of the movement in
17th-century France.[41] But Sainte-Beuve is very well aware that he
uses Port Royal as a kind of thread or point of reference and even
pretext for literary history.[42] One must rather admire the skill with
which he succeeds in enhancing the appeal of a subject that appears
so specialized and remote from imaginative literature. Among the
texts and writers discussed, Corneille's *Polyeucte* and Rotrou's
Saint-Genest are only tenuously related to Port Royal; Guez de
Balzac has hardly anything to do with it and serves rather as a foil, as
the antitype of the purely literary man; Molière's *Tartuffe* can be
brought in only for its anti-Jesuit overtones. But surely Montaigne,
though he precedes Port Royal, is needed for the discussion of
Pascal, and Racine can be legitimately treated in his relations with
the fathers.[43] Sainte-Beuve is necessarily concerned with the ideas
of the literary figures, their attitudes toward religion and the issues
of the times, and he makes no attempt to give a sense of literary

evolution and change. But he manages to convey something of the history of French literary prose—its metaphorical luxuriance in Montaigne, its struggle for classical clarity and composition, its triumph in Pascal—and to elaborate and substantiate his dislike of what today would be described as the "baroque" style of the age of Louis XIII. Rotrou is criticized for overemphasis, pomp, bombast, and moral improbabilities, and Francis de Sales for his "Euphuism and Gongorism of devotion." [44] There are a few excellent pages on the *Lettres Provinciales*, some on how Pascal's art of the dialogue serves his satirical purposes, and some almost lyrical passages on the perfect style of Racine which, in part, recant Sainte-Beuve's own early view of his elegiac tenderness.[45]

The interpretation of the thought of Montaigne and Pascal must attract the student of literature. Montaigne is seen by Sainte-Beuve as the pagan, "the natural man," the tempter of Pascal, as a malicious demon whose "method can be rightly called perfidious." [46] Pascal, in contrast, appears to Sainte-Beuve as the man of faith, "an Archimedes in tears at the foot of the Cross." [47] Sainte-Beuve rejects the attempt of Cousin to transform Pascal into a skeptic and a man of the world who saved himself only by a leap into faith.[48] Sainte-Beuve starts firmly with the assumption that Pascal's "faith precedes his doubt" [49]—that Pascal, like St. John, loved Christ the Saviour with an absorbing devotion. He emphasizes the clarity and sanity of Pascal's mind and style. His deplorable lack of charm and ascetic enmity toward art helped, moreover, to form his sober and bald, metaphorless style.[50] Finally, Sainte-Beuve suggests—somewhat hesitantly embracing the religion of progress and science—that Pascal might finally be disproved not by arguments but by history. The world, Sainte-Beuve hopes, will become a less frightening place and will cease to be a world of exile. To Sainte-Beuve's mind Buffon, biology, and evolution refute or shall refute Pascal.[51] But these limitations of his 19th-century horizon should not conceal the fact that Sainte-Beuve was extraordinarily successful in his task: with complete historical empathy he entered into the mind and feelings of a group of people very alien to the time in which *Port Royal* was written. Whatever minor criticisms may be directed against the inaccuracy of details or even misinterpretations, *Port Royal* remains a triumph of intellectual historiography. In combining history of religious sentiment, historical and biographical narrative, individual psychological portraiture, and forays into literary history, it may seem to constitute a hybrid genre. But what the books lack in purity of method and aim they amply compensate for by local life and by a unifying spirit that is the historical spirit at its best. *Port Royal* reflects Sainte-Beuve's basic convictions: his refusal to suppress the role of chance; his reverence for the mysterious core of human personality; and his distrust of a "philosophy of history" and grandiose schemes—a distrust which he also voiced against Guizot, whose "history is far too logical to be true." [52] There is a stubbornly irrationalistic, indeterministic streak in Sainte-Beuve that sets him apart from the new rationalists such as Taine or the orthodox positivists and naturalists.

Sainte-Beuve's third book of literary history, *Chateaubriand et son groupe littéraire sous l'Empire,* based on lectures at Liège in 1848–49 but not published until 1860, comes nearer to strict literary history. The "Opening Discourse" (1848) states quite clearly the case for literary history: "It is not enough to know the men if it is a question of works." While trying to "characterize the production of the mind as an expression of the time and the order of society, one must not neglect to seize on what does not belong to transient life, on what pertains to the immortal and sacred flame, the genius of Letters itself." [53] Sainte-Beuve approves the task of "reproducing, above all, the movement, the unity and the totality of a literary epoch" and rejects the old, external antiquarianism of classifications and catalogues in favor of a vivid sense of the tradition, a feeling for the true relations, for "what has influenced, for what counts." [54]

Elsewhere Sainte-Beuve protests against conventional literary history as a "necropolis" and describes its true aim as establishing "the succession and interplay of schools and groups, the names and the physiognomy of the real leaders, the characters and degrees of the main talents, the merit of the truly outstanding memorable works." [55] On occasion he draws rapid sketches of literary history. He surveys the main periods of French poetry and suggests that Ronsard, Boileau, and Lamartine were the real innovators rather than Malherbe (and implicitly Hugo).[56] But generally, in practice and certainly in the book on Chateaubriand, the organizing principle is biographical: "The soldiers count less and the captains are almost everything in literary history." [57] There are discussions of

Madame de Staël among the preliminaries, attention is paid to Chateaubriand's friends, Fontanes and Joubert, and there is an appendix on Chênedollé; but all the light falls on the hero, his spiritual evolution, and the stages of his style. In its time the book was resented, because of the suspicion it throws on Chateaubriand's sincerity and because of the contrast to Sainte-Beuve's earlier awestruck admiration for Chateaubriand during the latter's lifetime. Sainte-Beuve's curious apology that earlier he had been, like the cricket in La Fontaine's fable, "obliged to sing in the lion's mouth" [58] reflects poorly on his moral courage, but there is no need to accuse him of duplicity. The criticism directed against Chateaubriand is well-taken, acute, just, and even mild from a modern point of view. Sainte-Beuve still treats Chateaubriand as the great figure of the beginning of the century, still admires the harmony and rhythms of his style, the power and novelty of his imagery, the spell of his landscapes, and the impact of his fictive types and moods. But he defines him now as "an Epicurean with a catholic imagination" [59] and doubts whether Le Génie du Christianisme is convincing as an argument. Chateaubriand appears as a great seducer, a "magician," a great writer of the decadence. "Chateaubriand transferred the center of prose from Rome to Byzantium, and sometimes even further than Byzantium—from Rome to Antioch or Laodicea. The Lower Empire style in French prose dates from him." [60] Sainte-Beuve has arrived at the conclusion that his earlier hopes for a new French renaissance was mistaken, or rather refuted by later developments. Sainte-Beuve's ideal of criticism and standard of taste had changed.

It is impossible to establish a neat chronology of Sainte-Beuve's various concepts of criticism. On the whole he seems to move in two directions simultaneously: from an early, more subjective concept of personal expression to far greater objectivity, detachment, and tolerance, and at the same time from a rather uncritical, sympathetic acceptance to an increasing emphasis on the role of judgment, to a definition of taste and the tradition. These two movements of his mind are at cross-purposes. In theory, romantic historicism goes with tolerance, with relativism, but in Sainte-Beuve it is modified and often contradicted by partisanship in the literary battles of the time and by the egotism of a poet seeking for personal expression

even in his criticism. The objectivity, the detachment of the later
stage models itself rather on the pattern of science. The conversion
to a classical taste, however, brings about a reassertion of the judicial function and hence the tone of authority and often of acrimony
in Sainte-Beuve's criticism. It seems best to sort out the different
concepts of criticism without too much regard for chronology.

To Sainte-Beuve the first stage of criticism is "a delight in understanding everything that ever lived," [61] a joy in the variety of
humankind regardless of intellectual agreement. He brushes aside
Edmond Scherer's criticism of Joseph de Maistre, admitting its
truth, but saying, "I shall listen to him." "I love everything about a
man when the man is distinguished and superior, I let myself and
shall always let myself be carried away by curiosity for life and that
masterpiece of life: a great and forceful mind. Before judging, I
think only of understanding and enjoying the presence of a great
and brilliant personality." [62] If we want to understand all the variety
of humankind we must, as Sainte-Beuve prides himself in believing,
become impartial, even impersonal, indifferent. "I detach myself
from myself." [63] "I want to speak of a writer in a perfect spirit of
impartiality. This impartiality, even this neutrality, has become,
I confess, one of my last intellectual pleasures. If this is dilettantism,
I confess that I am affected by it." [64] He can even go so far as to say:
"I take pride in being nothing in particular, and I love myself
apparently better under this broken, multiple, and fugitive form
than under any other." [65] Thus he can, at least in later years, disavow
belonging to any sect or embracing any particular doctrine,[66] and
can speak of "generous indifference" [67] as his ideal. Yet even a fairly
early essay on Bayle (1835) favors equilibrium, the refusal "to be
fanatical or even too convinced, or obsessed by any passion." "This
basic indifference, one must say, this prompt, facile tolerance
sharpened by pleasure, is one of the essential conditions of the
critical spirit." The critical genius seems to him the "reverse of the
creative, poetic genius and the philosophical genius with system; it
takes everything into consideration, takes everything at its own
value. Critical genius is nothing too dignified, nothing squeamish,
nothing preoccupied. . . . It does not stay at its center . . . it has no
fear of misalliance." Sainte-Beuve doubts that the critic can be a
religious man, cultivating, as he does, "the critical and discursive,

relaxed and accommodating faculty." The vocation of the critic is "like a perpetual journey with all sorts of people and in all sorts of countries, undertaken out of curiosity." [68]

This power of surrender, Sainte-Beuve feels, implies the rejection of any specific creed, and even of Christianity. There is an additional argument for his deep-rooted skepticism as to a supernatural explanation of human life. "Literary criticism, especially the kind I practice, is alas! almost incompatible with Christian practice. To judge, always to judge others or to reproduce the others well, to transform oneself into the others as I do so often: that is basically a wholly pagan operation, the metamorphoses of Ovid." [69] But this is an entry in a private notebook. He rarely went quite so far in public. Mostly he thought of criticism as a school of tolerance. "A poet will understand only his own manner of being and proper individuality and by that alone will inform us that he is not a critic." "I have often thought that for a critic it is best not to have any artistic faculty, lest he carry into his diverse judgments the secret predilections of a father and interested author." [70] He himself felt that he had been a poet, but that resigning his poetic ambitions, while painful like any failure, meant finding a new freedom, a new largeness of mind and horizon.

The method of an understanding criticism will consist first in simply reading. "The art of criticism consists in knowing how to read an author judiciously and to teach others to read him in the same way." [71] "The critic is nothing but a man who knows how to read and who teaches others to read too." [72] And again: "To know how to read a book and meanwhile to judge it without ceasing to enjoy it is almost the whole art of the critic. But the art consists also in comparing and in noting well the points of comparison: thus, besides *Atala* read *Paul et Virginie* and *Manon Lescaut;* besides *René* read *Oberman* and *Le Lépreux;* besides *Les Martyrs* read the *Odyssey, Télémaque* and Milton. Do this and let yourself go. The judgment will result quite naturally; it will form itself from your impression." [73]

In his early stage, Sainte-Beuve thought of criticism as the work of an expositor, even a propagandist of the poets. "After the creation of works of genius there still remains to someone else the worthy task of propagating feeling and admiration for them. Enthusiasm, the Muse of the critic, resides in this." [74] Once he even thought of criticism in this sense as the main and novel function of the time. "We are far from thinking that the duty and task of criticism consists only in coming after the great artists, in following their luminous tracks, in collecting, ranking, listing their heritage, in decorating their monuments with everything that can make us value and illuminate them. This kind of criticism has no doubt claims to our respect: it is grave, learned, definitive; it explains, penetrates, fixes, and hallows the confused admirations, the partly veiled beauties, the difficult ideas, and also the letters of the texts it deals with." But now he believes that there is need of a criticism which will "attach itself to the new poets, shame the mediocrities, cry 'Make room!' around the poets, like a herald at arms; march in front of their chariot like a shield-bearer." [75] Though this surrender to a group of contemporary poets was of short duration, Saint-Beuve later even thought of the critic as a "secretary of the public," a kind of "confidential private librarian" who tells it what to take along on a trip—for the amount of baggage is severely limited.[76]

One can find many more passages of this general tenor which seem to minimize the judicial role of criticism, either subordinating the critic to the poets or to the public or making him some kind of neutral mirror or some all-comprehending dilettante and Epicurean. But Sainte-Beuve always eludes generalization. He increasingly disapproves of dogmatists such as Nisard and has his reservations about the new doctrinaire theory of Taine. He knows that the old rules are played out, and he has a strong feeling for the variety of literature, the infinite riches of the past, the enormous map of the world of literature. But he cannot be pinned down to such resignation and passivity as may seem to be implied in the pronouncements quoted above. They are often only avowals of modesty, disclaimers of absolute certainty, reservations, and possibly prevarications.

Sainte-Beuve, for one thing, believed that the critic was an artist. "Criticism, as I intend it and want to practice it, is invention and perpetual creation." [77] This was true for him personally. He can, in a letter at least, speak of his *Portraits* as "an annex of the elegiac and Romanesque genre." Their real order is that in which they were written, according to emotion and whim. Their real subject is Sainte-Beuve himself.[78] He can say publicly that his criticism is frequently only a particular form, a roundabout way of speaking his own feelings about the world and life, of "exhaling a hidden poetry in an indirect way." [79] "Under the pretext of depicting someone else, [the critic] often tries to catch his own profile." [80] At a certain stage especially, Sainte-Beuve regretted his failure as a poet so keenly that he tried to suggest that criticism is not only, as he admits, a *pis-aller* but also a progress, a necessary second stage of any mind, not really divorced from poetry.[81] Poetry can also be produced indirectly, can "penetrate a life like a secret perfume. The poetic spirit can exist there possibly in a more distilled form than in its more brilliant and specious manifestations." [82] He seems to suggest that he remained a poet, even that he had become more of a poet by becoming a critic.

Sainte-Beuve usually conceived the role of criticism in much more objective terms. Its function is primarily and basically judicial. While at certain times he minimized, in theory, the judicial role of criticism, he never ceased judging, and increasingly he affirmed and reaffirmed the role of judgment. The critic, he asserts, must discern with certainty, without any softness, what is good and what will live. He must tell us "whether in a new work, the real originality suffices to compensate for the faults? Of what order is the work? Of what scope and what flight is the author?" [83] Sainte-Beuve sees the need for authority; he alludes favorably to Malherbe, Boileau, and Dr. Johnson. "The true critic precedes the public, directs and guides it." [84] In discussing the state of criticism in 1845, he recognizes that the time for an apologetic, auxiliary, explicative criticism has passed; it is time for criticism to return to its ancient role of judge.[85] He even seems to admit a criticism of just repression, good policing as a remedy for present-day abuses, and he extols the allegiance of criticism to unembellished truth. He praises Boileau for hating "a foolish book," and finds in La Harpe and Johnson "a just and lively sense" of truth, a gift of nature that can be developed and to a certain point perfected.[86] Sainte-Beuve constantly comes back to these norms; he chides his contemporaries for "venturing everything except a judgment. They will not dare commit themselves to saying: this is good and this is bad." [87] The critic has a conservative and corrective function: he "maintains tradition and preserves taste," [88] defends "the degrees of art, the ranks of the spirit." [89] "True criticism consists in studying each being—that is, each author, each talent, according to the conditions of his nature, in giving a vivid and faithful description, but always providing that it classifies him and puts him in his place in the order of art." [90] The critic, Sainte-Beuve believes, has a direct influence upon the trend of literature. Boileau is now praised as a healthy influence.

> Let us greet and recognize today the noble and strong harmony of the Great Century. Without Boileau, and without Louis XIV, who recognized Boileau as his Controller General of Parnassus, where would we have been? Would even the greatest talents have yielded so much of what today forms the most enduring heritage of their glory? Racine, I am afraid, would have written more frequently plays like *Bérénice;* La Fontaine would have written fewer fables and more tales; Molière himself would have given us more Scapins and might not have attained the austere heights of the *Misanthrope.* In a word, each of these fine geniuses would have wallowed in their faults. Boileau—that is to say, the good sense of the poet-critic, authorized and doubled by that of the great king—restrained them all and forced them, by his respected presence, to produce their best and most serious works.[91]

Sainte-Beuve deplores the fact that his own time lacks a Boileau.[92] One senses that he was ready to play the role himself when he says that Balzac would have profited from a Boileau,[93] and when he hopes that Flaubert will learn from the criticism that he himself had written of *Salammbô.*[94]

But how is tradition defined? Sainte-Beuve appeals to the central concept of the French critical tradition—the concept of taste. At times, this "taste" means merely "tasting," a form of sheer Epicureanism. There is a curious passage in which Sainte-Beuve deplores the fact that one can no longer read reclining upon a couch like Horace during the dog days, or stretched out on a sofa like Gray, or walk through the countryside, book in hand, sunk in meditation. How very different are things today! "Epicureanism is forever lost. The last religion of those who had no other, the last honor and virtue of a Hamilton and a Petronius, how I understand and regret you in the very act of opposing and abjuring you!" [95] Taste "appears always noblest, most perfect, and most genuinely refined and elevated in a saintly moral nature. But it often appears highly developed in very different natures. A certain agreeable corruption (may one confess this?) is not unbecoming and even gives an extreme refinement to some of its rarer modes." [96] But Sainte-Beuve abjures this corrupted taste. His ambition is for the noblest, the most elevated, the most humane taste, a taste which he is willing to define as "the modesty of the mind," [97] which he sees as "the finest and most instinctive" of our organs,[98] as "the love of the simple, the sensible, the elevated, the great." [99] When he praises Eugénie de Guérin, he cannot think of anything better to say than: "She feared excess; she did not insist, she did not strive, she had taste." [100]

Good taste is thus a sense of moderation, of the sensible, the reasonable, combined with a recognition of greatness. It is simply the subjective side of what Sainte-Beuve elsewhere tries to define as the tradition, as the nature of the classical. In two well-known essays, "What is a Classic?" (1850) and "Of Tradition" (1858), Sainte-Beuve formulated his views most memorably. The earlier piece elaborates a double point of view: on the one hand, he insists on the Greco-Latin tradition, on a judiciously graduated veneration of the classics; and on the other hand, he recognizes the existence of something transcending this tradition: the works of Homer, Dante, and Shakespeare are classics though they do not conform to the demands of traditional classicism. Sainte-Beuve also sees, of course, that the usual French classicism, with its narrow rules, is a thing of the past, that his time must go beyond it and create a new literature, which will fulfill the demands of the age. His position is complex and possibly contradictory, but not incomprehensible. Throughout his life he revered the French 17th century as the great age: he recognized that it was a collective phenomenon, a social event, and not merely a matter of the fortuitous superiority of talents or geniuses. "The idea of a classic implies in itself something which has sequence and solidity, which forms a whole and makes a tradition, something which has composition, is handed on to posterity and lasts." [101] But he did not wish to erect the 17th century as a model. He would like us to understand tradition as something generous. A classic is any work, no matter what kind, that has lived up to the standards of beauty and sanity that the critic now demands. Sainte-Beuve is not content to define the classic quality in terms of wisdom, moderation, or reasonableness; it would then include largely writers of the second rank—correct, sensible, elegant writers. The important thing now seems to him to preserve the notion and the cult of the classics and at the same time to widen it. Sainte-Beuve quotes, "In my Father's house are many mansions," a quotation which seems to suggest an all-inclusive toleration; but he denies what in an earlier essay he had somewhat plaintively acknowledged, that the fate of the critic is to be a "vagabond gypsy, and almost a Wandering Jew." [102] Now he can say, "there must be choice, and the first condition of taste ... is not to roam ceaselessly, but once and for all to stay with a settled opinion. Nothing palls so much on the mind and is so injurious to taste as ceaseless roaming." [103]

In the later piece, "Of Tradition," the emphasis on the Latin tradition as it was usually understood is even stronger; perhaps because Sainte-Beuve was addressing an audience of students, giving the introductory lecture at the *École normale*. He expressly says that a "professor is not a critic"; he need not be aware (as a critic should be) of all novelty. The critic is "a sentinel always awake, always on the lookout," while the professor has smaller and different obligations: "he must not go far from the sacred places which it is his task to show and to tend." Though Sainte-Beuve thinks that the professor should know the chief new events and should have an opinion, he himself feels at that moment very much like a professor expounding the necessity of preserving tradition. He understands this task of the upholder of tradition as that of a humanist rather than that of an antiquarian. He complains of the overemphasis on research, which was beginning in France, of the disproportionate importance given to discoveries of unpublished documents. "People are proud of finds which are merely curious (when they are that), which cost no thought, no effort of the mind, but merely the trouble of going and picking them up.... One would say that the age of scholiasts and commentators was beginning anew; a man gets no less honor and consideration for this, nay, more, than if he had attempted a fine novel or poem and had tried the way of true invention, the lofty roads of thought." Sainte-Beuve would respect the degrees of art, the levels of intelligence. "Let us encourage industrious research, but let us in everything leave the master's place to talent, to careful thought, to judgment, to reason, to taste." He thinks that instead of boasting on the title page, "according to unpublished documents," a book should rather say, "according to judicious ideas and views, even if they are old." He suspects that if someone found the notes of Thucydides for his *History of the*

Peloponnesian War, they would be preferred to the finished book. "People have come to prefer the materials to the work, the scaffolding to the monument." [104] Though Sainte-Beuve was immensely erudite himself and, as his *Port Royal* shows, could engage in prolonged and sustained research among documents and out-of-the-way books, he was always suspicious of mere antiquarianism, especially the enthusiasm for French medieval literature. The enormous development of reasearch in that field left him cold. "By nature and by taste I have never been among those who reclaimed the ground of the Middle Ages." He disliked "the excessive enthusiasm of some, and the finicky complacency of others." [105] In reviewing some French medieval mysteries, he protests against their editors' comparisons of them to Racine and Sophocles. He shows that the two editors, Paulin and Louis Paris, are ignorant of antiquity and the French 17th century: "they have not the terms of comparison." "Anybody who had read Sophocles in the original would have been preserved from these eclipses or aberrations of taste." [106]

Sainte-Beuve upholds the tradition that descends from classical antiquity. He appeals to the French as heirs of the Romans: "we have to embrace, to understand, never to desert the inheritance received from those illustrious masters and fathers, an inheritance from Homer down to the latest classic of yesterday, which forms the brightest and most solid portion of our intellectual capital." He grants that, in a way, the poetic faculty is universal in humanity. He wants the French tradition not to be closed and exclusive, but he urges his audience never to abandon atticism, urbanity, the principle of good sense and reason combined with grace. "We must never lose sight of the feeling for a certain standard of beauty suited to our race, to our education, to our civilization." In this tradition, Sainte-Beuve refuses to make a distinction between the Greeks and the Romans. "For us, their legacy and their benefactions are fused together." He does not sympathize with the new Hellenism that would reject the Latin tradition, nor does he agree with the older purely Latin emphasis that would relegate the Greeks to an earlier primitive past. He tries to assimilate Shakespeare in the same tradition. He points out that Shakespeare read Montaigne and Plutarch and thus was not entirely outside of it. He grants the faults of Shakespeare's age, but sees him at the center of human nature, not mad or barbarous as Voltaire had depicted him. "Great men are never permanently extravagant, ridiculous, grotesque, ostentatious, boastful, cynical, or unseemly. . . . Tradition tells us, and the consciousness of our own civilized nature tells us still more plainly, reason must always have and definitely does have the first place among these favorites, these elects of the imaginative power." [107]

This reason is then defined more closely as sanity, as common sense, but also as lack of discontent, as harmony with society. Sainte-Beuve appeals to Goethe's famous saying: the romantic is the diseased, the classical the healthy. (He had a high if somewhat distant veneration of Goethe, whom he called repeatedly the "greatest of all critics." [108] though he knew little more than Eckermann's *Conversations* to support this view.) The classic, then, comprises all literature in healthy and happily flourishing condition, literatures in full accord with their times and with their social surroundings; literatures "satisfied to belong to their nation, to their age, to the government under which they come to birth and flourish . . . literatures which are and feel themselves at home, in their proper road, not out of their proper class, not agitating, not having for their principle discontent, which has never been a principle of beauty." "Classical literature never complains, never groans, never feels boredom." "The classic loves his country, his own time, and sees nothing more desirable or more beautiful." [109] We may miss today the overtones of these statements. They excited resentment because they implied an endorsement of the Napoleonic empire. Sainte-Beuve had become a symbol of acceptance and reconciliation with the regime. In an article entitled "Les regrets" (1852) [110] he had ridiculed those who were always weeping for the past. The 1848 revolution, which sent him, more or less voluntarily, to a temporary exile in Belgium, had given him a terrible shock.

He now looks back at romanticism as a sickness of the time. "Hamlet, Werther, Childe Harold, the pure Renés, are sick men of the kind who sing and suffer, who enjoy their malady . . . sickness for sickness' sake." [111] Criticism apparently can and has cured us of such a malady. Earlier, in a wry double-edged eulogy, he had praised Saint-Marc Girardin for fighting the malady: now people get married and have children and do not despise the world. "Youth, a party of youth, has become positive; they no longer dream." [112] Now this seems to him right: he wants people to be honestly happy. He hopes for a society where "we would find ourselves again in unison;

strife and moral sickness would cease, and literature would again of itself become classical, both in grandeur of line and in what is essential, its fundamental basis; . . . we should perhaps begin again to have works that last." [113] Sainte-Beuve's criticism has now become definitely social and even moral and, in its implications, absolute in its appeal to some broad but eternal standard. The differences of opinion among critics seem to him to derive simply from differences in perspective. "They don't look for the moment on the same object, on the same works of the author in question, on the same passages of his works. They have not the whole of him before their eyes, they are not for the moment taking him in entirely. A closer attention, a wider knowledge, will bring together different judgments and restore them to harmony." [114]

This broad eternal standard—Sainte-Beuve's taste anchored in the Latin tradition—can be made more concrete by a brief review of his preferences and aversions in the history of poetry and imaginative literature. *Causeries du Lundi,* the weekly essays that ran from October 1849 to August 1861, and *Nouveaux Lundis,* which ran from September 1861 to May 1869 almost continuously, contain 640 essays. Of these only 150 are supposed to be literary and only 55 critical in a strict sense. Whatever the statistics, Sainte-Beuve's criticism is bewilderingly rich in its scope and variety, and it ranges freely over all periods and genres of French literature. In the background loom the ancients, always revered and studied intensely. "Reread a canto of Homer, a scene of Sophocles, a chorus of Euripides, a book of Virgil!—grandeur or flame of feeling, glow of expression, and, if possible, harmony of composition and wholeness." [115] Sainte-Beuve admired Homer and the Greek tragedians greatly and knew them well; but he wrote rather of Theocritus, Meleager, Apollonius, and Quintus Smyrnus among the Greeks, for he loved the pastoral and the *Greek Anthology* and searched for something to interest a modern audience among Hellenistic epics. This choice, we must realize, was sometimes a matter of chance. Saint-Beuve was a journalist most of his life. He picked themes as they were suggested by the new publications that fell into his hands. He may have thought also that he had something more novel to say when he spoke of minor figures or of those who better suited his taste. Though he worked at Greek even in the last years of his life,[116] he obviously was a much better Latinist.

Virgil is the center of his cult and *Étude sur Virgile* (1857), though hardly distinguished as a book because it betrays too loudly its origin in lectures destined for the *Collège de France*, proclaims Sainte-Beuve a "priest of Virgil." He professes to belong by his secret predilections, to "that French school admiring antiquity in the manner of Fontanes, Chateaubriand, and Delille" and to see a "straight and uninterrupted vista from Virgil, Horace, Ovid, and Lucan to our own days." "Only through the majestic and triumphal Roman aqueduct have the fountains of Greece reached us." Virgil inspires even today the neglected "discrete religion of the beautiful, the natural, the refined, and the delicate in poetry." [117] Virgil is the first, in the order of epic poets, the most complete and the most perfect of the Racinian poets. His love of nature, his love of books, his piety, his patriotism, which is not incompatible with universal humanity, support "the unity of tone and color, of the harmony and agreement of the parts among themselves, of the proportion, of the sustained taste which is here one of the signs of genius because it pertains to the depth and the flower of the soul and which I may call a supreme delicacy." [118] Sainte-Beuve's ideal of poetry could not be better defined. The praise of Horace (1855) as a "breviary of taste, poetry, practical and mundane wisdom" is cooler: Horace is the source of the French lyric tradition, he is nearest to the French way of feeling, he is a man and not "an angel or a soul"; [119] but Sainte-Beuve sees limits to his range which he does not recognize in Virgil. Virgil wrote an epic, the highest and most majestic of all genres, and his tone is elegiac and melancholy, the mood that suited Sainte-Beuve best.

The worship of the classical tradition—however it may seem romanticized to us—hampers Sainte-Beuve's appreciation of medieval literature. He paid loving attention to the French historians, Villehardouin, Joinville, Froissart, and Commynes, but he is untouched by the great 19th-century fervor of medievalism. A discourse on the origins of French language and literature (1858) derives from Ampère,[120] and the *causerie* on Dante is little more than a sketch of Dante's reputation in France. Obviously Sainte-Beuve shares the view that he ascribes to Vico: the *Commedia* is "an expression of the history of the time." [121] In reaction to the increasing chorus of praise of Villon, Sainte-Beuve's essay is extremely cool. Villon is to Sainte-Beuve a type, a legend, an illusion, a collective individual. He finds, as Voltaire did in Shakespeare, only "two or three pearls in his dunghill." "La Ballade des dames du temps jadis" is the only poem that excites his enthusiasm.[122] It suits his general taste for elegy.

His attitude toward French renaissance poetry is also determined by the classical ideal. While Sainte-Beuve, in retrospect, praises his early advocacy of the Pléiade as "an act of taste," he restates his reservations about Ronsard and Du Bellay vigorously: Ronsard is a facile, too facile, poet; [123] Du Bellay, though on the right road to an antiquity without superstition, remains only a glorious promise.[124] Sainte-Beuve sees that the foreign romantic critics (with the Schlegels at their head) were right in considering the Pléiade as the beginning of French classicism rather than as an anticipation of French romanticism. Ronsard is thus between two fires: the French classicists do not want to recognize him as their ancestor; the foreigners think of him as the man who started French poetry on the wrong road.[125] Sainte-Beuve thinks that he started it on the right one.

Sainte-Beuve resolutely sides with the French classical line. The *précieux* and baroque poets are always ranked low: Saint-Amant, for instance, below Racan and Maynard. Conceits and bad taste are vices of Saint-Amant and the vices of the time.[126] Sainte-Beuve does not quite believe that "enfin Malherbe vint," since Malherbe was only a reformer in the wake of the revolution accomplished by Ronsard.[127] Sainte-Beuve deplores Malherbe's negative side, his rejection of the past, and sees his narrowness; though in two late papers Sainte-Beuve praises him as a great poet. "Even in his meagerness and dearth of matter he is always dignified and has his moments of perfect and entrancing elegance." [128] He initiates the age of Louis XIV which to Sainte-Beuve remains the greatest age of French literature and even—with the possible exception of the Augustan age of Rome—of all literature. (Shakespeare remains apart as "the greatest of natural poets," [129] and the Germans, notwithstanding Goethe, cannot produce classics.) Even Sainte-Beuve's first articles in the *Revue de Paris,* which were interpreted as an attack on the French classics, can hardly be described as anything but generous appreciations from a new point of view. The essay on Boileau (1829) complains of his lack of sentiment for nature and dismisses *L'Art poétique* as an "abolished code of poetry"; but still

Sainte-Beuve concludes that "Boileau is a sensible and refined spirit, polished and mordant, not very fertile, of an agreeable brusqueness, a careful observer of true taste, a good writer in verse." [130]

The early essays on Racine must strike us as highly laudatory, though Sainte-Beuve tries a curious revaluation, inspired by the romantic emphasis on the lyrical and by an oblique desire to minimize the purely dramatic authority of the classical French tragedy. Racine is made over into an elegiac and pious singer; his pure poetry is preferred to his drama. After *Athalie,* Racine did not express "the personal tender, passionate, and fervent sentiments" [131] he really felt. Sainte-Beuve objects to the dramatic system which at that time was still being imposed on the stage. He misses local color and Greek manners in *Phèdre,* Roman manners in *Britannicus.* Racine's kind of tragedy makes a bold and somewhat dry simplification of design. The contrast to romantic drama, to its local color, variety, and freedom is obviously in Sainte-Beuve's mind. Later he expressly recanted this view: "Alas, I myself once claimed that Racine was better fitted for elegy or the lyric than for the drama." [132] And he changed his view of Boileau sufficiently to recognize, as we have seen, his great role as a critic.

Sainte-Beuve's negative critique of neoclassicism was directed entirely against the mere imitators and camp followers of the classics in the 18th century. The essay on Jean-Baptiste Rousseau (1829) delivered a blow to Rousseau's reputation from which it has never recovered. The viewpoint from which the essay is written is that of romantic subjective lyricism. "The lyrical poet is a naked soul who goes forth singing in the midst of the world," he creates a "world apart, a poetic world of sentiments and ideas." There is nothing of this in Jean Baptiste Rousseau. He has no genius, he has a small mind, and with him everything is craft. "He was the least lyrical of all men in the least lyrical of all times." [133] His allegorical odes are baroque, metaphysical, sophistical, dry, inextricable. Similarly sharp are Sainte-Beuve's views about some of the last poets of the neoclassical tradition, e.g. Delille and Parny. As late as 1837 Sainte-Beuve attacks Delille as having "neither art nor poetic style," as coming late in an exhausted tradition.[134] Among the 18th-century poets Chénier wins Sainte-Beuve's admiration. Sainte-Beuve, more than any other critic, helped to establish Chénier's reputation (his poems were first published only in 1819) and to impress on his contemporaries the view that there is a continuity between Chénier and the romantics, that Chénier is "the revealer of a poetry of the future, that he brought a new lyre into the world." [135] Sainte-Beuve, is seems today, grossly overrates Chénier's technical innovations and considerably amplifies the elegiac tone over the erotic.

But then, at least initially, Sainte-Beuve was fighting the battle for romanticism. Among the poets, Lamartine was his early love. *Méditations poétiques* (1820) was a revelation: "One passed suddenly from a dry, meager, poor Poetry . . . to a large, truly inward, abundant, elevated, and wholly divine Poetry." [136] A long essay (1832) pays glowing tribute: it breaks into verse in an adoring epistle.[137] The review of *Jocelyn* (1835) could hardly be more favorable. Sainte-Beuve makes an elaborate attempt to set the poem in the tradition of idyllic poetry and to bring to bear his knowledge of Coleridge's conversation pieces and Wordsworth's descriptive poems in his praise of Lamartine's Alpine melodrama.[138] However, his disappointment with Lamartine is obvious in the review of *Recueillements poétiques* (1839): it shows dissatisfaction with the poetry which, to Sainte-Beuve's mind, had succumbed to the influence of Hugo, and it is especially critical of the preface, in which the poet seems to disparage his early work and loudly proclaims purely political and humanitarian preoccupations.[139] The later *Lundis* contain caustic attacks on the bad taste and false style of Lamartine's *Les Confidences* and the contrived love story of *Raphaël*.[140] Sainte-Beuve reviewed Lamartine's history of the Restoration with devastating wit [141] and later defended La Fontaine against Lamartine's disparaging remarks: "Lamartine raises his sight to the angel; and La Fontaine, though he seems to raise the beasts to the level of man, never forgets that man is nothing but the first of the animals." Lamartine's poetry is "noble, sublime, ethereal, and harmonious to a degree, but vague." [142]

> *Lamartine ignorant, qui ne sait que son âme.*[143]

This reaction is no doubt colored by his disgust with Lamartine's political career, but also Sainte-Beuve genuinely felt that he had recovered from an illness—the romantic melancholy caused by Lamartine and his kin.

Still, if one examines Sainte-Beuve's taste in 19th-century poetry, one wonders whether the recovery was complete. The relation to

Hugo can hardly be understood without a knowledge of the biographical facts. His love affair with Adèle estranged him from Hugo, and in later life Sainte-Beuve fell silent about Hugo both for personal and political reasons. He wrote nothing about Hugo's dramas (he never cared for the theater anyway) or about his later novels and collections of poems after 1835. Though Sainte-Beuve was for a time the "herald" of Hugo and praised his poetry extravagantly, one cannot say that he was uncritical even in the very beginning. His early review of *Odes et Ballades* (1827) admits that Hugo abuses force and antithesis and cannot avoid the bizarre and the puerile. In straining for an ideal, he overreaches himself.[144] After a period in which Sainte-Beuve was definitely under his and her spell, he began to complain publicly of Hugo's vanity and impiety; after the break, while preserving his admiration for Hugo's genius, he more and more saw Hugo as a crude force, as a Cyclops, "a Caliban who pretends to be Shakespeare," a barbaric titan [145] who fitted Sainte-Beuve's picture of French decadence.

Almost as unfortunate were the relations with Vigny, whom, after a somewhat distant friendship, Sainte-Beuve came to dislike as a colleague in the Academy. As early as 1826 he criticized *Cinq Mars* for its violation of historical truth and praised the poetry with many reservations. The prose seemed to him quite unreal.[146] Later the tone of his criticism (though hardly its actual content) changes to overt disparagement. Vigny's poetry is "like alabaster, artistically worked, but pale and colorless: life and blood do not circulate in it." [147] The obituary makes some amends, but still protests against Vigny's aristocratic pose, his false historical colors, and harps at great length on Vigny's long-winded speech at his reception to the Academy. Even *Les Destinées* seems to Sainte-Beuve, surely unjustly, a "well-sustained decline," though he greatly admires some pieces like "La Colère de Samson." [148] Personal coolness to the man and his grand airs made Sainte-Beuve harshly critical of his poetic achievement, particularly if one compares Sainte-Beuve's coolness with the praise he lavished on many minor contemporary poets—and particularly poetesses, such as Madame Desbordes-Valmore.

The most conspicuous case is that of Béranger, though we must not forget that Béranger was lauded by Goethe and many others in a tone that seems incomprehensible today. Even in a later article of tempered praise, Sainte-Beuve classes Béranger with the second rank of poets, which includes Burns, Horace, and La Fontaine.[149] Sainte-Beuve forgave much to the correct political tendency, and he also admired more strongly than we do the break with the French tradition of Alexandrine rhetoric. The *chanson* itself—popular singable poetry, long absent from the French tradition—charmed Sainte-Beuve and his age excessively. He was only echoing the general voice when, in 1842, he classed Béranger with Lamartine and Hugo as the greatest poets of the age.[150]

Sainte-Beuve, confronted with younger men and rivals, responded more and more coolly. He hailed Musset cordially, though he saw quite clearly the deficiencies of *Une Confession d'un enfant du siècle*.[151] In the obituary the tone of regret for a wasted life is possibly too audible. But Sainte-Beuve knew too much of Musset's habits and the decline of his last years.[152] He admired the four *Nuits* most, for he never ceased to enjoy elegiac and melancholy poetry, but he was lukewarm to the comedies. Gautier seems not to have interested him much, at least in the early years. The review of *Les Grotesques* points out errors of fact and deplores Gautier's attempt to rehabilitate the poets of the age of Louis XIII.[153] Another review attacks the doctrine of art for art's sake, the exclusive interest in color and image, "the exaggerated art in which form surpasses and so strangely annihilates content." [154] But it must be added that Sainte-Beuve always disapproved of a purely didactic, utilitarian attitude toward art, even though he admitted its social function.[155] The three later essays on Gautier (1863) give a much closer and more sympathetic survey of his work, but they convey the impression that Gautier is totally lacking in depth, and that his merits lie in a mere surface charm, which Sainte-Beuve now values more highly. Gautier's new and best book, *Les Emaux et Camées*, is praised only in passing.[156]

Sainte-Beuve's criticism of the romantics, though increasingly unsympathetic, seems fundamentally just if we consider the perspective of the times and the close relations which Sainte-Beuve enjoyed with almost all of them. He quite rightly insisted that his conversion from romanticism was not complete. In an essay on Banville he distinguishes three subtypes within what is usually called "romanticism." He speaks first of those who wanted to free all literature from conventional rules: Madame de Staël and her group (Fauriel included). He then speaks of those who could be considered Hellenists, those who turned to Greece, who may now appear classical, but who are also called, not without warrant, "romantic": Chénier and Chateaubriand. The latter did not like the younger romantics but was "a great romantic himself in the sense that he had returned to the direct inspiration of Greek beauty and also in the other sense that he had opened, by *René*, an entirely new vein of dream and poetic emotion." There are finally the romantics in the narrow sense, the school headed by Victor Hugo, who renewed poetry in the diverse modes and genres of free and personal inspiration. Gautier, with his emphasis on seeing, represents one branch, and Vigny, with his spiritual tendencies, another. Sainte-Beuve approves of the general tendency of romanticism, of its attempt to return truth, nature, even familiarity to French poetry. He reflects: "Let us think of modern lyrical poetry, in England, from Kirke White to Keats and Tennyson through Byron and the Lake poets, in Germany, from Bürger to Uhland and Rückert through Goethe, and let us ask what figure we would cut, we and our literature, in this comparison with so many foreign modern riches, if we did not have our poetry, the very poetic school which is now so much attacked.... Imagine it absent; what a gap!" [157]

The perspicuity of Sainte-Beuve's criticism greatly diminishes when he has to deal with his younger contemporaries and with the novelists of the new time whom we now value most highly: with Stendhal, Balzac, Flaubert, and Baudelaire. While he liked Stendhal as a critic, Sainte-Beuve did not think highly of him as a novelist. His faults as a novelist seemed to come from his "having arrived at this kind of writing by way of criticism, and according to certain anterior and preconceived ideas." [158] His characters are not living human beings but ingeniously constructed automatons. Julien in *Le Rouge et le noir* is only an odious little monster, a criminal resembling Robespierre. The picture of the parties and the intrigues of the time lacks that order and moderation in its development which alone could give the impression of a true picture of manners. *La Chartreuse de Parme* is Stendhal's best novel because of its charming early parts. But Fabrice is shallow and vulgar, like an animal governed by his appetites or a spoiled child indulging in his whims. He has no morals, no principle of honor. His extravagant flight and its consequences would be inexplicable if one should seek for order and probability in the story. From one end to the other (except for the beginning) the novel is hardly more than "a witty Italian masquerade." Sainte-Beuve asks for some part of the reasonableness, the sane emotion, the genuine simplicity that can be found in *I Promessi sposi* or any good novel of Walter Scott.[159] His judgment is repeated with somewhat stronger emphasis in an essay on Taine [160] and in an article on the *Souvenirs* of Delécluze. In these he also makes large reservations in his praise of Stendhal as a critic. "Stendhal uncrowns the human imagination. Out of aversion for tinsel he despises the splendors of the word and the legitimate grandeurs of passion, imagination, and eloquence." [161] The romantic in Sainte-Beuve protests against the 18th-century sensualist and hedonist. The classicist, insisting on unity, coherence, and probability, protests against Stendhal's ill-composed novels. While one should grant the justice of some of Sainte-Beuve's views, one must admit that he did not see the originality of Stendhal's mind, the acuteness of his psychology, or even the unconventionality of his fictional devices.

Balzac appeared to Sainte-Beuve at first as a sensational novelist of the stature of Sue, or Soulié, and he never quite changed his opinion. His final judgment of Balzac is obviously colored by a personal conflict. His first comment on Balzac, a review of *La Recherche de l'absolu* (1834), is favorable to the new novel itself and mentions *Eugénie Grandet* as Balzac's best book.[162] But the general emphasis of the article falls on Balzac as a fashionable writer for women. Balzac's reputation is ascribed to his connoisseurship of the female sex, to his *Physiologie du mariage*. Balzac has introduced himself as an intimate consoler, a confessor who is also something of a physician. Saint-Beuve also refers disparagingly to his occult tastes and several times alludes to his lascivious, *drolatique* interests. He quotes an anonymous friend (Ampère): "Whenever I read certain things [in Balzac], I want to wash my hands and brush my clothes." [163] The attention Sainte-Beuve pays to Balzac's early potboilers must have angered the latter even more. A little later, in the well-known article "De la Littérature industrielle" (1839), Sainte-Beuve ridicules Balzac for his proposal that the government should buy the works of the ten or twelve literary "Marshals of

France," beginning with those of Balzac himself, who "values his writings at two millions, if I understand him correctly." [164]

Balzac took his revenge and reviewed the first volume of *Port Royal* in a most contemptuous manner. Sainte-Beuve waited twenty years to reprint his review in the Appendix (1860) of the final edition, commenting, not unjustly, that Balzac had no right to judge the book, had no understanding of Christianity or of the 17th century, had committed many gross blunders, and had behaved, in general, like a charlatan. He takes the counteroffensive and calls Balzac rather a monster than a genius, something in between a great mind and a great jester. His lack of moderation, his gross point of view, his hallucinations have passed a certain point. He has not only depicted the vices of his society, he has flattered them.[165] It is surprising that Sainte-Beuve was asked by Balzac's sister to serve as one of the four pallbearers (the others were Hugo, Dumas, and the Minister of Education) at Balzac's funeral, and that he had a friendly interview with the sister before he wrote an obituary essay.[166] This essay,[167] while hardly perceiving Balzac's greatness, is far more moderate in tone and just in substance. Sainte-Beuve now calls him "possibly the most original, the most adequate and penetrating" painter of manners. He praises his characterization and even his fine, subtle, picturesque style. *Eugénie Grandet,* he repeats, will survive. But otherwise the article makes many points Sainte-Beuve had made before: the key to Balzac's success lies in his cultivation of the feminine public, especially in *La Femme de trente ans.* Balzac breathes delicious corruption, his style is completely Asiatic. His plots are frequently feeble, exaggerated, confused. It is not strictly praise when Sainte-Beuve accepts Chasles' saying (since then repeated in the title of a book on Balzac) that Balzac was rather a seer, a "visionary," than an observer and analyst. He was intoxicated with his work, his world is half-observed and half-created. He was constantly forcing his Muse and had no regard for criticism. Finally, Sainte-Beuve objects to *Cousine Bette* for its excessively black view of human nature. The heroine is a real Iago or Richard III, a monstrous criminal. "It does not happen that way in life," is a favorite saying of the later Sainte-Beuve, who more and more urged standards of probability and normality. The conclusion puts Balzac below George Sand, who is, in Sainte-Beuve's opinion, a "greater,

surer, and firmer writer." "She never gropes in her expression."
Even Sue seems probably "equal to Balzac in invention, fecundity,
and composition." But he "does not know how to write so well as
Balzac." [168] For a while after this, Sainte-Beuve feared that he had
admired Balzac incompletely, that perhaps he had been wrong
about him. But later remarks and reports of Sainte-Beuve's conversation show that he had not really changed his mind. In 1866 he
complained that Sue and Soulié did not exist any more and were as
if absorbed by Balzac.[169]

Sainte-Beuve's relations to Flaubert were happier. The article on
Madame Bovary, then being prosecuted for immorality, will strike
us as timid and lukewarm. Sainte-Beuve praises the book as being a
"composed, meditated book where everything holds together and
nothing is left to the chance of the pen." It has style, even a little too
much style for Sainte-Beuve's taste. But strangely enough he feels
that Madame Bovary herself is not depicted clearly, and he finally
confesses a lack of sympathy with what he considers an excessively
cold and cruel realism. He objects to a "method which consists in
describing everything and in dwelling on everything that he comes
across . . . After all a book is not and cannot be reality itself." Flaubert is too dry and ironical; the tone, he complains, is never tender
and understanding. Not a single character is good. In a strange
confusion of reality and fiction, and with a sentimentality rare in
his later writings, Sainte-Beuve holds out the example of a provincial lady whom he knew and who filled her life with charities and
thus escaped the fate of Madame Bovary. While Sainte-Beuve admits
the high qualities of the book—its style, design, and composition—
he declares his lack of sympathy with the new literature of science.
"Flaubert, the son and brother of distinguished physicians, holds
his pen like a scalpel. Nowadays, I find anatomists and physiologists
everywhere." [170]

After Sainte-Beuve's review, Flaubert called on him and they
struck up a friendship. But it can scarcely have been intimate.
When *Salammbô* appeared, Sainte-Beuve was evidently surprised
by the choice of subject. His three essays on the book show concern,
almost the attitude of an advising father. He thinks the whole idea
of the book an error and criticizes it in considerable detail. He first
reviews the source in Polybius, which gives a mere outline of the
plot and leaves free rein to Flaubert's imagination. But Flaubert

pretends to reproduce nothing but the exact image of the time. Sainte-Beuve is not convinced and demonstrates the moral anachronisms. He points to the romantic affiliations of Flaubert's characterizations and descriptions. Salammbô, in the beginning, is like a sentimental Elvira with a foot in *Sacré-Coeur*. She is like a sister of Velleda, the priestess in Chateaubriand's *Les Martyrs*. The landscapes remind one of Chateaubriand's *Itinéraire*. The amorous Matho, an African Goliath, is outside nature as well as history. The ceremonies described resemble Masonic initiations. The book is theatrical, operatic, and full of absurdities, as in the scene in which Salammbô caresses a serpent. The logic of the plot is weak. The whole book is paved with good intentions, with pebbles of various colors along with precious stones. Flaubert's imagination is sadistic: he heaps up horrors. "But our nerves are not ropes, and if there is too much of it, and they are bruised and tortured too much, they no longer feel anything." For fear of sentimentality, Flaubert cultivates atrocities.[171]

Sainte-Beuve objects to the genre itself. A historical novel presupposes a mass of information, a familiarity with moral traditions, and an affinity with the subject. Antiquity does not suit the historical novel. Flaubert's book is rather a *roman-poème,* a *pastiche,* a *tour de force.* Flaubert has failed to give real interest and life to it. It smells too much of oil and the lamp. The author applies himself too much; everything is forced, labored, and excavated. It is a purely abstract art, devoid of human sympathy; Salammbô herself in the end does not interest us. Sainte-Beuve argues that art is not entirely independent of human sympathy, that an artist should describe our analogues. He reflects on the contemporary distaste for emotion. Fearing to be like Gessner or Greuze or Fénelon, one becomes a wolf, a jackal, a tiger: one would not want to be suspected of playing the flute. Sainte-Beuve offers advice to all realists: Do not make things better than they are, but do not make them worse. Truth is all right, but do not be "eaters of unclean things." He solemnly declares that he loves the new realists individually, but that he cannot become a member of their sect. He hopes that Flaubert will return to a contemporary topic and in the future bother less about style.[172]

The relations between Sainte-Beuve and Baudelaire are those of a patronizing master to a gifted but naughty pupil. In 1857 Baudelaire was introduced to Sainte-Beuve and later that year he asked him to write on Baudelaire's translations from Poe. He sent Sainte-Beuve *Les Fleurs du mal* and Sainte-Beuve acknowledged the gift, putting into Baudelaire's own mouth some reflections explaining the choice of the subject matter. "I imagine you said to yourself 'All right, I have to find poetry and I shall find it where nobody else has tried to gather and express it.' And you took Hell, you made yourself over into the devil." But Sainte-Beuve warns him: "You despise passion too much, it is a theory of yours. You allow too much to intellect, to combinatory power. . . . Have no fear of being too common." [173] When the storm broke over *Les Fleurs du mal,* Sainte-Beuve did not come to its defense as Baudelaire had hoped, but remained silent. In a public letter (February 1860) he made his excuses: he was, after all, the author of *Port Royal,* a professor at the *École normale.* He wrote for the *Moniteur,* the official organ of the government.[174] When in 1860 Baudelaire sent him *Les Paradis artificiels,* Sainte-Beuve acknowledged it politely, regretting that he could not talk with him about this "very witty, very ingenious, very refined book," for Baudelaire was then in Brussels.[175] When Baudelaire became a candidate for the Academy, Sainte-Beuve in a review of the candidacies remarked that the Academicians were hardly likely to know that there are remarkable pieces of talent and artistry hidden in *Les Fleurs du mal* and that there are gems in the *Poems in Prose.* Baudelaire had "built himself a quaint and mysterious kiosk, in which one reads E. A. Poe, recites exquisite sonnets, becomes intoxicated with hashish in order to argue about it later, and takes opium and other abominable drugs in cups of exquisite china. To that peculiar kiosk, made in marquetry of an elaborate and intricate originality, which has for some time attracted our eyes at the extreme point of the romantic Kamchatka, I would give the name of 'Baudelaire's Folly.'" But Sainte-Beuve assures the Academicians that this strange, eccentric man is "a polite, respectful, exemplary candidate, a gentleman who speaks well and is quite classical in his manners." [176]

The relationship has excited much comment, mostly highly unfavorable to Sainte-Beuve. It has been suggested that Sainte-Beuve was a coward, that he was afraid to appear in Baudelaire's eyes as a Philistine.[177] A simpler explanation of Sainte-Beuve's attitude is that he was genuinely shocked by *Les Fleurs du mal*, or rather by certain poems in it, and that he was too timid to appear as a public defender of immorality. This seems rather a human than a critical failing: Sainte-Beuve was not cast in the role of a martyr, and disliked becoming a storm center. At the same time, it must be admitted that there was a serious critical failure in not recognizing the great power and originality of Baudelaire's poetry, even though Sainte-Beuve was not without sympathy either for the man or for the kind of feelings he was expressing. Sainte-Beuve shared the general human fate of a hardening of the critical arteries, a constant diminution, in spite of all attempts to keep abreast of the time, of his sympathy with the young and the new.

Except for a few excursions into classical antiquity, such as the book on Virgil, Sainte-Beuve wrote almost exclusively on French literature. He could, however, read English and Italian and knew a fair amount of English and Italian literature. On occasion he commented on German books available in French translations. On his mother's side he was of English descent and spent some time in England in 1828, though apparently he never learned the language well.[178] Still, he had some English interests: his poetry shows his love for Cowper and Wordsworth. There are some translations or imitations from Gray, Collins, Wordsworth, Keats, and Kirke White in his *Poésie de Joseph Delorme*. He obviously read something of Jeffrey, Lamb, and Hazlitt, and he quotes from Coleridge's *Biographia Literaria*. On the whole, he avoided criticizing foreign literatures, partly because he felt that he was not certain of his facts and understanding of the texts, and partly because he had little occasion to review foreign books for his audience. The English essays in the *Causeries* are not among Sainte-Beuve's most distinguished work: they are frankly descriptive and narrative, such as the piece on Lord Chesterfield,[179] or the fine, thoroughly prepared account of Cowper, who represented Sainte-Beuve's ideal of a "union between a poetry of the family and hearth with a poetry of nature."[180] The essays on Gibbon, which stress his French associations, are not very perceptive either about the man or about the purpose and style of *The Decline and Fall of the Roman Empire*.[181] Sainte-Beuve is, however, of some interest to students of English literature when he defends Pope against Taine's strictures. He thinks Pope much superior to Boileau in the extent of his ideas and in his taste for the picturesque, and he makes an excellent defense of Pope's poetry.[182] Sainte-Beuve is equally good when he defends Swift against a violent and rather silly attack by Saint-Victor.[183]

This survey of Sainte-Beuve's literary opinions, though far from complete, is sufficient to make his taste clear. It is a taste that can be described as a somewhat romantic classicism: the virtues of moderation, orderliness, wholeness, and good sense are central to his preferences. He is bored by the inanities of late academic neoclassicism, but neither does he care for the medieval and the baroque. He is repelled by the excesses of romanticism, its excursions into the purely gruesome and grotesque, the repulsive and the low, but remains basically romantic in his love for the elegiac, the melancholy brooding over man's condition and past. He has only a moderate sympathy with the new realism; he wants it to stay away from the violent and horrible, from the depressingly ugly or obscene. He objected to Zola and the novels of the Goncourts and was out of sympathy with Balzac. The beginnings of symbolism during his lifetime were not clearly understood by him: obviously he considered *Les Fleurs du mal* only a curiosity, a late descendant from the romantic poetry of the kind he had written himself.

Thus we can see at least three contending motifs in Sainte-Beuve's thought: a basic skeptical and sympathetic historicism, a taste that harks back to the classical tradition but wants it moderately liberalized, and an increasing preoccupation with the new naturalistic, "scientific" methods of studying literature. We can see why Sainte-Beuve has ceased particularly to interest our age. In the English-speaking nations he is little read, and, for decades none of his writings was in print in English translation. One cannot say that he has made a very distinct contribution to literary theory. His historicism was new or almost new only in France; his naturalism, mild as it is, must appear out-of-date; his taste will seem to us at once too conservative and too romantic. We love the baroque, the naturalistic, and the symbolistic (or most of us love some one of those styles), but we take the great Latin-French tradition for granted.

Yet it will not do to dismiss Sainte-Beuve lightly. The distinction of his work is imprinted on almost every page. He uses all methods and uses them skillfully and deftly, often in a very small space. He is averse only to cloudy speculation and to rigid systematization. He starts with the smallest detail and ends with the widest vista. Sainte-

Beuve never wrote a consecutive history or a monograph directly for print. *Port Royal* comes nearest to being such, but it grew out of lectures given at Lausanne. Even the *Tableau* is only a collection of newspaper articles, and the *Chateaubriand* is an almost unrevised transcript of lectures given at Liège. Thus we must judge his methods as primarily those of an essayist and occasionally those of a teacher. The audience is always before his mind, and he cannot and does not want to bore it with technical analyses or systematic theoretical disquisitions. Within the limits of his space and intention, he has his methods of "laying siege to a writer" [184] and knows how to document his readings. He sometimes starts, for instance, with the favorite words of an author. He reflects that Madame de Staël very frequently uses the word "life." Another great poet (Lamartine) constantly talks of "harmony" and the "waves." Another (Hugo) cannot but return to the world of "giants." The motto of Senancour is "permanence." De Maistre loves the phrase "point blank." [185] On occasions, though one must admit they are rare, Sainte-Beuve will inspect a poetic text quite closely. For example, he analyzes a poem by La Prade, showing that the images are incongruous, the symbols not perfectly just.[186] In the book on Chateaubriand he distinguishes three kinds and three stages in the history of images. He can give an example of what he calls a "vertical image." [187] Once in a while he analyzes a play like Corneille's *Cid*,[188] or goes through a novel like *Salammbô* carefully. But on the whole his method is rarely analytical. Sainte-Beuve alternates between historical confrontations, historical filiations and antecedents, and descriptions and evocations of an impressionistic manner. He is rarely picturesque or metaphorical in the manner of Hazlitt and Gautier, which many English and French writers adopted toward the end of the century. Lyrical passages such as that evoking the elegy of Chénier are rare and mostly confined to the early period.[189]

Sainte-Beuve's methods are too varied to be exhaustively described under standard headings. The scope of his subject matter, the lightness of his touch, the deftness of his presentation, the basic centrality of his outlook on human nature and literature, the mingling of the intellectual currents of the 19th century (certainly all those known in France), the flexibility and mobility of his mind—all should help Sainte-Beuve to recover his ground. One cannot disguise the shortcomings of his theory, which stresses biography and psychology, nor the limitations of his taste, which fears the grotesque, the extravagant, and tragically sublime. But Sainte-Beuve is too representative, too normal in the best sense, ever to be neglected.

DURING THE 1830's AND '40's the turn toward a political criticism of literature so conspicuous also in France, Germany, and Russia was carried to perhaps its most extreme degree in Italy. Literature, at least in theory, becomes almost completely subordinated to national ends. The preoccupation of Italy with the task of the liberation and unification of the nation was so all-absorbing that literature too could be seen only in terms of its contribution to the *risorgimento*. The nation, as today, was split into two camps: the conservative Catholic and the liberal secular; and criticism showed the same division between the followers of Manzoni and of Foscolo. Still, there must be discrimination within the two camps: two personalities who played a great role in history, Gioberti and Mazzini, stand out also as critics, and, from the point of view of criticism, the whole period is historically important because it prepared the ground for De Sanctis, the finest Italian critic of the century.

In Italy survivals of strictly romantic views were rather uncommon. Hardly anybody knew of Giovita Scalvini in his own time (1791–1843), who had published a few articles in *Biblioteca Italiana* (1818–20), a small essay, *Dei Promessi sposi* (Lugano, 1831) on Manzoni, and a prose translation with some of the lyrics in verse of Goethe's *Faust* (1835). Only in 1860 did a selection of his manuscripts appear, and today he has found a new editor and fervent admirers.[1] Foscolo was Scalvini's master: Scalvini as a youngster knew him in Brescia and later in London, but he revolted against him, partly for personal reasons but also philosophically and critically. Scalvini discovered German philosophy, particularly Schelling, and rejected Foscolo for his skepticism and aversion to speculation. In an early essay Scalvini had somewhat naively argued against the suicidal despair of Jacopo Ortis (1817), but in notes to the later manuscript he criticizes Foscolo as an artist for his classical

Alexandrianism. Even "I Sepolcri" seems to him lacking in unity; it is only "a mine of little poems." "There is a heavy odor of poetry; but it is an artificial odor." [2] Scalvini turns rather to Manzoni and Goethe, but with a sense of ultimate dissatisfaction leaves even them. In his fine essay on Manzoni's *I Promessi sposi,* Scalvini defends the novel against the charge of being an imitation of Scott by appealing to its concept of "inner form," to the "idea," the "soul," which is entirely different from Scott's. Only the outer form, that of the historical novel, is derivative, but one cannot object to Manzoni writing a historical novel after Scott as one cannot object to Sophocles writing tragedy after Aeschylus, or Raphael painting after Leonardo. Scalvini defends the choice of humble protagonists in a time of Italian decadence, stagnation, foreign rule, and pestilence as a parallel and contrast to Manzoni's own time, which implicitly enforces a lesson of patriotism. Still, Scalvini sees Manzoni's limits. "In his book there is something austere and even uniform, something which relentlessly pushes toward one aim: you do not feel that you are wandering freely in the great variety of the moral world; you notice often that you are not under the great vault of heaven which covers all various creatures, but rather you feel as if you were under the vault of a church which covers the faithful and the altars." [3]

Scalvini breathes more freely in the world of Ariosto, of Byron and Goethe. He admired Goethe as the supreme artist and tried to characterize *Faust* by emphasizing, for instance, the sudden changes and rapid transitions which still leave no feeling of incoherence. Goethe, however, came finally to represent, as he did to Heine and many others, a past period of pure art, a self-enclosed world. "Art must not resemble a universe governed by necessity," Scalvini reflects, "but must portray humanity, the life of humanity. Freedom is the foundation of art. Art rises out of life! . . . Art must serve the betterment of man." [4] This final turn toward "life," utility, contradicts, however, the aesthetic speculations in which Scalvini had indulged before. They sound Schellingian when Scalvini says that "in art the idea issues from the dark womb of the infinite without losing anything of its universality" or when he, alone among Italians of the time, appeals to the term "symbol" which he distinguishes from allegory. In interpreting works of art as symbols the critic, Scalvini argues, discovers aspects that might have been hidden from the artist himself. The sculptor of Laocoön could not have thought of everything that Lessing saw in it, nor did the first poets know anything of Herder's profound views of primitive poetry. Judgments need terms of comparison. "With their increase also the judgments increase." New aspects of truth come into sight, though truth is not revealed to us completely in any one time or place.[5] Though Scalvini's work is fragmentary and often only echoes his German readings, it shows a grasp of romantic doctrines and a sophisticated, frustrated, dissatisfied sensibility which was very rare in the Italy of his time.

The contrast with Vincenzo Gioberti (1801–52) could hardly be greater. A self-assured, fluid orator, a systematic thinker, a prime minister, and a priest, he seems at the other pole from the ship-wrecked exile Scalvini. But in aesthetics, Gioberti has the same affinities with Kant, Schelling, and the Schlegels. This German idealist thought, however, runs counter to Gioberti's Catholic training. His treatise, *Del Bello* (1841), is a curious hybrid between an ontological absolutism, which proclaims the existence of "absolute beauty" revealed in nature, and a psychological aesthetics of the imagination. Motifs from all intellectual history seem to cross. Lambs and lions, St. Thomas, Malebranche, Thomas Reid, Kant, Schelling, Hegel, and Cousin lie down together. There is little in the book that is relevant to literary theory, but there is at least ingenuity in Gioberti's attempt to apply Kant's aesthetics (not of the *Critique of Judgment* but of the introductory parts of the *Critique of Pure Reason*) to a classification of the arts and to speak of "aesthetic mathematics" and "aesthetic physics," of an aesthetic space and time conceived as containers of the poet's world of persons. Thus the question of the unities is solved if we realize that "the imagination of the spectators is the true and only theater," that the characters are not out of time and place but in their own aesthetic time and space, which the imagination can unify indefinitely. Susanne Langer's "virtual" time and space says the same, in substance.[6]

Del Bello contains two final chapters which sketch the history of art. All art is divided into heterodox (i.e. non-Christian) and orthodox art, reducing it to a contrast between pantheism on the one hand and reincarnation and the Christian view of creation and

incarnation on the other. Christ is the center, the "type" of orthodox art, its other types being the Virgin, the angel, and the saint.
The Divine Comedy is the most perfect poem. Dante represents the
complete man: he "could not have been the greatest poet and
writer if he had not been also an eminent philosopher and theologian." The current interpretation of Dante as a politician is
mistaken. "While the *Inferno* in a certain sense does serve the poet
as an allegorical veil to depict and to castigate the corrupt city of his
birth, which had almost become an inferno of the living, the genius
of the magnanimous exile rises to a grander concept and sees in the
theater of the world a shadow of higher truths considering the order
of immanent things as the ideal type of the things in time." This
concept, which orders and rules over the whole of the *Divine
Comedy,* constitutes the link between the three parts, the unity and
harmony of the whole poem.[7] Here, and much earlier in Gioberti's
marginal notes to Dante made in 1821–23,[8] the resolutely religious
interpretation of Dante comes to the fore. Dante is completely
orthodox, *cattolicissimo;* poetry is based on religion, *is* finally
religion, and the greatest poet is the philosopher-poet, the preacher-
poet needed also today.[9]

Dante, "the prophet of metaphysics and divine science," and the
Divine Comedy, "the universal Genesis of Christian letters and arts
in which all the typical germs of modern aesthetics are found,
enclosed, and first unfolded," [10] serve as the main claim for the pre-
eminence of Italian literature in *Del Primato morale e civile degli
Italiani* (1843), a strange book which does not merely assert fervidly
the historical greatness of Italy but blandly advises all other nations
to recognize Italy as the only creative nation and Rome as the seat
of spiritual and secular power. French, Gioberti concedes, may
remain the language of communication. The Germans should stick
to their abstruse erudition. England, to save itself, should be converted to Catholicism. Italian writers will reconcile religion and
science and make Italy again, under the leadership of the Pope, the
civilizer of the world and the Italian writer a priest of its ministry.
But the survey of Italian literature which bolsters this claim is,
fortunately, not merely a blowing of trumpets but a critical scheme
of history. Ariosto appears as the great contrast and counterweight
to Dante. Gioberti (surprisingly in view of his general outlook),
appreciates Ariosto's lack of practical purpose, his pure art, and

defines his ambiguous "sweet irony" as fluctuating between gravity and laughter.[11] "With Tasso the trumpet of Italian poetry fell silent . . . at last, it died, singing, one could say, among the stage properties, on the lips of virtuosos and sopranos and under the pen of a canon, the author of courtly wedding songs, of theater arias, a poet crowned by the Emperor [Metastasio]." [12] Italian literature was reawakened, in the spirit of Dante, only with Parini and Alfieri. Gioberti sees that Alfieri's adherence to the unities is not an artificial restraint but rather is in harmony with his character: the simplicity and even boldness and rapidity of action are due to an impatience that cannot brook any delay; he wants to reach his aim, without deviations, by the straightest line.[13] Only two recent writers elicit Gioberti's admiration: Manzoni, it is easy to guess, and Leopardi. Gioberti admires Leopardi, whom he had known personally, for his intense unsatisfied moral and religious quest, which Gioberti feels is similar to St. Augustine's or Pascal's, though he must deplore the very different conclusion. He sees that the "works of Leopardi are animated by a profound melancholy, by a quiet and logical desperation, which appears to the reader not like a disease of the heart but as a necessity of the spirit and the essence of a whole system." [14]

The same open mind animates also Gioberti's judgments of foreign writers, though he usually deplored their influence on Italy: he comments well on Shakespeare, Molière, Racine, Milton, Goethe, "the Rousseau of poetry and the creator of criticism," Schiller, Madame de Staël, and August Wilhelm Schlegel, whose *Course of Dramatic Literature* has "advanced by great steps criticism and all aesthetics and even almost entirely renovated the face of these sciences." [15] Gioberti's scheme of the history of Italian literature, which anticipates, in outline, De Sanctis', was widely influential, but possibly even more important was his interpretation of Dante as an orthodox philosopher-poet-priest.

Niccolò Tommaseo (1802–74) holds a similar Catholic romantic position, but he differs profoundly from Gioberti. He has a far more concrete relation to literature and the word, a refined though erratic sensibility, the crabbed erudition of a 17th-century scholar, and an irritable, uncharitable moralism that would be unthinkable in the bland and even unctuous Gioberti. Tommaseo, however, has no system of aesthetics—his *Dizionario estetico* (1840) is merely a collection of reviews arranged in alphabetical order of the authors treated. Tommaseo was an amazingly prolific writer on all subjects: his collected works would easily run to a hundred volumes. In his criticism, however, the fecundity is somewhat deceptive. Many later books are, under different titles, merely revampings of earlier ones.[16] The same arguments are repeated over and over. His central theory is the old identification of the good and the beautiful, a desire for the union of faith and art, morals and aesthetics. "A skeptical artist," we are told, "is the most ineffective, the most desperate, the most miserable artist." Byron is a poet only when he believes and hopes.[17] Leopardi, "elegantly desperate, diffusely mourning and learnedly disgusted with his miserable life" is ridiculed for his supposed argument for atheism: "There is no God because I am a hunchback; I am a hunchback because there is no God." [18] Foscolo's life was a "painful lie, a bitter comedy, a virulent satire on his time and of his works." These and many other writers seem dangerous to Tommaseo because they contradict his basic conviction that "without religion there is no poetry." [19] Manzoni clearly towers above his contemporaries as the renovator of Italian life and literature. Tommaseo, at least at first, even accepted Manzoni's complete identification of poetry and historical truth and, in discussing *I Promessi sposi,* dismissed its fictional action as a mere scaffolding for the historical evocations of the 17th century. Later he admitted, however, that the "imaginary and fictitious" is necessary in the historical novel.[20] Obviously Tommaseo's ideal poet is Dante, "the believing and hence great poet, popular because believing." [21] Tommaseo devoted an elaborate commentary to the *Divine Comedy* (1837), which contains his best criticism. Here he does not have to indulge in polemics; here he can come to grips with a text; here he can display his historical and philological erudition as well as his psychological acumen. The comments—e.g. on Francesca da Rimini's pain in seeing Paolo suffer for a love she cannot renounce or on Ugolino's mental agony for his sons which is far more acute than his hunger—anticipate De Sanctis in method. Tommaseo has also the merit of admiring and commenting in detail on the *Purgatorio* and *Paradiso,* not only in grammatical or rhetorical terms but on the harmony of scenes and settings and also on individual words—their musical effects, their associations and implications.[22]

Words in poetry are the theme also of the curious exchange of letters between Tommaseo and Gino Capponi (1833), which has elicited interest recently because it seems to anticipate the views of Poe or even Valéry. Capponi had written to Tommaseo that the material of poetry is feeling but that the "materialities" of life are arithmetic and that therefore poetry comes only in fragments and epic can be only craft. Tommaseo, in his answer, summarizes that "interjections are more poetic than epics, that the only poetry of us mortals is the lyric," but actually he corrects this, developing, I believe not quite seriously, the idea that "verse is calculus, and calculus is song and makes us sing; arithmetic is reinforced poetry; . . . poetry without calculus is vaporous, empty, or atheistic or Kantian." The next letter to Capponi, in French, is a mere *cappriccio:* poetry, Tommaseo fancies, "is the gilded cloud; it is in the heart, the throat, the arms, the voice, on the lips, in the smile, in the eyes, on the forehead. Poetry is action . . . it is the Word." [23] What seemed a promising contrast of feeling and ratiocination, song, and arithmetic peters out in Platonic vagueness and a final appeal to the Biblical Word.

These moralistic and linguistic motifs are in Tommaseo combined with romantic historicism. Tommaseo was the first Italian to collect folk songs, *Canti popolari toscani corsi illirici greci* (Venice, 1841–42), in the tradition of Herder's *Volkslieder*. Tommaseo, who was born in Dalmatia and lived in Corfu, Corsica, and Florence, translated and collected at first hand. All his life he kept this ideal of universal poetry, of world literature, in mind and wrote prolifically on many foreign authors: Goethe and Byron, Rousseau and Schiller, Lamartine and George Sand. Tommaseo prefers Byron to Goethe, the "gloomy, severe, and passionate doubt of the divine Englishman" to the "cold and derisive doubt of that courtier," as he prefers "a man to an actor." [24] Byron the man and Goethe the actor reverse surprisingly the usual contrast.

In exile in France, Tommaseo knew many literary figures and for a time had contacts with Sainte-Beuve. The novel *Volupté* excited Tommaseo's interest, but later he attacked it and thought Sainte-Beuve affected, cold, and immoral.[25] Tommaseo's historicism remains rather fitful, though he admired Vico and criticized him sensibly for enclosing the cycles of civilization too rigidly and hence breaking the continuity of history. His own long essays on Gasparo Gozzi and Pietro Chiari give a cultural history of Venice in the 18th century and detailed accounts of literary quarrels.[26] But the great historical learning is usually unrelated to the literary criticism. Tommaseo's almost inquisitorial moralism paralyzes his insights and sensibility. His learning becomes most alive when he contemplates an isolated passage or even a single word: "When I see a metaphysical or historical truth confirmed by a philological fact I say, this is the seal of truth." [27] Tommaseo, who compiled the first Italian *Dictionary of Synonyms* and a great *Dictionary of the Italian Language,* has, in spite of many mistakes, a sense of shades of meaning, a feeling for the poetry of words that is almost unique in his time. His tormented, bizarre, contradictory personality—best expressed in his letters, the diary, and the rather inept love novel *Fede e Bellezza* (1840)—is only at rare moments reflected in the criticism. What remains is a figure, even a "character," rather than a theorist: a commentator and journalist rather than a real critic.

Giuseppe Mazzini (1805–72) stands in clear contrast to the Catholic critics. Mazzini, who in his early years and the years of exile in England wrote much literary criticism also for French and English periodicals, lives in a totally different mental climate; he is nearest to the Saint-Simonians and particularly to Leroux in his views of the role of literature. Mazzini says the same thing over and over again. The aim of criticism is to prepare the art of the future, a new collective art which will reflect the new collective society. The poet fulfills a social ministry; he is or should be the prophet of the future. The glowing enthusiasm, the rhetorical pathos, the sentimental imagery of Mazzini's prose should not obscure the genuine appeal of his views and the not infrequent perceptiveness of his concrete criticisms. Mazzini has no use for materialism and constantly talks of God, Providence, the Idea; he wants vagueness and the infinite in poetry, in good romantic fashion. But actually he embraces the concept of a strictly deterministic, fatal, necessary law of progress which inevitably leads from the age of individualism to the age of collectivity. The poet is and cannot help being a representative of his age; literature is an expression of society, but at the same time Mazzini asks, with the contradiction that also was to permeate Marxism, that the poet should not only reflect his age but also anticipate the future of humanity.[28] Mazzini's concept of evolution is not that of the Germans; there is nothing specifically Hegelian in it. It is derived, rather, from Madame de Staël, De Bonald, the Saint-Simonians, and Leroux. It is an abstract, simple scheme. Classicism is past and dead. Romanticism did useful work of destruction but remained essentially negative. Its two greatest poets, Goethe and Byron, ended in indifference or despair. In France the two great romantic poets, Lamartine and Hugo, who had raised high hopes by their first works, were declining; each was retiring into his own ivory tower. Hugo, whose dominant concept had been the redemption of human personality, is left with only one faith: faith in himself. "He particularizes, segregates, concentrates, instead of universalizing life." "Everything is definite, determined, materialized." His cult of sensation, his religion of matter, his literary paganism is backed by the theory of art for art's sake, a "ruinous theory fatal to art" as it is "a negation of universal life and unity."[29] *Les Feuilles d'automne* was Hugo's apogee. Since then he has decayed, particularly in the dramas. Lamartine raised hopes with *Méditations,* but *Harmonies* offers no remedy except passive oriental pantheism. Neither Hugo, the more objective, more dramatic poet, nor Lamartine, the more subjective, more lyrical poet live up to Mazzini's expectation of a "religious-educator-poet, the poet of the future." Neither recognizes that there is only one "true and sacred art: the art for social perfection." It is a question of two definitions of poetry, Mazzini concludes: one which may be given in the words of Lamartine, "la poésie est un chant intérieur," and the other in the words of Shakespeare, who said it was "the prophetic soul / of the wide world dreaming on things to come."[30] The "things to come," so oddly twisted by Mazzini to suit his meaning, is collective poetry. It is sometimes conceived as synthesis, "encyclopedia" in the romantic sense. At other times it is simply a new sense of mission in the poet, who would be reconciled with his society and would found a literature, a poetry of the future, having a single "design," an "ensign."[31]

In other contexts, we read that the art of the future will be a new kind of drama, a collective art that would express a view of history as a Providential scheme. In one of his essays Mazzini sketches a schematic history of the drama distinguishing three stages with three representative authors: Aeschylus, Shakespeare, and Schiller, each dominated by a single idea: respectively, Fatality, Necessity, and Providence.[32] Mazzini, who had read the Schlegels with admiration (though he, of course, objected to their medievalism and Teutonism [33]) is attracted by Fatality in Greek tragedy and even in such a feeble modern imitator as Zacharias Werner, whose *24th of February* Mazzini thought to be like a "fragment of a recovered Aeschylus." [34] He was most adverse to Shakespeare, who represented to him the drama of the individual, of freedom, where the necessity is invisible. "There is no expiation [in Shakespeare] which could profit any other individual and which could raise itself to the majesty of sacrifice." "There is no common aim, no common progress. Solitude in life. Solitude in death." Mazzini quotes "Life is a walking shadow" as if it summed up Shakespeare's own view of the world. The new concept is that of Providence, as hinted at in Schiller's dramas. Schiller divined "the harmony between the individual and social thought, between liberty and the laws of the universe." [35]

Mazzini was a fervent Italian patriot, but his horizon was European. His judgments of Italian literature are all dominated by the political perspective. Alfieri is praised as an educator of Italy who does not, however, depict the paradise of the free man but wants Italians to embrace liberty out of hatred for tyranny. Foscolo is the one modern Italian writer admired almost unreservedly; Mazzini defended in detail his political record and accepted his flamboyant, passionate personality at its face value—surely also out of sympathy for his fellow exile in England, almost, one feels, in an effort to create a national legend. It is not surprising that Mazzini dismissed Leopardi as another voice of despair and that he judged Manzoni coolly. He criticized Manzoni's literal concept of factual truth in the novel, for he considered moral truth the only obligation of the poet.[36] Dante, of course, looms highest in the past. Mazzini rejected any partial interpretation, any attempt to make him Catholic or heretic, a Ghibeline or a Guelf. Dante is a "Christian and an Italian," the "type of a whole nation, mournful and grand as itself." [37]

In England Mazzini encountered Carlyle and was deeply impressed. But later he was disappointed by his skepticism and despondency and finally repelled by his inhumanity. Carlyle, in Mazzini's eyes, was corrupted by Goethe's indifferentism. "Adieu à Goethe, adieu à Byron," exclaims Mazzini in deliberate contrast to Carlyle's advice to open Goethe and close Byron. Mazzini quotes Emerson against Carlyle: there is a Universal Mind "of which each individual man is one more incarnation"; and he formulates again his own basic creed: "The great religious thought, the continued development of Humanity, by collective labour, according to an educational plan assigned by Providence." [38] All nations enter into this grand scheme, and all poets and writers must serve it. Mazzini, for instance, was intensely interested in the Slavic world, in Mickiewicz, whom he called "the greatest living poet," in Pushkin and even in Czech poetry, which he read in John Bowring's translations.[39] The Herderian ideal of universal poetry harmonizes with the anti-Austrian and anti-Russian liberalism, the ideal of humanity with the resurrection of Italy. Freedom and humanity, nationalism and collectivism are held together in Mazzini, both in politics and in literature.

The liberal version of Italian literary history suggested in Mazzini and before in Foscolo was elaborated by the two most influential literary histories of the century: Paolo Emiliani Giudici's *Storia delle belle lettere in Italia* (1845) and Luigi Settembrini's *Lezioni di letteratura italiana* (1866–72). Emiliani Giudici (1812–72) has the merit of writing the first narrative history of Italian literature except for the earlier French books of Ginguené and Sismondi. But his boasts, in the "Preliminary Discourse," of superiority over his predecessors is not justified by the actual performance. Emiliani Giudici admires Foscolo because he accomplished "the fusion of political and literary doctrine which we want from all historians of our literature," [40] but his own book can hardly be said to have carried out the program. Emiliani Giudici is, rather, a compiler who rarely shows critical originality or power of characterization. His literary creed is an extreme classicism, which indulges in polemics against foreign romanticists and Catholic reactionaries. But at the same time Emiliani Giudici embraces the romantic concepts of literary historiography as the history of a nation's conscience of liberty. It remains a declamatory scheme while the bulk of the book is sober reporting.

Luigi Settembrini (1813–77) uses an even more simplified historical scheme. The whole of Italian literature is seen as "a struggle of the Church against civil power, against art, against science, against liberty, against religion itself." Painting, music, architecture in Italy were dependent on the Church, hence "Guelf," while literature, "as Ghibeline, drew many inspirations from Paganism, rose against the authority of the Church, wanting to obey no other but reason, and finally achieved skepticism." [41] Italian literature is a continuation of Roman literature; it is national and classical, it harmonizes form and content. In Settembrini's conception, Christianity is purely destructive. Even St. Francis' love for "brother dog, brother wolf, brother sun, and sister moon" is distorted to mean a lowering of man to the status of a beast.[42] The absence of the Popes in Avignon is considered, in defiance of chronology and common sense, the explanation for the flowering of Italian literature in Dante, Boccaccio, and Petrarch. The *Divine Comedy* represents "the upsurge of reason against authority"; Boccaccio reflects the popular revolution; Petrarch's homelessness and ambiguous status as a cleric without vows is a sign of anticlericalism.[43] But oddly enough, in spite of this pamphleteering character, comprehensible only in the context of his long years of imprisonment in Bourbon jails, Settembrini is a better critic than Emiliani Giudici; he has courage and an independent taste. For example, he admires Petrarch's *Africa* as an attempt to restore classical national poetry; he describes Marino's *Adone* in detail as an extended episode from Tasso's *Jerusalem;* he defends Goldoni's apparent superficiality; he recognizes that Foscolo's *Grazie* is his finest poem.[44] Settembrini's luscious "pagan" sensibility clashes with the doctrinaire framework.

One critic, Carlo Tenca (1816–83), attempted the task of mediation between liberal and Catholic views; he overcame this cleavage by a grasp of the nature of art and of the reconciling and pacifying power of the historical spirit. In his early writings, Tenca seems clearly a follower of Mazzini. An article, "Delle condizioni dell'odierna letteratura in Italia" (1846), alludes discreetly to the views of a "valiant Italian" and asserts the task of criticism in Mazzini's terms: it should prepare a new literature, reestablish the lost "harmony between writers and the multitude," prepare the unity of the nation as "poetry should express the general sentiment of an age," and find "a literary formula." The reasons for the greatness and decline of literature are in history. "Literature will become spontaneous and fertile with civic institutions." But literature is not completely subservient to the historical process: "Art is still one and immutable in its essence, and the times can modify it in its manifestations but not change its nature or falsify it." [45]

Tenca accepts the achievement of Italian romanticism, its breaking of the shackles of tradition; he praises the *Conciliatore* group. He admires Manzoni, defending *I Promessi sposi* against Manzoni's own rejection of the historical novel. He generously reviews the lifework of the devout Silvio Pellico and is surprisingly lenient to the medieval and sentimental Tommaso Grossi. But he accepts also Foscolo's self-portrait as a fiercely independent hero-poet.[46] Romantically, with political overtones for Austrian-occupied Milan, Tenca exalted the Slavs and informed the Italians about Russian, Polish, and Czech literature.[47] He criticized sharply only the late romantics, particularly Prati, whom he could convict of pantheism, sentimentality, egotism, and mystical irrationalism.[48] He rises above the parties in a striking essay on Emiliani Giudici (1852). History will be, he feels, the universal, conciliating power in Italian life. The philosophical deism and sentimental Catholicism inherited by the early 19th century need to be superseded. Emiliani Giudici is criticized for "deducing from the external events of the nation those causes of the greatness and decay of literature" that should rather be sought for in the intimate existence of the people. "This historical materialism shows a distrust of the great destinies of literature." Tenca sketches an outline history of modern Italian literature in which he defends the romantic revolt and sees continuities where others have seen only enmities. Manzoni is not so far from Parini. There are germs of the new age in Foscolo and Leopardi. The task of criticism is "to bring together, to harmonize the intellects." Literary history thus will become "an active instrument of aesthetic evolution." [49] It was, however, almost twenty years before De Sanctis' *History* fulfilled this demand. Still, the roots of De Sanctis are in this time: he has its scheme of history, similar to Gioberti's; he has the liberal ideology of Mazzini's critic-educator; but he differs from all of them by going directly to the Schlegels and Hegel, by grasping firmly the nature of art, by overcoming the limitations of a political time.

IN ENGLAND the thirties and forties of the 19th century can be described as an age of transition. This, it has been objected, is true of any period; but these two decades fit particularly well John Stuart Mill's description in his *Spirit of the Age* (1831): "Men have outgrown old institutions and old doctrines, and have not yet acquired new ones." There was an anarchy of opinions and an aversion to system and theory. "He is a *theorist:* and the word which expresses the highest and noblest effort of human intelligence is turned into a bye-word (sic) of derision." [1] Mill is thinking in general terms, but his diagnosis also applies to the situation in literary criticism. The 18th-century system of poetics and aesthetics had decayed, but it lingered on with many writers. The romantic creed systematically propounded by Coleridge had not taken firm root in England, though it was upheld, in various versions, by Lamb and Hazlitt, and after their death by a few survivors such as De Quincey and Leigh Hunt. New or comparatively new ideas and emphases emerge with several writers who achieved eminence in other activities than strictly literary criticism: with Carlyle, John Stuart Mill, Macaulay, and Ruskin. But the idea of a coherent literary theory disappears almost completely and with it any technique of analyzing literature and any interest in form. The nature of literature is misunderstood. Literature becomes, for most critics, a purely didactic or emotive activity. Slowly the attitude which has been called "Victorian" was crystallizing: a didacticism rooted either in a utilitarianism that extended far beyond the Utilitarian group, or an Evangelicalism that distrusted art as secular and frivolous. The standard of utility, of social use, was combined with a distrust of the intellect, the free play of the mind, the speculative, the theoretical. Art became suspect either as mere amusement, or worse, as a stimulus to sensuality or as a revolutionary subversive force. The violence of the

English reaction to the French novel [2] can be explained only in that it was felt to challenge the basic assumptions and proprieties of the society. Those who still exalted the arts either transformed literature more and more into a branch of religion, or defended it against the contempt of a scientific and industrial age as a domestic culture of the emotions—a nook in which man preserved his privacy. The distrust of the intellect implied by didacticism and emotional theories meant, in criticism, a reliance on natural shrewdness, on the common sense of every individual, and thus, in practice, led to an anarchic impressionism. The personal caprice was, however, usually concealed behind the enormous self-assurance of the Victorian prophet and sage, behind the dogmatism of his *ipse dixit*.[3] The critic who believes in the infallible evidence of his common sense or prophetic insight will lose all patience with analyzing a work of art or formulating a general theory. He will look for the same tone of authority in the writer he discusses. He will study his life for evidence of "sincerity," the new cant word of the criticism of the time, as if conviction, sincerity, belief could assure good art, as if "the worst" were not "full of passionate intensity."

The comparative decline of literary theory was, however, accompanied by an enormous expansion of literary antiquarianism and literary history. It was precisely the breakdown of critical standards, the lack of theoretical interest, which favored an all-embracing tolerance and encouraged an indiscriminating accumulation of mere information about literature. The process had begun in the 18th century but intensified enormously in the first decades of the 19th. Book clubs reprinting early English books [4] in limited editions, reviews such as *The Retrospective Review* [5] devoted expressly to the excerpting and describing of older English literature, and the popular lecture series on English literature addressed to a mixed metropolitan public were all new developments. The intense interest in older English literature had its patriotic overtones, connected with the resurgence of English nationalism during the Napoleonic wars, and reflected a general change of taste: the new enjoyment of medieval and particularly of Elizabethan literature. But these motives behind the revival of older English literature quickly decayed, and its study became, more and more, the exclusive domain of the literary antiquarian whose ethos was an indiscriminate love of the past, a worship of new facts, and a mildly scientific curiosity. During the 19th century English literature became an academic subject of instruction. But, significantly, English literature was first taught in Scotland, Ireland, and the United States and was not established fully at the old English universities until the 20th century.[6] There was in English studies hardly anything of the corporate national enthusiasm that inspired "Germanistik" in Germany. Anglo-Saxon studies had a very old tradition in England, dating back to the Elizabethan age, but they had decayed in the later 18th century.[7] Only under the impact of the new Danish and German scholarship, its discoveries in Germanic philology and its enthusiasm for Teutonic antiquity, did Anglo-Saxon studies revive also in England. *Beowulf* had been edited in Denmark and Germany before John Mitchell Kemble (1807–57), who had studied with Jakob Grimm in Göttingen, brought out the first English edition in 1833.[8] The other eminent early student of Anglo-Saxon literature, Benjamin Thorpe (1782–1870), had learned his Anglo-Saxon in Copenhagen from Rasmus Rask. But Anglo-Saxon literature remained an academic specialty in England.

Much more enthusiasm was engendered by the study of medieval romances, ballads, and folk songs. The interest had been prepared by the very half-hearted endeavors of Bishop Percy and Thomas Warton. Such a meritorious antiquary as Joseph Ritson thought "legends and fables constantly fabricated for the same purpose, and with the same view: the promotion of fanaticism" and treated the old poems merely as illustrations of antiquity.[9] George Ellis retold medieval romances with a condescending jeering irony.[10] Only the enthusiasm of Sir Walter Scott for the ballads and his own imitations of metrical romances stimulated a whole band of researchers, collectors, and imitators. Though the word "folklore" dates only from 1846,[11] early in the century an enormous body of miscellaneous knowledge of fairy tales, romance themes, ballad and folk-song types came into being. Scott had freely contaminated and rewritten his ballads, but accurate and faithful methods of editing were slowly established. In ballad lore William Motherwell's *Minstrelsy: Ancient and Modern* (1827) represents the turning point.[12] Richard Price, in his remarkable preface to a new edition of Thomas Warton's *History of English Poetry* (1824) was apparently the first to introduce the idea of general literature as a huge treasure house of themes, which spread, multiply, and migrate according to laws similar to those established for language by the new Germanic philology of the Grimms. Price believes that "popular fiction is in its nature traditive" and represents an age-old symbolic wisdom.[13] Many new students devoted themselves to what we would call international *Stoffgeschichte:* Sir Francis Palgrave (1788–1861) and Thomas Wright (1810–77) in particular were scholars of stupendous though often unorganized learning on all such subjects. Enthusiasm for romances and ballads nourished even much later poets, such as Tennyson, Rossetti, and Morris; but the study itself became an antiquarian specialty proliferating in text societies and local historical groups, with less and less critical discrimination toward the masses of uncovered materials.

The Elizabethan age attracted the most critical attention. It was generally exalted as the greatest age of English literature, not only by romantic poets but also by many critics of conservative taste, such as Jeffrey and Gifford. The flood of new editions is staggering: almost all poetical miscellanies were reprinted, there was a complete edition of Elizabethan critical essays,[14] and there was no end to the reprinting of plays. Marlowe, Greene, Middleton, Ford, and Webster were identified as proper subjects for criticism for the first time in the early decades of the century; and there were solid annotated editions of Ben Jonson, Beaumont and Fletcher, and Massinger.[15] The interest began to extend to the comparatively neglected parts of 17th-century literature. Though the metaphysical poets remained under a cloud, there were exceptions to their general disfavor: occasional praise was bestowed on Donne, Herbert, Marvell, and even Crashaw;[16] and Sir Thomas Browne was widely admired and well edited by Simon Wilkin.[17] The enthusiasm for the plays often seems especially undiscriminating. But in these first decades of the century were accumulated all the materials (or almost all) that made the writing of English literary history for the first time an urgent possibility.

The interest in older literature extended also to foreign literatures, which before had hardly been known, at least in these newly discovered periods. There were, for the first time, translations from the troubadours and the German *Minnesänger*.[18] J. G. Lockhart's *Ancient Spanish Ballads* (1823) belongs to the ballad movement initiated by Scott. Dante's entire *Divine Comedy* was translated in Miltonic blank verse by Henry Francis Cary (1772–1844).[19] The

Nordic fashion, which dates from the 18th century, led to substantial accounts of Teutonic antiquities and finally to translations of the poetic *Edda* and the Danish ballads.[20] Individual enthusiasts even began translating and reporting on the literatures of the Slavs, the modern Greeks, and the Magyars,[21] and there was a purely literary side to the growing interest in Oriental literatures.[22]

But, surprisingly, this strong antiquarian movement was *not* accompanied by anything that could be described as a flowering of literary historiography: there is no comparison with Germany or France in this respect. In England no history of literature was produced to replace and supplement Warton's. The first very elementary general *History of English Language and Literature* (1836) was a little handbook by Robert Chambers which was later expanded to his popular *Cyclopaedia*.[23] Historiographical conceptions were still extremely backward: either Warton's progress from imagination to reason or a seesaw scheme was adopted.

The most eminent literary historian of the time, Henry Hallam (1777–1859), provided in his *Introduction to the Literature of Europe in the 15th, 16th and 17th Centuries* (1838–39) little more than a well-informed catalogue of books, a descriptive survey of everything of any importance published in all subjects from mathematics and medicine to poetry and novels. Hallam has no concept of imaginative literature and thus devotes more space to Grotius and Hobbes than to any other authors. He is essentially a skeptic who distrusts all theories, all psychological or social explanations. "If there are no great writers at a certain time and place, we must simply ascribe" their lack to "a pause in natural fertility." "Nature does not think fit to produce them." Hallam concludes, for instance, that "the scarcity of original fiction in England of the 17th century was so great as to be inexplicable by any reasoning." [24] Still, he holds firm to a standard of neoclassical taste. He defends Malherbe, complaining that "we narrow our definition of poetry too much if we exclude from it the versification of good sense and select diction." Hallam constantly asserts that the historical point of view cannot change the judgment of taste. "It will not convert bad writing into good to tell us, as is perpetually done, that we must place ourselves in the author's position and make allowances for the taste of his age, or the temper of his nation." He thus objects to the current overrating of "our old writers," bluntly lists the faults of Shakespeare, and can say that "it is impossible not to wish that Shakespeare had never written his Sonnets." [25] It is hardly surprising that Hallam despises Donne, Góngora, and Calderón, and that he praises not only Montaigne but Sir John Davies and Massinger as "second to Shakespeare." [26] His ideal is a "general diffusion of classical knowledge." Milton seems to him "the first writer who eminently possessed a genuine discernment and feeling of antiquity." Hallam, with his refusal to generalize about national literatures or epochs, with his concept of genius as mere accident, with his rejection of all "sophistical theories which assume a causal relation between any concomitant events," [27] belongs intellectually to an earlier age.

Some literary historians of the time grasped the necessity of a historical scheme but failed in their practice. Thus J. P. Collier (1789–1883), who is today discredited because of his later forged entries in Elizabethan documents, wrote a *History of English Dramatic Poetry up to the Time of Shakespeare* (1831) which, in intent, aims at the writing of a formal genre history. He wishes to show that the mystery plays "almost imperceptibly deviated into the morality, by the gradual intermixture of allegory with sacred history," while the morality plays, in turn, "gave way to tragedy and comedy, by the introduction, from time to time, of characters of actual life, or supposed to be drawn from it." [28] But Collier's book does not fulfill this program. He is hunting too many hares at the same time: he gives long lists of plays and performances, information on actors and theaters, and loses sight of the history of the genre as an art form.

The social explanation of literary history as propounded by Madame de Staël did find an English (or rather Scottish) practitioner. John Dunlop's *History of Fiction* (1814) was planned in close correlation with the history of society. Dunlop relates, for instance, the mercantile spirit and the Italian *novelle,* and contrasts the courts of Louis XIV and Charles I in order to account for the respective states of heroic romance. "From the very nature of domestic fiction, it must vary with the forms and habits and customs of society, which it must picture as they occur successively." [29] The theory behind the book is sound, but the practice suffers from his vague conception of social history and its relation to literature.

Only Thomas Carlyle imported the concept of a national literature unified by a national mind, the concept of literary evolution, and the whole ideal of narrative consecutive literary history.

THOMAS CARLYLE (1795–1881)

Today Carlyle excites hatred or boredom rather than admiration. He is considered a forerunner of Hitler, a worshiper of supermen-heroes for whom "might makes right." The defense would argue that Carlyle's hero is a vessel of God who possesses might only because he conforms to the law of God's universe.[1] But this argument fails to convince, since there is abundant evidence of Carlyle's recommending the use of brute force against the oppressed and glorifying the ruthless and unscrupulous wielders of power.[2] Besides, Carlyle's style militates against any revival of his writings. Its repetitive, loud-voiced, emphatic, mannered grandiloquence, the whole biblical pathos—incongruously shot through with grotesque trickeries—repels the present-day reader who does not know the quieter stretches of Carlyle's writings and does not recognize or relish the deliberate method with which Carlyle attempted to build a half-mythic, half-humorous figure of the prophet behind the masks of Teufelsdröckh and Sauerteig.

But whatever may be our final opinion of Carlyle as a social thinker, historian, or stylist, we should recognize his importance as a literary critic, as an interpreter of German literature, as an expounder of historicism and transcendentalism, and as a moralistic critic with great powers of characterization who exalted sincerity, reality, and "fact." This last motif was there from the beginning, but it outgrew all the others and finally turned Carlyle against all literary criticism. This struggle of heterogeneous elements in his mind enhances his representativeness. Carlyle is the Hercules at the crossroads of intellectual history, choosing virtue and fact over art and fiction.

Carlyle as an interpreter of German literature is immeasurably superior in knowledge and insight to all his contemporaries. Coleridge, De Quincey, and such professional intermediaries as William Taylor of Norwich or Mrs. Sara Austin. *The History of German Literature* that Carlyle began in 1830 but abandoned as unpublishable would have been largely a compilation from German sources: only the part from the beginning to Luther was finished, and from it Carlyle extracted two articles for publication, one on the

Nibelungenlied, the other on "Early German Literature," mainly of the 14th and 15th centuries (1831). These essays provide substantial information, quotations, and abstracts of plots, but hardly any criticism.[3]

Carlyle's scheme of a history of German literature was mainly the consequence of his intense interest in a few great figures of recent German literature. His first book, a *Life of Schiller* (1825), is not very distinguished, judged by modern standards.[4] It conceals its frequent dearth of biographical information behind Johnsonian moralizings, and its lack of critical discernment and courage by descriptive accounts of the plays and clumsy translations. The perspective on Schiller is still very narrow. His relation to Kant is described vaguely, and the aesthetics is almost ignored. Carlyle finds Schiller's concept of history too cosmopolitan and argues in favor of nationalism. The poetry is barely mentioned, and the plays are ranked often perversely. Thus *Maria Stuart* excites Carlyle's old prejudice against the wanton Scottish queen. The later article on Schiller (1831) makes, however, ample amends in critical severity. It elaborates a judgment confirmed by posterity: "Often, it seems to us, as if poetry were, on the whole, not [Schiller's] essential gift; as if his genius were reflective in a still higher degree than creative, philosophical and oratorical rather than poetic."[5]

Carlyle's relationship to Goethe is primarily personal—that of a pupil to a teacher and even savior. Carlyle thought of Goethe as a sage who rescued himself and his time from Wertherian unbelief and despair, who taught the world and Carlyle a new secular gospel of resignation, reverence, toleration, and action. "Work and despair not," "the grand secret of Renunciation," "The Worship of Sorrow"—such phrases and saws sum up Carlyle's indebtedness. But as literary criticism Carlyle's several essays on Goethe vary greatly in closeness of contact with the texts and in power of characterization. The earliest piece on *Faust* (1822) does little more than retell the story, complain of its lack of unity, and describe the characters: Faust as another young Carlyle "with the head of a sceptic and the heart of a devotee," Mephistopheles as "some French *philosophe* of the last century."[6] The preface to Carlyle's translation of *Wilhelm Meister* (1824) is a skillful plea for the book with which Carlyle himself was not altogether happy on moral grounds and which he felt obliged to expurgate.[7] He complains of the lack of "romance

interest" and of the "milksop hero," but ranks Goethe, "the greatest
genius in our times," with Homer and Shakespeare.[8] In the introduction to the translation of the *Wanderjahre* included in the
second volume of *German Romance* (1827), Carlyle discovers his
central interest and tone: Goethe is a "teacher and a reverencer;
not a destroyer, but a builder-up." [9] The article on Goethe's
Helena (1828) comes to grips with a difficult text: it is remarkable
as an early sympathetic consideration of a section of the second part
of *Faust*. Carlyle succumbs even to the "strange, piquant, quite
peculiar charm of these imitations of the old Grecian style" and
understands that Goethe moves in "a phantasmagoric region where
symbol and thing signified are no longer clearly distinguished." [10]
The long essay on Goethe (also 1828) states most sharply Carlyle's
concept of Goethe's change from Unbelief to Belief, from the
suicide of Werther to the Sanctuary of Sorrow in the Pedagogical
Province. Incidentally, Carlyle corrects the current sentimentalized
view of *Werther* and does at least something to characterize Goethe's
"emblematic intellect; his perpetual never-failing tendency to
transform into *shape*, into *life*, the feeling that may dwell in him." [11]
"Death of Goethe" (1832) is hardly more than a funeral oration; but
the last long article that followed soon afterward, though it starts
rhapsodically, is built around a solid account of *Dichtung und
Wahrheit* and describes Goethe's evolution in three stages: the early
Wertherian, despairing, unbelieving period, the middle Pagan
period with *Wilhelm Meister* as a "warm, hearty, sunny human
Endeavour," and a third serene, triumphant final stage of the
Wanderjahre and the *West-östlicher Divan*. The evolution is seen
almost completely in moral terms, and the literary issues are ignored.
But the quotations from the gnomic and epigrammatic poetry show
that Carlyle relished not only Goethe's wisdom but also the "figurativeness which lies in the very centre of his being." [12] Significantly
Carlyle translated and interpreted Goethe's *Das Märchen* (1832),
which he saw not as an allegory with a single key but as a "phantas-
magory, wherein things the most heterogeneous are, with ho-
mogeneity of figure, emblemed forth" and would require a dozen
keys.[13] Carlyle was primarily, as Goethe remarked, "aiming at the
spiritual and moral core" [14] of the German writers; but the essays
on Goethe, while concerned with the exemplar of wisdom, with
the historical figure of the European regeneration after what

seemed to Carlyle the depths of the 18th century, do contain good literary criticism in their novel emphasis on the multivalent symbolism of the late Goethe.

The third German writer discussed by Carlyle with admiration and sympathy is Jean Paul. This taste for Jean Paul is usually treated as an aberration, but it may appear in a different light considering the Jean Paul revival in Germany since Stefan George's praise, and realizing that many of the most important German prose writers of the 19th century—E. T. A. Hoffmann, Börne, Heine, Stifter, Raabe, Gottfried Keller—were deeply indebted to Jean Paul. The influence of Jean Paul on Carlyle's prose style (though later and less important than that of the Bible and Sterne) and novelistic technique (in *Sartor*) is undeniable and merely confirms the evidence of the criticism. The three articles on Jean Paul (the introduction to *German Romance,* 1826, and two essays, 1827, 1830) characterize Jean Paul's art and outlook elaborately and concretely. Jean Paul's style is analyzed in detail: his parentheses, dashes, and subsidiary clauses, his neologisms, images, metaphors, allusions, sardonic turns, quips, and puns, the whole "wild complicated Arabesque." [15] Jean Paul's techniques and general formal principles are examined sympathetically: a "living and life-giving, rather than a beautiful or symmetrical order." [16] His humor, compared with Sterne's and Cervantes', is defined in terms of Schiller's theory of "inverse sublimity" whose "essence is love." [17] In a striking metaphor, Jean Paul's total method is expounded: "His movement is essentially slow and cumbrous, for he advances not with one faculty, but with the whole mind; with intellect, and pathos, and wit, and humour, and imagination, moving onwards like a mighty host, motley, ponderous, irregular, and irresistible." [18] Carlyle also understands Jean Paul's world view and his historical affinities with Herder and Jacobi rather than with Kant or Fichte: "Philosophy and Poetry are not only reconciled, but blended together into a purer essence, into Religion." Carlyle's formula for Jean Paul's achievement could serve also as a summary of his own ambition. Needless to say, Carlyle admires Jean Paul as a person, for his long heroic struggle with poverty, and as an example of "Christian greatness." [19]

Compared with Goethe, Schiller, and Jean Paul, all other German writers excited only perfunctory interest in Carlyle. His sympathies with the romantic movement proper were scant. Carlyle doubts Madame de Staël's contention that three young men (the Schlegels and Tieck) in the little town of Jena could have effected a sweeping change in literature. He does not recognize a conflict between German romanticism and the German classics. Carlyle sees the German literary revival as a unity: largely as a reaction against the Enlightenment of the 18th century. The German movement, Carlyle knows, has its parallels in England and France. He cites the new enthusiasm for Shakespeare and the Elizabethans and the decline of the reputation of Pope. He knows that even in France critics are beginning to doubt the three unities and that the authority of Corneille is waning.[20] Though Carlyle refers to the Schlegels frequently, he has nothing to say of them as distinct personalities or as propounders of specific doctrines.[21] When Carlyle came to review Friedrich Schlegel's *Philosophische Vorlesungen* (1830), he merely used it as a springboard for a contrast between German and British philosophy: Schlegel is praised only for his spiritualism and his supposed denial of the reality of space and time, in total neglect of his real, very different teachings.[22]

Carlyle translated some of Tieck's fairy tales for his collection *German Romance* (1827), which was hardly more than a bookseller's venture, and felt required to say something of Tieck in his introduction. Carlyle himself admits ingenuously that the first paragraph of his characterization could equally apply to any true poet,[23] and the rest of his account is equally vague and helpless. Only a late, closely analytical letter on Tieck's historical novel, *Vittoria Accorombona*, can be considered criticism.[24]

Among the German romanticists Novalis exercised the greatest attraction for Carlyle. His essay (1828) genuinely tries to understand an alien point of view: Carlyle labors at a general defense of mysticism, and rather simply characterizes German speculative philosophy as a phenomenalism, a belief in the unreality of space and time and the capacities of Reason in contrast to the humble Understanding. He sees Novalis as a champion of these ideas, without attempting to distinguish him from his German contemporaries. Carlyle quotes some aphorisms on self-annihilation, on the body as a temple, on the self-grinding mill of the Universe envisaged by the 18th century (often with a slight distortion of the original meaning), and welcomes Novalis "as an Anti-Mechanist—the most perfect of modern spirit seers." [25] But he is highly critical of Novalis as poet and man. *Heinrich von Ofterdingen* displays "a degree of languor, not weakness, but sluggishness." Novalis "speaks in a low-voiced, not unmelodious monotony." "He *sits,* we might say, among the rich, fine, manifold combinations which his mind almost of itself presents him" in what Carlyle feels to be the passive contemplation of an "Asiatic" character.[26]

It seems a pity that Carlyle read the *Life* of E. T. A. Hoffmann by Hitzig for the introduction to his translation of *Der Goldene Topf.* He drew from it only a sermon on the terrible fate of artistic Bohemia that met poor Hoffmann. Carlyle paraphrases Goethe's judgment on the early 18th-century poet Günther when he concludes: "In fact, he elaborated nothing: above all, not himself." [27] In surprising contrast, Carlyle treated the dubious Zacharias Werner with sympathy: in a long essay (1828), he talks tolerantly of Werner's conversion to Roman Catholicism because the phenomenon interested him psychologically. Werner's plays are praised much too generously, especially if one compares the treatment of Werner with the condescension Carlyle bestowed on the far better dramatist Franz Grillparzer. He treats him, with Klingemann and Müllner, as a mere "playwright," not a proper dramatist, with a "small vein of tenderness and grace." Carlyle knew *Die Ahnfrau, Sappho,* and *König Ottokar,* the last a "harmless tragedy . . . without any discernible coherence." [28]

In these articles on German literature Carlyle has in mind a general conception of criticism and of literary history. Earlier than anyone else in England, Carlyle had understood the German historical and organological view. This achievement has not been adequately recognized by modern scholars, who have sometimes praised his early historiographical views as anticipations of "sociology" and modern historical science, mistaking his antecedents and affinities.[29] Carlyle shares the basic methods and insights of German romantic criticism and historiography. Criticism to him is identification with the author, intuition, even divination, not demonstration of cause and effect relations and not a search for general laws or theories. He consistently disparages 18th-century poetics and aesthetics, genetic schemes, theories of association, social explanations. "Man is not the product of his circumstances but, in a far higher degree, the circumstances are the product of the man." [30] Thus poverty and even lack of education is considered rather a stimulus than an obstacle to a poet. The critic's aim is "transposition into the author's point of vision": he must work his way into the poet's "manner of thought, till he sees the world with his eyes, feels as he felt and judges as he judged." [31] In the act of enjoying a work of art "we partially and for the time become the very Painter and the very Singer." Sympathy, "an open loving heart which is the beginning of all knowledge," and even divination, "a blazing radiant insight into the fact," are required. "To know; to get into the truth of anything, is ever a mystic act" [32] is Carlyle's triumphant conclusion—a gesture toward a problem, though hardly a solution.

If sympathy, identification is the critical method, we ask for a criticism of intentions, an examination of "what the poet's aim really and truly was" and for a criticism of beauties as "no man can pronounce on the faults till he has seen the very last and highest beauty." [33] Carlyle, at this early period, advocates universal tolera- tion, a view of literature which would allow "space for all true singers out of every age and every clime." He hopes for "free literary intercourse with other nations," for Goethe's "World Literature, instead of isolated, mutually repulsive National Literatures." [34] Carlyle's ideal world literature does not, of course, require an abolition of national literatures, but rather looks forward toward a harmonious symphony of the nations. The way to humanity leads through nationality, and this is true also of literature. In *German Romance* (1827) Carlyle had proclaimed his principle for treating German literature: "Germanhood I have all along regarded as a quality, not a fault," as "every nation has its own form of character and life." [35] In the essay on Burns (1828) he had praised the new Scottish literature of Burns and Scott as growing no longer "in water but in mould, and with the true racy virtues of the soil and climate" in contrast to writers like Hume or Kames who "had nothing truly Scottish, nothing indigenous" in them.[36] In the same article that proclaimed the ideal of world literature, he chided William Taylor of Norwich for having "no theorem of Germany and its intellectual progress," for not offering "a por- traiture of the national mind"; and there he formulates the new ideal of literary history most impressively:

The History of a nation's Poetry is the essence of its History, political, economic, scientific, religious. With all these the complete Historian of a national Poetry will be familiar; the national physiognomy, in its finest traits, and through its successive stages of growth will be clear to him; he will discern the grand spiritual Tendency of each period, what was the highest Aim and Enthusiasm of mankind in each, and how each epoch naturally evolved itself from the other. He has to record the highest Aim of a nation, in its successive directions and developments; for by this the Poetry of the nation modulates itself; this *is* the Poetry of the nation.[37]

Similarly in the then unpublished preface to the *History of German Literature,* Carlyle calls literature "the truest emblem of the national spirit and manner of existence." The historian should bring nearer "the essential life of the nation," should "decipher and portray the spiritual form of the nation at each successive period" and thus see clearly into the "hidden inward structure of that nation." [38]

Here all the key words of German historicism are assembled: individuality, nationality, development, the spirit of a nation and an age, inward form and structure, continuity. There is nothing sociological or Saint-Simonian or Hegelian about these concepts at this time: they all can be found in the Schlegels, in Novalis, Jean Paul, and, with more naturalistic affinities, in Herder and Goethe. Carlyle is well aware of his sources: in tracing the beginnings of the "new epoch in classical studies" to Christian Gottlob Heyne, Carlyle refers to the *Lectures* of the Schlegels as their culmination.[39] In the "State of German Literature" (1827) he characterizes the new criticism of the Germans as not concerned "with the qualities of diction, the coherence of metaphors, the fitness of sentiments, the general logical truth in a work of art," nor with the psychology, with the desire to discover and delineate "the peculiar nature of the poet from his poetry," but "properly and ultimately with the essence and peculiar life of the poetry itself." Citing the dramas of Shakespeare as an example, Carlyle makes the Germans ask:

Wherein lies that life; how have [the plays] attained that shape and individuality? . . . Are these dramas of his [Shakespeare] not verisimilar only, but true; nay, truer than reality itself, since the essence of unmixed reality is bodied forth in them under more expressive symbols? What is this unity of

theirs; and can our deeper inspection discern it to be indivisible, and existing by necessity?... What and how was the
poem, and why was it a poem and not rhymed eloquence,
creation and not figured passions? [40]

Carlyle knows that there are differences between the aesthetic
theories of Kant, Herder, Schiller, Goethe, and Richter, and that
Tieck, and especially the two Schlegels, have labored meritoriously
in reconciling these various opinions.[41] But he is not himself interested in these distinctions, just as he did not draw clear distinctions
between the German philosophers whom he read and used—Kant,
Fichte, Schelling, and Jacobi. In his early criticism Carlyle freely
adopted the Germans' concept of the meaning and creation of
poetry. Poetry is primarily a kind of knowledge, an insight into
the reality behind appearances, into the mystery of the universe.
"Poetry is nothing but higher Knowledge," "another form of
Wisdom." The true Poet is the Seer, "whose eye has been gifted to
discern the godlike Mystery of God's Universe, and decipher some
new lines of its celestial writing ... for he *sees* into the greatest of
secrets, 'the open secret,'"[42] says Carlyle, speaking of Goethe and
using Goethe's favorite phrase. Similarly he says of Shakespeare:

> He does not look *at* a thing, but into it, through it; so he con-
> structively comprehends it, can take it asunder, and put it
> together again; the thing melts, as it were, into light under his
> eye, and anew *creates* itself before him. ... For Goethe, as for
> Shakespeare, the world lies all translucent, all *fusible* we might
> call it; the Natural in reality is the Supernatural ... What are
> the *Hamlets* and *Tempests,* the *Fausts* and *Mignons,* but
> glimpses accorded us into this translucent, wonder-encircled
> world; revelations of the mystery of all mysteries, Man's Life as
> it actually is? [43]

Thus poetry is "the essence of all science," since it aims "at incorporating the everlasting Reason of man in forms visible to his Sense." [44]
The poet is necessarily universal, a "living, real Encyclopaedia" as
"the whole world lies imaged as a whole within him." [45] He will,
just as inevitably, be an objective poet, entirely free of subjective
mannerism. "Philina and Clärchen, Mephistopheles and Mignon,
are alike indifferent, or alike dear" to Goethe. Shakespeare the Man

is inscrutable: he is "a Voice coming to us from the Land of Melody." Homer is "the *Witness;* we hear and believe, but do not behold him," whereas Byron, in contrast, "painted nothing else than himself, be his subject what it might." [46] Poetry thus has only one theme: the central mystery which Carlyle often calls, in a phrase common in Schelling, the Infinite in the Finite. "The poet should inform the Finite with a certain Infinitude of significance." [47]

At this early stage Carlyle was able to describe the means and methods of art in general terms. The work of art is a whole, a unity, and achieves this unity by an identity of form and content, a system of symbols. The wholeness may be the poet's, who must have a harmony of faculties, must be a universal man and not only an Intellect; or it is the wholeness achieved in the work itself: "a real self-supporting Whole, which is the highest merit in a poem." [48] Carlyle compares it with a thousand-year oak, "no leaf, no bough superfluous," [49] in the biological analogy that had been worked so hard by many Germans. It is the unity of form and content, "for body and soul, word and idea, go strangely together" and "language is the express image of thought, or rather it is the body of which thought is soul." [50] A word is not a mere arbitrary sign. It is still "a magic formula, whereby man rules the world." It used to be "a real name with meaning" [51] and Carlyle seeks to restore the word to its ancient sacred dignity. He could not understand criticisms of those who asked him to abandon his own peculiar style. "Those poor people seem to think a style can be put off or put on, not like a *skin* but like a coat." [52] If words are not merely arbitrary signs, then they are symbols. Symbol—not only artistic or linguistic symbol, of course—is the central concept of *Sartor.* In a symbol there is "concealment and yet revelation . . . embodiment and yet revelation of the Infinite; the Infinite is made to blend itself with the Finite, to stand visible, and is as it were, attainable there." The Universe appears as one vast Symbol of God. "The Poet, Prometheus-like, shapes new symbols." [53] "All History and all Poesy is but a deciphering of the Bible of World History out of that mystic heaven-written Sanscrit." [54] Carlyle distinguishes symbol from allegory: Dante's *Divine Comedy* is not an allegory—man does not believe an allegory but a symbol, "an emblematic representation of his Belief about this Universe." [55] Many terms of German romantic criticism are assembled: wholeness, or unity like that of a tree; symbol rather than allegory. Carlyle adds also "music," with him a highly metaphorical term, an alternative to harmony, melody, or song: something like the Greek *mousike* when he speaks of poetry as "musical thought," as "a melody which leads us to the edge of the Infinite" or calls Harmony "the essence of art and science." With an easy shift of meaning music can become merely meter or song. Dante is Song, Homer is Music, as is Burns.[56]

This coherent view of criticism and poetry conflicted from the very beginning, however, with other motifs in Carlyle's thought that were more deeply rooted in his personality and that finally won out: religious and ethical motifs contradicted, overlaid, and ultimately destroyed the system of thought we have outlined. Carlyle remained basically a Puritan who was unable fully to accept the idealistic monism of the German philosophers or the historicism of much of German criticism. He had, for a time, particularly from 1827 to 1832, assimilated their point of view, mainly because he had found in them allies in his struggle to overcome the skepticism of his youth and to find a new religion freed from orthodox ties. But Carlyle's new religion—which cannot be described as Christianity, since he did not accept the role of Christ or the Church—was neither German monism nor historicism. It was, rather, a dualism in which history appeared as a battlefield of God and the Devil, of Fact and Sham, of Reality and Illusion, and in which literature had only one function: the assertion of this creed and the propagation of this message. Carlyle was, or increasingly became, a curious kind of "existentialist" who believed that there is only one reality: that of lived experience, which he called "fact," and that there is only one task of art, the depiction of this fact. History becomes the only poetry, biography the only history.

The essence of idealism, or the belief in a reality behind the phenomena, and the possibility of reading and interpreting reality in the symbols of art, are abandoned. Carlyle ceased to understand the nature of art. "Fiction partakes, more than we suspect, of the nature of lying." [57] The one reality that Carlyle worships, with an odd, almost superstitious awe, is an event, a fact. "How impressive the smallest historical fact may become, as contrasted with the grandest fictitious event." That something actually happened, that it was not a dream but a reality, is a constant object of Carlyle's wonder. Charles I actually stayed the night in a hayloft with a peasant, and that peasant, in 1651, was born, was a son, was a father, toiled in many ways, and died. Johnson actually told a streetwalker: "No, no, my girl, it won't do." "Do but consider that it is true; that it did in very deed occur!" exclaims Carlyle, surprised at a commonplace that is to him the beginning of wisdom.[58] King Lackland was verily there at St. Edmundsbury and left *"tredecim sterlingii,* if nothing more, and did live and look in one way or the other, and a whole world was living and looking along with him. There, we say, is the grand peculiarity; the immeasurable one; distinguishing, to a really infinite degree, the poorest historical Fact from all Fiction whatsoever." [59] This worship of fact, of events in the past, explains Carlyle's turn to history, away from "lying" literature. When Mill lent him French memoirs of the Revolution, he commented glowingly: "This were what I should call the highest kind of writing, far higher than any kind of Fiction even of the Shakespeare sort. For my own share I declare I now enjoy no other Poem than the dim, shadowy as yet only *possible* Poem, that hovers for me in every seen Reality." [60] The past, in the eyes of Carlyle, assumes an aura of holiness that makes him, at least theoretically, suspend his ethical preoccupations. "Whatsoever has existed has had its value: without some truth and worth lying in it, the thing could not have hung together, and been the organ and sustenance, and method of action, for men that reasoned and were alive." This tolerance becomes even a general absolution: "The Past is all holy to us; the Dead are all holy, even they that were base and wicked while alive." [61]

More and more, with increasing age, Carlyle condemned all fiction and art. He not only deprecated novels, as he had long before attacked the "fashionable novels" of Bulwer, the erotic stories of George Sand,[62] or the sentimentalities of Dickens,[63] but he came to reject even Goethe and the whole seduction of art. "Fiction, even in the Fine Arts, is not permissible at all." [64] Many reports tell us that the older Carlyle disliked verse, that he advised poets to write in prose, and that he had no use for criticism, theory, or philosophy of any kind.[65]

But the violence with which the later Carlyle rejects fiction and aesthetics should not obscure the fact that he still concerned himself with literature and was able to reconcile this exaltation of fact with some function of the written word. The shift from a concept of poetry as a revelation of the reality behind the appearances to a "disimprisoned soul of fact" seems not too radical. It was only a further easy step to say that poetry itself simply is fact, that history is true poetry.[66] Exceptions are only apparent in Carlyle's mind. Homer's *Iliad* is "nothing of a fiction," as Homer believed his stories to be strictly true. Dante speaks truth, not fiction, and Shakespeare's plays are a kind of epic, history, fact.[67] The source of this idea is A. W. Schlegel's view that Shakespeare's histories are an epic of England, but Carlyle metaphorically expanded its meaning and would have included plays that, in technique, are quite unrealistic and are not histories in any sense of the traditional classification. "Fact" becomes a sacred word which, in practice, may be the art of Dante, Shakespeare, or Homer—anything that seemed to Carlyle grand and true. If poetry is history or epic, then "at bottom" poetry is a heroic poem, a biography, the life of a man.[68] The work of art as an artifact disappears, even the distinctness of the poet as a poet vanishes. Earlier he had identified the poet and the thinker, but later the poet becomes absorbed into the hero, into the great man, into any great man, and finally the poet seems nothing distinct from any good man at all. "Wherever I go or stand, I find the inarticulate dust of Poets, (of Makers, Inventors, great struggling souls, who never higgled for Copyright in the Row, and merely tended towards Heaven and God, and *from* Hell and the Devil); and I say to myself 'There have been millions and millions of Poets, and hundreds of them have been Shakespeares, perhaps thousands, or a higher ratio, since Adam first put on fig-breeches.' " [69] The poet is simply a good man, even an inarticulate good man, since everything great is unconscious and finally silent.

Carlyle, more extravagantly than any reputable critic, believes in Unconsciousness, in Nature, in Inspiration. "The uttered part of a man's life bears to the unuttered unconscious part a small unknown proportion." Only a "thin rind of the Conscious covers the deep fathomless domain of the Unconscious." "From that mystic region, and from that alone, all wonders, all Poesies, and Religions, and Social Systems have proceeded." [70] This applies not only to individuals but also to ages. A self-conscious age is an uncreative, inferior time. Literature appears, as far as it is a self-conscious literature, almost as a kind of disease. The difference between believing and unbelieving ages, which is the same to Carlyle as the difference between creative and the critical, or sterile, applies also to individuals: Virgil is inferior to Homer because of his "fatal consciousness"; [71] Boswell succeeded because he had "unconscious talent." [72] Unconsciousness, for Carlyle, is the sign of creation. Night is nobler than day. Speech is silvern, silence is golden. "Perhaps our greatest poets are the *mute* Miltons." [73] John Morley's jibe at Carlyle's "gospel of silence in thirty volumes" misses this meaning of unconscious creation, but it suggests the self-defeat of such extreme irrationalism. It ends with complete bafflement in the face of man's objective creations, which are, after all, the articulate life of reason.

The complete rejection of art, fiction, and theory grew out of Carlyle's original assertion of activism and concern with personality. With Carlyle the interest in criticism from the first shifted definitely to biography. In speaking of Burns, Carlyle says: "Far more interesting than any of his written works are his acted ones." "In the Art we can nowise forget the artist" since no "poem is equal to its poet." [74] Simultaneously a similar shift was being accomplished in France with Sainte-Beuve. Criticism had been formal or affective or philosophical and was always primarily concerned with the work. With Carlyle it became resolutely personal. Though Carlyle was often concerned with the biography of his German favorites, he was genuinely interested in their writings and teachings. With the English writers of his time it was different. He knew most of these writers personally: they obtruded themselves by their physiognomy and behavior and became victims of Carlyle's satirical portraiture. The mumbling Coleridge drawling and snuffling "om-m-mject" and "sum-m-mject," "a moaning singsong of theosophico-metaphysical monotony," "a helpless Psyche overspun with Church of England cobwebs; a weak, diffusive weltering, ineffectual man." [75] Wordsworth, "a man of immense head and great jaws like a crocodile's, cast in a mould designed for prodigious work," but actually "a rather dull, hard-tempered, unproductive and almost wearisome kind of man." "Franker utterance of mere garrulities and even platitudes I never heard from any man." Still, "a natural man" "with a fine rustic simplicity and dignity about him." [76] Lamb, "the leanest of mankind, with spindle legs ... of a Jew type rather, spoke with a stutter; in walking tottered and shuffled; emblem of imbecility, bodily and spiritual (something of real *insanity* I have understood) and yet something too of humane, ingenuous, pathetic, sportfully much-enduring." "Usually ill-mannered (to a degree), screwed into frosty artificialities, ghastly make-believe of wit." [77] Landor, "a tall, broad, burly man, with gray hair, and large, fierce-rolling eyes: of the most restless, impetuous vivacity, not to be held in by the most perfect breeding—a wild man, whom no extent of culture had been able to tame," or, in a more favorable mood, "a proud, irascible, trenchant, yet generous, veracious, and dignified old man, quite ducal or royal in the temper of him." [78] De Quincey, "one of the prettiest talkers I ever heard: of great, indeed diseased acuteness, not without depth, of a fine sense too, but no breadth, no justness, weak, diffuse, supersensitive; on the whole, a perverted, ineffectual man." "One of the most irreclaimable Tories now extant; despising Poverty with complete contempt; and himself, alas, poorer than ever Job was who at worst never got *gazetted*." [79] The harshness and malicious wit in many of Carlyle's opinions should not obscure his real insight and power of characterization. Yet this insight is seldom based on extensive reading of the writer's works, but seems simply physiognomic instinct, hearsay, or impression. Wordsworth's "divine reflections and unfathomabilities [are] stinted, scanted; palish and uncertain;—perhaps in part a feeble reflex (derived at second hand through Coleridge) of the immense German fund of such?" [80]

Even when Carlyle did not know the men personally, he judged them mainly by ethical standards applied to their persons. Burns is praised for spontaneity, sincerity, and lyrical immediacy but is considered as spoiled and ruined by worldly ambition. "His morality is that of a mere worldly man; enjoyment, in a finer or coarser shape, is the only thing he longs and strives for." Carlyle has a surprisingly low opinion of his work. "We can look on but few of these pieces as, in strict critical language, deserving the name of Poems; they are rhymed eloquence, rhymed pathos, rhymed sense; yet seldom essentially melodious, aërial, poetical." [81] Carlyle singles out "The Jolly Beggars" for praise as the most strictly poetical of all his poems. But he objects to "Tam o' Shanter" as "mere drunken phantasmagoria, a piece of sparkling rhetoric." [82] Burns' poetry is praised, with references to texts, for its warm sentiment of love, its melodiousness, its graphic descriptions of nature, its clearness of sight. Though Carlyle hints at the failings of the man and deplores his lack of religion, the emphasis and tone of his criticisms are positive. The feeling of kinship with a poor Scottish peasant and the recognition of the lyric as a genre of limited pretensions make the essay mainly one of appreciation, especially as it elaborates the contrast between Burns' sincerity and Byron's falsehood.

Carlyle never wrote the essay he had planned on Byron, but it is obvious from the many scattered comments on Byron [83] that he would have treated him as the representative of pessimism, despair, and even moral nihilism. Carlyle constantly chides Byron for what we might call a failure of nerve, and even, surprisingly, passivity and inaction, notwithstanding Byron's Greek record. Byron represents "feelings which arise from passion incapable of being converted into action." [84] The famous advice "Close thy Byron, open thy Goethe" [85] is based on this contrast between action, love, work, and despairing gloom and sloth. Carlyle was puzzled by Goethe's admiration for Byron and refused to believe that Euphorion had anything to do with Byron.[86]

Scott, a "robust, thoroughly healthy and withal very prosperous and victorious man," [87] is also treated in contrast to the sick, poor Byron. But what in the essay on Burns was a cause for praise—earthiness and local Scottish feeling—becomes, with Scott, a cause of blame. The emphasis has changed because Scott was successful, had become a Baronet, and as a novelist had, in Carlyle's eyes, more serious obligations than a song writer. "His life was worldly; his ambitions were worldly. There is nothing spiritual in him; all is economical, material, of the earth earthy." He "must kill himself that he may be a country gentleman, the founder of a race of Scottish lairds." Writing daily like a steam-engine, that he "make £15,000 a-year, and buy upholstery with it." [88] The life of Scott is used as a text for a sermon on the vanity of worldly ambition and success and the uselessness of all work written in a hurry, extemporaneously, for amusement only. "The great Mystery of Existence was not great to him." "One sees not that he believed in anything." This "substantial, peaceable, terrestial man" had "no message whatever to deliver to the world." [89] The novels are judged very harshly as "theatrical scene-paintings." Scott's art of characterization is quite external: "He fashions his characters from the skin inwards, never getting near the heart of them." Surprisingly, Carlyle sees in Scott's historical pictures nothing but antiquarian enjoyment in old fashions of arms and dress. But "buff-belts and all manner of jerkins and costumes are transitory; man alone is perennial." [90] Grudgingly, Carlyle admits that the historical novel was an important innovation, but he does not see Scott's profound insight into historical conflicts nor the solidity of his picture of 18th-century Scotland. He treats him, almost as severely as Croce was to do, as a mere hero of commerce, and as an "artist," a virtuoso provider of entertainment.

The occasional remarks on Shelley and Keats are even harsher and less discerning, though one must admit, as always, Carlyle's power of unforgettable phrasing. A sentence such as "Hear a Shelley filling the earth with inarticulate wail; like the infinite, inarticulate grief and weeping of forsaken infants," suggests that he knew only "O Life O World O Time." [91] Carlyle thanked Browning for his essay on Shelley introducing a collection of forged letters and told him bluntly:

> Shelley always seemed to me an extremely weak creature, and lamentable more than admirable. Weak in genius, weak in character (for these two always go together); a poor, thin, spasmodic, hectic, shrill and pallid being . . . his universe is all vacant azure, hung with a few frosty mournful if beautiful stars; the very voice of him (his style, etc.) shrill, shrieky, to my ear has too much of the ghost.[92]

Similarly, Carlyle has no use for Keats. In the Burns essay he referred to Keats' "weak-eyed maudlin sensibility, and a certain vague random tunefulness of nature," [93] and the *Life* of Monckton Milnes increased his contempt. "The kind of man that Keats was gets ever more horrible to me. Force of hunger for pleasure of every kind, and want of all other force—such a soul, it would once have been very evident, was a chosen 'vessel of Hell.' " [94] The limits of literary criticism seem to be reached. The Inquisitor has taken over. These violent pronouncements show that Carlyle cannot be identified with the English Romantic Age: not a single literary figure escaped his scathing indictment. Historically he comes out of an older past.

Carlyle's fierce hatred of the Enlightenment is even stronger. The condemnation of the 18th century is sweeping and general, though in detail Carlyle is far more charitable to 18th-century writers than to contemporaries. Dryden, Pope, and Sterne are praised: Sterne "for the immense love of things around him." [95] Swift and Hume excite his admiration, though Swift seemed to him no Christian, and Hume was the great opponent of all Carlyle stood for. Still, there is a strong vein of stoicism in Carlyle and Hume was a stoic, "a heroic, silent man." [96]

But Carlyle's principal admiration was reserved for Dr. Johnson, "one of the greatest heroes," "one of our great English souls." [97] Johnson the writer did not interest Carlyle much: he finds in his books "the indisputablest traces of a great intellect and a great heart," and "a wondrous buckram style," [98] but he cares only for the man as reported by Boswell. Carlyle's recognition of Boswell's "open loving heart," of his voluntary hero worship, of his "ingenuity, a figurativeness and fanciful sport, with glimpses of insight far deeper than the common," is tempered by a low opinion of Boswell's morals and intellect: "a gross liver, a vain, heedless babbler, a coxcomb," full of "sensuality, pretension, boisterous imbecility." [99] Carlyle propounds substantially the same paradox as Macaulay's slightly earlier essay. Foolish Boswell unconsciously produced the greatest book of the 18th century: the gospel of "the Prophet of the English." [100] This paradox has since been resolved by the discovery of Boswell's papers which demonstrate his conscious artistry.

The French 18th century is for Carlyle the great Age of Unbelief. Still, the essays on Voltaire and Diderot and the comments on Rousseau in the lectures on *Heroes* are not devoid of human sympathy and some literary perception. Rousseau seems oddly out of place among Carlyle's heroes: "a morbid, excitable, spasmodic, mean, vain" man whom he seems to admire only because Rousseau was in earnest and had "a spark of heavenly fire" in him.[101] Voltaire, in an early essay (1828), excites Carlyle's praise for his tolerance, his "keen sense of rectitude." He was "a perfectly civilized man," but his nature was "positively shallow. We find no heroism of character in him, from first to last; nay, there is not, that we know of, one great thought in all his six-and-thirty quartos." "He is no great Man, but only a great *Persifleur*." [102] He is no poet, no philosopher, but his writings must be praised for lucidity, order, skill in overcoming difficulties, for wit and "taste" (which is not, however, genuine love for poetry). Yet Carlyle recognized that Voltaire is inferior to Diderot as a thinker.[103] The Diderot essay warmly acknowledges his intellectual eminence. *Le Rêve de D'Alembert* is dismissed, *Les Bijoux indiscrets* is alluded to as "the beastliest of all past, present or future dull novels," but there is ample praise for *Jacques le Fataliste* and especially for *Le Neveu de Rameau*. Carlyle had read something of Diderot's art criticism and criticizes its naturalism in the terms of Goethe's comments.[104] But the essay is mainly biographical, expressing proper horror at Diderot's relation with Sophie Volland and at the low company he kept, and ideological, with a fervid sermon against atheism and the philosophy of mechanism.

Strickly from the point of view of literary criticism, one must deplore that Carlyle chose the path of virtue: the shift to biography, didacticism, moralism, and the criterion of "sincerity" have not advanced the cause of criticism. Carlyle's temporary adoption of the creed of historicism and of German romantic symbolism brought him much closer to an understanding of poetry. But on the other hand one should recognize that Carlyle's moralism was basic to his personality and that there was some deep insight in his rejection of the anarchy of values and blind trust in change implied by romantic German historicism. Carlyle's harsh dualism of good and evil in man, his recognition of catastrophes and cataclysms in history, and even his worship of lived experience as "fact" represents a view of the world (and thus of art) that must be faced in order to be refuted.

THOMAS DE QUINCEY (1785–1859)

De Quincey has been often described as a minor Coleridge and has even been called "the adjective of which Coleridge was the substantive."[1] De Quincey no doubt had a glowing admiration for Coleridge as a philosopher and psychologist: he thought him comparable to Plato and Schelling and "absolutely unrivalled on earth" as a psychologist.[2] But he was also the first to expose his plagiarisms from Schelling.[3] He wrote most uncharitably of Coleridge's opium habit, and he does not seem to have understood his poetry at all. He asserts, in his only lengthy comment on one of the poems, that "the ancient mariner had slain the creature that, on all the earth, loved him best. In the darkness of his cruel superstition he had done it, to save his human brothers from a fancied inconvenience."[4] Nor did De Quincey agree with Coleridge on aesthetics or literary theory: he has none of his preoccupations with the imagination, with wholeness, or with symbol, and he definitely rejected Coleridge's criticism of Wordsworth's theory of poetic diction and his account of illusion.[5] Rather, in criticism, De Quincey's allegiance is to Wordsworth: "For most of the sound criticism on poetry, or any subject connected with it that I have ever met with, I must acknowledge my obligations to many years' conversation with Mr. Wordsworth." [6] He called the 1800 *Preface* "beyond all comparison the subtlest and (not excepting even the best of the German essays) the most finished and masterly specimen of reasoning which has in any age or nation been called forth by any one of the fine arts." [7] Later De Quincey complained about Wordsworth's failure to document or to limit his case against the old prescriptive diction of poetry, and even accused him of entirely "misconceiving his own meaning." [8] But in literary theory, De Quincey belongs not to the Coleridgean and German dialectical symbolism but to the empirical psychological tradition of the British and to the emotionalist trend, descending from Dennis through Hartley to Wordsworth. De Quincey had high hopes in future advances of psychology. "In the sense of absolute and philosophic criticism, we have little or none; for, before *that* can exist, we must have a good psychology, whereas, at present, we have none at all." [9]

There are, in De Quincey, occasional echoes of the symbolic view (as there are in Wordsworth). Poetry teaches as nature teaches: "as forests teach, as the sea teaches, as infancy teaches,—viz. by deep impulse, by hieroglyphic suggestion . . . through symbols and actions." [10] Even here "the impulse from the vernal wood" is recognizable in the symbolic alphabet. But usually in De Quincey poetry does not teach but rather communicates emotions. The famous distinction between the literature of power and the literature of knowledge (for which De Quincey cites Wordsworth as a source) [11] is, at first sight, a mere reformulation of the distinction between poetry and science made by Wordsworth and Coleridge. "Literature of power" allowed De Quincey to subsume imaginative lyrical prose under this term and thus to avoid the implications of "fiction" by grouping together what the Germans call "Dichtung" irrespective of meter. "Power" in De Quincey means emotional impact and is surely allied to similar distinctions drawn by Hazlitt [12] and possibly even to Herder's attempt to make "power" the central concept of poetry when, in the first *Kritisches Wäldchen* (1769), he tried to overthrow Lessing's *Laokoön*. De Quincey had translated the *Laokoön,* in part, with comments, and had written a brief account of Herder.[13] But De Quincey seems not to have been aware of the German debate and may rather have drawn on the 18th-century discussions of the sublime. He himself somewhat shifted in his use of the distinction between power and knowledge. The early passage (1823) emphasizes the difference between "power" and "pleasure" and sees the function of literature in the exciting of unawakened feelings. "I say, when these inert and sleeping forms *are* organized, when these possibilities *are* actualized, is this conscious and living possession of mine *power,* or what it is?" [14] But later (1848) De Quincey defines the distinction differently: literature of power speaks to the human *spirit,* literature of knowledge to the meager understanding.[15] Power is called "deep sympathy with truth," "exercise and expansion to your own latent capacity of sympathy with the infinite." It lives in relation "to the great *moral* capacities of man." It is identified with "the *understanding heart,*" with intuitive knowledge. "Peace" and "repose" [16] are proclaimed to be essential to great works of art, in an attempt to counteract the merely affective, overpowering implications of the early use of "power." Like Longinus, De Quincey tries to keep both *ekstasis* and *katharsis.* But the term "literature of power" has not survived in criticism because "power" does not clearly suggest emotional impact and because "knowledge," in a well-known saying, *is* power.

This central conception of De Quincey's theory of literature is oddly matched with ideas of quite different provenience and consequences. In two essays, "Rhetoric" (1828) and "Style" (1840–41), De Quincey draws a distinction between rhetoric and eloquence (or oratory). Eloquence is the art of persuasion, the power of moving (which one would think should appeal to him), while rhetoric means playing with ideas for their own sake, mental gymnastics or pyrotechnics, an "art of rejoicing in its own energies." [17] De Quincey often recognizes the view that ideally style or "manner is confluent with the matter," that style is or should be, in Wordsworth's term, not the dress but the "incarnation of thoughts." [18] In practice, however, De Quincey is interested in the variety of style that manages language for its own sake, style that has "an absolute value . . . quite distinct from the value of the subject about which it is employed." [19] He finds examples of this "rhetoric" in Donne, Jeremy Taylor, and Sir Thomas Browne, whereas the Greeks had only oratory, and no rhetoric in his special sense.[20] De Quincey consistently disparages two kinds of style: the plain style of a Swift for its "coarse inartificiality," which seems to him in no way superior to that of Defoe and hundreds of other writers; [21] and the choppy, discontinuous style of Hazlitt and Lamb. Thus Hazlitt is not eloquent in De Quincey's sense. "No man can be eloquent whose thoughts are abrupt, insulated, capricious, and (to borrow an impressive word from Coleridge) non-sequacious." [22] Lamb suffers from short breath. "The gyration within which his sentiment wheels, no matter of what kind it may be, is always the shortest possible. It does not prolong itself—it does not repeat itself—it does not propagate itself." Lamb has "no sense of the rhythmical in prose composition." [23] De Quincey extravagantly concluded, possibly because "rhythm" for De Quincey meant only the drawn-out rhythms of the Ciceronian and baroque periods he admired in Taylor, Milton, Browne, and Burke, and practiced himself in his "impassioned" dream fantasies. But his conception of "style" and rhetoric vacillates disconcertingly between what he calls "organology"—style as an organ of thought, style in relation to the ideas and feelings—and "mechanology," a science of style considered as a machine, in which words act upon words.[24] Rhythm, independent of meaning, and mind play, independent of its subject or its truth, combine in his concept of "rhetoric," which is so peculiar and so contrary to all historical usage that it is difficult to see why it should be hailed as "the most original contribution to rhetorical theory since Aristotle." [25] De Quincey merely wrenched an accepted term into a new meaning. Incidentally, he sketched a trend in the history of English style in the 17th century. But even De Quincey had to recognize that the divorce of rhetoric from meaning and eloquence is not quite tenable.[26]

The two basic conceptions of "literature of power," in the sense of emotional impact, and of "rhetoric," defined as unemotional mental pyrotechnics, do not fit together and are even more strangely combined with other historical ideas. De Quincey propounded his own version of the classical and the romantic and embraced a cyclical concept of the history of literature. On both points he is, however, quite unoriginal and does not deserve the extravagant praise that has been heaped on him for his "profound grasp of what may be called the organic conception of literature." [27] De Quincey seeks to replace the contrast between classical and romantic with a contrast between pagan and Christian literature. The main distinction between antiquity and Christianity De Quincey sees in their different attitudes toward death: the pagan is full of gloomy uncertainties and therefore tries to disguise the idea of death; the Christian faces its horrors firmly because he believes in resurrection. De Quincey pompously claims that he "has ascertained the two great and opposite laws under which the Grecian and the English tragedy has each separately developed itself" and disparages the Schlegels, who "barely indicated the distinction of Classical and Romantic" but "are not entitled to credit of any discovery at all." [28] But surely De Quincey's claims to originality on this point are quite unsubstantiated: the Schlegels, Jean Paul (whose *Vorschule* De Quincey admired [29]), and many other Germans thought that romantic poetry could just as well be called Christian. De Quincey's emphasis on the different conceptions of death in antiquity and Christianity—his contrast between the youths extinguishing a torch represented on ancient sarcophagi and the skeletons with scythes on Christian tombs—echoes a long debate in which Lessing, Herder, and Schiller took prominent parts.[30] What is peculiar to De Quincey is only his violent disapproval of pagan religion. Like a group of German romantics who revolted against the Hellenism of the great German classics, De Quincey was fanatically anti-Greek. In his view the Greek gods inspired only blind terror, were feared as "public nuisances," as "rattlesnakes." Greek religion had a degrading influence: the ancients had no conception of spirituality, none of sin, or even of charity.[31] De Quincey systematically attacks Greece, "uninventive Greece, for we maintain loudly that Greece, in her poets, *was* uninventive and sterile beyond the example of other nations." [32] He disparages Homer as far inferior to Chaucer, Pindar as unreadable, Demosthenes as empty, and Plato as "by no means remarkable for his opulence in ideas." [33] The Greek tragic poets were, however, the only rays of moral light in the pagan darkness. Greek tragedy is praised by De Quincey but conceived as *tableaux vivants* that know no conflict and "represent a life within a life: a life sequestrated into some far-off slumbering state, having the severe tranquility of Hades; a life symbolized by the marble life of sculpture; but utterly out of all symmetry and proportion to the realities of that human life which we moderns take up as the basis

of our Tragic Drama." [34] De Quincey's "Theory of Greek Tragedy" (1840), for which he claims complete originality, simply
carries to absurd lengths the Schlegels' parallel between Greek
sculpture and Greek drama. Though De Quincey thought of himself as the second Greek scholar in the country, he represents
rather an extreme romantic Christian reaction against Hellenism.

This doctrinaire and unhistorical philosophy of history is combined in De Quincey, at times, with a rationalistic concept of
inevitable cyclical progress, with the view, familiar in England
since Warton and Hurd, that poetry declines from an early age of
passion to an age of reason, or the view that there is a seesaw of
creative and critical ages. De Quincey himself traces this idea back
to Velleius Paterculus, and he could have met it in Goethe and
Carlyle.[35] He makes particular use of this concept in an attempt to
disprove the view that there was a French period in English literature, or that Pope was dependent on French classicism. Instead,
De Quincey's argument runs, "no section whatever of the French
literature has ever availed to influence, or in the slightest degree to
modify our own." [36] As for Pope and Dryden, "that thing which they
did they *would* have done though France had been at the back of
China. The school to which they belonged was a school developed at
a certain stage of progress in all nations alike . . . a school depending
on the peculiar direction given to the sensibilities by the reflecting
faculty and by the new phases of society." [37] De Quincey chides Pope
for saying

> We conquer'd France, but felt our captive's charms:
> Her Arts victorious triumph'd o'er our Arms [38]

Yet he considers the English Augustan age to be an unpoetic minor
age, followed, in the time of Johnson, by an "age of collapse." [39] De
Quincey harshly criticized Addison, Swift, Dr. Johnson, Fielding,
and Crabbe,[40] but expressed, surprisingly, high admiration for
Pope. He can do so because he assimilates Pope—particularly in
the 1848 essay—in his concept of rhetoric. "I admire him as a pyro-
technic artist for producing brilliant and evanescent effects out of
elements which have hardly a moment's life within them." [41] The
subject matter in Pope is irrelevant: the style of the archery counts,
not the choice of victims.[42] De Quincey does not believe Pope was a
proper satirist, since he lacked malice and indignation, was satisfied

with his society, and had really a pacific and charitable frame of mind. Though "a careless and indolent assenter" to Christianity, "he had drunk profoundly from the streams of Christian sentiment."[43] In his poetry he deliberately assumed "the license of a liar for the sake of some momentary and farcical effect," indulging in brutalities and audacious falsehoods because he was "incapable of a sincere thought or a sincere emotion."[44] *The Dunciad* is by far his greatest work, while *An Essay on Man* is "a dream of drunken eclecticism" without central principle.[45] De Quincey overstates his view and spoils it by the final disparagement of Pope's sincerity. But at a time when Pope was usually seen either as a "correct" didactic poet and grave moral thinker or as a venomous malicious scoundrel,[46] De Quincey recognized something of Pope's technique of assuming a masque or *persona* and had a genuine insight into his character and his social and religious relations.

These main theoretical concepts in De Quincey's writings are in themselves incompatible and are merely the highlights scattered over an enormous body of miscellaneous writings. The bulk of De Quincey's practical criticism is quite unrelated to theory and is often biographical or a mere capricious laying down the law. He makes a display of recondite, sometimes inaccurate, erudition, or of hairsplitting polemical acuteness interrupted by incredibly tasteless clowning and bumptious boasting. There is no more exasperating writer than De Quincey; he never seems to be able to keep to a point, digresses constantly, pads blatantly, and obviously aims at startling his reader at any price. We are told that Dr. Johnson "had studied nothing," that Hazlitt "had read nothing," that Kant "never read a book in his life,"[47] and so forth. It would be an easy game to make De Quincey an example of mere caprice, of pure John Bullish provinciality, of narrow-minded moralism, of complacent anti-intellectualism: a model of the worst features of the criticism of the time. Certainly his views of French literature cannot be taken seriously,[48] and his writings on German literature, though less prejudiced, are hardly more balanced. One may laugh at the highly amusing moralizing about Wilhelm Meister and his lady-loves,[49] but it is harder to excuse (except as potboilers) the lives of Goethe and Schiller written for the *Encyclopaedia Britannica* (1838). De Quincey dismisses *Faust* as unintelligible and does not mention Goethe's lyric poetry; he ignores all Schiller's prose and poetry and all the dramas after *Wallenstein*.[50] De Quincey thought Goethe "far inferior to Coleridge in power and compass of intellect" and prophesied that "posterity will wonder at the subverted idol, whose basis, being hollow and unsound, will leave the worship of their fathers an enigma to their descendants."[51] Only the few sympathetic pages on Jean Paul[52] alleviate De Quincey's frequent but curiously inept excursions into German literature.[53]

He was at home only in modern English literature. The "Life of Shakespeare" for the *Encyclopaedia Britannica* (1838) is, however, hardly superior to the German lives; it is incredibly prolix, is devoid of information, and indulges in sentimental speculations about Shakespeare's "nuptial disappointments."[54] The little essay "On the Knocking at the Gate in Macbeth" (1823) is rightly admired as a perceptive analysis of a sound effect. De Quincey uses examples from everyday life—such as the silence and desertion of the streets after a great funeral suddenly broken by the sound of wheels rattling away from the scene—to explain the effect of the knocking in *Macbeth:*

> The retiring of the human heart and the entrance of the fiendish heart was to be expressed and made sensible. Another world has stept in ... But how shall this be conveyed and made palpable? In order that a new world may step in, this world must for a time disappear. The murderers and the murder must be insulated—cut off by an immeasurable gulf from the ordinary tide and succession of human affairs—locked up and sequestered in some deep recess ... time must be annihilated, relation to things without abolished ... the knocking at the gate is heard, and it makes known audibly that the reaction has commenced; the human has made its reflux upon the fiendish; the pulses of life are beginning to beat again; and the reestablishment of the goings-on of the world in which we live first makes us profoundly sensible of the awful parenthesis that had suspended them.

De Quincey has put his finger on a crucial turning point of the play and has analyzed the sudden change, though one may doubt whether the effect of the knocking works retroactively to isolate the criminal pair. Might not the effect be more simply explained by our sharing in the apprehension and the terror of the guilty couple?

The knocking is like the voice of doom, the herald of retribution; and everyday reality is rather re-established by the speech of the porter, who is never even referred to in De Quincey's essay. The essay culminates in a peroration on Shakespeare that is a characteristic piece of romantic bardolatry:

> O mighty poet! Thy works are not as those of other men, simply and merely great works of art, but are also like the phenomena of nature, like the sun and the sea, the stars and the flowers, like frost and snow, rain and dew, hail-storm and thunder, which are to be studied with entire submission of our own faculties, and in the perfect faith that in them there can be no too much or too little, nothing useless or inert, but that, the farther we press in our discoveries, the more shall we see proofs of design and self-supporting arrangement where the careless eye had seen nothing but accident! [55]

Shakespeare is nature—but nature revealing God's design in every smallest detail: nature reconciled with art.

De Quincey felt no such reverence toward his contemporaries. The essay on Keats (1846) is lukewarm: he condemns *Endymion* as "the very midsummer madness of affectation, of false vapoury sentiment, and of fantastic effeminacy," a poem belonging to the "vilest collections of waxwork filigree or gilt gingerbread." Keats shockingly abused the English language, trampled on it "as if with the hoofs of a buffalo" but still produced one immortal work, *Hyperion,* which has "the majesty, the austere beauty, and the simplicity of a Grecian temple enriched with Grecian sculpture." [56] But then, a year afterward, De Quincey remembered that being like a Greek temple is no compliment, since Greek mythology is "feeble," incapable of breeding anything so deep as depicted in *Hyperion,* which draws on far older, far darker creeds.[57] And not a word about Keats' odes or other narrative poems!

Considering his politics and religion, Shelley fared slightly better. De Quincey makes an effort in his essay (1846) to recognize "the admirable qualities of his moral nature," his sincerity and purity. But he can do so only by explaining Shelley's behavior and views as "partial lunacy"; he displays his smug bigotry by suggesting that Shelley perished in a "holy hurricane," raised by a "religious sea" in order to avenge the cause of a "denied and insulted Deity." Nothing at all, in the long essay, is said of the works except of *The Cenci,* which De Quincey defends for the "angelic nature of Beatrice," "the light shining in darkness." "Even the murder, even the parricide, though proceeding from herself, do but deepen that background of darkness which throws into fuller revelation the glory of that suffering face immortalised by Guido." [58]

De Quincey did not know Keats or Shelley personally; he did know Wordsworth and admired him as the greatest poet of the age. But he knew Wordsworth too well and could write of him and his family only with an odd mixture of genuine affection and gossipy malice. Mrs. Wordsworth was "very plain" and had "a considerable obliquity of vision." Dorothy stammered, walked ungracefully and knew very little. William had "certainly not ornamental legs," drooped about the shoulders, was prematurely aged, and was incapable of "the humilities and devotion of courtship." [59] He was favored by outrageous luck in all financial matters, getting bequests and sinecures just when they were needed, as if people died in order to help him. But these reminiscences (1839) were followed by some genuine criticism on the poetry in a later essay (1845). Some of the essay consists of carping and jesting: that Margaret in *The Excursion,* for example, should have written to the War Office to ascertain the whereabouts of her husband. [60] He praises, of course, Wordsworth's discoveries in nature, his "learned eye." Like Coleridge before him, De Quincey made much of such observations as a cataract looking as though "frozen by distance," or twilight having an abstracting, removing power, or of cattle grazing

> Their heads never raising;
> There are forty feeding like one. [61]

But De Quincey can also characterize Wordsworth's poetry more perceptively; his way of dealing with passions obliquely, his "suddenly unveiling a connexion between objects hitherto regarded as irrelate and independent," and finally his seeking systematically "sadness in the very luxury of joy," looking for an "influx of the joyous into the sad, and of the sad into the joyous—this reciprocal entanglement of darkness in light, and of light in darkness." [62] De

Quincey calls it "the principle of antagonism," [63] apparently on the analogy of the laws of association. We might call it irony or paradox.

Such perceptive comments, mostly aimed at an analysis of the reader's response to literature, compensate for the dreary wastes of jaunty jocularities, learned oddities, and turgid declamations of De Quincey. Still, through every article, however prolix, digressive, and bumptious, there shines an oddly winning impish personality and an alert mind. But De Quincey lacks the system, coherence, and objectivity of a great critic.

LEIGH HUNT (1784-1859)

De Quincey, we have seen, is nearest to Wordsworth in literary theory. Leigh Hunt, if one can generalize about his enormous output of some fifty-five book titles and hundreds of articles, seems nearest to Lamb and Hazlitt in method and certainly derives his theory of imagination from Coleridge. Hunt praised Coleridge's criticism of Wordsworth as "the finest lecture on the art of poetry in the language"; [1] he wrote glowingly of Lamb's "masterly" criticism; [2] and he admired Hazlitt, even though he often disagreed with the harshness of his judgments. [3]

Hunt's most systematic pronouncement of principles is the introduction, "In Answer to the Question: What Is Poetry?," to *Imagination and Fancy* (1844), an anthology of extracts from Chaucer to Keats. He attempts to show "what sort of poetry is to be considered as *poetry of the most poetical kind*," poetry "in its element, like an essence distilled," or "pure poetry," as he sometimes calls it. He seeks the answer in the Coleridgean distinction of imagination and fancy. But Coleridge's distinction, with Hunt, has lost its anchorage in an idealistic epistemology: Imagination has ceased to be creative imagination, and has become again merely invention, inventiveness, or image-making. Remnants of Coleridge's distinction are still discernible: Imagination is a "perception of sympathies in the natures of things"; fancy, "a sporting with their resemblance, real or supposed." But the gulf between the two faculties is widened: Imagination with Hunt belongs to tragedy, or the serious muse; fancy to the comic. One of the teachers of imagination is melancholy. Fancy is "without the other's weight of thought and feeling." Fancy is "a lighter play of imagination, or the feeling of analogy

coming short of seriousness." It is the "poetical part of wit." [4] The
deterioration of fancy to mere comic wit has gone much further
than in Wordsworth or Coleridge. In Hunt's companion anthology,
Wit and Humour (1846), wit is even equated with "fancy in its most
wilful and strictly speaking, its least poetical state." Humor differs
by dealing "in incongruities of character and circumstance, as Wit
does in those of arbitrary ideas." [5] These loose distinctions are not
improved by frequent statements that a passage can illustrate both
imagination and fancy or by jumbled classifications of the workings
of the imagination and wit according to rhetorical categories.
Natural and unnatural fictions, similes, metaphors, animating
metaphors, small touches such as Priam's grey chin as he kneels
before Achilles, are the subdivisions of imagination; simile, metaphor, irony, burlesque, parody, exaggeration, puns, and nonsense
verse are some of the subdivisions of wit. In practice, imaginative
poetry is broken up into "imagery" and "music": either the union
of painting and music Hunt admired in Spenser, or the sheer music
of Coleridge. But the theoretical consequences of this ideal of "pure
poetry" are never drawn. Hunt considers epic (with drama), not the
lyric, as the highest genre.[6] "Music" in poetry he understands superficially as smoothness, "sweetness" of versification, or simply as the
free accentual balladic verse described by Coleridge. Hunt, in his
early reaction against the "cuckoo song verses, half up, half down" [7]
of Pope, praised the run-on line of Dryden, and practiced a loose,
colloquial rhymed couplet in his own trivial retelling of the Paolo-
Francesca episode, *The Story of Rimini* (1816). But later, in the
posthumous *Book of the Sonnet* (1867), Hunt can insist on narrowly
technical requirements for a verse form, on the Italian rhyme
scheme for the sonnet, on one leading idea, and can recommend the
composition of sonnets as "wholesome recreation" that "need not
interfere with the ordinary business of life, any more than the meal
or the walk." [8] Pure poetry, at first conceived as imaginative poetry,
has become inconsequential poetry, poetry as escape, amusement,
as a refined game. No wonder that Hunt saw no conflict between
poetry and science, fiction and fact. He chides Keats for deploring
the "unweaving of the rainbow," the touch of cold philosophy.
"There will be poetry of the heart, as long as there are tears and
smiles: there will be a poetry of the imagination, as long as the
first causes of things remain a mystery. A man who is no poet, may

think he is none, as soon as he finds out the physical cause of the rainbow; but he need not alarm himself; he was none before." "An age of poetry has grown up with the progress of experiment." [9]

Hunt contemplates this separate realm of poetry with affectionate admiration. Criticism—and he must mean judicial censoring criticism—is "for the most part, a nuisance and an impertinence." He disparages the critic, who is "often an unsuccessful author, almost always an inferior one to a man of genius." [10] He admires Lamb's criticism precisely for being "anti-critical," for aiming to "reconcile us to all that is in the world." [11] There is thus no distinction between taste and judgment. "Taste is the very maker of judgment." [12] All varieties of poetry are allowed: "exclusiveness of liking" is deplorable. In the preface to another anthology, *A Book for a Corner* (1849), which cultivates the "soothing, serene and affectionate feelings," he defines "a universalist, in one high bibliographical respect, as the only true reader. For he is the only reader on whom no writing is lost . . . the only reader who can make something out of books for which he has no predilection." [13]

Leigh Hunt himself was such a universalist. He wants to evoke enthusiasm for poetry; he introduces, anthologizes, comments, and praises generously and warmly. His good humor and cheerful optimism about human nature give out only when he feels injured by Byron's conduct toward him in Italy or when he protests against the virulent Tory reviewers, who had dubbed him "King Cockney" and had persecuted Keats, Shelley, and Hazlitt for political reasons. [14] But there are limits even to Hunt's catholicity of taste: he admires Dante for his imagination and the intensity of his passion, but he dislikes him for his "ferocious hatreds and bigotries," his religious and political fanaticism. The *Inferno* seems to him "the dream of an hypochondriacal savage." [15] He has the same kind of reservations about Milton: he dislikes Milton's "gloomy religious creed," which "wants the highest piety of an intelligible charity." [16] Needless to say, Hunt does not care for the "morbidity and coarseness" of the "loveless misanthrope" Swift. [17] After some initial hostilities, Hunt recognized Wordsworth as "the greatest poet of the present age," but he retained his objections to Wordsworth's politics and, in a late letter, found him deficient in "the musical side of a poet's nature,—the genial, the animal-spirited or bird-like, the happily accordant," [18]—a neat, inadvertent rehearsal of his own qualities.

It would be hard to name an author of any standing whom Hunt did not praise. Still, his special preferences are clear enough: he loves the tradition of the pastoral, the sonnet, and the Italian verse romance, to each of which he devoted a separate book of anthology or retellings.[19] Among the English poets Spenser is his favorite; he is "the greatest painter England has produced," "his versification is almost perpetual honey." Hunt exhibits "pictures in a Spenser gallery"; that is, he selects stanzas from *The Faerie Queene* and assigns them to painters who might have painted them: Raphael, Coreggio, Titian, Guido Reni, Poussin, Claude Lorrain, even Michelangelo and Rembrandt.[20]

Hunt's taste was critically most fruitful in his admiration for the poetry of Coleridge, Shelley, and Keats. There was genuine merit in his early recognition of Keats, of whom he wrote the first favorable reviews and the first biographical sketches; [21] with undeviating devotion, he championed Shelley as a man and a poet; [22] and Hunt was one of the first to emphasize the peculiar greatness and fineness of Coleridge's poetry. "Of pure poetry, strictly so called, that is to say, consisting of nothing but its essential self, without conventional and perishing helps, he was the greatest master of his time. If you could see it in a phial, like a distillation of roses (taking it, I mean, at its best) it would be found without a speck." [23] Hunt reviewed the early collections of the Tennysons very favorably [24] and praised Elizabeth Barrett Browning, both for *Aurora Leigh* and the *Sonnets from the Portuguese,* as "the greatest poetess that ever existed." [25]

Hunt's catholicity was almost all-embracing. His own kindly "religion of the heart" prompted the praise of Uncle Toby as "the high and only final Christian gentleman" and of Sterne as "the wisest man since the days of Shakespeare." [26] But he could also admire Voltaire as the greatest French writer. He edited the *Dramatic Works of Wycherley, Congreve, Vanbrugh, and Farquhar* (1840), expressing only a minimum of horror at their immorality; and in spite of his early objections to the "French school" in English poetry, he enjoyed Dryden, liked *The Rape of the Lock,* and granted every possible good point to Pope's character.[27] With Lamb and Hazlitt, Hunt shares the enthusiasm for the Elizabethan and Jacobean dramatists; he edited a selection from Beaumont and Fletcher "to the exclusion of whatever is morally objectionable" (1855) and extracted appealing passages from many other dramatists in his anthologies. He thought Webster and Decker "the greatest of the Shakespeare men" and apparently was the first to appreciate the character of De Flores in Middleton's *Changeling*.[28] In Shakespeare he was most attracted by what used to be called his "fairy way of writing" and his "most beautiful and impartial spirit of human-ity."[29] Hunt's early theatrical criticism, which anticipates or runs parallel to Hazlitt's and Lamb's, is constantly concerned with Shake-speare and Shakespearean acting. Much of it is advice to the actors on the interpretation of their roles. He sharply criticizes the pomp-ous style of John Philip Kemble and admires Kean's conception of Othello. The latter seems to him perfect "in the desperate savage-ness of its revenge, in its half-exhausted reception of the real truth, and lastly in the final resumption of a kind of moral attitude and dignity, at the moment when it uses that fine deliberate artifice and sheathes the dagger in its breast." Sometimes Hunt attempts a defense of Shakespeare's characters against moral aspersions: he praises Desdemona and Ophelia, for instance, as if they were real, very charming women. In general, Hunt's Shakespeare criticism reflects the growing romantic worship of Shakespeare's text: he justifies the tragic ending of *King Lear* or ridicules the stage version of the sepulcher scene by which Romeo survives the poison long enough to speak to Juliet.[30] And one must not forget Hunt's lifelong championship of Chaucer: "Not an old poet except in chronology: he is young, and sunny, and full of the bloom of life."[31]

Hunt's method is thus nontheoretical, laudatory, what has been loosely called "impressionistic," "appreciative" criticism. Occasion-ally we simply get criticism by metaphor: he calls Allan Ramsay's admired pastoral, *The Gentle Shepherd,* "a dog-rose, if you will; say rather, a rose in a cottage garden, dabbled with the morning dew, and plucked by an honest lover to give to his mistress."[32] But usually Hunt's criticism is much more like that of a guide in a gallery: little sentimental whimsies or exclamations of wonder; a pointing to fine passages that he has marked with a pen, or singled out by italics;[33] and sometimes a commentary that allows him to make observations on small details. Thus he draws attention to the vowels in a stanza of Shelley's "Ode to a Skylark" or comments sensitively on a passage in Keats' "Eve of St. Agnes": "Madeline is asleep in her bed; but she is also asleep in accordance with the legends of the season; and therefore the bed becomes *their* lap as well as sleep's." [34] (A "new critic" could be proud of this "explication.")

Hunt has historical importance as a propagandist of imaginative "pure" poetry, as a mediator of older Italian literature, as an early champion of Keats and Shelley. But he lacks theoretical power, as his loose derivative theory of the imagination shows. He has little judgment, though a definite taste for the fairylike, the glowingly imaginative, or the sentimentally charming. He has even little power of characterization or evocation, though he can observe details with sensitivity. However important as a middleman of romantic ideas and tastes, as a genial, diligent, widely read introducer and taster, he lacks real distinction of mind. He would hardly need such full discussion if Saintsbury had not thought of him as "on a level with Coleridge, with Lamb and with Hazlitt," [35] and if in recent years he had not found his champions who put him next to Coleridge and Hazlitt "above Lamb, De Quincey and Carlyle." [36] He seems to me clearly inferior to every one of these critics.

THOMAS BABINGTON MACAULAY (1800–1859)

Macaulay's enormous reputation as a critic has declined more sharply than that of any of the other major Victorian writers. In Croce's *Aesthetic* he is mentioned, as the representative of English criticism, alongside of Lessing, Sainte-Beuve, and De Sanctis.[1] But Macaulay himself had no illusions about his talents. In a letter declining to write an article on Scott for the *Edinburgh Review* in 1838, he told the editor that "I am not successful in analysing the effect of works of genius. I have written several things on historical, political, and moral questions, of which, on the fullest reconsideration, I am not ashamed, and by which I should be willing to be estimated; but I have never written a page of criticism on poetry, or the fine arts, which I would not burn if I had the power." [2] It would be unjust not to take this self-criticism seriously. Macaulay is a historian, a biographer, a political and social publicist, but only occasionally a literary critic. He is rarely interested in the analysis of a work of literature or in a theory of literature. A strong anti-theoretical bias is central to his view of politics and life in general. In the essay on Bacon he proclaims all theory "useless" and ridicules Greek philosophy—and, by implication, all speculative philosophy and theology—as having "filled the world with long words and long beards." Macaulay cherishes utility and progress, deeds, not words, the "philosophy of fruits" against the "philosophy of thorns." [3] The distrust of theory grows out of his hatred for the French Revolution and the constant effort of the Whig reformer to distance himself from the radicals of his time: the utilitarians with whom he seems to have many aims in common, but whom he criticized for their rationalism and utopianism.

Macaulay rejects theoretical speculation, yet is equally suspicious of close analysis, of dissecting what seems to him beyond the reach of the understanding. "One element must forever elude the researches of criticism; and that is the very element by which poetry is poetry." "What the description of a naturalist is to a real porcupine, the remarks of criticism are to the images of poetry. What it so imperfectly decomposes it cannot perfectly reconstruct." [4] Such anti-intellectualism seems to leave nothing for criticism but pronouncements of taste, or an abandonment of its tasks to history and biography. This happened to Macaulay as it happened to much criticism in the 19th century.

Actually this is true only of the later, mature Macaulay. In his early essays he expounded a highly speculative scheme of the history of poetry, a scheme that implies a concept of poetry and some standards of criticism. The historical scheme was formulated in Macaulay's very first essay, that on Dante (1824). It is also the theme of the Milton essay (1825) and is repeated in the essay on Dryden a few years later (1828). Though Macaulay seems to have read Hazlitt or Peacock,[5] his scheme is similar to such 18th-century critics as Warton, whose double point of view combined primitivism and belief in progress. "A rude society is that in which great original works are most frequently produced." "As civilization advances, poetry almost necessarily declines." [6] Macaulay embraces a collectivist view quite unreservedly. "The laws on which depend the progress and decline of poetry, painting, and sculpture, operate with little less certainty than those which regulate the periodical returns of heat and cold, of fertility and barrenness." There is a "spirit of the age" against which the individual can struggle, "we will not say absolutely in vain, but with dubious success and feeble applause." [7] The poet in modern society is a survival from a more primitive age. "He who, in an enlightened and literary society, aspires to be a great poet, must first become a little child." A modern poet will have "a certain unsoundness of mind," a fine frenzy, since poetry is conceived as "an art to produce an illusion on the imagination"—illusion here meaning a fictitious world which violates all common sense. "Those first suppositions [of poetry] require a degree of credulity which almost amounts to a partial and temporary derangement of the intellect." [8] Coleridge's "willing suspension of disbelief" has become voluntary insanity. One must recognize that the essay on Dryden moderates the extremities of this view. There is still the familiar scheme of the alternation of creative and critical ages. "Our judgment ripens, our imagination decays." Imagination, Macaulay still holds, is "strongest in savages, children, madmen and dreamers." But he now sees that the two principles cannot exclude each other completely. He sees that "men reasoned better in the time of Elizabeth than in the time of Egbert, and they also wrote better poetry." He now admits a distinction between poetry as a mental act and poetry as a species of composition and sees the need for experience in communication. "The first works of the imagination are . . . poor and rude, not from the want of genius, but from the want of materials. Phidias could have done nothing with an old tree and a fish bone, or Homer with the language of New Holland." [9]

The primitivistic view, however, dominates Macaulay's early literary judgments. Shakespeare is "the greatest poet that ever lived" when he abandons himself to the impulse of his imagination. "But as soon as his critical powers come into play, he sinks to the level of Cowley; or rather he does ill what Cowley did well. All that is bad in his works is bad elaborately, of malice aforethought." The few great works of imagination which appeared in a critical age are the works of uneducated men: Bunyan, Defoe, Burns. [10] Milton, both "a man of learning and of imagination," is thus an exception in an age of philosophers and theologians. Macaulay tries to account for this escape from the spirit of the time by Milton's isolation in his blindness and by the independence of his mind, in theology and politics. But Milton not only rebelled against his time: he also found a compromise solution for the assumed conflict of imagination and reason by writing "suggestive" rather than "pictorial" poetry. Dante is far more pictorial, far more concrete: but Milton, intentionally, leaves his world of spirits in ambiguity. "His fiends, in particular, are wonderful creations. They are not wicked men. They are not ugly beasts. They have no horns, no tails." [11] Macaulay shares the 18th-century view that early language was pictorial, a language of images and hence poetic, while modern language in becoming an abstract language of symbols (in the sense of arbitrary signs) becomes less suitable for poetry. Dante is to Macaulay the poet of images, of strong pictures, and the *Divine Comedy* is "beyond comparison the greatest work of imagination since Homer." [12] Macaulay, a stout Protestant, calls "the Catholic religion the most poetical" because it is the most pictorial and defends the grotesque details of Dante as "more affecting" than "the vague sublimity" of Milton. He praises Dante's "humanized representation of supernatural beings," his "pagan fictions" in the other world, and sees that Dante's metaphors and comparisons drawn from earthly objects "harmonize with the air of strong reality" that Dante succeeds in establishing. [13] Milton, though devising by his very suggestiveness a means of attaining his end, must be considered an inferior poet. "The narrative of Milton in this respect differs from that of Dante, as the adventures of Amadis differ from those of Gulliver." The constant underlying assumption is that the "business of poetry is with images, and not with words. The poet uses words indeed; but they are merely the instruments of arts, not its objects. They are the material which he is to dispose in such a manner as to present a picture to the mental eye." [14] The justification of Milton is thus historical. In a critical time he devised the only means of persuasion for skeptical minds: suggestion rather than pictorial representation.

The dichotomy of image and sign, or imagination and criticism, allows Macaulay to continue with his scheme of literary history. An age of criticism follows after the age of imagination. But in their eagerness to correct the bad taste of the age of imagination, the early critics blundered into the extremity of devising "arbitrary canons of taste," rules of correctness. Macaulay condemns neoclassical criticism almost without reservation. Rymer is "the worst critic that ever lived." Addison's criticism is "as superficial as Dr. Blair's." Johnson's observations on Shakespeare's plays and Milton's poems are as "wretched" as Rymer's. His edition of Shakespeare is "worthless," and all his judgments are vitiated by prejudices and superstitions. [15] Obviously Macaulay had no use for Byron's defense of the unities and of the correctness of Pope. [16]

Macaulay's *History of England* concerned the Restoration period and the expulsion of the Stuarts. Most of his literary essays treat late 17th- and 18th-century figures (Bunyan, Dryden, Temple, the Restoration comic dramatists, Addison, Johnson, Boswell, Horace Walpole, Goldsmith, Fanny Burney). Here Macaulay's biographical and historical knowledge as well as human sympathy were strongest. Though he was a wide reader of the classical writers, of the great Italians, and even of several Germans such as Schiller, we always feel that the late 17th and the 18th centuries are his spiritual home. Yet because of his scheme of the history of poetry, he saw the period as one of decline. Even Dryden, whom he admired as the greatest of the "critical" poets, as an "incomparable reasoner in verse," seemed to him not "a man of a creative mind," lacking "in the highest sense of the word, any originality." [17] Macaulay has hardly a good word for the wit of the Restoration dramatists, who shocked his moral sensibility and appeared to him as the "mouthpiece of the most deeply corrupted part of a corrupted society." He rejects Lamb's defense, for he sees that the moral code propounded by the dramatists is not a product of their imagination but a "code actually received and obeyed by great numbers of people." [18] Macaulay disliked Pope as a man and ranked him below Defoe in originality and native power of imagination.[19] Though he gave an extremely sympathetic account of Addison as a person, moralist, and essayist, he had no illusions about the value of his poetry and drama. With all his sympathy for the charm of Oliver Goldsmith he could not help saying that the fable of the *Vicar of Wakefield* "is indeed one of the worst that ever was constructed" and that "The Deserted Village" is historically quite untrue.[20] He thought the actual writings of Dr. Johnson justly falling into oblivion and he does not overrate even his favorite, Fanny Burney. He recognizes that she is inferior to Maria Edgeworth as well as to Jane Austen, who seemed to him the novelist nearest to Shakespeare in subtle characterization.[21] His dislike for the skeptical and worldly Temples and Walpoles is both temperamental and political.

Only the tremendous admiration for Boswell's *Life of Johnson* stands out as a paradox. Macaulay prefers it to Tacitus, Clarendon, Alfieri, and Johnson's *Lives*. It has achieved its eminence almost unconsciously in spite of its author. Boswell was "a man of the meanest and feeblest intellect," who lacked "logic, eloquence, wit and taste." "If he had not been a great fool, he would never have been a great writer." [22] Here is the same unreconciled, unexplained, and unexplainable antithesis which was to be the theme of the Bacon essay: a servile corrupt judge, a mean human being who at the same time was the greatest benefactor of mankind; man's glory and his shame. These bundles of antitheses are both imperceptive as psychology and superficial as history.

The years 1750–80 seem to Macaulay the lowest ebb in English literature. The revival comes with Cowper, whom Macaulay compares in his historical position to Alfieri. He welcomes the new imitation of the Elizabethans as he praises Monti for his imitation of Dante.[23] He sees the unity of the new movement even though he does not call it "romantic." The essay on Byron argues that Byron, though perhaps unconsciously, was "the interpreter between Mr. Wordsworth and the multitude," that Byron "founded what may be called an exoteric Lake School." [24] Macaulay praises Byron's letters, and makes the usual criticisms of Byron's gloomy egotism, his system of ethics in which "the two great commandments were, to hate your neighbour and to love your neighbour's wife." Still, he recognized that Byron cannot be put down as a mere showman: "The affectation reacted on his feelings. How far the character in which he exhibited himself was genuine, and how far theatrical, it would probably have puzzled himself to say." [25] Though Macaulay as a historian and ballad writer must have been deeply affected by the general influence of Scott, he would have said nothing favorable about him had he written the essay he was asked to write. "In politics, a bitter and unscrupulous partisan; profuse and ostentatious in expense . . . perpetually sacrificing the perfection of his compositions and the durability of his fame to his eagerness for money: writing with the slovenly haste of Dryden." [26] It is hard to see whom among his contemporaries Macaulay admired, or on what grounds, except those of a doctrinal critical liberalism, he sided with the romantic movement. In this respect Macaulay's position is similar to that of his master Jeffrey, whom he praised as "more nearly an universal genius than any man of our time." [27]

With the years, Macaulay's views of his contemporaries became even harsher. Especially in letters and in the Journal (never published in full), he let himself go. Carlyle was an "empty headed bombastic dunce." His "philosophy is nonsense and the style gibberish. I have the profoundest contempt for him." [28] *Aurora Leigh* is "trash—unredeemed trash—bad philosophy, bad style, bad versification, gross and sometimes indecent imagery." Melville's *The Whale* is "absurd." [29] He did not care for Dickens and the "sullen socialism of *Hard Times*." [30] He seemed, however, to have liked Thackeray, both as a novelist and as a person.

The negative attitude extended to the romantics. He thought nothing of Coleridge, his "cloud of gibberish," and the "hocus pocus" about reason and understanding.[31] He read the *Prelude* on publication and thought it "a poorer *Excursion*. There are the old raptures about mountains and cataracts; the old flimsy philosophy about the effect of scenery on the mind; the old, crazy, mystical metaphysics; the endless wilderness of dull, flat, prosaic twaddle." [32] Only the ancients, Shakespeare and some novelists such as Richardson and Jane Austen remained constant companions.[33] But the enjoyment and knowledge seem curiously distant, with little or no transfer into his own views and sensibility.

The critic had become the judge, or "a king at arms versed in the laws of literary precedence, who must marshal [the author] to the exact seat to which [he] is entitled." [34] But the grounds of the title remain obscure: they are, at most, something so vague as "common sense," as the truth of "imitation," "the exhibition of human characters." [35] Macaulay apparently had seen the insufficiency of his early historical scheme and had come to distrust any evolutionary theory. He had recognized the impossibility (for him) of rational analysis and imaginative appreciation. He was more and more satisfied with the arbitrary pronouncements of likes and dislikes, and seized by the exact failing of which he had accused Dr. Johnson—an extraordinary passion for ranking authors and their works in numerical order.[36] "He decided literary questions like a lawyer, not like a legislator. He never examined foundations." [37]

The sheer ability of the writer must always impress us: his knowledge and memory, the clarity of his prose, the expository skill, the vividness of the presentation. But his intolerance and cocksureness, his lack of analytical patience, and his contempt for theory point to the limitations of his mind. He had no access to the highest reaches of the intellect, nor to the deepest recesses of the soul. In Arnold's sense, he was a Philistine.

JOHN STUART MILL (1806-73)

At least since Plato banished the poets from his republic, poetry
has had its detractors. Throughout history it has been called lying,
immoral, or useless and has been defended by arguments and
counterstatements as true, good, and beneficial. In England, early
in the 19th century, this debate assumed a new urgency and new
form. The earlier moralistic objections voiced by evangelical circles
seem to have weakened. The disparagement of poetry as useless and
untrue found, however, a new systematic justification in the utilitarian doctrine, which crystallized attitudes widely held by a society
worshiping commerce, science, and technological progress.

The founder of utilitarianism, Jeremy Bentham (1748–1832),
was the most extreme case of a man devoid, at least in theory, of any
feeling for history, tradition, imagination, or even ordinary human
sympathy. With his pedantic terminology he classified the arts as
"anergastic" (nonwork-producing) and "aplopathoscopic" (regarding mere sensation). In his calculus of pleasure poetry ranks very
low. "The quantity of pleasure being equal, push-pin is as good as
poetry." Besides, of course, poetry is not true, is "misrepresenta-
tion," [1] exaggeration.

John Stuart Mill (1806–73) was educated by his father, James
Mill, Bentham's most prominent disciple, strictly in this rationalistic spirit. In his *Autobiography*, written late in life, Mill describes
his mental crisis when, at twenty, he discovered the insufficiency of
the system and rebelled, intellectually, against his father. There
Mill ascribes great importance to the reading of Wordsworth (in
1828) as "a medicine for my state of mind," and as "a source of
inward joy" [2] assisting him in overcoming his dejection. In the
inaugural address at St. Andrews (1867) Mill recommends, next to
intellectual and moral education, "the education of the feelings and
the cultivation of the beautiful." [3] The brilliant essay on Bentham
(1838) criticizes Mill's early master severely for his "deficiency of
Imagination," his "want of poetical culture," "the general incom-
pleteness of his own mind as a representative of universal human
nature." [4] In retrospect, poetry is always valued as education of the
feelings, as a liberation from arid rationalism, as an element needed
for a total humanity.

About five years after his crisis Mill felt the need of formulating a theory of poetry and wrote an article, "What Is Poetry?" (1833), that gave a different and much more unusual account of the nature of poetry. There, more radically than any contemporary (with the possible exception of Leopardi), he argues not only that poetry is a representation of feeling and not a science, but also that it is not "rhetoric" but soliloquy, pure self-expression, with no regard for an audience. Poetry not only does not convey scientific truths, it does not even describe objects or narrate events. In Mill's consistent phenomenalism the whole referential side of art, the whole imitation theory is denied. "Descriptive poetry consists . . . in description of things as they appear, not as they are." "If a poet describes a lion, he does not describe him as a naturalist would, nor even as a traveller would, who was intent on stating the truth, the whole truth, and nothing but the truth." Rather, the poet must describe the "state of awe, wonder or terror" of the man confronted with the lion. "Now this is describing the lion professedly, but the state of excitement of the spectator really. The lion may be described falsely or with exaggeration, and the poetry be all the better." The only truth required is emotional truth. "If the human emotion be not painted with scrupulous truth, the poetry is bad poetry, i.e. not poetry at all, but a failure." [5] Neither does poetry consist in invention, fiction, narration, or incident, which appeal to children and people in the early stages of society. "An epic poem, in so far as it is epic (i.e. narrative) is not poetry at all," says Mill, though he recognizes that it is an all-inclusive form which allows every "kind of poetry to find a place in it." The drama is also admitted as a "union of poetry and incident," but incident is clearly the inferior ingredient. "To the many Shakespeare is great as a story-teller, to the few as a poet." [6]

Mill realizes that this focus on emotion does not yet establish a distinction between poetry and rhetoric. As he has cut off poetry from external reality, so he cuts it off from any effect on the reader. In a famous phrase he states the contrast: "Eloquence is *heard*, poetry is *overheard*." "Eloquence supposes an audience; the peculiarity of poetry appears to us to lie in the poet's utter unconsciousness of a listener." Thus "all poetry is of the nature of soliloquy." The poet must "succeed in excluding from his work every vestige of lookings-forth into the outward and every-day world," and must "express his emotions exactly as he has felt them in solitude, or as he is conscious that he should feel them though they were to remain for ever unuttered." "When the expression of his emotions is tinged by a desire of making an impression upon another mind, then it ceases to be poetry, and becomes eloquence." "Poetry," Mill formulates strikingly, "is feeling, confessing itself to itself in moments of solitude." [7]

This is an extreme position which, if thought through to its consequences, would lead to a concept of the poet as a solitary, and to poetry as emotional overflow without plot, incident, or even description, and to a listener as an eavesdropper at private soliloquies. But Mill, in his letters to Carlyle at that time, saw the difficulties of this view and wrote soon an additional piece, "The Two Kinds of Poetry" (1833), which expands and somewhat modifies his doctrine. He now recognizes two kinds of poets: poets of nature and poets of culture, with Shelley and Wordsworth as their respective representatives. Shelley, rather oddly, appears as the poet wanting in culture, the pure, spontaneous, passive poet fulfilling the requirements of the early definition. The conclusion follows that "lyrical poetry is more eminently and peculiarly poetry than any other." Wordsworth, however, is the poet of culture. "Poetry," with him, "is almost always the mere setting of a thought." It has an "air of calm deliberateness"; it is willed and hence unspontaneous. "The genius of Wordsworth is essentially unlyrical." But this is not, as one would expect from the logic of the first essay, a disparagement of Wordsworth. Rather, Shelley as a "mere poet" contrasts with the "philosopher-poet" who ideally combines the two endowments. This concept of the "philosopher-poet" allows Mill to admit thought into poetry but always in a subordinate position. Mill even gives a mechanistic explanation of the poetic temperament in terms of association psychology: "Poets are those who are so constituted that emotions are the links of associations by which their ideas, both sensuous and spiritual, are connected together." [8]

Clearly the antecedents of this point of view are in the empirical psychological tradition of British aesthetics: in Jeffrey, Thomas Brown, Dugald Stewart, and Hartley, and certainly in some aspects of Wordsworth's theory.[9] Mill had visited Wordsworth in 1831 and reported that he "has advanced [the theory of poetry] beyond any other man, being probably the first person who ever combined, with such eminent success in the practice of the art, such high powers of generalization and habits of meditation on its principles." [10] There seems no reason to assign any importance, at that time, to the influence of Coleridge or to Carlyle, whom Mill met in 1831, since Mill shares neither their views nor their vocabulary.[11] There is genuine though perverse originality in Mill's emphasis on soliloquy, which runs counter to the whole affective tradition of British aesthetics.

All the later, scattered pronouncements of Mill on poetry either repeat and expand the views of the two early essays or seek compromises with contradictory positions. The essay on Vigny (1838), though largely an account of the prose, accepts, without qualm, the function of political poetry. Mill reflects that joy in the "intrinsically beautiful," in "beauty in the abstract" that he finds in Goethe, is rare today and does not assuage the thirst for real-life feelings of our time. Mill even defends the exhibition of hideousness in Balzac as presenting a form of real life. But poetry is set apart, since it is ascribed, in a good 18th-century manner, to a strong flow of feeling that almost physiologically forces a rhythmic utterance. Mill knows that this view "demands *short* poems, it being impossible that a feeling so intense as to require a more rhythmical cadence than that of eloquent prose, should sustain itself at its highest elevation for long together." "A long poem," therefore, "will always be felt (though perhaps unconsciously) to be something unnatural and hollow." [12] In the Bentham essay (1838), the concept of imagination in the sense of empathy is introduced to allow a new contrast between the lyrical poet, who "melodiously utters his own actual feelings," and the dramatist, who has "the power by which one human being enters into the mind and circumstances of another." [13] A review of *Poems of Many Years* by Richard Monckton Milnes (1838) praises the poet's sincerity but betrays an interesting recognition of the difficulty of this favorite criterion of English criticism. "Properly speaking, it is only a man's whole life which is sincere—*that* alone is the utterance of the whole man, contemplative and active taken together." [14]

More frequently Mill tried to reconcile poetry with knowledge and philosophy. As early as 1833, possibly under the influence of Carlyle, Mill speaks of the artist as "conversant with intuitive truths," which it is his office "to declare and to make impressive." "Poetry is higher than logic, and the union of the two is philosophy." [15] Mill's review of *The French Revolution* (1837) praises

Carlyle as a great poet endowed with "the essential element of the poetic character—*creative imagination* which, from a chaos of scattered hints and confused testimonies can summon up the thing to appear before it as a completed whole." [16] Though Mill endorses here the romantic term, he objects that Carlyle goes too far in his distrust of analysis and generalization, for Mill demands a science of history that would establish causes and laws with which to predict the future.[17] In a review of Tennyson's *Poems* (1835) Mill, though highly appreciative of Tennyson's artistry, recommends that the poet become a philosopher. Mill recognizes that "The Palace of Art" is an attempt at a poem "symbolical of spiritual truths." But the poet must see that "his theory of life and the world be no chimera of the brain, but the well-grounded result of solid and mature thinking; he must cultivate, and with no half-devotion, philosophy as well as poetry." [18]

For the rest of his life Mill cultivated, with full devotion, logic, economics, and sociology. The essay on Coleridge (1840), which names Coleridge and Bentham as the two poles of English philosophy, scarcely alludes to the poet and critic. Apparently Mill succeeded more and more in putting poetry into a corner of his mind. A diary entry (1854) protests that the "artist is no Seer," that "art in relation to Truth is but a Language." [19] The interesting extremism of the first essay remains Mill's single important contribution to a theory of poetry.

JOHN RUSKIN (1819–1900)

Ruskin seems hardly to belong to a history of *literary* criticism. One can of course collect his opinions on poets and writers and come up with a body of pronouncements that, not unexpectedly, reflects the taste of the early Victorian age: Shakespeare is admired for his universality and objectivity; Wordsworth for his love of nature proclaiming the glory of God; Scott, "the greatest literary man whom that age produced," [1] for his humanity, sanity, and landscape painting. Ruskin appreciated Tennyson and the two Brownings, and he supported and defended Dante Gabriel Rossetti both as a painter and poet. He was carried away by Swinburne, though he thought him "a Demoniac youth." [2] But Ruskin's sympathy failed when confronted with the new novel: an image of the ugliness and corruption of modern city life and the craving for excitement at any price. Ruskin has little use for Dickens and none for Thackeray, and even the high-minded George Eliot is berated: *"The Mill on the Floss* is perhaps the most striking instance extant of this study of cutaneous disease. Tom is a clumsy and cruel lout while the rest of the characters are simply the sweepings out of a Pentonville omnibus."[3] More surprisingly, Ruskin came to appreciate Pope, though he had begun by disparaging his "Twickenham classicism." Pope, with Virgil, he felt, is "the great master of the absolute art of language"; he is "the most representative we have, since Chaucer, of the true English mind," and "in many respects," he even says, "a greater man never lived."[4]

Among foreign poets Homer, of course, loomed large, and Dante is studied closely as the "central man of all the world" and certainly the "great prophetic exponent" of the Middle Ages.[5] Ruskin loved *Don Quixote,* which he understood in romantic terms;[6] his interest in Goethe, though somewhat reluctant, was considerable, and his admiration for the second part of *Faust* was unusual in England at that time.[7] A specialty of Ruskin was the recommendation of Jeremias Gotthelf, the Swiss village pastor who has been recognized only in recent decades as a major novelist.[8]

But all these are *obiter dicta,* rankings, evaluations—the kind of pronouncements Ruskin made when he answered the usual request to list the Hundred Best Books and to praise the reading of good books in general.[9] They contribute toward the total picture we may try to form for ourselves of the man, but do not immediately concern the development of literary criticism. More interestingly, quotations from the poets are occasionally used by Ruskin to illustrate his schemes for a history of feeling. For example, he reviews the mode of regarding death from the battles of Homer to modern sensational drama. Homer, Dante, and Scott serve to represent the distinctions between ancient, medieval, and modern landscape feeling.[10] Ruskin also can focus on a single passage in a poet to give what today would be called its "explication"; thus he nicely defends the accuracy of "blind mouths" in Milton's *Lycidas*[11] or explains the reference to a psalm in Matilda's speech at her first appearance in the *Purgatorio.*[12]

Still, Ruskin's significance in a history of criticism is not due to any of his scattered opinions or comments. Rather, it is due to the aesthetics propounded in the first three volumes of *Modern Painters*

(1843, 1846, 1856) and later to his social teachings, in which art assumes a central place. Ruskin's importance is today obscured by our rejection of his taste in painting and architecture: his praise of such pictures as Landseer's "The Old Shepherd's Chief-Mourner" or Hunt's "Light of the World" damns him out of hand; the Oxford Museum he helped to decorate and the "streaky" Venetian Gothic he encouraged find few admirers today. It is impossible to agree with his wholesale condemnation of the late Renaissance, Baroque, and Rococo artists, his distaste for the Dutch painters, including Rembrandt, and his contempt for Whistler, which led to the famous libel suit, after Ruskin had said that he "never expected to hear a coxcomb ask two hundred guineas for flinging a pot of paint in the public's face." [13] It is difficult to refute the evidences of sheer will-fulness and perversity—particularly, in the later writings, the charge of fantastic etymologizing or the obsession with pet theories on climatic changes—or to dispute the disagreeable impression of unctuous or angry pathos and mawkish whimsicality. A taste for Kate Greeneway's drawings and other sentimentalities of the time has been put into a pathetic light by the story of Ruskin's uncon-summated marriage and his infatuation for the little girls at Winnington and Rose La Touche.

But all these considerations, which have made Ruskin the most obsolete and remote of all the Victorian "sages," should not obscure the fact that he held a theory of art (and literature) which is far from incoherent or even old-fashioned, but is an impressive restate-ment of romantic organicism. Ruskin's aesthetics apply to liter-ature, for he always refused to draw a line between painter and poet: he uses the word "poetry" often in the wide Platonic sense, and he moves indiscriminately from painting or sculpture to poetry and back again. Homer and Dante are quoted to illustrate landscape feeling, side by side with Claude Lorrain and Turner. The unity of the arts is not merely assumed; it follows from a theory that makes creation an internal act of intuition and imagination. The central doctrine of organicism is held by Ruskin consistently throughout his life, even though there were shifts of emphasis. The early ambi-tion to establish infallible laws of criticism receded: the later Ruskin had little use for the details of his system elaborated with some scholastic ingenuity in the first volumes of *Modern Painters*. His distaste for "metaphysics" and unnecessary distinctions became

stronger with the years. The unctuous tone of the first volume of
Modern Painters disappeared: the mature Ruskin could hardly have
written of the "angels who feel an uncomprehended pain as they try
and try again in vain, whether they may not warm hard hearts with
the brooding of their kind wings." [14] For a period at least, he
revolted against his early evangelicalism and expressed an embar-
rassed and puzzled admiration for the robust and sensual in art.
Homer, Shakespeare, Tintoretto, Titian, Michelangelo were boldly
animal, while St. Francis and Fra Angelico were poor weak creatures. "I don't understand it," Ruskin confesses in an 1858 note
after hearing a dreary nonconformist sermon in Turin. "One
would have thought that purity gave strength, but it doesn't. A good,
stout, self-commanding, magnificent animality is the make for poets
and artists." [15] Later, however, he returned to his earlier view and
found that "Religion" in Giotto, "instead of weakening, had solem-
nised and developed every faculty of his heart and hand." [16] But
the basic theory remains the same.

It is obviously drawn largely from Wordsworth and Coleridge
and from Carlyle, whom Ruskin acknowledged as his master.[17]
Details of the discussion of imagination and fancy resemble Leigh
Hunt's. Despite strenuous denials, Ruskin must have been impressed by Pugin's defense of the Gothic, and have read Rio and
other exponents of medievalism.[18] He recognized how much of
Emerson sounds similar and even thought it worth while to defend
himself against the charge of plagiarism.[19] Romantic German aesthetics filtered through to him from English sources, though he
rejected it when he saw it: partly out of ignorance, as he distorts
Schiller completely,[20] and partly out of genuine revulsion against
the terminology and what may have seemed to him the antireligious
implications of the German doctrines.

The outlines of the theory are clear: Ruskin tries to combine
naturalism and symbolism: a worship of nature even in its minutest
aspects with a supernaturalism which allows a "typical," or, as we
say, "emblematic" and "symbolic" representation of nature. The
basic motivation is religious: "The Heavens proclaim the glory of
the Lord." Nature is the work and word of God and the artist's
function is to relay this message. It is an error to consider Ruskin as
an advocate of a simple transcription from nature. He always clearly
distinguishes between "copying" and "imitation," and disapproves

of deception, or *trompe l'oeil*. He always rejects Dutch art and considers the modern realistic novel a low genre. When, in a well-known and often misused passage, he recommends that the artist "should go to nature in all singleness of heart having no other thoughts but how best to penetrate her meaning, rejecting nothing, selecting nothing: believing all things to be right and good, and rejoicing always in the truth," [21] he is advising young artists to train themselves in observation, but he is not restricting the great man of imagination. Ruskin fights academic classicism, the belief in generalities, the recommendation of a Reynolds to paint drapery as such (not silk or velvet), the convention of the "brown tree" system, the "dark lantern," which he rejects as much as he detested Dutch literalism. The polemics on two fronts is comprehensible if we understand Ruskin's central idea: art is an analogue of nature, is as alive, "organic," as nature, and must reflect the truth of nature—a truth that Ruskin feels to be violated both by the deadness (or what he feels as deadness) of Dutch art and the "classicalism" of the French and Italian 17th- and 18th-century landscape painters.

It would be easy to assemble passages that seem to imply an obsolete view of art as merely illustration or records—e.g. of buildings or scientific phenomena—, functions that have since been taken over by photography, though Ruskin himself thought the photography of his own time more a falsifier of nature than an accurate instrument of transcription.[22] In many contexts Ruskin's standard is, in fact, that of observational truth. He praises much in Turner for its scientific accuracy: with a drawing of rocks by Turner before him, "a geologist could give a lecture upon the whole system of aqueous erosion." [23] Much of the violent criticism of Claude Lorrain and Salvator Rosa expresses annoyance at "instances of mountain calumniation," [24] wrong cloud formations, poorly observed trees, flowers, and animals, and false light effects. Much of *Modern Painters* does not concern itself with works of art at all, but for long stretches discusses cloud formations, tree shapes, rock surfaces, etc., quite apart from pictures, with only the vague rationalization of teaching the artist to recognize truth in nature.

Ruskin can shift to what seems an "impressionist" view of the subject matter of art. Nature is not simply given but created in collaboration with mind: there is "a truth of aspect" as the artist deals "exclusively with things as they affect the human sense and the

human soul." "To art," Ruskin admits, "facts are of use only as they
lead to phenomena." [25] But this phenomenalism is based on the
assumption that there is a final harmony between man and nature,
as both are creations of God. Nature speaks to man in a symbolic
language and the artist interprets this language: he devises works
that reproduce nature proclaiming these symbols. In *Modern
Painters* this conception is often put in terms of the old argument
from design: the kind of "physico-theology" which in England has
had a long tradition since Derham and Paley. Ruskin says expressly
that a preacher and a painter have the same duty. "Both are commentators on infinity," and Ruskin claims naively that "there is not
a moment of any day in our lives, when nature is not producing
scene after scene, picture after picture, glory after glory, and
working still upon such exquisite and constant principles of the
most perfect beauty, that it is quite certain it is all done for us, and
intended for our perpetual pleasure." [26] But in his less pious
moments he seems to think that this language of God is not simply
conveyed or revealed to us but is found, discovered, and even created
by the artist.

Ruskin's concept of the imagination—mainly expounded in the
second volume of *Modern Painters* (1846)—suffers from a lack of
clarity in distinguishing between viewer and artist, between man in
general and the artist, and between the artist's mind and the finished
work. At the same time, it is too elaborately ingenious in its classifications, which have become meaningless since they are tied to an
obsolete faculty psychology. Ruskin starts with the viewer: he distinguishes between *aesthesis* and *theoria,* with *aesthesis* becoming
pure sensuous impression (hence "aesthetics" is a misnomer) and
theoria "the exulting, reverent and grateful perception of beauty."
"It receives the pleasures of the sense but with thankfulness and
reference to God's glory." [27] The theoretic faculty is contemplation
(which he equates with the German *Anschauung)* of ideas of beauty,
accompanied, however, by "full perception of their being a gift and
manifestation of God." The use of this theoretic faculty is one of the
duties of man. "Men have no right to think some things beautiful,
and no right to remain apathetic with regard to others." [28] Ruskin
recognizes, however, that this theoretic imperative can be fulfilled
only by a process of aesthetic education: that we do not necessarily
recognize the right beauty immediately, but only after proper

preparation and training. Beauty is, as in Kant, sharply distinct from the true and the useful, and of course Ruskin must reject the genetic explanations of the sense of beauty by association or habit which were common in the British psychological tradition. The concept of beauty has two stages: "naturalist" and "symbolic": There is "vital," natural beauty recognizable in animals and even plants and primarily in the beauty of the human form. Ruskin rejects, of course, the classical ideal of generic beauty and prefers the "characteristic," but at least in this context the classical ideal survives in religious disguise: the right ideal can be reached only by "the banishment of the immediate signs of sin upon the countenance and body." [29] All grief, all passion are unfit for high art, are ugly or low. But beyond vital beauty is "typical" beauty, symbolic of the attributes of God's infinity, unity, repose, symmetry, purity, and moderation. "The fact of our deriving constant pleasure from whatever is a type or semblance of Divine attributes . . . is the most glorious of all that can be demonstrated of human nature." [30]

All that has been said about the theoretic faculty and the two types of beauty is then paralleled and repeated in terms of the imagination. The distinction between the theoretic faculty and the imagination is, however, abandoned in practice, and the very same gradations from the senses to the highest insight are expounded with a different terminology. Imagination is higher than fancy. Fancy is disparaged as sensual, frivolous, and mechanical in the manner of Leigh Hunt. "Fancy," says Ruskin in his picturesque way, "plays like a squirrel in its circular prison, and is happy; but Imagination is a pilgrim on the earth—and her home is in heaven." [31] But elsewhere Ruskin grants the continuity between fancy and imagination, and later he completely repudiates the distinction.[32] Imagination, however, is divided into three functions, which Ruskin calls "totally distinct": penetration, association, and contemplation. "Penetration" is insight into reality, not as a general scientific truth but as concrete individual essence—another version of the "characteristic" beauty demanded before. "Association" is Ruskin's misleading name for the combinatory power of the imagination: Coleridge's esemplastic power. "Contemplation" is the process of holding and preserving the activities that preceded.[33] It includes what we would call the whole process of symbolization and externalization—that is, the work of art itself.

As in the whole tradition of Platonism, in Coleridge, Carlyle, and
Emerson, the distinction between the imaginative act and the work
of art is minimized; imagination transforms reality into the ideal,
and the ideal is simply the work itself. In a new series of distinctions parallel to those made of the types of beauty, Ruskin lists
three ideals: the purist, the grotesque, and the naturalist ideal.
Purism is represented, for instance, by Fra Angelico. It is angelism,
"spiritual" beauty uncontaminated by nature. The grotesque ideal
is imagination preoccupied with the contemplation of evil; while
the naturalist ideal is the achieved organic art: art created on the
analogue of nature. The emphasis on the grotesque is the most
striking novelty of this new series of distinctions, as it was necessarily missing in the discussion of beauty. Ruskin distinguishes again
between the false grotesque, the merely playful or morbid or sinister, and the noble or symbolical grotesque, which he admires in
the details of Gothic cathedrals and palaces, and in Dürer and
Holbein. At times grotesque seems simply to mean what used to be
called "tragicomedy" or the juxtaposition or mixture of styles;
e.g. in Shakespeare "Prince Henry is opposed to Falstaff, Titania to
Bottom . . . Imogen to Cloten." [34]
   The whole elaborate scheme is clear enough: outside in nature
there is beauty which man must grasp by his theoretic faculty in
order to see it as more than sensual beauty, as also divine. Within
man and the artist in particular, there is the faculty of imagination,
which penetrates, synthesizes, and contemplates and realizes different ideals in works of art: purist, grotesque, or naturalist. But
actually all these distinctions collapse into one overriding relationship: that of man to nature and the God in nature. The function of
art is to present this nature and the divinity in it in many styles:
from the humblest imitation to the most imaginative flights. Only
one criterion must be observed: art must be organic, "vital," open
to empathy or what Ruskin calls "love," even when it is symbolical
of God, who is the God of nature. Ruskin simply does not recognize
God as a geometer, the deviser of the Newtonian world machine.
Ruskin detested "the deteriorative power of conventional art," the
ornaments of the Alhambra, Egyptian and Byzantine art, classicist
perfection, the Crystal Palace, iron construction, anything that
struck him as mechanical, as turned out by rote, as inhuman and
abstract. This is why he preferred the unrepeatable, slightly inac-

curate carvings of the medieval craftsman to modern factory goods. He would, as it was said wittily, "have preferred a God who got all his calculations a little wrong." [35] Also, Renaissance art falls under this condemnation of the unspiritual, the inhumanly perfect, the surface art, though it is difficult to reconcile Ruskin's dislike for the Apollo Belvedere, his coolness to Raphael, and his distaste for Palladio with his enormous admiration for Michelangelo and the Venetian colorists Titian, Veronese, and Tintoretto, who belong to the Renaissance if anybody ever did.

In Gothic art Ruskin is systematically looking for the naturalist or grotesque undercurrent or for anticipations of later more illusionist art. Thus he compares an early extremely stylized angel with a later much more human Eve and the serpent or two griffins, [36] always preferring the image with the more human—that is, "rational"—expression. But the naturalist standard is not held consistently. It can always be overridden by religious symbolism. Thus Tintoretto is defended for painting an angel in "The Expulsion from Paradise" casting a shadow before him toward Adam and Eve in defiance of the source of light. [37] Titian's "Bacchus and Ariadne" is allowed to display the "magnificently impossible blue of the distant landscape," as Ruskin grants that "the whole value and tone of the picture would be destroyed if this blue were altered." [38] Ruskin gives permission to Canaletto, "had he been a great painter," to cast "his reflections wherever he chose, and to paint his sea sloping if he chose." [39] Tintoretto is admired for his allegorical or emblematic devices: the angelic hosts taking "the shape of the head of a fish" in "The Baptism" or the ass feeding on the remnants of withered palm leaves in "The Crucifixion." [40] Ruskin as strongly as the most visionary romantic asserts the rights of imagination which "scorns all shackles and fetters of mere external fact that stand in the way of its suggestiveness." [41]

The norms of poetry seem strictly parallel to those established in the other arts. Ruskin dislikes realism as trivial and ugly; he criticizes conventional classicism and finds untruth to nature, even to topography, distasteful. For anybody who has seen the Castle of Chillon, Byron's description of its "snow-white battlements" and of Lake Geneva as "a thousand feet deep" below it [42] would seem disturbing, as it was to Ruskin, though it is hard to see why this should be so on aesthetic grounds. Homer, Shakespeare, Wordsworth, and Scott are constantly quoted for accurate observation. Examples from poetry illustrate the different stages of the imagination rising above mere imitation. Coleridge in "Frost at Midnight," gazing at the film fluttering on the grate, documents the operation of contemplative imagination.[43] Spenser's image of Envy represents the noble grotesque, while Dante's devils in the 21st and 22nd Canto of *Inferno* are "the most perfect instances of the terrible grotesque," even though Ruskin is too squeamish to tell us why.[44] He can be very pedantic about these distinctions, assigning with strange confidence, line by line, Milton's adjectives and apposites for his flowers in *Lycidas* to either imagination or fancy.[45] But on the whole Ruskin relishes all kinds of accurate art: everything strongly visualized, however unreal. Dante's centaur, Chiron, dividing his beard with his arrow before he can speak must have "actually trotted across Dante's brain, and he saw him do it." [46] Puck, Ariel, Caliban, Milton's devils, the whole universe of Dante are all praised as great feats of poetic imagination, even though Ruskin can allegorize *The Tempest* pretty crudely into a conflict of liberty and slavery.[47] The distinctions between high imaginative art and myth disappear more and more in Ruskin's mind. In his weird interpretations of Greek myths, *The Cestus of Aglaia* (1865) and *The Queen of the Air* (1869), much of the documentation comes from Aeschylus and Pindar, as well as Homer. The physical existence, sun or sky or cloud or sea, is the root of myth; out of it grows the personal incarnation, "a trusted and companionable deity"; and lastly comes "the moral significance which is in all the great myths eternally and beneficently true." [48] Ruskin literally believed and defended the "idea of a personal being in the elemental power" of the Greek gods and even of the figures of "The Apocalypse": the pale sister on the horse must be conceived as a "real and living angel" and not merely as a symbol of the power of death.[49] However fantastic and superstitious this creed may strike us, it follows from the basic romantic animism which Ruskin, in different versions of literalness, embraced all his life. Even mountains are conceived as "loving." "You may," he answers the inquiring girls in *The Ethics of the Dust* (1865), "at least earnestly believe, that the presence of the spirit which culminates in your own life, shows itself in dawning, wherever the dust of the earth begins to assume any orderly and lovely state. You will find it impossible to separate this idea of gradated manifestation from that of the vital power." This animism is projected beyond the empirical world: "the idea of gradation admits the idea of a life above us, in other creatures, as much nobler than ours, as ours is nobler than that of the dust." Ruskin came to believe, or again believed, in the "multitudinous ministry of living angels." [50]

It is thus all the more surprising that Ruskin attacked what he labeled the "pathetic fallacy." After all, anthropomorphism is the basic method of all metaphor, and it seems impossible to draw the kind of distinctions that Ruskin draws when he objects to specific verses. Oliver Wendell Holmes' lines

> The spendthrift crocus, bursting through the mould
> Naked and shivering, with his cup of gold

are called "very untrue. The crocus is not a spendthrift, but a hardy plant; its yellow is not gold, but saffron." [51] Ruskin does not recognize that the crocus is called "spendthrift" because he is imagined to spend his gold profusely. Nor can one see why Kingsley's verse:

> The cruel, crawling foam

must be condemned because "the foam is not cruel, neither does it crawl," but also defended as dramatically appropriate to the speaker in the ballad, as his reason is "unhinged by grief." Why is Coleridge's

> The one red leaf, the last of its clan,
> That dances as often as dance it can

considered false? Coleridge, Ruskin complains, "fancies a life in the leaf and will, which there are not; confuses its powerlessness with choice, its fading death with merriment, and the wind that shakes it with music." Ruskin prefers a simile of Dante: spirits "falling as dead leaves flutter from a bough," because it is a simile which not "for an instant loses Dante's clear perception that *these* are souls, and *those* are leaves." [52] This criterion, however, denies the very nature of metaphor or substitution, which is not "confusion." The distinction drawn between an animistic metaphor devised deliberately and one justified by emotional stress seems quite unverifiable and in practice untenable, even by Ruskin. Thus Pope's lines, well known through Handel's setting,

> Where'er you walk, cool gales shall fan the glade,
> Trees, where you sit, shall crowd into a shade

are condemned as a "definite absurdity, rooted in affectation, and coldly asserted in the teeth of nature and fact," as there is "no greater baseness in literature than the habit of using these metaphorical expressions in cool blood." [53] But it is impossible to see why Pope's conceit, which before occurs in Edmund Waller, Ben Jonson, and Persius and may very well go back to a Greek myth of Aphrodite's birth from the sea,[54] should be worse than Wordsworth saying

> The floating clouds their state shall lend
> To her; for her the willow bend . . . ,

lines that Ruskin approves for their "exquisite rightness." [55] Ruskin's own writings and those of his favorite poets, Wordsworth, Scott, and Tennyson, are full of the pathetic fallacy, and so are those of all poets in varying degree. Miss Josephine Miles has shown and statistically analyzed the progress of this all-pervasive device in 19th-century English poetry,[56] but attribution of emotion to things is of course as old as the hills: it is a prevalent device of folk poetry, a reflection of the belief in an active universe, which is, after all, Ruskin's own central creed. It seems a paradox that his fundamental vision should have been obscured by a standard either of literal-minded observational naturalism, which objects to scientific untruth, or of "sincerity," which denies literary tradition and making. Playfulness, frivolity, neatly turned compliments for a lady must be false or be inferior fancy, in Ruskin's view. The great poet must be a good man, a serious man, a seer and prophet, as art must serve God and Man—hence society and morality.

Especially in his later writings, Ruskin sees art primarily as a moralist and social reformer. In the *Lectures on Art* (1870) he defined the purpose of art as threefold: "(1) enforcing the religion of men, (2) perfecting their ethical state, and (3) doing them material service." [57] Its nature and main function seems forgotten. Still, the view of art's involvement in society and its symptomatic value for the health of a society has never been so fully and persuasively stated as by Ruskin, at least in England. *Stones of Venice* may be idiosyncratic in its judgments, but it is a fully presented story of the rise, flowering, and undeniable fall of a city in the mirror of its art. Art is "the exponent of the mind of a nation," "the mirror and index of national character," "the most noteworthy national autobiography." [58]

Ruskin was one of the first to see industrialization in terms, not only of human suffering but also of the blight it inflicts on art and free creativity. He saw through the vaunted blessings of the division of labor. "It is not, truly speaking, the labour that is divided, but the men: Divided into mere segments of men—broken into small fragments and crumbs of life." [59] Ruskin's criticism of the "economic man" is valid even today, and his horror at the spread of ugliness and the insensitive barbarity with which the evidences of the past, its buildings and sculptures and paintings are being destroyed or restored to nonrecognition are many times as urgent today as in his lifetime. But we must admit that Ruskin's remedies were dreams: St. George's Guild was mismanaged, the idyllic view of the Middle Ages—to Ruskin not the Dark but the bright ages [60]— and of the happiness of their craftsmen is untenable. The resistance against the city seems often sentimental or simply a lost cause. But there is a basic truth in his plea for art as a "joy for all," [61] achievable only in a good society. Ruskin's immediate English followers, G. B. Shaw and William Morris, who did restore beauty to English book production and inspired the garden suburb movement, owe much to him in fundamental ideas. Frank Lloyd Wright's conception of organic architecture is unthinkable without his inspiration.[62] Rather surprisingly, Ruskin found a fervent admirer and fine translator in Proust, who learned from him that "the universe is something of infinite value," though later Proust doubted Ruskin's sincerity and said even that his works are "often stupid, fanatical, exasperating, false and irritating, but are always praiseworthy and always great." [63]

This seems to me the precise truth. Ruskin has almost all the most unpleasant features of the Victorian prophet: the claim of infallibility, the pulpit eloquence, the capricious whimsicality, the squeamish prudery and frequent mawkishness which must repel us, amidst passages of wonderful sensitivity, deep feeling, acute analysis, and genuine profundity. In his time Ruskin achieved almost singlehandedly the aesthetic education of Englishmen. He put art in its central position in civilization by his grasp of the nature of organic art and its part in society. Many of his contemporaries felt that he had taught people to recover "the innocence of the eye" [64] and to see both art and nature for the first time. He could not and did not want to escape the Platonic identification and confusion of art, morality, and religion, but he rejected rightly the alternatives offered at his time: the art for art's sake doctrine and the exclusion of art from the utilitarian concerns of the age. Art with Ruskin, as with Kant and Schiller, was again seen as the great humanizing activity and achievement of man.

IN RECENT DECADES American scholars have studied the early history of criticism in the United States closely and have demonstrated that even Colonial times produced some criticism in the sense of literary opinion about authors and the function of literature. In the early 19th century the great bulk of criticism reflected the concern of the new nation with its identity and its definition of a national literature. In the United States, the problem of nationality was possessed of a peculiar character not easily paralleled elsewhere. Here was a new nation that spoke the same language as its mother nation but had broken away from it in anger. Here was a nation that, in contrast to Europe, was a republic, a free democracy, which could not accept the class distinctions and the hierarchies of an older civilization. And here also was a society that struggled hard for its material existence. The cultivation of literature, and especially of poetry and fiction, had constantly to be vindicated against moralistic and utilitarian preoccupations of the people. The United States had none of the resources on which much Continental literary nationalism drew: no long romantic history, no folklore, no picturesque cities. As Hawthorne was to admit, ours is "a country where there is no shadow, no antiquity, no mystery, no picturesque and gloomy wrong, nor anything but a commonplace prosperity, in broad and simple daylight." [1]

These circumstances explain some of the salient features of early American criticism. A highly self-conscious attitude toward English literature was based partly on the desire of the provincial to demonstrate intelligence and talent against jibes like that of Sydney Smith, who asked, in 1820, whether anybody "in the four quarters of the globe reads an American book." [2] At the same time a defiant optimism discovered American geniuses at every step, or placed buoyant hopes on the future, when liberty, equality, and the spread of democracy would bring the literary millennium. Especially after 1815 Americans turned to the Continent and particularly to Germany in reaction to their dependence on England. In criticism the influx of ideas from German romanticism, from Schelling and A. W. Schlegel and the whole German historical school, became most important, especially since similar ideas came also from British sources, from Coleridge or Carlyle, or from French intermediaries such as Cousin. William E. Channing, in his pompous discourse on "The Importance and Means of a National Literature" (1830), complained that "our reading is confined too much to English books" and that we should "cultivate intimacy" with the literature of Continental Europe.[3] Longfellow prophesied in 1849 that "as the blood of all nations is mingling with our own, so will their thoughts and feelings finally mingle in our literature. We shall draw from the Germans, tenderness; from the Spaniards, passion; from the French, vivacity, to mingle more and more with our English solid sense. And this will give us universality, so much to be desired."[4] We may smile at the simplicity of Longfellow's recipe but should recognize that some of this universality was the great feature of American criticism in the century which followed. Criticism in America has remained closely related to that of the Continent without having lost its English ties; the vantage point across the ocean has allowed it to be something like a synthesis of European criticism, exempt, at least, from the particular limitations of the main national traditions.

At this early period the search for nationality turned rather to simpler remedies: to demands for American topics and settings, to claims for the unique inspiration of the American landscape, to the American Indian and his traditions, and to the recent American past—the Revolutionary War and the dimmer New England legends which Hawthorne, the finest American writer of the time, was to draw upon. The debate on American literary nationalism was of great local importance but hardly needs consideration in a general history of criticism.

The same is true of the more narrowly literary theories of the time before the emergence of Poe and Emerson around 1836. As theories they are of little interest, since they echo the respective British developments. There was something like an American neoclassicism in the 18th century—that is, writers adopted the English orthodoxy, with Pope or Johnson at its head. There was also some-

thing like an American preromanticism in criticism; the Scottish
critics, Kames, Blair, and Alison, whose books were used in American schools and were reprinted with astonishing frequency, dominated the scene before the new English romantic taste made them
outmoded.[5] One can trace the new cult of Shakespeare, the growing
reputations of Wordsworth, Coleridge, Byron, and Scott, and later
of Shelley and Keats, and one can study the reflections of their
literary ideas in many writers. The poet William Cullen Bryant, in
well-phrased lectures on poetry,[6] echoed all the main motifs of
romantic theory. Poetry is not an imitative art but is "suggestive";
it appeals to the imagination, but, more importantly, its "great
spring" is emotion. Poetry does not differ from eloquence except by
its metrical form, and poetry is not, of course, divorced from morality. Poetry "delivers direct lessons of wisdom"; [7] it contributes to the
happiness of mankind by inciting us to love our fellow men, to love
human glory and the glories and wonders of nature. There is no
need to trace the sources of these hoary commonplaces; they were
restated over and over again—by Longfellow, for instance, in a
florid and expansive review of Sidney's *Defence of Poetry*.[8] Poetics
was a "defense of poetry," and it had to be so in a commercial and
Puritan society. Aesthetic theory and literary taste were necessarily
derivative. The same ideas could be found in all the magazines of
the time—with different emphases, in different combinations, but
without any essential novelty.

EDGAR ALLAN POE (1809–1849)

It could easily be shown that Edgar Allan Poe was a reviewer who
reflected the taste of his times and who used the methods and styles
of the contemporary British magazines and their American counter-
parts. The image of Poe's intellectual loneliness in a commercial
civilization, fostered in Europe mainly by Baudelaire's highly
colored articles, is belied by Poe's frenetic and successful activity as
a literary journalist who complied with the demands of his audience
and the conventions of his trade. He "slashes" his enemies in sar-
castic "executions," or he praises and glorifies "fair authoresses,"
seriously ranking and comparing Mrs. Osgood with Mrs. Norton, or
Miss Talley with Mrs. Welby.[1] He voices his admiration for the
glories of his own time in comparison with the past. "This is
emphatically the thinking age;—indeed, it may very well be ques-

tioned whether mankind ever substantially thought before." [2] He disparages Greek tragedy for its "shallowness and uncouthness" [3] and speaks of the "dramatic inability of the ancients." [4] He finds the older English poets overrated [5] and tells us that "for one Fouqué there are fifty Molières." [6] He feels it also necessary to display historical erudition, though this is often secondhand and inaccurate.[7] Poe admires poets such as Tennyson, "the noblest poet that ever lived," [8] Elizabeth Barrett Browning, Thomas Moore, Thomas Hood—and R. H. Horne for his *Orion,* a work that has never been excelled or even equaled "in all that regards the loftiest and holiest attributes of the true Poetry." [9] He admires novelists such as Dickens, Godwin, Bulwer, and Disraeli. He detests Carlyle and Hugo as "asses," [10] Emerson as a "mystic for mysticism's sake." [11] He has no love for Cooper, persecutes Longfellow for alleged plagiarisms, and turns sharply against Lowell for a gibe against him, asking that "no Southerner should ever touch a volume by this author," since Lowell is an abolitionist.[12]

Though much of Poe's reviewing is repetitive, prejudiced, sentimental, or simply dull, a case can be made for his frequent rightness and occasional perceptiveness. His championing of Hawthorne's early stories is a feather in his cap, though his admiration is not unmixed—he accuses Hawthorne of plagiarism from Tieck,[13] dislikes his allegory, and complains of his monotony. The review of Dickens' *Barnaby Rudge* [14] deserves praise not because Poe detected the murderer in advance but because of his sensible analysis of the plot and characters by standards of probability and coherence. His dramatic criticism also has some merits for its time: contemporary plays are attacked mostly for their "deficiency in verisimilitude" [15] and for their absurd stage conventions and lack of construction.[16] Even his criticism of poetry, which is much more erratic, contains shrewd analyses of imagery, rhyme, and diction. Poe, on the whole, is very sensible about literary nationalism. Though he is a good patriot, he sees that "we daily found ourselves in the paradoxical dilemma of liking or pretending to like a stupid book the better because (sure enough), its stupidity was of our own growth, and discussed our own affairs." [17] There is merit also in his frequent assertion of the high function of criticism, especially in the importance he places on its judicial role.[18] Yet Poe hesitates whether to consider criticism a science or an art.[19] Criticism requires art in the sense that each essay should be a work of art, but it is also "an art based immoveably in nature," [20] on principles, and thus it aspires to be a "science."

Whatever the merits of this enormous activity in its time and place (there are 258 articles in the Virginia edition), they would not give Poe a claim to a place in an international history of criticism. But the claim *is* justified and can be substantiated by an appeal to two essays, "The Philosophy of Composition" (1846) and "The Poetic Principle" (1848, published 1850). Some further support is given by entries in the "Marginalia" and scattered remarks in the book reviews. Seen from the vantage point of our time, and through the eyes of the French symbolists in particular, Poe appears as the propounder of theories that in themselves may not be original and may not be defensible as a coherent critical system, but have the distinction of suggesting the main motifs of much later thought on poetry.

Poe restates the idea of the autonomy of art so sharply that he comes near the full doctrine of "art for art's sake." In practice, he challenged the oppressive didacticism of his time and country. He invented the famous phrase "the heresy of the Didactic" [21] and thought it right and proper to write a "poem solely for the poem's sake." [22] He doubts that "the ultimate object of poetry is truth" and asserts "radical and chasmal differences between the truthful and the poetical modes of inculcation." It is impossible "to reconcile the obstinate oils and waters of Poetry and Truth." [23]

More surprisingly, Poe emphasizes that poetry is not passion. In part this means simply a recognition of the Wordsworthian "recollection in tranquility," a sense that grief, for instance, must be "chastened" or, as we might say, distanced before it can become poetic material; and in part it means that "poetry, in elevating, tranquilizes the *soul*. With the *heart* it has nothing to do." [24] Poetry is spiritual and not passionate—and not erotic. Nor is poetry of course an imitation of the external world; at most it is "the reproduction of what the senses perceive in nature through the veil of the soul." [25] Thus poetry does not depend on society: "The poet in Arcady is, in Kamschatka, the poet still . . . nor can any social, or political, or moral, or physical conditions do more than momentarily repress the impulses which glow in our own bosoms as fervently as in those of our progenitors." [26]

Thus far, in its exclusion, this delimitation of the realm of poetry seems well in the tradition of Kant's *Critique of Judgment,* however filtered through Coleridge, A. W. Schlegel, and other intermediaries. But Poe's concept of the autonomy of art is in practice greatly modified and weakened. Though he condemns didactic poems and persistently criticizes Longfellow for the moralistic tag ends of his ballads, he admits a "didactic moral" as "the under-current of a poetical thesis" [27] and grants that poetry "is not forbidden to depict—but to reason and preach, of virtue." [28] In writing of the drama he reasserts his hostility to overt didacticism. "The conveying of what is absurdly termed 'a moral'. . . should be left to the essayist and the preacher. It is not in the power of any fiction to inculcate any truth." But he freely grants a standard of lifelikeness. "The truthfulness, the indispensable truthfulness of the drama, has reference only to the fidelity with which it should depict nature . . . the drama, in a word, must be truthful without conveying the true." [29] Thus Poe readmits truth and morality, though in a subordinate position, and apparently with reference to only two genres of literature, the drama and the novel, which are, in his mind, inferior to poetry precisely because they are imitative.

Though Poe protests against the imposition of utilitarian criteria on art, he actually can see and even glorify the social role of art. Taste is placed by Poe, in a good Kantian manner, between intellect and moral sense, in "intimate relations with either extreme . . . waging war upon Vice solely on the ground of her deformity—her disproportion—her animosity to the fitting, to the appropriate, to the harmonious—in a word, to Beauty." [30] In the remarkable "Colloquy of Monos and Una" (1841), in which he envisages the triumph of intellectualism, democracy, and industrialism as a last horrible stage before the destruction of the earth, he sees the perversion of taste as the final horror. "Taste alone—that faculty which, holding middle position between the pure intellect and the moral sense, could never safely have been disregarded—it was now that taste alone could have led us gently back to Beauty, to Nature and to Life." [31] This aesthetic salvation of man, reminiscent of Schiller's aesthetic education, is an opportunity regretfully missed even in a fanciful dream.

Most frequently Poe offers us the idea of beauty, of "supernal" beauty, as the aim and center of art. His concept of beauty is not, as some pronouncements seem to suggest, completely divorced from knowledge; it is Neoplatonic in its reference to harmony, to mathematical proportions, to the ideal or ideality.[32] The concept assumes a romantic cast in the insistence that beauty is vague, suggestive, and strange, sad or melancholy, but also "supernal," "ethereal," and "mystic." There is in man an "immortal instinct," a thirst unquenchable that belongs to immortality.

> It is the desire of the moth for the star. It is no mere appreciation of the Beauty before us—but a wild effort to reach the Beauty above. Inspired by an ecstatic prescience of the glories beyond the grave, we struggle, by multiform combinations among the things and thoughts of Time, to attain a portion of that Loveliness whose very elements, perhaps, appertain to eternity alone. And thus when by Poetry—or when by Music, the most entrancing of the Poetic moods—we find ourselves melted into tears—we weep then—not as the Abbate Gravina supposes—through excess of pleasure, but through a certain, petulant, impatient sorrow at our inability to grasp *now*, wholly, here on earth, at once and for ever, those divine and rapturous joys, of which *through* the poem, or *through* the music, we attain to but brief and indeterminate glimpses.[33]

Poe's severest critic, Yvor Winters, complains that Poe "would rob us of all subject matter, and would reduce poetry from its traditional position as the act of complete comprehension to a position of triviality." [34] But for Poe there is nothing trivial or even playful about this concept of beauty: however narrow in its exclusiveness, it surely asserts a metaphysical claim to a glimpse of the highest truth. In a similar context and not by chance, Poe quotes Shelley's Platonic "Hymn to Intellectual Beauty" [35] and refers to its "awful Loveliness." He contends that "the struggle to apprehend the supernal Loveliness has given to the world all *that* which it (the world) has ever been enabled at once to understand and *to feel* as poetic." [36] But obviously Poe's grasp of the metaphysical was feeble. The sense of "petulant, impatient sorrow" suggests a mere feeling for the mystery behind the universe combined with a conviction of its inscrutability. His hopes for immortality rested on a vague theory of cosmic progress, a palingenesis on another planet.[37] Poe, basically an agnostic, tried to base an aesthetics on remnants of religiosity.

With Poe, moreover, beauty and poetry are often something much more commonplace—the mere sentiment of sadness, the thought of death, or the yearning for love. The catalogue of beautiful subjects in "The Poetic Principle" is in part an enumeration of natural beauties and in part a list of ethical values: "all noble thoughts—all unworldly motives—all holy impulses—all chivalrous, generous, and self-sacrificing deeds." It includes the beauty of women, both physical and spiritual: "the harmony of the rustling of her robes" as well as her "gentle charities, her meek and devotional endurances, the faith, the purity, the strength, the altogether divine majesty of her love." [38] The sentimental rhetoric of the passage is complemented by the assertions in "The Philosophy of Composition" that "Beauty of whatever kind, in its supreme development, invariably excites the sensitive soul to tears" [39] and that "the death of a beautiful woman is, unquestionably, the most poetical subject in the world." [40]

In practice, Poe has a much wider view of the highest poetry; a list of "ideal" poetry includes Aeschylus' *Prometheus Bound,* Dante's *Inferno,* Cervantes' *The Destruction of Numantia,*[41] Milton's *Comus,* Coleridge's three great poems, Keats' *Ode to a Nightingale* and "most especially *The Sensitive Plant* of Shelley and the *Undine* of De La Motte Fouqué." [42] This list appears elsewhere minus the *Undine* and with the *Rape of the Lock* and *Tam o' Shanter* added.[43] The roster is varied and incongruous enough to exclude the reduction of poetry to one topic or even one mood, and it is not even reconcilable with Poe's usual insistence on the identity of poetry with song or its affinity to music. In Poe "music" often means simply musical, mellifluous, or even singable verse, the union of poetry and music he admired in Thomas Moore's singing his own songs.[44] But just as often "music" is a variation on the "mystic," "supernal" theme. A letter states: "I am profoundly excited by music, and by some poems, those of Tennyson especially—whom, with Keats, Shelley, Coleridge (occasionally) and a few others of like thought and expression I regard as the sole poets. Music is the perfection of the soul, or idea, of Poetry. The vagueness of exaltation aroused by a sweet air (which should be strictly indefinite and never too strongly suggestive) is precisely what we should aim at in poetry." [45] Poe means nothing definable in musical

or metrical terms but is using only a new locution for mystic long-
ing, fulfilled, insofar as it can be fulfilled at all, by "the notes
stricken from an earthly harp which *cannot* have been unfamiliar
to the angels." [46] These creatures, we feel, are even more hypothetical than Rilke's angels.

Poe's concept of poetry is thus in no way symbolist. Since he distrusts even metaphor and simile, he has no concept of correspondences or analogy, no grasp of the poetic symbol.[47] Poetry allows us
only a glimpse of something beyond, ideal, supernal, unearthly.

An examination of Poe's concept of imagination and the nature
of the creative process verifies this conclusion. Imagination for Poe
is not creative. Though Poe speaks of novelty and originality as
requisites, imagination with him is always only a combinatory
power. At its highest it is a power of intuition, in the sense of
skipping the laborious steps of induction and deduction.[48] Though
imagination is "supreme among the mental faculties" and brings
us "to the very verge of the great secrets" [49]—as does poetry—still it
is strictly noncreative, combinatory. Once, very early (1836), Poe
alluded to the theory that Coleridge borrowed from Schelling
when he spoke of the primary and secondary imagination: "Imagination is, possibly, in Man, a lesser degree of the creative power in
God." But Poe immediately interprets this in a pre-Kantian sense
by appealing to an 18th-century Prussian *encyclopédiste,* the Baron
von Bielfeld.[50] "What the Deity imagines, *is,* but *was not* before.
What man imagines, *is,* but *was* also. The mind of man cannot
imagine what is *not.*" [51] Poe's later, most elaborate discussion of
imagination turns around this one idea of combination and choice.
"The pure Imagination chooses, *from either beauty or deformity,*
only the most combinable things hitherto uncombined; the com-
pound as a general rule, partaking (in character) of sublimity or
beauty, in the ratio of the respective sublimity or beauty of the
things combined—which are themselves still to be considered as
atomic—that is to say, as previous combinations." It is true that
Poe then contradicts his insistence on atomism by admitting chemical combinations in which the result has "nothing of the quality
of one of them or even nothing of the qualities of either." [52] But
neither physical nor chemical compounds are genuine creations.
Thus it is only logical that Poe rejects Coleridge's distinction
between imagination and fancy, calling it "a distinction without a
difference—without even a difference of degree. The fancy as

nearly creates as the imagination, and neither at all. Novel conceptions are merely unusual combinations." [53] It is also true that Poe himself occasionally uses the distinction between imagination and fancy in his criticism. Thus Joseph Rodman Drake's "Culprit Fay" is said to show only "Fancy, the faculty of comparison," mere ingenuity.[54] And elsewhere Poe even draws a fourfold distinction between imagination, which "even out of deformities fabricates [again a mechanistic term] that Beauty which is at once its sole object and its inevitable test," fancy, which introduces a subelement of unexpectedness, of difficulty happily overcome; fantasy, which is characterized by an avoidance of proportion; and humor, which seeks "incongruous or antagonistical elements." [55] But whatever the vacillations of Poe's terminology may be, he is not—contrary to the usual opinion of American Poe scholarship— a follower of Coleridge or A. W. Schlegel. He read them, no doubt, and profited from their ideas,[56] but centrally he rejected the dialectical and symbolist romantic creed and remained an 18th-century rationalist with occult leanings. An examination of *Eureka,* Poe's cosmological prose-poem, gives the same results; Poe assumes a Newtonian-Laplacian world-machine but grossly confuses gravitation with love and describes God as existing "only in the diffused Matter and Spirit of the Universe." [57]

Since Poe considers imagination merely combinatory, he cannot easily distinguish between scientific speculation and imaginative insight. Though Poe takes, at different times, different positions on the relation of speculation and imagination,[58] he arrives at the view that the "truly imaginative are never otherwise than analytic," [59] rejecting the old dogma "that the calculating faculties are at war with the ideal." "The *highest* order of the imaginative intellect is always preeminently mathematical; and the converse." [60]

Thus Poe insists on the share of the intellect in the creative process, and by intellect he means the combinatory power. "There is no greater mistake than the supposition that a true originality is a mere matter of impulse or inspiration. To originate is carefully, patiently, and understandingly to combine." [61] The share of judgment and reason acceptable to good classicism becomes in Poe something different, a defense of technological manufacture, of calculated contrivance. In the "Philosophy of Composition" Poe purports to describe the process of composing "The Raven" in order to show that "no one point in its composition is referrible either to accident or intuition—that the work proceeded, step by step, to its completion with the precision and rigid consequence of a mathematical problem." [62] There follows the famous deduction of the process of composition; the decision to choose beauty, then melancholy as "the most legitimate of all poetical tones"; then the refrain "Nevermore"; then the idea of a bird repeating the refrain; then the choice of a raven followed by the argument that the death of a beautiful woman is the most poetical topic in the world; then the decision to make the poem a series of questions put by a lover to the raven; then the choice of the stanza (Poe boasts of it as an invention unheard-of for centuries though he derived the scheme from Chivers); then the selection of an indoor locale, a tempest outside, a white bust contrasting with the black raven, etc. Even Baudelaire, who quoted Poe's essay as if it were his own, asked: "Did he make himself, by a strange amusing vanity, much less inspired than he naturally was? Did he diminish the spontaneous faculty in himself in order to give will a larger share? I should be rather inclined to think so." And Baudelaire suggested that "after all, a little charlatanism is always permitted to genius, and is even proper to it." [63] Obviously the exact order of Poe's calculations cannot be taken seriously. The step-by-step deduction is an *a posteriori* stunt (if not a hoax), psychologically quite improbable in its flitting from theme to meter and back again, and refuted by the fact that Poe wrote fifteen different versions of the poem. But the basic idea is obviously meant seriously, however much Poe was trying to shock his readers out of their naive belief in inspiration. The fine description of the creative process at the beginning of the essay is much nearer the truth than the "deduction."

> Most writers—poets in especial—prefer having it understood that they compose by a species of fine frenzy—an ecstatic intuition—and would positively shudder at letting the public take a peep behind the scenes, at the elaborate and vacillating crudities of thought—at the true purposes seized only at the last moment—at the innumerable glimpses of idea that arrived not at the maturity of full view—at the fully matured fancies discarded in despair as unmanageable—at the cautious selections and rejections—at the painful erasures and interpolations—in a word, at the wheels and pinions—the tackle for

scene-shifting—the step-ladders and demon-traps—the cock's
feathers, the red paint and the black patches, which, in ninety-
nine cases out of the hundred, constitute the properties of the
literary *histrio*.[64]

The elements of groping, experimenting, hard work, craftsmanship,
even play-acting, putting on masks, and pretending did need
emphasis after the great romantic trust in the winds of inspiration.
But ratiocination, calculation, step-by-step deduction is another
matter. Actually the method in which Poe prided himself failed him
consistently; he did not really deduce that a man was hidden in
Maelzel's chess automaton, he did not solve the mystery of Marie
Roget by deduction, and he could decipher only simple crypto-
grams.[65] "The Raven," which has impressed many readers, especially
in France and Russia, must be described as a *tour-de-force*, a
virtuoso exercise which, in its detail, is often shoddy and slipshod.[66]

Poe's ideal of planning for effect is, basically, a rhetorical concept
that places aesthetic value on the emotional excitement caused by
the poem. "The value of the poem is in the ratio of this elevating
excitement." [67] Arbitrarily and narrowly Poe decides that there
must be a single pure, uniform, and unique effect, produced by a
single mood, a single emotional tone. This explains his famous
rejection of the long poem and his advocacy of the short tale dominated by one mood, aimed at one effect. A poem must intensely
excite, and Poe means by excitement literal nervous tension. He
observes that such excitement can be only brief and transitory.
Hence "a long poem does not exist," [68] or rather a "long poem is, in
fact, merely a succession of brief ones." "At least one half of the
'Paradise Lost' is essentially prose." [69] Milton and Homer give us
only a "series of minor poems." "But the day of these artistic anom-
alies [epics] is over." [70] Poe even sets the proper length of a poem at
100 lines and speaks of the necessity of being able to read a poem
or a tale at one sitting,[71] since interruption constitutes a disturbance
of the illusion, a breaking of the spell. Poe has influenced all subsequent theories of the short story by this insistence on unity of effect,
hence on brevity and point. He finds the long novel as objectionable
as the long poem. "As the novel cannot be read at one sitting, it
cannot avail itself of the immense benefit of totality." "During the
hour of perusal [of a short tale], the soul of the reader is at the

writer's control." [72] The short-story writer should "deliberately conceive a certain single effect to be wrought." He then "invents such incidents—he then combines such events as may best aid him in establishing the preconceived effect." [73] "His very initial sentence" should suggest this effect. "In the whole composition there should be no word written, of which the tendency, direct or indirect, is not to the one pre-established design." [74]

The assumptions of the theory, however, seem highly questionable. The argument against the long poem and the novel is only plausible on a psychological theory that makes aesthetic effect depend on a momentary nervous excitement rather than on the contemplation of a possibly extensive verbal structure. Even on psychological grounds, the continued immersion for days, the living with a work of art, might be successfully defended. The insistence on a single mood is based on the assumption inherited from neoclassicism that the genre must be pure, and that mixtures and contrasts of mood are inartistic. Poe's concept of unity is clearly not an organic one. An organic concept allows a reconciliation of contradictions, a multiplicity in unity, while Poe's is merely a unity of effect achieved by calculation. There is some poetic justice in the fact that Poe is often quoted in handbooks for short-story writing that provide recipes for the types of stories current in popular American magazines, whether slick or pulp, detective or adventure.

Contrary to the usual view, Poe seems to have had no grasp of organic unity. He found the term "unity of interest" in A. W. Schlegel. Schlegel had derived it from an 18th-century French critic, De La Motte, knowing full well that he was translating a term used for the psychology of the audience into a term for the structure of a work of art.[75] Poe reverts to the 18th-century idea of unity as an impression or effect on the reader and not as something organically grown in the mind of the poet under the laws of nature. It is either a unity of tone—the "keeping," as Poe likes to call it, using a painter's term; [76] or it is simply a coherent, closely knit plot, pointed toward a dénouement. The plot must have "its indispensable air of consequence, or causation" [77] so perfect that—in terms closely following Aristotle's description—"no one of its component parts shall be susceptible of removal without detriment to the whole." [78] The most perfect plot would be one that conceals the causality. "We should aim at so arranging the points, or incidents, that we cannot distinctly see, in respect to any one of them, whether that one depends from any one another, or upholds it." But "in this sense," Poe admits, "perfection of plot is unattainable *in fact*,—because Man is the constructor. The plots of God are perfect. The Universe is a Plot of God." [79] In this bold metaphor Poe glimpses the idea of organicity, but again he asserts that man is merely a constructor of causal sequences, and not a creator.

What plot is to the prose tale, measure or "music" is to the lyric. Poetry is "the rhythmical creation of beauty." [80] In a long paper— Poe's longest piece of criticism—"The Rationale of Verse" (1848), he develops a prosody which, from a modern point of view, seems strangely confused even on elementary matters. He does not recognize accent in English verse at all and seems to work toward a rudimentary musical prosody as it was later formulated by Sidney Lanier. Poe defends a kind of verse that can be read in a monotone, with feet of equivalent time, producing a singsong impression. This would achieve the suggestive, mystic, and incantatory effects he seeks. In practice he favors a regular meter, intricate though irregular stanzaic forms, alliterations, internal rhymes, and onomatopoeic devices.[81]

"Music" for the lyric and "plot" for the short tale are his two favorite devices. They represent the two sides of Poe's poetic theory: the occult and mystic, the contrived and calculated. His strange combination of mysticism and mathematics, sentimental aspiration and deliberate plotting for effect provided two important motifs for the theories of symbolism—music, with its suggestiveness and indefiniteness, and conscious craftsmanship, calculating virtuosity. Occultism and technology are the oddly assorted strands woven even more closely together in the theories of the French symbolists. Fortunately, they could add something else, the concepts of symbol and creative imagination—concepts which, even in the time of Poe, had been restated in the United States by Emerson and his fellow transcendentalists.

RALPH WALDO EMERSON (1803–1882)

Ralph Waldo Emerson expounds a most extreme symbolist theory of poetry. With him, art is drawn completely into a monistic world view in which it functions as a language of ciphers revealing, in fluid transformations, the essence of a nature that is divine and good and luminously beautiful. The poet is exalted as genius and prophet. His imagination, relying on inspiration and even instinct, submits in wise passiveness to the streams emanating from the Over-soul and thus creates works of organic, healthy, proportionate beauty reflecting and embodying the central Idea of the universe. In Emerson's theory of literature we hear nothing of imitation, or pleasure, passion, and association, and hardly anything of tragedy, the epic, the novel, or other genres. In his identification of beauty, goodness, and truth, of the act of vision and creation with the act of reception, such distinctions disappear. But one thing remains indispensable: the web of convertible symbols, the rhetoric of metamorphoses speaking of the divinity of nature and man. This highly spiritual ideal of poetry, apparently so remote and abstract, allows Emerson to plead for an equality of all subject matters, for contemporaneity, and for a democratic, American art. A Christian egalitarianism inspires his prophecy: "America is a poem in our eyes; its ample geography dazzles the imagination, and it will not wait long for metres." [1] Whitman could feel that he had answered Emerson's call, and Emerson was the first to welcome *Leaves of Grass* as "the most extraordinary piece of wit and wisdom that America has yet contributed." [2]

Emerson has often been charged with inconsistency and incoherence. Santayana even told us that he "had no doctrine at all." [3] Sliding over the word "foolish," one can quote in answer Emerson's own "a foolish consistency is the hobgoblin of little minds." [4] Emerson confessed to "a little distrust of that completeness of system which metaphysicians are apt to affect." [5] He even humbly admitted his "incapacity of methodical writing" and apologized for not knowing "what arguments mean in reference to any expression of a thought." [6] Most commentators on Emerson have criticized the loose organization of his essays, and Emerson himself, in letters to Carlyle, called each sentence in them "an infinitely repellent particle " and his writing "a brick-kiln instead of a house." [7] He even prayed for improvement. "If Minerva offered me a gift and an option, I would say: give me continuity. I am tired of scraps.

> *The Asmodean feat be mine*
> *To spin my sand heaps into twine.*" [8]

Granted that all this is true: one would still have to face the fact that, at least in aesthetics and criticism, Emerson presents a single coherent doctrine, which shows, as we shall see, one important inconsistency but is on the whole open to the charge rather of monotony, repetitiveness, and inflexibility than of random eclecticism. Emerson has been rightly described as primarily a diarist, "a preacher to himself." [9] His *Journal* could almost be called his only work: it overlaps with the *Essays* and flows over into them. Emerson's distinct style and personality, his candor, purity, serenity, and sometimes bland aloofness, but also his consistent angle of vision, create a central insight, a uniform conception of the world and hence of art.

There is no evidence that Emerson's view of art and poetry underwent any important change once his basic point of view was established; not even as much change as one can trace in his abandonment of subjective idealism, in his slow loss of the early prophetic hopes, in his growing preoccupation with evolutionary science, and in his final resignation to a "beautiful necessity." [10] The essays on "Art and Criticism" (1859), on "Beauty" (1860), and on "Poetry and Imagination" (1872) say substantially the same as the section on "Beauty" in the first little book on *Nature* (1836) or the essays on "Art" and "The Poet" apparently composed in 1836 and 1841. The late essays all draw on earlier drafts and together with many entries in the *Journal* form a single kaleidoscope in which the gaily colored sentences are constantly reshuffled in new dazzling patterns. But the glass pieces always remain the same.

Basically, Emerson's concept of the universe is Neoplatonic. It is an emanistic pantheism—modernized, however, by a certain fluidity and imaginative freedom opposed to literal mysticism and scholastic rigidity. "Nature is the incarnation of a thought, and turns to a thought again." "The world is mind precipitated." [11] There is a "universal mind" common to all men of which each man is one more incarnation. Each individual has access to the Oversoul through self-surrender, which, while making him lose his individuality, restores his pristine divinity. There is a scale of nature from the lowest mineral to the universal spirit, or, within the individual, from brutish sensation to the vision of the seer. But the social implications of a hierarchical scheme are minimized by Emerson's insistence on equality and ubiquity. Beauty is everywhere. "God is the all-fair. Truth, and goodness, and beauty, are but different faces of the same All." Nature is beautiful: "the standard of beauty is the entire circuit of natural forms,—the totality of nature," [12] which in

turn "points at identity." [13] Art occupies only a narrow segment on
the scale; man's creation of beauty adds to the works of nature. In
Emerson a work of art is not only "organic," analogous to nature,
but strictly "a new work of Nature, as a man is." [14] He can say that
"Shakespeare made his Hamlet as a bird weaves its nest" and that
"temples grew as grows the grass." [15] The analogy to the creation of
nature is asserted with insistent literalness. "For it is not meters, but
a meter-making argument that makes a poem,—a thought so passionate and alive that like the spirit of a plant or an animal it has an
architecture of its own, and adorns nature with a new thing." [16] This
new thing is beautiful and true because it is "an abstract or epitome
of the world," because it "concentrates this radiance of the world
on one point," and "sequesters one object from the embarrassing
variety." "Thus Art is a nature passed through the alembic of
man." [17]

Emerson, however, is often aware of the distinctness of the realm
of art. The verse "Beauty is its own excuse for being" refers to the
flowering rhodora in the woods, but Emerson also draws a theoretical distinction between "thought [which] seeks to know unity in
unity" and "poetry [which seeks] to show it by variety; that is,
always by an object or symbol." [18] Emerson even knows, in theory,
"the peril of didactics to kill poetry"; [19] but, in general, on the high
level of his meditations, he blandly asserts that "the true philosopher and the true poet are one, and a beauty, which is truth, and a
truth, which is beauty, is the aim of both." [20] "The poet contemplates the central identity" as does the philosopher and seer. Poetry
is "the perpetual endeavor to express the spirit of the thing," hence,
"if perfected, is the only verity, is the speech of man after the real,
and not after the apparent." [21] The poet "lifts the veil; gives them
[mortal men] glimpses of the laws of the universe." [22] All the arts
are really identical: "Raphael paints wisdom, Handel sings it,
Phidias carves it, Shakespeare writes it, Wren builds it, Columbus
sails it, Luther preaches it, Washington arms it, Watt mechanizes it.
Painting was called 'silent poetry,' and poetry 'speaking painting.'
The laws of each art are convertible into the laws of every other." [23]
But it is obvious from Emerson's list, which includes an explorer, a
general, and an inventor, that these laws have nothing to do with
canons of criticism but are laws common to all great men, "representative" men, laws that pervade the universe.

Emerson believes that nature, "the immense shadow of man," [24] is a system of symbols; that even men are "symbols and inhabit symbols"; [25] that the world, in a different term, is "emblematic"; and that "the whole of nature is a metaphor of the human mind." [26] Analogy is the key to the universe, and correspondence is "in the core of things." Nature is an alphabet that the poet deciphers. But Emerson, different from the Swedenborgians on whom he drew, insists on the "accidency and fugacity of the symbol." In a simile drawn from Plotinus, he compares the poet with Lyncaeus, whose eyes were said to see through the earth. "The poet turns the world to glass . . . he stands one step nearer to things, and sees the flowing or metamorphosis." [27] Swedenborg and Böhme are explicitly criticized for making "the symbol too stark and solid," for "nailing it to one sense," for mistaking "an accidental and individual symbol for an universal one." For Emerson all symbols are "fluxional." [28] "The central identity enables any one symbol to express successively all the qualities and shades of real being. In the transmission of the heavenly waters, every hose fits every hydrant." [29] Emerson elaborates the pervasiveness and shifting convertibility of symbolism, beginning with the smallest metonymy, a "low idealism." Everything for Emerson has "two handles," [30] i.e. both a literal and a symbolic meaning. There is an "endless passing of one element into new forms," an "incessant metamorphosis." [31] Emerson recites a whole list of names for nature. "The world is a Dancer; it is a Rosary; it is a Torrent; it is a Boat; a Mist; a Spider's Snare; it is what you will; and the metaphor will hold . . . Swifter than light the world converts itself into that thing you name . . . Call it a blossom, a rod, a wreath of parsley, a tamarisk-crown, a cock, a sparrow, the ear instantly hears and the spirit leaps to the trope." [32]

In constant variations Emerson celebrates the feat of the poet and his imagination in transforming the world. "My boots and chair and candlestick are fairies in disguise, meteors and constellations. . . . Every word has a double, treble or centuple use and meaning. . . . Chaff and dust begin to sparkle, and are clothed about with immortality." [33] If the good old shoe box is a jewel case to the imagination, all subject matters are equal for poetry. "Is a rail-road, or a shoe-factory, or an insurance office, bank or bakery outside of the system and connection of things, or further from God than a sheep-pasture or a clam-bank?" [34] Everything goes into the stockpile of a

writer, "a war, an earthquake, revival of letters, the new dispensa-
tion of Jesus, or by Angels; Heaven, Hell, power, science, the *Néant,*
exist to him as colors for his brush." [35] The plea for the power of art
to handle all subjects easily passes into an argument for contemporaneity, democracy, and American art. "Give me insight into to-day,
and you may have the antique and future worlds." [36] Thus "the test
or measure of poetic genius is the power to read the poetry of
affairs,—to fuse the circumstance of to-day; not to use Scott's antique
superstitions, or Shakespeare's, but to convert those of the nineteenth century and of the existing nations into universal symbols...
to convert the vivid energies acting at this hour in New York and
Chicago and San Francisco, into universal symbols." "There is no
subject that does not belong to [the poet]—politics, economy, manu-
factures and stock-brokerage, as much as sunsets and souls." [37] Much
of the older literature seems to Emerson hopelessly obsolete because
of the advent of democracy: pastoral poems, for example, have
perished. There is no use in imitating historical styles. "Why need
we copy the Doric or the Gothic model? Beauty, convenience,
grandeur of thought and quaint expression are as near to us as to
any." [38] The high and the low, the good and the evil, the beautiful
and the ugly are all equal in the eyes of the poet. "A dog, drawn by a
master, or a litter of pigs, satisfies and is a reality not less than the
frescoes of Angelo." [39] "Art lives and thrills in new use and combining of contrasts, and mining into the dark evermore for blacker
pits of night. What would a painter do, or what would poet or saint,
but for crucifixions and hells? And evermore in the world is this
marvelous balance of beauty and disgust, magnificence and rats." [40]

It would, however, be a mistake to draw the obvious inference
from these pronouncements; to see in them a recommendation of
"realism" or genre painting or of a reconciliation of opposites, a
subjugation of the ugly and tragic in art, not to speak of "formalism," which Emerson seems to advocate when he says that "subject
is absolutely indifferent." [41] He plays his variations on one theme
only: the unity of the world, the equality of things and men before
God, the all-pervasive symbolism, the universal metamorphosis. He
relies on the simplest method of metonymy, on an analytic spread-
out, an accumulation of examples, illustrations, similes, and metaphors all held together only in eternity. The equality and democracy of subject matter is a religious equality. All things live and have

their being in God, all in each and each in all. Emerson's method of composing his essays, by proliferating examples circling around one theme, exemplifies the theory; his poems also have this incremental structure, which Emerson felt to be "wildest freedom." He wanted to write "rhyme which builds out into Chaos and old night a splendid architecture to bridge the impassible, and call aloud on all the children of morning that the Creation is recommencing." [42]

This view of a free fluid symbolism, where "every hose fits every hydrant" is, however, in Emerson, often crossed and somewhat contradicted by a different set of ideas: the view that there is a fixed relation between words and things; that there is a necessary style, reflecting an organized unity; in short, that there is a single ideal of classical beauty. His symbolist vision obviously subordinates art to nature, or, at best, hardly distinguishes art from nature; but at times, especially in discussing the fine arts, Emerson would rather view art as nature idealized. He probably did not sense the contradiction between saying that "in happy hours, nature appears to us one with art; art perfected" [43] and his admiration for idealized art, for Greek sculpture, Michelangelo, Raphael, and, in proper distance, for Canova, Thorvaldsen, and Horatio Greenough. He can quote Bacon (who in turn rephrases commonplaces of Renaissance Platonism) that "poetry . . . seeks to accommodate the shows of things to the desires of the mind, and to create an ideal world better than the world of experience." [44] He does not see that this other "idealism" and its world of perfect forms are incompatible with the concept of fluid symbolism in which art disappears in the web of correspondences. Nor does he see the contradiction between such a fluid, suggestive symbolism and the theory of language he seems to hold rather steadily.

Emerson often asserts that "words are things," that words should become one with things, or that "there is always a right word, and every other than that is wrong." [45] Every word is necessary. "Good poetry sounds as if copied out of some invisible tablet in the Eternal mind." All great poets have "found the verse, not made it." [46] Emerson supports the 18th-century theory of original picture language. "As we go back in history, language becomes more picturesque, until its infancy, when it is all poetry." [47] Thus "language is fossil poetry," a view that appealed to Vico and would have appealed to Croce. The poet "is the Namer, or Language-maker." [48]

"Wise men pierce this rotten diction [of our time] and fasten words again to visible things." [49] Thus the words of the poet "must be pictures, his verses must be spheres and cubes, to be seen and smelled and handled." [50] In some contexts, Emerson seems to think that only one hose fits a hydrant, that a happy symbol is "a sort of evidence that your thought is just." [51] In apparent contradiction to his usual trust in the individual, in self-reliance, in utter freedom, Emerson recognizes, at times, the power of tradition, the pressure of the age, the "voice of the fable" that has something divine in it. [52] He remembers Goethe speaking of the highest works of art: "whatever is beautiful rests on the foundation of the necessary. Nothing is arbitrary, nothing is insulated in beauty." A work of art is "spiritually organic," has "a necessity, in Nature for being . . . is now only discovered and executed by the artist, not arbitrarily composed by him." [53] Emerson then appeals even to the classic-romantic distinction in Goethe's formulations: "Classic art is the art of necessity; organic; modern or romantic bears the stamp of caprice or chance. The classic unfolds, the romantic adds. The classic *should*, the modern *would*. The classic is healthy, the romantic is sick." [54] Classical unity becomes Emerson's ideal, "a single tone," "regnant through the whole." [55] The world is dissolved into a final harmony. "The poet, who reattaches things to nature and the Whole . . . disposes very easily of the most disagreeable facts." [56] Tragedy and the tragic disappear. "All sorrow dwells in a low region. It is superficial. . . . All melancholy, as all passion, belongs to the exterior life." Greek tragedy is disparaged for its belief in a brute fate or destiny, in an "immense whim." [57] Emerson reaches here the thin heights of optimism. The elder Henry James could say that Emerson had "no conscience"; and Lowell thought that "when one meets him the Fall of Adam seems a false report." [58]

This easy trust in the goodness of nature and the harmony of the universe permeates also Emerson's view of genius. He most frequently conceives of genius as entirely passive, will-less surrender to the stream of inspiration emanating from above. The greatest poets, Homer or Shakespeare, are "channels through which streams of thought flowed." [59] The poet "disindividualizes" himself: he is "one through whom the soul of all men circulates," an "organ through which the universal mind acts." [60] Emerson can even say that "our moral nature is vitiated by an interference of our will" and that "the poet works to an end above his will, and by means, too, which are out of his will." [61] Thus he defends "private and household poetry," verses from diaries, because technical faults do not matter. Such faults testify "that the writer was more man than artist, more earnest than vain; that the thought was too sweet or sacred to him, than that he should suffer his ears to hear or his eyes to see a superficial defect in the expression." [62] Logically, Emerson asks for spontaneous, sincere art. Art is personal expression, although, paradoxically, the greatest art is as completely impersonal as Providence. One passage sounds extremely "expressionistic": "The more profound the thought, the more burdensome. Always in proportion to the depth of its sense does it knock importunately at the gates of the soul, to be spoken, to be done. What is in, will out." [63] We find innumerable recommendations of "sincerity": the poet should write from "real experience," should have not a "labial but a chest voice." Poetry should have "a necessary and autobiographic basis." [64] Emerson can go so far as to say that "Strasburg cathedral is a material counterpart of the soul of Erwin of Steinbach. The true poem is the poet's mind: the true ship is the shipbuilder." [65] As with the Renaissance Platonists, the work of art is identified with the inner vision, the Idea.

Surprisingly, considering this basic outlook, Emerson does sometimes take more practical considerations into account. Art is not always joyous self-expression; Emerson knows that "the finest poems of the world have been expedients to get bread, or else expedients to keep the writer from the mad-house." [66] We must pardon literature for "the effort of man to indemnify himself," and recognize that a poet may be "able to cast off his sorrows into [his] writings." Emerson sees that "there is no deeper dissembler than the sincerest man," and that "many men can write better under a mask than for themselves." [67] He lost patience with the younger William Ellery Channing for his refusal to revise his poems and for his trust in mere inspiration. "He should have lain awake all night to find the true rhyme for a verse." Emerson hates "this sudden crystallization," [68] the refusal to change even one letter. He proposed something like hygiene or gymnastics for the poet when he listed the stimuli for writing poetry, e.g., getting up early, writing letters, solitude, conversation, and even listening to the Aeolian harp. [69]

But these moods of the practicing poet and adviser to others are all canceled out by the overriding view that all poetry is one and will disappear in the one. "One master could so easily be conceived as writing all the books of the world. They are all alike." "One person wrote all the books." All literature is "plainly the work of one all-seeing, all-hearing gentleman." [70] But even this single gentleman writing a single book can be dispensed with, for the same reason that we do not need sculptors and painters. The artist is asked the embarrassing question: "If he can draw every thing, why draw any thing?" "Painting and sculpture are gymnastics of the eye," and hence "there is no statue like this living man, with his infinite advantage over all ideal sculpture, of perpetual variety." "Away with your nonsense of oil and easels, of marble and chisels; except to open your eyes to the masteries of eternal art, they are hypocritical rubbish." [71] Art is all in the mind and no external action is needed. "If we felt that the universe was ours, that we dwelled in eternity, and advance into all wisdom, we should be less covetous of these sparks and cinders. Why should we covetously build a Saint Peter's, if we had the seeing Eye which beheld all the radiance of beauty and majesty in the matted grass and the over-arching boughs? Why should a man spend years upon the carving an Apollo, who looked Apollos into the landscape with every glance he threw?" [72] The old puzzle about "a Raphael without hands" is solved very easily: he can look Apollos into the landscape. Also language is ultimately superfluous: "With all progress . . . speech becomes less, and finally ceases in a noble silence." [73] All the arts are only "initial," literature is "ephemeral," and we can "easily entertain the supposition of its entire disappearance." This strange consummation will be achieved when "a true announcement of the law of creation, if a man were found worthy to declare it, would carry art up into the kingdom of nature, and destroy its separate and contrasted existence." [74] Everything will be poetry—or we could say the opposite: that nothing will be poetry or art, but everything will be nature or God.

In such a scheme there is hardly any place for criticism. Criticism can only be empathy and identification. Emerson quotes the old saw that "every scripture is to be interpreted by the same spirit which gave it forth" as "the fundamental law of criticism," [75] and he boldly asserts that "the reader of Shakespeare is also a Shakespeare." This means "the ultimate identity of the artist and the spectator." [76] But there is apparently another kind of criticism, too: "transcendental criticism," which judges books "by absolute standards." [77] The term must be interpreted not as any reversion to authoritarian criticism but as a development of the idea of the supersession of art by nature. "The legitimation of criticism [is] in the mind's faith that the poems are a corrupt version of some text in nature with which they ought to be made to tally." Whimsically Emerson suggests that "the pairing of the birds is an idyl, not tedious as our idyls are: a tempest is a rough ode, without falsehood or rant; a summer, with its harvest sown, reaped and stored, is an epic song subordinating how many admirably executed parts." [78] Like the critic, the philosopher is "a failed poet"; [79] the poem is a failed pairing of birds, an inferior tempest, or unsuccessful summer. What seemed a fervent defense of poetry, its exaltation to wisdom and vision and of the poet to a seer, has turned into a complete subordination of poetry to nature, and a confounding of the poet with all men.

Since all literature is seen as one entity it cannot have any real history. "The history of literature—take the net result of Tiraboschi, Warton, or Schlegel—is a sum of very few ideas and of very few original tales." [80] Fancifully, he suggests that "poetry was all written before time was . . . we hear those primal warblings and attempt to write them down, but we lose ever and anon a word or a verse and substitute something of our own, and thus miswrite the poem. The men of more delicate ear write down these cadences more faithfully, and these transcripts, though imperfect, become the songs of the nations." [81] Emerson seems to have in mind something like the old idea of primeval folk poetry of which all written poetry is only a fragment or echo. He often thought of the poet as "bard"; he read about the Welsh bards and had the magician Merlin speak with the voice of the ideal poet.[82] But usually he does not think in terms of decay from some dim glories in the past; rather he conceives of literature as an immobile totality: we should "treat the entire extant product of the human intellect as only one age, revisable, corrigible, reversible by him." [83]

This does not mean, however, that Emerson was unable to discriminate among poets and had no definite literary preferences. He has often been accused of "thinness of culture," and his curious indiscriminate lists of writers and selections of poems have been quoted as proofs for his lack of taste.[84] Though he hardly pretended to systematic scholarship, he was a wide reader, especially in English poetry; he translated Dante's *Vita Nuova*,[85] read much of Goethe in the original, and knew his beloved Montaigne, the "grand old sloven," in Cotton's translation.[86] One misunderstands the aims and workings of his mind if one examines his lists for logical affinities or rigorously criticizes the choices in *Parnassus* (1874).[87] He reads for use, looks for sentences, phrases, lines, "lustres"; and when he includes Beaumont and Fletcher in such lists, he does not "rank" them but remembers some songs and heroic repartee he admired.[88] Still, a definite pattern of exclusions and inclusions, a set of standards for his criticism, can be worked out. Obviously Emerson has little use for romantic *Weltschmerz* and mere subjectivism. Byron is "no poet." "What has Lord Byron at the bottom of his poetry but, 'I am Byron, the noble poet, who am very clever, but not popular in London.'?" Byron "revenges himself on society for its supposed distrust to him." [89] Shelley seemed to Emerson "a man of aspiration, heroic character," but not a poet. Strangely enough, he thought of him as lacking imagination, as "uniformly imitative." [90] Wordsworth, after initial objections, impressed Emerson mainly for the Neoplatonic "Immortality Ode," "the high-water mark which the intellect has reached in this age." Wordsworth and Swedenborg were "the agents of a reform in philosophy, the bringing poetry back to Nature,—to the marrying of Nature and mind, undoing the old divorce in which poetry had been famished and false, and Nature had been suspected and pagan." But often he criticizes Wordsworth for something "hard and sterile in his poetry," for provincialism and narrowness, for writing by theory, for lapses into newspaper style.[91] There is a kind of minute realism that Emerson disliked, whether in Wordsworth, the English novelists, or Goethe. Emerson despised Jane Austen: "vulgar in tone, sterile in artistic invention, imprisoned in the wretched conventions of English society, without genius, wit, or knowledge of the world. Never was life so pinched and narrow." [92] He has little use for Dickens ("the poor Pickwick stuff") and thought *Oliver Twist* all surface.[93] One would expect Emerson to sigh as he wrote, "What a notable green-grocer was spoiled to make Macaulay!" [94] Obviously Emerson admires Milton for his idealism and applauds Burns for his independence. More unusual at that time was his great love for

George Herbert, whose emblematic view of nature appealed to him; he also took interest in Donne, Herrick, the songs of Ben Jonson, and Marvell.[95] But the comment on them is sparce and hardly close. Only the essays on Goethe and Shakespeare add up to sustained criticism.

The essay on Shakespeare is remembered mainly for the conclusion in which Shakespeare seems disparaged as "master of the revels to mankind." Emerson regrets that "the best poet led an obscure and profane life, using his genius for the public amusement." But this survival of the Puritan suspicion of the stage should not obscure the fact that Emerson calls Shakespeare "the first poet of the world"—so much beyond compare that "all criticism is only a making of rules out of his beauties." [96] Shakespeare is the synthetic, objective genius, free from mannerism and egotism. He is properly optimistic since "no man can be a poet" without cheerfulness. He worked "the miracle of mythologizing every fact of the common life." Emerson recognizes Shakespeare's great debt to his predecessors, observes his power of adaptation and assimilation, and sees that he is deeply indebted to traditional morality and to the Bible.[97]

Emerson had his difficulties with Goethe, highly recommended as he was by Carlyle and many Americans. Goethe seemed to him often prosy and artificial, and repelled him morally. Emerson did not feel the reverence that Carlyle felt for Goethe's character. *"Faust,"* he says, "abounds in the disagreeable. The vice is prurient, learned, Parisian. In the presence of Jove, Priapus may be allowed as an offset, but here he is an equal hero." Emerson can speak of Goethe's "vicious subjectiveness," his "total want of frankness," and even call him "artistic, but not artist." [98] Then, surprisingly, he is swept off his feet by *Helena.* Goethe is "an Indian of the wilderness, a piece of pure nature like an apple or an oak, large as morning or night, and virtuous as a brier-rose." What seems to us the most contrived antique in Goethe's work appears to Emerson a piece of nature. Organicism can mean very different things to different minds. Emerson comes back to Goethe over and over again for sentences and saws, for *Maximen und Reflexionen,* for his insight into analogy in nature, and for his theory of art. "He has defined art, its scope and laws." [99]

Emerson himself has here put the finger on the source of his aesthetics, and he quotes Goethe in all kinds of contexts to this purpose. Goethe, who drew the parallels of art and nature as closely as Emerson, is also the source of his views on necessity, health, the classic, and the ideal, views that often clash with the more fluid and fervent symbolism of his central doctrine. [100] The general source of that doctrine is Neoplatonism. Plotinus he knew directly through the translations of Thomas Taylor and indirectly through the Cambridge Platonists, particularly Cudworth, and through Coleridge. In a general history of aesthetics Emerson's position may appear nearest to Schelling's, but the evidence of direct knowledge of Schelling's writings is scarce.[101] Emerson drew rather from Coleridge and Carlyle and had the fervent, mystic, and whimsical coloring associated with Swedenborg and his followers; Böhme; Novalis; a Frenchman, Oegger; and a local worthy, Sampson Reed, one of his earliest admirations. But though every single idea may be traced to some precedent, Emerson's view of art and of poetry is still an original combination. Particularly for his time and place, Emerson represents a sharp break with a past of conventional rationalism, common sense, and emotional romanticism. The very extremity with which he held his views makes him the outstanding representative of romantic symbolism in the English-speaking world. He cannot be compared to Coleridge in dialectical power and engagement with actual texts, but he is free from Coleridge's eclecticism and maintains his angle of vision much more steadily. He does not share Carlyle's worship of fact and has nothing of Carlyle's historicism. Emerson is quintessential, and almost frightening in the purity of his doctrine.

THE OTHER TRANSCENDENTALISTS

Emerson is generally considered the founder and head of the transcendentalist movement; but there seems little evidence that his peculiar ideas on aesthetics and criticism were shared by others or even widely understood and admired in his time. The transcendentalist movement itself was primarily a religious awakening: a turn toward an emotional, intuitive, undogmatic religion, which sought philosophical support (as far as it needed it) in a philosophy of faith, in Coleridge, and the French eclectics, rather than in the Neoplatonic masters of Emerson. Literary interests and theories were secondary and often served as disguises for a central preoccupation with religion. In a history of criticism a brief glance at three figures

associated with Emerson may suffice to illustrate different relationships to the master and different attitudes toward literature.

Henry David Thoreau (1817–62) stands nearest to Emerson in
spite of what their temperamental and social disagreements may
have been. One can compile quotations from Thoreau's journals
that duplicate, parallel, or exaggerate motifs from Emerson's aesthetics. Thoreau, for instance, is possibly even more insistent than
Emerson in treating art as nature. Poetry is "a natural fruit." "As
naturally as the oak bears the acorn, man bears a poem." [1] Thoreau
also believes in the symbolic meaning of nature and in the poet's
function of finding such symbols. "I would so state facts," Thoreau
formulates his ambition, "that they shall be significant, shall be
myths or mythologic." [2] Language, as in Emerson, has a close relation to things, even to the body and the senses. The most poetic
name of an object is given by the man "whose life is most nearly
related to it, who has known it longest and best." [3] As in Emerson,
all languages are only provisional. A time will come when "the
present languages, and all that they express, will be forgotten." [4]
Thoreau constantly identifies knowing and doing, writing and
living. "Expression is the act of the whole man" and "the divinest
poem is the life of a great man." [5] He offers similar identifications in
his only long piece of literary criticism, "Thomas Carlyle and his
Works" (1847). Thoreau does not attempt "to discriminate between
Carlyle's works," but regards them all "as one work, as is the man
himself." He praises Carlyle's "rugged, unwearied, and rich sincerity" and curiously (though not unjustly) considers Carlyle not
a *"seer,* but a brave looker on and *reviewer"* who has a "just appreciation of any, even inferior talent." [6] But he objects to the stylistic
mannerisms that he sees described in Carlyle's own account of Jean
Paul's style, the exaggerations and scurrilities that seem to Thoreau
so many faults of character. The best style is that "in which the
matter is all in all and the manner nothing at all." [7] He himself read
and admired the metaphysical poets and the great 17th-century
prose stylists—Sir Thomas Browne in particular—who cannot be
considered as interested only in matter; and Thoreau's own literary
style and poetic sensibility is too subtle, involved, and even idiosyncratic to make us accept his own recommendations in the "Reading" chapter of *Walden* (1854). There he extols the ancients and the
"still older and more than classic but even less known Scriptures of

the nations," the *Veda* and *Zendavesta,* so that "by such a pile we may hope to scale heaven at last." [8] Books are oracles; scaling heaven, Thoreau's and all men's chief concern. Poetry is subordinate to the artist's life. "The true poem is not that which the public read. There is always a poem not printed on paper, coincident with the production of this, stereotyped in the poet's life. It is *what he has become through his work*. Not how the idea is expressed in stone, or on canvas or paper, is the question, but how far it has obtained form and expression in the life of the artist." But Thoreau had a sense of his own failure, which he formulated in odd doggerel:

> My life has been the poem I would have writ
> But could not both live and utter it.[9]

Life absorbed his art: what place was there for criticism?

Another transcendentalist flew away in a different direction: Jones Very (1813–80) has recently found fervent admirers for his mystical poetry and some attention for his criticism.[10] Sending Emerson his essays on Shakespeare, he wrote that "you hear not mine words but the teachings of the Holy Ghost." [11] But I hear only the voices of Coleridge and August Wilhelm Schlegel muffled by pious declamations. Even the slightly earlier essay on "Epic Poetry" (1837) is a diluted version of Schiller and Schlegel: modern poetry has progressed from the epic to the dramatic because poetry has changed from Greek sculpturesque poetry of the senses to the Christian inward poetry of sentiment. "The inability of the human mind, at the present day" to represent an action objectively is a cause of rejoicing, since it testifies to the triumph of Christianity.[12] The essays on Shakespeare and on *Hamlet* (1838) develop the idea of Shakespeare's complete objectivity. "With the ever-surprised mind of a child, he was always transformed into the object he saw." But then, inconsistently, Shakespeare is identified with Hamlet alone. Jones Very is "continually hearing the poet himself speaking out through the words of Hamlet." Hamlet's voice is summed up in the soliloquy "To be, or not to be." All of Hamlet, his indecision and attitude toward Ophelia, are accounted for by his preoccupation with the thought of death, by his doubts of immortality. "With him the next world by the intense action of his thoughts, has become as real as the present." Shakespeare similarly was a man "too weak to contend with his own unaided strength against the destroyer of our own race, unable to find the way, the truth, and the light." [13] Presumably Jones Very found the way, but left literature, Shakespeare, and the text of *Hamlet* far behind.

Margaret Fuller (1810–50) left criticism for the Roman revolution and the Marquess of Ossoli. Reflecting on her early transcendental years, she felt that "so much strength has been wasted on abstractions which only came because I grew not in the right soil." [14] But, from a historical perspective, her critical work for the *Dial* (1840–44) and her reviewing for the New York *Daily Tribune* (1844–46) are a solid achievement. Transcendental phraseology tinges it only superficially, and even her turgid and often high-pitched and sentimental rhetoric should not divert attention from her basic good sense and her clear critical discernment. The "Letter to Beethoven" written seventeen years after the composer's death, in which she speaks of the "swell of her soul as deep as thine," [15] is happily not characteristic of her work. Actually Miss Fuller reflected more concretely on the nature and office of criticism than any of her American contemporaries, and she faced literary works more intimately and more frequently than anyone else in the New England group. Her distinction of three kinds of criticism is still valid, though we do not use her terms: "subjective" critics who indulge in personal caprice, "apprehensive" critics who can go out of themselves and enter fully into a foreign existence, and finally "comprehensive" critics who must be also apprehensive, must enter into the nature of another being, but must, besides, judge the work by its own law. Miss Fuller sees and defends the spirit of inquiry and need of generalization in criticism.[16] Though she sighs, transcendentally, for a "perfectly natural state in which the only criticism shall be tacit rejection," she wants a criterion, standards, "Protestantism," not only praising and appreciating but also saying "No." As things are, she "must examine, compare, sift, and winnow." "I cannot pass on till I know what I feel and why" [17] is not a bad description of a critic's conscience.

Margaret Fuller spoke out bravely and reviewed her American contemporaries severely. She recognized the problem of nationality and individuality, the novelty of the American synthesis of Europe, but sadly reflected that she would not be "present at the gathering-in of this harvest." [18] Emerson is her hero—"the harbinger of the better day," "a father of the country"; but she also sees his limitations and expresses them in her picturesque way. He "raised himself too early to the perpendicular and did not lie along the ground long enough to hear the secret whispers of our parent life." [19] She had wanted to "pray" to his image at her "oratory," but he had rejected her ardor almost apologetically.[20] Hawthorne she recognized as "the best writer of the day." [21] Though she had been a victim of Poe's critical asperity, she had a sense of his talent: the "intellect of strong fiber," the "well-chosen aim," the virtuosity of the poems.[22] The New England poets fared in her hands almost as badly as in Poe's: Longfellow is imitative and artificial, "a dandy Pindar"; Lowell is "absolutely wanting in the true spirit and tone of poesy." [23]

Her views of the English poets are less sure. She is taken in by Bailey's *Festus* and by Henry Taylor's tragedy *Philip van Artevelde,* and she understandably ranks Elizabeth Barrett "above any female writer the world has yet known." [24] On the other hand, she was also one of the first admirers of Robert Browning in America.[25] Her survey of the English romantic poets (1846) is silent on Keats; but she praises Shelley and the Lake Poets. One can expect that the highest praise would go to Wordsworth; but it is good to hear that she does not miss a moral in the *Ancient Mariner.* Only her extravagant ranking of Southey is disconcerting. "Expansive and fervent piety" and "tearful depth of expression" [26] are telltale praise to our unsentimental ears.

Sentimentality permeates also her survey of the French novel (1845). George Sand—the "glow of her heart"—and Eugène Sue come in for praise; but she has some admiration for Vigny's tales and for Balzac, though she calls the latter a "heartless surgeon" and "a Mephistopheles." [27] Her interest in things Italian was mainly political; but she was surprisingly enthusiastic about Alfieri, not only about the autobiography but also about the austere tragedies, which she preferred to Manzoni's and to Schiller's.[28]

Goethe was the one writer who occupied her most. She translated *Tasso,* Eckermann's *Conversations,* and several poems. She planned a life of Goethe and read widely in and around him. Bettina von Arnim attracted her particularly, and she translated her Correspondence with Miss Günderode (1842). She wrote several articles on Goethe and discussed him at length in *Woman in the Nineteenth Century* (1845).[29] Miss Fuller had great difficulties with Goethe, some due to her background and environment and some raised by

Goethe's German critics. The letter invented by Bettina describing the meeting of Beethoven and Goethe with the Emperor Franz in Teplitz was a stumbling block; and her liberalism made her share even the political objections of Wolfgang Menzel, though she saw the shoddiness of the man.[30] She makes much of Goethe's aristocratic sympathies and Olympian heartlessness but penetrates always to the works themselves. She sees that Goethe's self-control is acquired, and that *Tasso* should be interpreted as a victory over his self and its dangers. She defends the *Wahlverwandtschaften* rightly for its severe moral; she gives sympathetic accounts of *Iphigenie* and *Wilhelm Meister,* for their ideal of humanity and the characters of the women.[31] She admires the first part of *Faust,* but, as many critics since, has her troubles with the conclusion of Part Two. She wishes Faust had conquered rather than cheated the devil: that there would be no "loophole redemption." [32] Miss Fuller deplores that Goethe ever went to Weimar and wasted his time in court entertainments, but she does not sympathize with the pre-Weimar young Goethe either. *Werther* baffles her: she misses the "point to a tale got up with such an eye to effect." [33] Her Goethe is the classical Goethe, the sage whom she criticizes for lacking insight into the Emersonian "sacred secret," but admires for his worldly wisdom and toleration, his knowledge of human nature and art. "As a critic on art and literature, not to be surpassed in independence, fairness, powers of sympathy, and largeness of view," [34] Goethe helped emancipate her from strait-laced morals and sentimental piety. She did not succeed completely. In spirit she comes closest not to Goethe, with his universality, not to Emerson, with his rarefied vision, but rather to Bettina and George Sand—in short, to the generous, frank, and somewhat overfervid spirit of Young Germany and liberal France.

THE DEATHS of Jean Paul (1825), Friedrich Schlegel (1829), Hegel (1831), and particularly Goethe (1832) marked the end of a great period in Germany. The contemporaries felt this break keenly, since it coincided with the change in the whole intellectual and political atmosphere after the July revolution. Goethe himself, in his last years, had frequently expressed his sense of the end of old Europe; and Hegel had prophesied the imminent demise of all art. In criticism the reaction was directed against Goethe and the romanticism of what now appeared the period of conservative *Restauration*. The new national and liberal movements adopted such slogans as "life" rather than "art," service to the nation rather than individual culture, contemporaneity rather than a return to the past. Trust in the future, belief in inevitable progress, faith in the spirit of the age became the almost universally accepted creed. German criticism became more and more subservient to the national, political, and social aims of the time. In criticism things were certainly astir. A whole gamut of views is represented, from the most conservative to the most advanced, from theories that can be described as still dependent on 18th-century assumptions to a Marxism that is still very much alive today. We shall survey the critics of the time according to the historical position of the ideas to which they professed allegiance. This will also yield a roughly chronological order, by age group and public appearance.

Franz Grillparzer (1791–1872), the Austrian dramatist, is most clearly a survivor from the 18th century. His extensive notebooks, to which we should add an autobiographical sketch (written in 1853–54) and a few scattered articles, were published only after his death and, in some cases, long after. They constitute a body of reflections and opinions that has excited not only interest for the light it throws on his dramatic work but also admiration for its sturdy common sense, its independence of judgment, and the evidence it shows of wide-ranging, unusual reading.[1] In general, Grillparzer shares the attitudes and views of the German classics: of Goethe, Schiller, and Lessing. Many of his notes are polemics against the new literature: the romantics, particularly A. W. Schlegel, the speculative philosophers, particularly Hegel, and the political and nationalistic literary historians, particularly Gervinus. A large number of notes are devoted to Lope de Vega and the other Spanish dramatists whom Grillparzer studied closely beginning about 1824. He read dozens of Lope's plays, made abstracts of plots, drew from them for his own dramas, and constantly preferred Lope de Vega for his "naturalness," inventiveness, and careless abundance, to the "mannerist" Calderón.[2] But these unpretentious notes, a monument of devotion, rarely attained the level of criticism in the sense of analysis and evaluation.

Grillparzer is primarily a poet who feels a strong aversion to system, theory, prescription, and dogma. He cannot believe in the historicist doctrine of continuity, evolution, collective creativity, or "national mind" and holds fast to the role of chance and lucky genius. He complains of Gervinus' *History of German National Literature:* "Everything that happened had to happen that way; there is no room for caprice, mood, genius, whim; everything is explained to death."[3] Grillparzer denies the close connection of poetry and history. "The progress of the arts depends on talent and not on historical events. Goethe would have become the same great poet even if there had been no Frederick the Great; and the French revolution (which was a sufficiently violent business) did not produce a single poet."[4]

The common view that art is being superseded seems ridiculous to Grillparzer. "Genius is always something of a miracle and cannot be explained naturally."[5] Nor do sources and traditions account for a poet. Grillparzer criticizes, for instance, the view that Ariosto's *Orlando Furioso* represents the culmination of the Charlemagne cycles. Ariosto has nothing to do with the medieval romances: he cared for the stories only as mere matter for his treatment. One could just as well "classify Yorick's *Sentimental Journey* among travel books."[6] Gervinus, Grillparzer comments, lacks the prime requisite of a literary historian: he does not understand poetry. Just as a historian of chemistry must be a chemist and a historian of astronomy an astronomer, so an author of a book on the poetic literature of Germany must be a poet—or at least have a feeling for poetry.[7] This lack of poetic sense is why most critics are inferior. Theatrical critics are usually bad students who vent their resentment against the playwright. "He who knows something and can do something, writes *something* and not *about* something." The argument that there is a special critical talent does not impress Grillparzer. "Critical talent is a result of productive talent. Whoever can make something can also judge what others have made." [8] The poet's point of view could not be stated more strongly. There seems to be little use or hope for criticism.

Nevertheless, the notebooks show Grillparzer's lifelong struggle to achieve a useful comprehension of aesthetics. From entries scattered over decades, often made in close conjunction with his reading, no really coherent theory emerges. The identification of beauty with "perfection" comes from Baumgarten; Lessing and Kant are constantly in mind. Some ideas derive from Bouterwek, whom Grillparzer praised as the best aesthetician.[9] But romantic motifs are also rehearsed: the distinction of fancy and imagination (with the German reversal of the terms), the infinity of the feeling for beauty, the organicity of the work of art, the view that genuine poetry is one great *tropus* or figure "but as it were, symbolic, not allegorical." [10] Grillparzer's speculations become more original when he is concerned with drama and particularly the concept of fate. He feels strongly that Schiller's concept of tragedy as a victory of freedom over necessity is inadequate. He criticizes A. W. Schlegel's relegation of fate to antiquity. Fate in Greek tragedy means a number of different things. Providence, its supposed Christian counterpart, would make tragedy impossible. Fate, Grillparzer argues, can very well be used in modern drama as the determinism of nature, as a *tropus* of the world order. It can appear as the "obscure dread" of the characters themselves.[11] But Grillparzer, who had begun with a crude tragedy of fate, *Die Ahnfrau* (1816), complete with errant ghost and family curse, later turned away from this strict determinism. On the one hand, as a good classicist he still argues that probability, strict causality, and the "feeling of necessity" constitute the "inner form of the drama." Drama must achieve "presence"; even the unities are defended as a means toward this end. On the other hand, Grillparzer loves Lope de Vega and admires Shakespeare and even Beaumont and Fletcher, and accordingly exalts as the highest type of drama that which succeeds in making "valid and real" even contingencies, chance events, "the incongruences of nature." A successful play "forces belief by its mere existence." Hence Grillparzer makes much of gesture and pantomime in his plays and oddly enough considers even dialogue "epic." [12] This is the advantage of historical drama or drama drawn from accepted myths. Medea, we know, will murder her children, and the dramatist therefore need not bother to motivate the act as carefully as he would the act of a fictional character. But, in Grillparzer's view, there is nothing sacred about history. The dramatist is no historian as the Hegelians or Hebbel would have us believe. Asking the playwright to be faithful to history is as unreasonable as asking for a close imitation of nature. Harassed by petty Austrian censorship and upset by the nationalistic resentments aroused by his tragedy on *King Ottokar of Bohemia,* he defended his right to change history at will, as Schiller and Shakespeare had done.[13] Drama, Grillparzer pleads, must be judged by its effect on the stage. Art or form is simply "the complex of means, to pass one's thoughts vividly to the listener." The public may not be a good judge, but it is an infallible jury.[14] His later failures on the stage reduced him to premature silence.

Grillparzer's strong patriotism and loyalty to the Habsburgs made him sharply conscious of the difference between Austria and Germany in literature. He distrusted the virulent Teutonic nationalism rising in Germany; he did not share the admiration for folk poetry and German medieval literature. He even defended the French classics, especially Corneille.[15] He disliked the German romantics, though he admired the wasted talent of Zacharias Werner as potentially that of the third greatest German poet.[16] He detested the Young Germans, their political liberalism and time-serving journalism. He had called on Heine in Paris and found him living with two *grisettes.* In spite of his wit and good sense, he is, in Grillparzer's eyes, "a disreputable fellow." [17] Grillparzer avoided the young Hebbel, who had become his rival in Vienna. He refused an invitation to a dinner where Hebbel was to be present, saying: "The man knows everything. He knows, for instance, how Our Lord originated; but I don't know it and so I cannot talk with him." [18]

Humility, common sense, genuine feeling, Grillparzer hoped, were the old Austrian virtues.[19] They are certainly the virtues of Grillparzer's criticism. Though it lacks speculative analytical power, it is a fine record of an artist's struggle to defend his practice to himself, to set down his feelings about works of art unpretentiously, simply, though often acidly, as it suited his lonely, embittered, inhibited temperament.

Grillparzer, in criticism at least, belongs to an age preceding romanticism in the strict German sense: even his love for Lope de Vega makes a point against the Schlegels' idolatry of Calderón. The Schlegels themselves had no immediate followers; but the younger romantics, especially the Grimms, stimulated an enormous learned activity directed at medieval literature and Teutonic antiquities. Ludwig Uhland (1787–1862), in his time a poet of great reputation, was the most eminent scholar-critic in their wake. His work did not have the impact it should have had, because much of it was either not published or was published in remote places during his lifetime. Only the posthumous *Schriften zur Geschichte der Dichtung und Sage* (1865–73) revealed the extent and distinction of his work. As a very young man Uhland wrote a piece "Über das Romantische" (1807) which rehearses the main slogans of the time: the infinite, the Nordic, the Christian. When Uhland went to Paris in 1810, he studied Old French manuscripts and wrote a remarkable dissertation on the Old French epic. It is the earliest attempt, still based on very insufficient knowledge, to show that there existed an Old French heroic epic that was totally different in style from the chivalric romances and that was rather analogous to the Homeric poems and the Nibelungen cycle. Uhland postulates an ancient *Chanson de Roland,* which had not yet been recovered, and anticipates, on the whole, the theories of Pio Rajna concerning the old Teutonic base of the *chanson de geste.*[20] Uhland's first published book of scholarship, *Walther von der Vogelweide* (1822), was also a solid achievement. Before Uhland, German *Minnesang* was almost always thought of as love poetry, and the individual poets did not stand out clearly. Uhland resolutely treated Walther as a political poet who "grasped his own age" [21] and as a poet of sensual "low" love rather than as a *Minnesänger* sighing for his ideal lady.

When Uhland was made professor at the University of Tübingen

in 1829, he launched into a lecture course which, if it had been published at that time, would have been by far the best history of older
German literature. The introduction draws up a striking program
of literary historiography. A good history must display poetic ideas,
figures, and forms and trace the "course of this development." [22]
Mere description of works according to genres, or explanation of
the conditions and influences from which the works arose, or even
critical appraisal, is not sufficient. Uhland calls his method "organic," or developmental, but in practice he concentrates on the
reconstruction of the heroic myth of the ancient Teutons and sets
this apart and ahead of a consideration of religious legends, chivalric
romances, courtly love poetry, and didactic verse. These diverse
types are assumed to have arisen roughly in chronological order,
which corresponds to the changes in the social status of the producers—from the mythic folk to the cleric, the knight, and finally
the burgher. Like the Grimms, he tries to reconstruct the "poetic
kernel," the primeval myth behind the actual works. Myth must be
extricated, purified, its spirit freed, its figures and forms made to
stand out clearly.[23] Thus Uhland can retell its stories and make
them frequently more appealing than they are in their diffuse or
crude originals, and he can also give a fervent description of their
ethics of loyalty, which often confuses poetic ideal with historical
fact. While Uhland's method and beliefs are the same as the Grimms,
he has a more realistic view of the composition of the *Nibelungenlied,* arguing that the author, while not an inventor of the myth, was
still the poet of the song as we know it.[24]

As the lectures progressed, Uhland's competence and interest
flagged. He describes Wolfram von Eschenbach sympathetically but
skips Gottfried von Strassburg. The sections on German literature
of the 15th and 16th centuries are disappointing because Uhland
has little understanding of humanism and theology. Only the
section on Fischart, the German adapter and imitator of Rabelais,
is original and valuable. With a right instinct Uhland went back
and lectured on *Sagengeschichte der germanischen und roman-
ischen Völker* (1831–32), treating heroic myth on an international
scale. Uhland's scholarly career was then interrupted by politics,
and only later did he turn to collecting and editing German folk
songs. In contrast to *Des Knaben Wunderhorn,* his *Alte hoch- und
niederdeutsche Volkslieder* (1844) is confined to early texts preced-

ing the 17th century and is edited with scrupulous honesty. It was a queer romantic idea for Uhland to imagine that the songs arose according to some speculative order of feelings, yet the grouping into "Summer and Winter Songs," "Animal Fables," "Riddles and Wishes," and "Love Poems" is no worse than any other. Unfortunately, in his later years Uhland became less critical and more provincial. He devoted much energy to proving Swabia the original country of Germanic myths and indulged in allegorical interpretations. The large, eight-volume collection of his prose contains only the beginnings of enormous projects: a Middle High German literary history, a Germanic mythology, studies of German folk songs and legends. But there is enough finished work to make Uhland, after the Grimms, the most distinguished early student of *Germanistik*.

The fine lyrical poet Joseph von Eichendorff (1788–1857) was a student at Heidelberg when Arnim and Brentano published the *Wunderhorn* and shared in the enthusiasm for folk poetry. Late in his life Eichendorff wrote four books on literary history, of which *Geschichte der poetischen Literatur Deutschlands* (1857) is the most extensive.[25] These books deserve notice as early attempts to judge literature from a consistently Roman Catholic point of view. Eichendorff elaborates a simple historical scheme: all history since the Middle Ages is a falling off from the ideal union of poetry and religion. After the Reformation there appears a split in man. Either feeling or reason claims exclusive sway. Sentimentalism, didacticism, and the pantheistic religion of humanity are the dire result. The romantic movement (and this would surprise present-day critics of a "dissociation of sensibility") appears to Eichendorff the one great and valiant effort to restore the union of poetry and religion. Eichendorff stresses the converts to Roman Catholicism, Friedrich Schlegel, Zacharias Werner, and Adam Müller; he commends those who were born Catholics and found their way back to the Church, like Clemens Brentano; and looks for Catholic leanings in the remaining Protestants, Tieck, Novalis, and Arnim. Keeping in view the final outcome, Eichendorff judges the long aberrations of Brentano and Werner leniently and without prudery. In the case of the staunchly Protestant Arnim, where he has no evidence to go on, Eichendorff rather easily accepts ethical fervor as a substitute for Catholicism and proclaims him "essentially more Catholic than most of his professedly Catholic contemporaries." [26] The ship-wrecked lives of E. T. A. Hoffmann and Kleist are used as warning examples: they could not find the sheet anchor of faith.

Eichendorff's books are mostly straight criticism of men and their behavior and sentiments, but he also applies aesthetic criteria to literary works. Poetry must be symbolic and must always solve the central problem of incorporating the eternal in the real. The idea must become an image.[27] Eichendorff extols Wolfram's *Parzival* as the summit of medieval poetry, praises Calderón (whose *autos* he translated) as the greatest dramatist, and is severely critical of Schiller's plays, which seem to him rhetorical and abstract.[28] The detail of these books is often shoddy, or derivative from Gervinus and other scholars, and the preconceptions are imposed too relentlessly. Thus Shakespeare is made to mourn the decay of Catholicism, and the fact that Hamlet went to Wittenberg is interpreted to mean that Shakespeare saw there the seat of corroding skepticism.[29] Eichendorff's literary histories belong to the new atmosphere of the mid-nineteenth century, when ideological issues became sharply drawn and aesthetic criteria became minimized or forgotten. Eichendorff's taste and human charity save him from the worst consequences of his doctrinal point of view. Still, he reflects the general transformation of literary criticism into an instrument of ideological warfare.

This warfare had begun to rage around the figure of Goethe. Goethe's fame (after the passing vogue of *Werther* and *Goetz*) had been established largely by the Schlegels early in the century. Goethe had also found other devoted admirers and expositors. As early as 1799 Wilhelm von Humboldt (1767–1835), the great linguist, wrote an incredibly pedantic, long-winded book on *Hermann und Dorothea* as an illustration of the theory of the epic. F. W. Solger made a pretentious analysis of the *Wahlverwandtschaften* (1809) as a tragedy. There was a fervent cult of Goethe in Berlin, of which Varnhagen von Ense (1785–1858) and his wife Rahel Levin (1771–1833) were the center. Books on Goethe multiplied even in his lifetime. Carl Ernst Schubarth (1796–1861) wrote a two-volume work (1820) that gave the first extended allegorizing interpretation of *Faust*.[30] Of these early interpreters, Carl Gustav Carus (1789–1869)—a doctor, *Naturphilosoph,* landscape painter, and psychologist—[31] seems to have had the profoundest understanding and sympathy of Goethe's mind. Carus corresponded with Goethe, mostly on matters of anatomy, and visited him once in Weimar. His two small books on Goethe, *Briefe über Goethes Faust* (1835) and *Goethe zu dessem näheren Verständniss* (1843), are written from a scientific, "physiological" point of view. He looks at Goethe as a totality, physical and mental, as he would on a "plant, a palm tree, an eagle, or a lion." [32] Carus emphasizes Goethe's physical and mental health (which does not preclude occasional illnesses), his beautiful physique, and with it, his capacity for evolution and transformation. Goethe's life is a "work of art," the "pyramid of his being" (Goethe's own term), the result of an inner organic evolution that is both physical and spiritual. Carus is not completely uncritical of Goethe's achievement. Goethe's resignation reflects an inability to give of himself, and the hardness of his formal shell in old age is a cover-up for his inner softness. This view of Gothe as a person is skillfully supported by a study of his writings. Carus interprets Goethe's saying about the single confession of his works as meaning not autobiography but purgation, getting rid of what endangered his mental health. Carus vigorously opposes the identification of Goethe with Tasso or Faust or Meister. He interprets Faust by the "genetic" principle: through a series of transformations. But in contrast to many commentators, Carus recognizes that Faust achieves only a premonition of the happiness of unselfish love for humanity and is saved only by supernatural grace. The poem *Faust* is "rather finished than concluded." [33] Carus' books are not close enough to the texts to be great criticism, but their method is an interesting variation on the leading themes of German romanticism: organicity, evolution, and individuality, understood as both a physical and mental entity. Goethe has become an exemplary man, the representative German.

Nevertheless, opposition to Goethe came from almost every quarter. Conservative Lutheran circles had judged him severely on moral and theological grounds for many years.[34] Wolfgang Menzel (1798–1873), however, was the first to elaborate the criticism from a nationalistic point of view. Menzel's *Die deutsche Litteratur* (1828) is not so simple as it might seem from the noisy attacks on Goethe. Menzel had some unusual perceptions. He was, for instance, one of the early admirers of the fine Swiss peasant novelist Jeremias

Gotthelf, and he praised Hölderlin at a time when Hölderlin was almost forgotten. At bottom, Menzel was a romanticist nurtured by the spirit of the wars of liberation against Napoleon. He admires Schelling and Tieck as the greatest masters of philosophy and fiction. He praises the Germans for "inwardness, sensibility, contemplativeness," [35] though he criticizes them for lack of national and civic pride. The attack on Goethe is partially political: Goethe was not a good German because he retired in the time of national need into the study of Chinese. The attack is also moralistic, censuring Goethe's sensuality and paganism; and it is literary: Goethe is the great eclectic, the great imitator of all foreign literary movements and fashions—a master of feminine surrender, with the talent of a Greek "courtesan," a chameleon.[36] Goethe's power of metamorphosis and growth, Goethe's openness to the influences of world literature, and Goethe's understanding of women are merely so many negative traits set against Menzel's ideals of doctrinal rigidity, untouched nationalism, and masculinity. Menzel's crude but eloquent book met the demand for a readable account of German literature at that time. It was, for example, translated by Margaret Fuller, and it elicited a long polemical article by Belinsky. Heine praised it in an early review, making only slight reservations against the judgment of Goethe. Mundt and Gervinus, in their histories of German literature, obviously learned from Menzel.[37]

The equally violent rejection of Goethe by Ludwig Börne (1786–1837) was motivated very differently. Börne, the radical journalist and essayist, was a straightforward moralist and liberal doctrinaire. He was really of two minds: a relativistic or skeptical aesthetic mind, and a political mind devoted to the eternal truths of republican freedom. He wrote a great deal of dramatic criticism and reviewed many books, but stated bluntly that he knew nothing of dramatic theories and cared even less.[38] He wants only one thing: the union of civic life, science, and art or, in practice, the absorption of art by "life," which to him is politics. He looked back on his own theatrical criticism in these terms:

> "I saw the mirror of life in drama, and when I did not like it, I struck it, and when I was disgusted with it, I broke the mirror into pieces. Childish anger! I saw the same picture a hundred times over in the pieces. I soon discovered that the Germans

have no theater and a little later that they *cannot* have one. The first left me indifferent—one can be a very noble and very happy nation without a good theater, but I grieved about my second insight." [39]

The Germans cannot have a theater, we need hardly amplify, because they are not free and freedom is the foundation of all art. But Börne has no historical perspective. Even a review of *Hamlet* treats Hamlet as an allegory of will-less Germany. A performance of Schiller's *Wilhelm Tell* serves only as a pretext for ridiculing Tell as a German Philistine. [40] A speech in praise of Jean Paul after his death (1825) celebrates him, with fervent eloquence, as the "poet of the lowly born, the singer of the poor, the Jeremiah of his captive nation." [41] The *Letters from Paris* praise P.-L. Courier, Béranger, Hugo, and even Paul de Kock, mainly because they are liberals.

The famous attacks on Goethe must also be seen as political action. Börne never criticizes a work of Goethe; he judges only his character and his politics. He is most effective when he collects from *Tags- und Jahreshefte* all the deferential expressions of Goethe's feelings for aristocrats and the Weimar court; but he reverses the meaning of Bettina's hero-worshiping *Goethe's Briefwechsel mit einem Kinde* (1835) when he considers it an unmasking of Goethe as a mean egotist and cold-hearted Olympian. [42] Börne is basically a man of the Enlightenment who would like to rival Lessing, the polemicist, though hardly Lessing the aesthetician. He has somehow eluded the entire German development from Herder to the romantics: he is a didactic moralist, new and important only in the exclusively political (which are to him moral) standards that he brought to the discussion of literature. Heine, whom Börne attacked in later years, is usually coupled with him but differs profoundly. Heine never ceased to be a poet, and he never lost grip on the nature of art.

HEINRICH HEINE (1797–1856)

Heine is so much more brilliant, witty, nimble, and hard-hitting a writer, and his standing as a poet (especially outside Germany) is so much greater than his German contemporaries, that even his critical writing has survived the neglect accorded to theirs. One may view Heine's criticism as a commentary on his ideological, political,

and religious development—as the polemics of his self-definition.
The many pronouncements on Goethe remove him into the irre-
vocable past as an admired but superseded "Olympian" classic. The
brutal satire on Platen, in *Die Bäder von Lucca* (1829), settles
accounts with virtuoso academic formalism, even though the attack
largely concerns Platen's homosexual leanings. *Die romantische
Schule* (1833), Heine's most sustained piece of critical writing,
repudiates his own past. Here he breaks with the Schlegels, Tieck,
Jean Paul, Novalis, Hoffmann, and Arnim and Brentano, who were
the models of his youth, and rejects all medievalism, mysticism,
sentimental dreaming, and Teutonic patriotism. *Der Schwaben-
spiegel* (1838) extends the antiromantic criticism to the local, provincial, trivial imitators of German folk poetry. The book on *Ludwig Börne* (1840) draws a line against the radical and revolutionary
allies, with whom Heine had become identified in the public eye
because of his exile in Paris and the label "Young Germany," forced
on him by the decision of the *Bundestag*. Heine sees in Börne the
type of a new fanatic. The Nazarenes, the Jews, the ascetic spiritual-
ists plot to destroy the Hellenes, the pagans, the sensualists, the
artists who are Heine's party. Heine, a Jew by birth and a liberal
by lifelong conviction, embraces the Saint-Simonian doctrine of the
"emancipation of the flesh" and fears that "the whole modern
civilization, the painful accomplishments of so many centuries, the
fruit of the noblest works of our predecessors," is endangered by a
victory of Communism or egalitarian democracy.[1] The scattered
pronouncements ridiculing Freiligrath, Herwegh, and Dingelstedt
as cautious poets of "liberty in general" are attempts to shake off the
association with the new rhetorical, political poetry. But we have in
this *History* always refused to treat criticism merely for the light it
sheds on the biography and the other writings of a critic.

We might also consider Heine's prose writings (or the bulk of
them after his arrival in Paris in May 1831) as an episode in Franco-
German cultural relations. *Die romantische Schule* (1833) and the
companion book, *Zur Geschichte der Religion und Philosophie in
Deutschland* (1834), served in their French versions as counter-
strokes to Madame de Staël's *De l'Allemagne*. Heine wanted to
correct the picture of Germany Madame de Staël had presented to
the French. Inspired by her hatred for Napoleon, Madame de Staël
has glorified German spirituality, honesty, virtue, and culture and

has not seen "our prisons, our brothels, our barracks." [2] Her
approach to German philosophy is completely dilettantish: "She
swallowed Kant as a vanilla sherbet, Fichte as pistachio, Schelling as
tutti-frutti ice." Her admiration for the German romantics blinds
her to their real meaning.[3] Heine tells the French that German
philosophy is far from harmless: that it is disguised atheism, that it
prepares for the greatest revolutionary upheavals; and German
romanticism is merely thinly veiled Roman Catholic obscurantism.
The German romantic poets are "a heap of worms . . . which the
Holy Fisherman in Rome knows how to use for baiting souls." [4]
Heine's other reports from Paris—*Französische Maler* (1831),
Französische Zustände (1832), and the later articles collected as
Lutezia (1854)—tell the Germans not only about the politics of the
metropolis of Europe but also about the painting, music, theater,
and literature of the time. The excellent, witty, shrewd journalism
is nourished by Heine's extensive personal contacts in Paris. He
manages to convey a sense of the tremendous ferment of these years
in France, a feeling of the richness of the time in comparison with
what he felt to be the stifling atmosphere of censor-ridden Germany.
Today, however, Heine's rankings and values seem distorted by his
political and personal perspective. He consistently praises George
Sand as "the greatest writer whom the new France has produced." [5]
He considers Musset, "certainly after Béranger," the greatest living
French poet, though he attacks him also as a "street urchin" and
alludes to the ruin of his personal life. Praising his comedies as
Shakespearean in their whimsicality, Heine considers Musset's early
Byronic pessimism mere affectation—though an affectation which
life had sadly confirmed as a reality.[6] The praise of Balzac as a
student of women who examines them as "a scientist does an animal
species or a pathologist a disease" [7] sounds rather patronizing. It is
also hard to take seriously the extravagant praise for Edgar Quinet
as a great poet and a "good German" when Heine ridicules Quinet's
person and his boots; [8] or to find very convincing a characterization
of Vigny's talent and mind as "directed toward the finicky and mini-
ature-like." [9]

Heine had many reservations toward things French: he never
gave up his dislike for the French alexandrine, which seemed to him
merely rhymed "belching"; [10] and he condemned the French

romantic drama quite consistently. Hugo excited his dislike for many reasons: his plays seem to Heine contrived, cold, and without taste; Hugo is a hunchback spiritually as well as physically; *Les Burgraves* is "versified sauerkraut." [11] Sainte-Beuve is like the fore-runner of the king of Darfour in darkest Africa who shouts with the loudest voice: "See the buffalo, the descendant of a buffalo, the steer of steers; all others are oxen, only this one is the genuine buffalo!" With every new work that Hugo put before the public Sainte-Beuve "blew the trumpet and praised the buffalo of poetry to the skies." [12] One can hardly be surprised that Heine considers Chateaubriand a downright fool, a "Pulcinello who shoves his bauble in the face of people: *'Ecco il vero croce.'*" [13] If Heine waxes suddenly enthusiastic about Lamartine, whom he confesses to have disliked for his spiritualism, he does so only because of the properly liberal *Histoire des Girondins*.[14] The political alignments override all other considerations: the literary perceptions are secondary.

Neither the polemics with his German contemporaries nor the role of a Franco-German intermediary would make Heine an important critic. Nor can one say much in favor of a bookseller's enterprise such as *Shakespeares Mädchen und Frauen* (1838). Heine's commentary on the romantic illustrations draws heavily on Hazlitt, Mrs. Jameson, and Guizot.[15] Its interest is purely incidental, e.g. the defense of Shylock or the attacks on Tieck's interpretations of Lady Macbeth and Ophelia. The long introduction to an illustrated edition of *Don Quixote* (1837) is on the same level—a lively rehearsal of the German romantic view.

The real importance of Heine's criticism is rather in the curious ambiguity of his theoretical position. The personal and ideological coloring of nearly everything he wrote makes all the more remarkable Heine's insight into the nature of poetry and the position of art. Alone among the new liberals who broke with the romantic past, he rescued a coherent theory of poetry. His malicious denigration of A. W. Schlegel—for which Schlegel's vanity, his relations with Madame de Staël, and the scandal of the second marriage were the chief occasion—did not constrain Heine from endorsing the basic doctrines of his old teacher. Heine theoretically condemns mere *Tendenzpoesie* and asserts the autonomy of art. "It should not serve as a handmaid for religion or politics; it is itself its last aim, as the world is its own aim." [16] In discussing Goethe, Heine originally agreed with "the sublime view" that art creates "an independent second world." "In art there are no ends—as in the universe itself, where only man imposes the concepts of 'ends and means': art, like the world, exists for its own sake." Later Heine amended, "I cannot unreservedly agree with this point of view." [17] Without any question he contradicts the independence of art many times. He praises the writers of "Young Germany," who "do not want to make a distinction between life and writing, who do not want to divorce politics from scholarship, art, and religion, and who are at the same time artists, tribunes, and apostles." [18] When confronted with contemporaries, Heine judges mostly by ideological criteria. Anticlericalism, liberalism, dislike of Teutomania color every pronouncement. Quite genuinely, he felt himself first and foremost a "soldier in the war of humanity."

These contradictions are resolved, however, if one realizes that Heine holds an evolutionary view of history that is Hegelian and Schlegelian in derivation. The arts are conceived as evolving in close parallelism, each representing its period, each informed by a unifying spirit. Heine plays with the romantic analogues, comparing the *Nibelungenlied* to a versified cathedral, explaining distorted medieval paintings as the result of Christian spiritualism. He disapproves of Neo-Gothic building because we cannot and must not revive an older mentality.[19] Commenting on a visit to the cathedral at Amiens, he complains that we moderns have only opinions and not convictions, and "you need something more than mere opinion to erect a Gothic cathedral." [20] This organic unity he sees also in the Renaissance, when the works of artists were the "dreaming mirror image of their time," when artists lived in "sacred harmony with their environment, when they did not divorce their art from the politics of the day." But the German classical age was a period of the artificial divorce of art from life, of contradiction to the spirit of the time. His own age represents a stage of transition in which subjectivity and individuality may and must riot unchecked. There is barely hope for a new art that will again reconcile art with life and society. It will not borrow its symbolism from the past and may even discover a new technique.[21] Thus Heine can judge and juggle with three periods and three criteria: the world of classical, objective, universal art which is in the past; the present, subjective, ironical, divided art of which he himself is an exponent and victim; and the art of the future, which he sees dimly as an emancipation from romantic divisions, as a new reconciliation with society and life. The autonomy of art remains for Heine a postulate of a particular time. The merger of art with contemporary life can be seen as the task of a new age. But this reconciliation is not envisaged as a movement toward didacticism or realism.

Heine always objects to the realist dogma. Art is not an imitation of reality. In art "form is everything, matter nothing." [22] In a passage later to be quoted by Baudelaire, he proclaims himself a "supernaturalist in art" (in contradistinction to his naturalism in religion). "I believe that the artist cannot find all his types in nature, but that the most significant types, as inborn symbolism of native ideas, are revealed, as it were, in his soul." "Colors and forms, tones and words, appearance in general, are only symbols of the idea, symbols that arise in the soul of the artist when it is moved by the Holy Ghost of the world." [23] Heine goes so far as to speak, almost like Oscar Wilde, of the transforming power of art over life: the beautiful features of the Italian women must be due to the influence of the plastic arts. Nature, which supplied the artist with models in the distant past, today copies the works of the master artists.[24] Though this may be only a *jeu d'esprit,* a joke, there is no doubt that Heine shares with Goethe and Schelling the idea of the close collaboration of art and nature—the conception of the second world of art, an objective world of universal significance, created spontaneously as an analogue of the processes of nature. Heine believes in inspiration. Reason has only a policing power in art.[25] Though art is, we have been told, supernatural, it is also natural— spontaneous, original, primeval. Heine never wearies of praising German folk songs and legends. He criticizes Platen for his lack of "deep natural sounds, as we find them in popular songs, children, and other poets," for the "frightening constraint he put on himself to say something which he calls 'a great deed in words.' Ignorant of the nature of poetry, he does not even know that the word is a deed only with the orator, but for the true poet an event." [26] Heine chides Goethe for not preserving the true legend of Faust, for lacking in piety toward its "inner soul." [27] He believes strongly in the creativity of the "folk," and he remains, in spite of all anticlerical reservations, a student and lover of medieval German literature and folklore. Though he praises the Grimms highly and draws from their *Deutsche Mythologie* much information for his *Götter im Exil, Elementargeister,* and the ballet scenario *Faust,* his views are nearer to those of the Schlegels, Arnim, and Rosenkranz.[28] Folk poetry is not completely dead, as it was to the Grimms; it can be revived and is being revived by Heine himself. Song, music, and dance are the themes and models of many of his poems.[29]

The greatest works, in the past, were objective, universal, and often, like the *Nibelungenlied,* anonymous. Objectivity is for Heine always an ideal. He chides Börne for his subjective prejudice: Börne could not understand "objective freedom," since he considered "artistic form" in Goethe mere heartlessness.[30] Shakespeare is praised for his universality; he is not a mirror of nature but contains an inborn world within himself; the merest fragment of the world revealed the whole universal connection to the poet.[31] Heine, who often rehearses the Schlegels' contrast of the romantic and the classical, rejects their duality of plastic and musical art because all art should be plastic.[32] Poets have preserved the beautiful beings of Greek mythology. Since the victory of the Christian church, poets were "a quiet community where the joy of the old image worship, the jubilant idolatry, was transmitted from generation to generation." [33] Goethe, though he is harshly criticized for his political servility, his indifference, and his preference for mediocrities, remains the object of admiration as a creator of plastic figures of living men and women, for his "clear Grecian eye" and pagan image-making.[34]

Heine's concept of irony, another feature of ideal art, is in theory the objective irony of Friedrich Schlegel. In a deleted passage Heine deplores that the Schlegels abandoned the view, later elaborated by Solger, of irony as the "essence of art" in favor of Schelling's philosophy of identity.[35] Irony seems to Heine "the main element of tragedy": he demands even that every romantic comedy should be tragic.[36] Irony is the antidote to sentimentality and medievalism. Modern poets do not want to fake "a catholic harmony of feelings," but rather want "like Jacobins to dissect feelings inexorably, for the sake of truth." [37] His praise of Aristophanes, of Shakespeare's *Troilus* for its "jubilant bitterness, world-jeering irony," of Cervantes, of Molière, and of Sterne, suggests Heine's predecessors. He had become more and more critical of his own more immediate models, of Hoffmann, Jean Paul, and the theorist of irony, Friedrich Schlegel, whom he could not forgive for his conversion and his service to reactionary Austria.[38]

For Heine style is also an objective quality. Masters of the word handle style freely: they "write objectively, and their character is not betrayed in their style." [39] Though Heine constantly exploited biographical information, often very unfairly, in his own criticism, he resented it strongly when it was used against him.[40] He must have regretted formulating the divorce of life and work so sharply in *Atta Troll:* "Kein Talent, doch ein Charakter." He was thereafter said to have a "talent" and no "character." On occasion he himself exploits the assumed opposition of style and personality. Buffon's saying "Le style, c'est l'homme," Heine argues, is completely wrong. Villemain's style, he tells us slyly, is "beautiful, noble, well-grown, and clean." [41] But the harmony of man and work is only a distant ideal. In our time, the poet cannot help being "subjective, lyrical, and reflective." [42] Byronic *Weltschmerz,* inner division, *Zerrissenheit,* is a necessity of the time. "The world is torn in two, and as the poet's heart is the center of the world, it must be torn pitiably in this present age." [43] Heine plays with, laughs at, but, deep down, believes in the poet as martyr, since he is both the representative of his age and the unacknowledged, persecuted prophet of a new one. But the future of poetry remains obscure. Certainly it was not to be the didactic poetry of the Young Germans. Rather, the future was adumbrated in Heine's own late poetry, written in the *Matratzengruft*—a very real prosaic martyrdom. This poetry anticipates modern complex contradictory sensibility: bitterness and horror, irony and wit, dream and drab reality. It anticipates Baudelaire and Laforgue.

Heine's position in a history of poetic theory is thus transitional and ambivalent: romantic *and* liberal, aesthetic *and* didactic. But in the theory and method of criticism there is no question of his affinities. In criticism he defends consideration of the artist's intentions. The critic should not ask what the artist should do, but rather: "What does the artist want, or, better, what cannot the artist help doing?" [44] Criticism should be sympathetic. The Schlegels, Heine acknowledges, had great merits in aesthetic criticism. "In 'reproducing' criticism where the beauties of a work of art are vividly realized, where a subtle feeling for peculiarities matters . . .

the Schlegels are quite superior to old Lessing." [45] A. W. Schlegel is reprimanded, however, for ignoring historical relativity when he compared Bürger's ballads unfavorably with those collected by Percy: "The Old English poems yield the spirit of their time, and Bürger's yield the spirit of ours." [46] The final ideal is Herder's cosmopolitanism: "Herder saw all mankind as a great harp in the hands of the Great Master; every nation seemed to him a specially tuned string of this giant harp, and he understood the universal harmony of their diverse chords." [47]

The method of Heine is primarily metaphorical rather than speculative or analytical. Only two early reviews of plays by friends struggle, scholastically, with the Aristotelian categories: events, passions, character, diction, etc.[48] Later, drawing on Jean Paul, Görres, and Hazlitt, Heine's criticism becomes almost entirely characterization by metaphor, unless it is ideological polemics or personal satire. But when he speaks of a literary text, he can evoke its mood by elaborate similes without regarding too closely the actual contents of his text. Thus in Tieck's fairy tales:

> the reader feels as if in an enchanted forest; he hears the subterranean springs murmur melodiously, he fancies, at times, hearing his own name in the rustling of the trees. Broad-leaved clinging vines sometimes entangle his foot frighteningly; wild and strange wonder-flowers look at him with their colorful longing eyes; invisible lips kiss his cheeks with teasing tenderness; tall mushrooms, like golden bells, grow up ringingly at the roots of trees; large silent birds rock on the branches, and nod down with their pensive long bills. All breathes, all listens, all is full of awesome expectation—when suddenly the soft horn of the forest sounds and on a white palfrey a beautiful lady rides past, with waving plumes on her cap, a falcon on her wrist.[49]

Similarly, Goethe's *West-Östlicher Divan* is described as if it were a lush Oriental picture in the style of Thomas Moore.[50] Heine's criticism is often arabesque, fantasy, charming decorative art which quickly changes to witty, caustic, and often vulgar and coarse satire. At his best Heine can be glowingly evocative or pointedly aphoristic; at his worst he can descend to mere scandalmongering, sentimentality, or tiresome, cheap witticisms. One side points ahead toward Nietzsche, the other toward guttersniping sensational journalism.[51]

YOUNG GERMANY

A resolution of the German Diet of December 10, 1835, suppressed "a literary *coterie* known under the name of Young Germany." Five authors—Heine, Gutzkow, Wienbarg, Laube, and Mundt—were singled out. Not only were all their published writings banned but also anything they might write in the future. Even reviewing or mentioning their names and the titles of their books became an offense. Opinions about the origins of this amazing edict differ even today: some effect must be ascribed to the indignant articles Wolfgang Menzel had launched against the erotic novel *Wally die Zweiflerin*, by his former collaborator Karl Gutzkow. Suspicions were aroused by the plan of an ambitious *Deutsche Revue*, for which, however, many other harmless authors had promised collaboration. The name *Junges Deutschland* had been bandied about before and must have sounded like Mazzini's revolutionary *La Giovine Italia*. But there was no coherent German group. Heine, in Paris, corresponded fitfully with Laube, inquiring about the others. The rest hardly knew each other, disagreed, and even quarreled; the persecution intimidated them thoroughly.[1] The Diet revoked the resolution in 1842, and nothing remained of Young Germany but the label. Politically these men were quite ineffectual, and they made their peace with the authorities very quickly. Gutzkow later in his life became secretary-general of the Schiller Foundation. Laube was for years director of the Vienna Court Theater. Mundt became a Prussian professor. Wienbarg early fell silent, suffering from mental illness. In spite of all the differences and the looseness of their association these men shared one ideal: liberalism, which meant trust in progress, in the spirit of the time, in the social role of literature.

Ludolf Wienbarg (1802–72) apparently had done most to propagate the name of the group by dedicating his *Aesthetische Feldzüge* (1834) to Young Germany. These once-famous lectures appear today rather vague declamations, which in aesthetic ideas are completely derivative from Lessing, Goethe, Schiller, Jean Paul, Solger, and Schelling.[2] But the tone of a new time is heard in Wienbarg's constant pleas for a "poetry of life" that would express the social situa-

tion, and in his complaints about the bookishness of German culture, its lack of a center and common cause. Aesthetics for Wienbarg
has ceased to mean anything specifically concerned with art. It is
identical with world view, or ideology.[3] When, toward the end of
the book, Wienbarg comes to grips with concrete critical problems,
he judges Goethe with a divided mind. Goethe is servile and free,
great and small, a genius and a courtier. Faust is interpreted alle-
gorically as "Germany struggling for liberation." Faust is a revolutionary; Faust *is* Goethe, but only the early Goethe. For love of a
princess Goethe changed and conformed.[4] The book concludes with
praise for Heine's prose, and the wit that prophesies civic freedom.
But Heine, unfortunately, is a foreigner and an enemy; he had a
Jewish father and a Christian mother from whom he inherited the
gift of imagination and the tincture of German *Gemüt*.[5] In another review Wienbarg praised Heine's book on Germany as
"bold, grand, and thoroughly genetic." The juxtaposition of the
philosophical revolution in Germany with the political revolution
in France is "the high point of his world-historical wit." [6]

While Wienbarg had pretensions to an aesthetic theory, Karl
Gutzkow (1811–78) and Heinrich Laube (1806–84) were frankly
publicists, prolific pamphleteers, reviewers, debaters of literary
opinions. Gutzkow was strongly anti-Hegelian, against fatalism,
"historical torpor," and quietism. He was antiromantic, bluntly
antilyrical.[7] Without embracing any clear creed of realism, he was
concerned with the novel as a rising art form. He recommended
and practiced what he called "der Roman des Nebeneinander," a
novel representing the whole variety of the world, "the whole age,
the whole truth, the whole reality." His ponderous novel *Die Ritter
vom Geiste* (1850) is a series of complex, interwoven, or contrasting
plots from different social spheres, which by their correlation presumably convey the simultaneity of life rather than the mere succession of events which Gutzkow assigns to the drama.[8] Gutzkow
suggests, at least, the problem of space in the novel, though he could
not solve it in theory or in practice.

The same sense of suggestiveness, improvisation, and topicality is
conveyed by the many volumes of Gutzkow's criticism. Gutzkow,
with advancing years, turned against almost all his contemporaries.
Büchner, whom he knew slightly, was the one discovery in which
he could take pride.[9] But he came to hate Hebbel and, after Heine's

book on Börne, despised Heine as a "Judas." "Heine pretends to be
a poet but writes like a guttersnipe." [10] A little book *Über Goethe
am Wendepunkte zweier Jahrhunderte* (1836) keeps an uneasy balance between regrets for Goethe's politics and admiration for his
work, particularly for that of the early period. Gutzkow sees
Goethe's base in the "domestic," to which he could always retreat.
His "guilelessness," distrust of theory and lack of dialectics, his
"egoism of health," and his mental economy are the qualities that
explain his strength and his weakness.[11] Gutzkow endorses Goethe's
ideal of world literature; it should, however, validate, rather than
replace, nationality. "Everything belongs to world literature that
is worthy of being translated into foreign languages." [12] Gutzkow
discusses acutely Goethe's strange relationship to Byron, who seems
to him "only a character who took poetry by force." [13] Goethe, in
short, is to Gutzkow no critical, moral, or political model; he is still
the master. "The age of tendentiousness can only begin when we
have settled accounts with the age of talent," [14] that is, the age of
Goethe. Talent means artistry, craftsmanship, qualities that are
woefully lacking in the fuzzy, flabby, diffuse writings of Gutzkow.

Heinrich Laube has much more superficial competence. His early
Geschichte der deutschen Literatur (1839), however, is a shoddy
compilation of which only the parts devoted to current literature
preserve some documentary value. The same is true also of his
prolific theatrical criticism, which covered several decades (1829–
75) and several cities (Breslau, Leipzig, Berlin, Vienna).[15] In reminiscences and books devoted to the theater Laube chronicled and
defended his activity as a theatrical manager, adapter, and *regisseur*.
To Laube the Vienna *Burgtheater* owed a period of flowering and
Grillparzer got a resuscitation on the stage.

Among the Young Germans condemned by the Diet, Theodor
Mundt (1808–61), though least known today, seems to me by far the
best literary critic and historian. His *Geschichte der Literatur der
Gegenwart* (1842) is a brilliant sketch, ostensibly a continuation of
Friedrich Schlegel's Vienna lectures.[16] The political purpose is of
course entirely different. Mundt is a Protestant and liberal who
nevertheless writes in the true spirit of romantic historiography.
Literature is "a coherent national science, a concrete part of the
true reality of the national mind." [17] Since about 1800 modern liter-

ature has centered around the revolution, which is "the myth of the present age." Mundt contrasts the age of individualism, that of Goethe and Schiller, with the romantic age that is national and universal at the same time. While Mundt condemns romanticism on many counts, political and literary, he defends it as necessary and progressive because it returned literature to the life of the nation. Romanticism must not be identified with reaction and Roman Catholicism.[18] But Mundt, of course, hopes that the rising liberal literature, democratic and Protestant, will find the proper synthesis of individualism and collectivism, nationalism and cosmopolitanism. The concept of *Weltliteratur* does not contradict nationality; rather, nationality is "the real core and highest charm of literature," and each nation should develop its nationality to the utmost in order to become part of a world literature.[19] Unfortunately just this generous ideal of comparativism proved damaging to Mundt's book in practice.

The first three retrospective lectures incisively characterize the German classics and romantics. Novalis is like "a miner who lost his way in his shaft and was found there buried among all his riches." [20] Hölderlin (who was little known then) is highly praised: "Hardly any poet has felt and recognized so deeply the true need of the modern spirit." [21] Jean Paul, in his disproportion of mind and body, is the symbol of modern Germany. Kleist is "the political Werther of his age." [22] The later chapters become, however, encyclopedic surveys laudable for their effort to pay attention even to the minor literatures: Spanish, Russian, Polish, Swedish, even Hungarian and Czech. But Mundt pays a heavy price for inclusiveness: he becomes thin and superficial. He dwells at length on the woman's question; he gives laborious résumés of George Sand's novels; he attacks the politician Gentz; in short, he loses sight of his original aim.[23] The liberal Protestant ideology overlies actual literary criticism. At his best Mundt achieves the tone and attitude of Adam Müller and Friedrich Schlegel and sketches a boldly speculative scheme of large ideological forces playing on literature. Mundt's position and method are, in some ways, remarkably similar to that of the first full-scale historian of German literature, G. G. Gervinus.

GEORG GOTTFRIED GERVINUS (1805–1871)

Gervinus would have been horrified to be grouped with Young Germany. Among his early writings was a sharp attack on Börne, and he showed his contempt for Heine and his consorts even late in life.[1] Still, as a literary historian he belongs to the political liberalism of the time, shares the belief in the end of the poetic period, and aims at a reconciliation of literature and life, politics and art. His monumental *Geschichte der poetischen Nationalliteratur der Deutschen* (5 volumes, 1835–42) loudly proclaims that "the flowering of our poetry is over, has run to seed," that we must wish our country "great events," the transformations and revolutions that Goethe had feared.[2] "The contest of art is finished; now we should set ourselves the other aim which none of our marksmen has hit hitherto. Apollo grant us the glory here as he did not refuse it to us there."[3] Such are the last words of Gervinus' *History*.

There is irony and pathos in Gervinus' involvement in politics. In 1837 he was one of the seven professors of the University of Göttingen who resigned in protest against the abrogation of the Constitution; in 1853 he was prosecuted for treason. The preface to the fifth edition of the *History* in 1870 warned of "incalculable dangers" in the unification of Germany under Prussian hegemony.[4] His passionate democratic liberalism surely contributed to the sudden decline of his reputation after the establishment of the new Reich.

The political enthusiasm, the concern for the nation's grandeur and moral health, permeates the whole *History*. In the introduction (1835) Gervinus expressly repudiates all aesthetic standards: "I have nothing to do with the aesthetic judgment of things; I am no poet and no belletristic critic. The aesthetic judge shows the origins of a poem in itself, its inner growth and perfecting, its absolute value, its relation to its genre and possibly to the nature and character of the poet. The aesthetician does best to compare a poem as little as possible with other and foreign poems; the historian uses comparison as a principal means toward his end."[5] Comparison, often in a set and tiresomely antithetic manner, is Gervinus' almost obsessive procedure. He uses it throughout the volumes to make historical and social explanations and to define historical and social groupings; he examines the changes in the producers of poetry from the clergy to the knights and burghers, and the "retreat of poetry from the people to the scholars"[6] in the 16th and 17th centuries; he pays systematic attention to the contributions of the diverse German provinces and towns, and to the associations and contacts of the poets and, though he focuses clearly on belles-lettres, he discusses historiography, criticism, political writings, and the state of the theater quite fully as background. No doubt, social and intellectual rather than poetic history is his forte.

Still, he goes beyond this interest in the totality of national life. He believes, like Hegel, in a necessary relation between poetry and national evolution, in some fatal exhilarating or cramping power of the historical process. Thus in *Faust* he tries not merely to find "the leading moments in the ideas of the time, to suggest the historical interconnection," or to see it as a "symbol" of the *Sturm und Drang* period,[7] but to see it as a poem that grew, "like a plant out of its soil, out of the situation of the nation and the time, whose unfolding is completely dependent on the cultivation of the soil." [8] The limitations of the poem are the limitations of the time. Goethe "stood still at the spot where he made his hero stop; he had no feeling for active life and the forces of will in man. . . . He stopped at that spot necessarily because the country itself had stopped there— the country that even today has not crossed the gulf between the life of feeling and thought and the life of action." [9] A new *Faust* is impossible without "an essential progress in the great life of the nation." [10] Similarly, Schiller's tragedies evoke the reflection that "everything has its time and condition; thus tragedy has never had a great age unless the state of the real world has offered a school to the tragedian." Schiller got that schooling. "Our tragedy went hopelessly astray until the French affairs [i.e. the Revolution] set it on the right path." [11] The moral is always that "if our youth would first take care to *make history,* it could promise better luck for the business of poetic creation." [12] In a dedication (1840) to the historian F. C. Dahlmann, Gervinus calls for the end of poeticizing and quotes Hotspur, strangely misusing his words: "I had rather be a kitten, and cry mew / than one of these same meter balladmongers." [13]

If Gervinus were only an enemy of "mincing poetry," a preacher of political action, or even a moralist who must condemn the lewd Wielands and obscene Heinses, he would have to be classed as another Wolfgang Menzel, as a political historian of literature, as a publicist. But he was a real critic and a great scholar. His *History* is not only the best history of German literature before Hettner and Scherer but, it seems to me, the best literary history in any language before Taine and De Sanctis. In factual erudition, skill of narration, power of exposition and characterization, and the coherence, lucidity, and basic truth of its general scheme, it is clearly superior to the histories of Warton and Hallam, of Emiliani Giudici, of Ticknor, or even of Villemain, Ampère, and Nisard. In spite of political perorations and a didactic undercurrent, in spite of an awkward shyness in coming to grips with concrete analyses of works of art, the *History*, especially in its first edition (before its flow and unity was interrupted by expansions, corrections, and the incorporation of erudite materials) [14] is animated by a firm aesthetic creed and a strong, though often dour, critical spirit. Gervinus successfully combines history and criticism, the crowded survey of genres and mass movements, with intellectual biographies of the great writers: Klopstock, Wieland, Lessing, Herder, Goethe, Schiller, and Jean Paul.

Only the last chapter, on "romantic poetry," seems excessively unsympathetic and polemical. Gervinus criticizes the romantic movement for its alienation from reality and life, its support of the political reaction, its Catholic leanings, its vague lyricism, its moral irresponsibility, its escape into fairyland and prehistory. To Gervinus the actual poetic achievement of the time seems exceedingly small: Tieck seems the most representative figure; Novalis is disparaged; Kleist is praised very coolly; and E. T. A. Hoffmann, a "sickly being," is seen producing, at most, raw materials for future works of art.[15] Gervinus' revulsion against the idols of his youth, particularly Jean Paul, who was his great solace during his early years in a drapery shop,[16] protrudes too much to make for good criticism of his immediate elders. But Gervinus concedes that while "in romanticism our poetry began to putrify, it became the manure for a seeded field, from which the sciences of literary history, of art-history, mythology, and philology sprouted." [17] Gervinus sees the value of the aesthetic criticism of the Schlegels, who "stimulated rather than created a totally new science, literary history." [18] He himself felt that he had *created* that science almost singlehanded, that he was the first to project a "narrative work of art" [19] in place of the older erudite compilations. Certainly, in his practice, Gervinus is the lineal descendant of the Schlegels, in spite of his very different ideology and the many objections he brought against their writings and opinions.[20]

Gervinus *has* aesthetic criteria and makes aesthetic judgments constantly, even though he disclaimed any formal aesthetics. He argues that aesthetic judgment must be taken for granted in a historian. On theory, he refers only in general terms to his sources in Aristotle and Lessing, Goethe and Humboldt (and he should have added Schiller).[21] A definitely German classical taste informs the book: an unbounded admiration for the Greeks and in particular for Homer; a love for Shakespeare; a reverence for Lessing, and deep sympathy for the classical stage of Goethe and Schiller. The antiquarian Teutonic spirit is felt only in the treatment of the Middle Ages. Though he pays much attention to international relations and foreign sources, he always arrives at the conclusion that the German elaboration is superior to its model—that, for instance, the *Minnesang* is somehow deeper, more "inward" than troubadour poetry, though later he admitted that its range of themes is much more narrow.[22] Still, considering the atmosphere in which he wrote (with the Grimms as his colleagues in Göttingen), he preserved a remarkably critical attitude toward German medieval literature. He deplores the exaggerated cult of the *Nibelungenlied*, which cannot be put aesthetically on a level with Homer and cannot serve as a model of national emulation.[23] The discussions of Walther von der Vogelweide, Wolfram, and Gottfried do not lose sight of aesthetic considerations; and the volumes on the 15th, 16th, and 17th centuries, which could be and are more purely historical, constantly pass critical judgments, marred only by a lack of sympathy for the learned Latin tradition and baroque Catholic taste.

The high point of the books is the treatment of the great classical age: of Lessing, who, for Gervinus, most clearly defined German art as situated "between North and South, the Netherlands and Greece, Nature and the Ideal" and who, in *Nathan der Weise*, in spite of its bad verse, "created the most characteristic and most German work of our modern poetry next to Goethe's *Faust*"; [24] of Wieland, who is condemned but analyzed at great length; of Herder, who suffers from his pietism and cosmopolitanism; and finally of Goethe and Schiller, whose parallel intellectual biographies are traced with great care. Special shrines are set apart for Gervinus' favorites: the revolutionary Georg Forster, whose writings he edited with a long introduction; and J. H. Voss, whose translation of Homer seems to him the great wellspring of German classicism.[25] Gervinus judges the *Sturm und Drang* period severely and describes Goethe's role in it, emphasizing Goethe's distance from his fellows. Contrary to the

usual German assumptions, Gervinus knows that "experience" is
no standard of poetry. Goethe was always "at the brink of lived experience: ready to conclude, able to master it, before he started on his
[poetic] labor." He stood "at the dangerous boundary between feeling and reflection, instinct and consciousness," knowing that the gift
of "enjoying things deeply and still putting them at an objective
distance" is the true power of the poet.[26] Gervinus sees the journey
to Italy as an ethical and aesthetic purgation, as a step "from lawless-
ness to order and clarity, from Nordic barbarism to Southern culture." [27] Gervinus hails the friendship with Schiller, expounds
Goethe's aesthetics (including the symbol) meticulously, and then
pays glowing tribute to *Hermann und Dorothea,* the "only poem
which all the modern centuries could hand to a Greek risen from the
dead without commentary and apology." [28] Goethe is then primarily
an epic poet, incapable of writing tragedy, compelled by his nature
to objectivity, detachment, and finally quietism, the Olympic cold-
ness and the "painful tolerance" of his later years.[29] Gervinus makes
much of Goethe's horror of history, his blindness to the significance
of the French revolution, his comic servility to royalty, his solemn
exaltation of the most trivial occurrences and objects.[30] Goethe
could have been a Virgil but was only an Ovid—or rather, if we may
correct his saying, considering Gervinus' exclusive taste for *Hermann und Dorothea,* a Theocritus.[31] *Faust* is also an epic, full of
"gaps, riddles, and contradictions" that reflect the diverse moods
and styles of Goethe's life, rather than a unified drama.[32] Like many
of his contemporaries, Gervinus deplores the whole of Goethe's
later development. "The orphic period," as he calls it, is only "a
psychological curiosity." The *Divan* is "bodiless, nebulous"; the
Novelle "unspeakably trivial"; [33] the second part of *Faust* merely an
allegory of Goethe's life: "The origin, nature and interpretation of
this poem is as repellent as Dante's or Tasso's commentaries on their
own compositions." It will be "set aside like Milton's *Paradise
Regained* or Klopstock's forced dramas." [34] Even Goethe's classical
works are often judged severely with a yardstick of classical unity
and coherence of tone. In *Egmont* there is incongruity between the
Flemish folk scenes and the operatic effects; *Wilhelm Meister* splits
into two uneven parts. Only *Iphigenie* is the "purest flower of
modern culture." [35]

Schiller is contrasted with Goethe as the tragic against the epic, the subjective against the objective, the sentimental against the naive poet, with Schiller's own distinctions in mind. Gervinus' admiration for Schiller's aesthetic writings and for his political and patriotic significance could hardly be greater. The whole enterprise of historical tragedy seems to Gervinus the highest aim of the modern poet. Schiller, situated between the typical art of Sophocles and the individualizing art of Shakespeare, effects the reconciliation of nature and culture, antiquity and modernity, that Gervinus considers the highest aesthetic ideal.[36] But his critical sense is not satisfied with an abstract solution, with the elaborate parallel he draws between Goethe and Schiller, or even with his conclusion that the quarrel for preference between them cannot be settled, as that between Plato and Aristotle, Ariosto and Tasso, Rousseau and Voltaire, cannot be settled.[37] In practice, Gervinus sees the shortcomings of Schiller's plays—not only of the early plays, among which he prefers *Fiesco* for its historical theme [38] but also of *Wallenstein*. In the latter Schiller succumbs to fatalism, surrenders "the pure relation between action and catastrophe, which is always flawless in Shakespeare and Goethe." [39] As Goethe could not, in his time, achieve a Homeric epic, failed with the *Achilleis*,[40] and achieved perfection only in the modest idyll *Hermann und Dorothea*, so Schiller could not achieve Shakespearean tragedy nourished by history, because his Germany lacked true history. Thus Gervinus has devised a scheme (which might have been imagined by the young Friedrich Schlegel or Hegel) that is aesthetic and historical at the same time. It is based on the classical hierarchy of the genres, with tragedy and epic as the highest. Epic, which is objective and calm, is turned toward the past. Tragedy, subjective and involved in its time, faces the present.[41] Lyric and didactic verse are considered inferior genres. Lyric poetry seems to Gervinus always a sign of dilettantism, since the dilettante "flees the objective." [42] "Lyrical poems are like the childhood of a poet and have interest in themselves only if the poet has advanced further," he tells us apropos of Hölderlin, who seems to Gervinus merely a romantic dreamer.[43] Gervinus draws a distinction between the national poet, who "leisurely spins his threads from the distaff of time," and the personal poet, who "laboriously draws them from his innards like a spider." [44] What matters is only drama and epic, tragic or heroic

action—the ideals Lessing defended while Herder, a soft lyrical
soul, "trembled at the blood bath that Lessing's saying 'actions are
the subject of poetry,'" would have caused among the poets.[45]
Gervinus does not shrink from the slaughter. Homer, Shakespeare,
Goethe, and Schiller would survive. The Germans in their golden
age, great in retrospect but departed forever, achieved, alone
among the modern nations, the union of Hellenism and Christianity, the true modern "culture." [46] They achieved it in spite of a
wretched national life, in a time of national shame, in the isolation
of a world of beautiful dreams. Gervinus envies the Greeks and the
English, who in the age of Pericles and of Shakespeare achieved the
ideal union of national glory and freedom with art.

Accordingly, Gervinus' next book was the four volumes on
Shakespeare (1849–50), which, when introduced by F. J. Furnivall
in 1874, attracted much attention in the English-speaking world,
until it was overshadowed by A. C. Bradley's subtler and closer
reading of the tragedies. Gervinus' *Shakespeare* still preserves a
certain interest as the first attempt after Ulrici's to make a detailed
survey of all of Shakespeare's plays and to give a systematic account
of Shakespeare's moral outlook. Whereas Ulrici emphasizes Shakespeare's Christianity, the secular Gervinus develops at great length
the theme of Shakespeare's moral sanity, equanimity, justice, lack
of prejudice, and common sense. To him "morality is indivisible
from true poetry." Shakespeare's plays "present that higher order,
the eternal justice in human affairs, the finger of God." [47] Though
Gervinus does not believe in poetic justice in the sense of a system of
exact retribution, he sees justice fulfilled even in apparent viola-
tions. The *manner* of death is decisive: Cordelia "dies in the glory
of a transfigured savior, Lear, in reconciliation, Gloucester smiling,
Kent with joyousness." [48] Shakespeare's evolution (divided into
periods) is also conceived as a moral one. Gervinus interprets the
sonnets as a record of moral purgation and closely identifies Shakespeare with Prince Hal. He thus defends the rejection of Falstaff
and disparages Falstaff as "the personification of man's animal
sensual nature." [49] *Antony and Cleopatra* disturbs him, for it shows
a temporary relaxation of Shakespeare's moral fiber. He sees a flaw
in the very subject matter, the conflict "between political duty and
immoral passion," and deplores the lack of nobility in the two pro-

tagonists.[50] Curiously enough, Gervinus ranks *Cymbeline* very high: with *Lear* it appears as a "poetic theodicy," akin to an epic placed in prehistory.[51]

The moral scrutiny becomes identical with a search for artistic unity. Gervinus looks everywhere for the "leading thought," the unifying theme,[52] and finds his critical task accomplished when he can find a generalized formula for a play or a group of plays, when he can say that *The Merchant of Venice* concerns man's relation to property or that *Cymbeline* turns around two opposite concepts or moral qualities, faithfulness and truth versus falsity and untruth.[53] Gervinus is well aware of the dangers of intellectualism, dislikes Hegelianism, and frequently protests against reductions to abstract formulas; [54] but in practice his criticism is vitiated by his inability to escape his high didacticism, his whole psychological-moralistic conception of the plays. He can make good observations on the contrasting and interlocking of scenes and states of mind: Claudius' speech when kneeling in impotent contrition as a parallel to Hamlet's own state of mind; Volumnia's appeal to Coriolanus as anticipated in the earlier scene that leads to his banishment.[55] All too often, however, Gervinus does not see the plays as plays but examines only characters in isolation. He must derive action from character, since he cannot allow Shakespeare what he would consider fatalism.[56] Even the witches in *Macbeth* are "the mere embodiment of inner temptation." [57] There must always be a moral flaw in tragic characters. Much is made, absurdly, of Cordelia's calling a *French* army to invade England, of Desdemona's guilt in causing the death of her father, of the passionate rashness of Romeo, and even of the devious ways of Hamlet that bring about the final wholesale slaughter.[58] The analyses of characters and situations are often ponderously dull and belabor the obvious. In general, Gervinus keeps his eyes on the plays and only rarely makes contemporary applications of Shakespeare. But he does develop the theme that Germany is Hamlet, a saying popularized by a poem of Freiligrath's (1840), and he ends by recommending Shakespeare to the Germans as a "freethinking teacher" of indisputable authority who "keeps the breach of progress open." [59] As in the *History of German Literature,* contemporaneity, or the duty to his own time, has destroyed the critic Gervinus, as it did so many of his countrymen of that age.

THE HEGELIANS

Of all the systems of German idealistic philosophy, Hegel's had by far the widest reverberations in literary criticism. Hegel's *Vorlesungen über Ästhetik* was published posthumously only in 1835, but his earlier pronouncements and, more important, the whole method of dialectics and the general scheme of historical evolution stimulated many pupils and adherents to try their hand at literary theory and interpretation even before the death of the master. Unfortunately, few understood Hegel's carefully balanced position: his emphasis on the union of idea and image, content and form. His followers seized, so to speak, only one side of the handle, the "idea," which quickly became nothing but the philosophical, moral, or religious content of a work of art. The Hegelians, whether or not accepting his total system, were, in literary criticism, the most relentless hunters of "central" or "leading" ideas: allegorizers who reduced a work of art to an illustration of a philosophical theory or a document in the history of intellectual change.

Goethe's *Faust,* even before the publication of the second part, lent itself to this approach. Carl Friedrich Göschel (1784–1862), in his *Über Goethe's Faust und dessen Fortsetzung* (1824), interpreted *Faust* simply as a poetic anticipation and confirmation of Hegel's philosophy. "The way that Faust goes is the necessary way which thought must take, for it goes in the course of its evolution through all the modes of conflict and difference between man and God, subject and object, the individual and the general, this world and the world beyond."[1] A year later, Hermann Friedrich Wilhelm Hinrichs (1794–1861) published his *Aesthetische Vorlesungen über Goethe's Faust* (1825), which attracted Goethe's respectful though puzzled attention and may have stimulated his resumption of work on the second part.[2] Hinrichs "construes" *Faust* according to the Hegelian triads, finding them in every act, scene, situation, and character. He knows from theory that the content of every true tragedy must be a reconciliation of God and man and thus confidently predicts that Faust would be saved after "freely confessing that he had sinned."[3]

Shakespeare became the other victim of this approach. Eduard Gans (1798–1839), a philosopher of jurisprudence, interpreted *Hamlet* as a tragedy of the understanding, or the understanding made independent of reason: Hamlet violates morality by his dissection of morality. Reason triumphs at the end with Fortinbras, the personified state.[4] The same arid conceptualism also pervades the first systematic German interpretation of Shakespeare since A. W. Schlegel's: Ulrici's *Über Shakspeare's dramatische Kunst* (1839). Hermann Ulrici (1806–84) was not technically a Hegelian; indeed, he criticized Hegel's philosophy and erected his own system of philosophical theism.[5] His early work, *Geschichte der hellenischen Dichtkunst* (1835), was, however, completely steeped in Hegelian (and possibly Schellingian) dialectics: "developing" the idea of art and the distinct genres of art "in their necessity."[6] The Shakespeare book contains much historical information drawn from English sources, including information about other Elizabethan dramatists, but is mainly concerned with proving that Shakespeare held a coherent Christian view. Tragedy in Shakespeare "presents always the immediate ordinance of divine justice and moral necessity."[7] The plays are examined for their fundamental ideas and presented in "an ideal order" that passes from the "bridal love" of Romeo and Juliet, through Othello's "married love," Lear's "parental love," Macbeth's tragedy of will and action in the state, to Hamlet's loftiest, most universal tragedy of thought. Ulrici seems the first writer to condemn Hamlet's task of revenge from a Christian point of view. Hamlet's inaction is virtue rather than guilt. He perishes because he tries "to elude the directing hand of God," because he wants to be "absolute master," wants to be "God."[8] In practice, Ulrici's search for Shakespeare's philosophy leads often to the assertion of the crudest kind of poetic justice: Juliet, Cordelia, Desdemona are punished for their sins or peccadilloes; Paris, Juliet's suitor, for the shallow way in which he conceives of love; Ophelia for her "dreams of sensual pleasure and worldly happiness."[9]

Heinrich Theodor Rötscher (1802–71) is very similar to Ulrici in his interpretations of Shakespeare. He deserves attention because of his theoretical defense of the Hegelian method and because of the influence he exercised on two great writers, Belinsky and Hebbel. Belinsky admired him and on occasion paraphrased him; Hebbel saw in him a critical mentor and for a time listened to his advice.[10] In later years (1845–63) Rötscher was an influential theatrical critic in Berlin and wrote also on the theory of acting.[11] But his early essays, mainly on Shakespeare and Goethe, represent orthodox Hegelian criticism in its purity. The collection *Abhandlungen zur Philosophie der Kunst* (1837–42), is introduced by an analysis of "the relation of the philosophy of art and criticism to the individual work of art" [12] that shows a clear awareness of the issues. The aim of criticism, Rötscher asserts, is "to understand the great works of art in their inner reasonableness, in the unity of thought and representation," to provide us with an "insight into the necessity of the organism." The difficulty, he recognizes, consists in showing "how the freely intuited thought achieves form and limitation, how the infinite assumes finite shape." [13] In practice, Rötscher, like the other Hegelians, formulates first a general, leading idea and then tries to dovetail every detail into the formula. Thus the "idea" of the *Merchant of Venice* is the self-defeating "dialectics of abstract law." Even Launcelot Gobbo's desertion of his master, Jessica's elopement, and the business of the rings in the last act must be shown to fit the scheme. The melancholy of Antonio is interpreted as arising out of an "unconsciously working contradiction between his ideal nature and the interests and aims of his mercantile activity." Portia's obedience to her father's last wish in the matter of the three caskets raises an arbitrary decree to a moral obligation: she trusts in divine Providence, in the quality of Christian mercy.[14] With similar relentless ingenuity Rötscher defends every detail in *Romeo and Juliet* and *King Lear*. He easily rebuts the charge that only an evil chance brought about the deaths of the two lovers. In his dialectics, "the chance only contributes to revealing the Inevitable." [15] Lear suffers for his original guilt, the "terrible delusion of putting the word in place of the deed, the speech in place of sentiment." His madness, which must not be explained psychologically, is due to this same inner divorce of word and deed.[16] But one should acknowledge that Rötscher, in spite of much abstract verbiage, raises real problems in *King Lear*. The conclusion seems to him like a last judgment: Lear and Gloucester "relieved of their sins by the very excess of their suffering, become figures sanctified by misfortune." [17] Much in Rötscher would please modern interpreters of Shakespeare who look for symbols, correspondences, and Christian doctrine. They pay much closer attention to Shakespeare's text than Rötscher did, but they share with the Hegelians the intellectualist misunderstanding of art.

Compared with Rötscher, Karl Rosenkranz (1805–79), Hegel's biographer, seems the much more learned historian. His *Geschichte der deutschen Poesie im Mittelalter* (1830) applies a Hegelian scheme to German medieval literature. Literature passes from intuition (the epic) to sentiment (the lyric) to thought (the didactic poetry) and, within these stages, shows again triadic progressions. The lyric, for example, progresses from the *Minnesang* to the *Meistersang* to the folk song. Spiritual forces—the individualism of the primitive Teutons, the universalism of the Church, the mysticism imported from the Orient—shadowbox in literature; but within this schematism Rosenkranz manages to convey much concrete information and some criticism. He places, for instance, high value on *Titurel*.[18] The *Handbuch einer allgemeinen Geschichte der Poesie* (1832–33) is even more schematic and arbitrary in its classifications. When in prison in the Castel del'Ovo in the bay of Naples, De Sanctis translated the work into Italian; he wished to learn German and had plenty of time on hand.[19] Rosenkranz, in his later works, emancipated himself slowly from the heavy armory of Hegelian concepts. A substantial book on *Goethe und seine Werke* (1847) still moves within an Hegelian scheme of evolution: Goethe progressed from culture to nature, to the ideal and hence to the "idea."[20] But *Diderots Leben und Werke* (2 volumes, 1866) is simply historical, psychological, and descriptive. It is a pioneering work, remarkable in the Germany of that time for the sympathy and understanding Rosenkranz devotes to Diderot, an atheist and materialist, a writer with a lurid reputation for immorality.

Rosenkranz' most interesting book is the *Aesthetik des Hässlichen* (1853), which shows, if not speculative power, at least great classifying ingenuity. The mere idea of an aesthetic of the ugly (though not entirely new)[21] is striking. Rosenkranz argues that the ugly not only serves as a foil for the beautiful in art but is, in the Hegelian sense, a genuine negation of beauty, requiring a theory—just as evil does in ethics, or disease in biology.[22] Rosenkranz construes a progressive scale of the ugly: from the "formless" to the "incorrect" and finally to the "deformed." The "formless" is divided into the "amorphous," the "asymmetrical" and the "disharmonious." The "deformed" ranges from the "common" (the "petty," the "weakly," the "low") to the "repellent" to "caricature." The "repellent" is also classified in a triad: the "clumsy," the "dead and empty," and the "horrible," which in its turn is subdivided into the "jejune," the "nauseating," and the "evil," (which is also scaled in three grades: the "criminal," the "ghostly," and the "diabolical," the furthest point the ugly can reach.) But even the "diabolical" is broken down into the "demonic," the "witchlike," and the "satanic." [23] Rosenkranz tries also to define and to exemplify such categories as the bizarre, the baroque, and the grotesque and to give an account of caricature and parody. The baroque, which he has difficulty in distinguishing from the bizarre, consists "in an attempt to give significance to the commonplace, to the fortuitous and arbitrary by an extraordinariness of form." [24] Much of this is psychological or lexicographical discussion on the meaning of terms, but Rosenkranz enlivens it by many recondite illustrations, drawn mainly from literature, and does not shy away from the obscene or scatological—a sign of rare audacity in his time and place. The final relation between the ugly and the beautiful remains unsolved, however, and the clumsy dialectical apparatus seems hardly justified. Rosenkranz recognizes that "the violent contrast can become beautiful," that there is a legitimate "synthesis of heterogeneous contraries" (he obviously knew Solger); and he is fascinated by the manifestations of the ugly in all its forms. But his training in German idealism and his classical convictions lead him to the conclusion that art "must idealize the ugly, i.e. must treat it according to the laws of the beautiful." [25] He cannot get away from the ancient identification of art with the creation of ideal beauty.

The same desire to expand and modify the scheme of Hegelian aesthetics animates the work of Friedrich Theodor Vischer (1807–87). But it leads him further away into empirical psychology, into the new realism. Vischer composed an *Aesthetik oder Wissenschaft des Schönen* (1846–57), a kind of *summa aestheticae* in six large quarto volumes. Besides this monumental encyclopedia Vischer wrote much concrete criticism, on Goethe and Shakespeare and his own immediate contemporaries—Eduard Mörike and Gottfried Keller, Hebbel and Uhland.[26]

Throughout his life Vischer violently criticized the second part of Goethe's *Faust* as willfully obscure, arbitrarily allegorical, ethically suspect, "absurd, affected, stiff, repulsive, ridiculous." [27] He not only wrote a fullscale parody of *Faust* (*Der Tragödie dritter*

Teil, 1862) but even had the bravado to outline a continuation of *Faust I* as Goethe should have written it. This curious exercise in "positive criticism" [28] reveals the limitations of Vischer's taste and imagination. It is a contrived scheme according to which Faust has to pass through a set of fixed spheres: religion, politics, and science. Faust must commit a real crime, he must experience abject poverty, he must die a hero's death as a voluntary sacrifice to his nation. Vischer admires the first part greatly, abstracts from it a concept of the figure and the style, and confronts the second part with this pattern. He knows but ignores the fact that Goethe had changed and had achieved something in the second part very different from the first.

Vischer's enterprise fails even as a mental experiment, for he does not properly understand the style of the first part and tries to correct and improve Goethe in the direction of his aesthetic ideal: a "purified," less "baroque" Shakespeare—an ideal that dominates also the essays and lectures on Shakespeare.[29] These exalt Shakespeare as the great original "realist" but make constant reservations about his mannerisms, bombast, forced wit, and negligent plotting. In practice, Vischer's interpretations are largely psychological. Hamlet is seen as a man of excessive imagination rather than sensibility, intellect, or paralyzed will. Hamlet is hard, impulsive, even malicious and crafty, an ironist and actor reduced by his self-consciousness to an "inveterate stutterer of action." [30] Shakespeare's "histories" are the great model recommended to the Germans: a new national drama, historical and political, should be created, a cross between Schiller's and Shakespeare's.[31]

Much more vital than this academic concern for an ultimate reconciliation of idealism and realism, of German classicism and Shakespeare, was Vischer's concrete taste for the intimate lyric art of his friend Eduard Mörike and particularly for the humorous realism of Gottfried Keller. His own whimsical novel, *Auch Einer* (1879), shows how far he had moved away from German classicism. Vischer wants realism, but humorous, good-natured, "sunny" realism, "poetic realism" that shuns harsh satire, bitter social criticism, or repulsive ugliness. In the huge structure of the *Aesthetik* the comic spirit is also Vischer's highest ideal, and comedy the ultimate genre.

The *Aesthetik* consists of numbered paragraphs stating a thesis in bold letters interspersed with lengthy commentaries in smaller print which digest and discuss all previous German aesthetics. The entire fifth volume (1857) is devoted to an elaborate system of poetics. The *Aesthetik* is ostensibly only a modified, corrected exposition of Hegelian aesthetics, but fundamentally it upsets the whole scheme. In contrast to Hegel, Vischer devotes great attention to natural beauty. An entire volume analyzes the "objective existence of the beautiful," beginning with the beauty of light, color, air, water, and earth, through the beauty of plants, fishes, birds, and so forth, up to man. This scale is contrasted with the "subjective form of the existence of beauty," the imagination, which Vischer analyzes, divides, and subdivides without apparent regard to art. Art appears, at last, as the synthesis of nature and imagination.[32] Though Vischer still moves in Hegelian triads, he has actually abandoned the dialectics and the peculiar Hegelian implication of art in history. Vischer grants that the history of the arts, for the most part, coincides with an enumeration of their kinds, but he introduces a concept of "chance" which, allowing for the irrational and fortuitous, destroys the claim of dialectics to a deduction of its concepts.[33] With "chance" comes a much greater emphasis on the "image" rather than the idea, on art as the "eternalization of the individual," and the related emphasis on the comic in its "negative position toward the idea." The comic "resists the penetration by the idea" because its spirit is "the spirit of immanence." [34] Whereas Hegel treated satire, comedy, and the modern comic novel as moments in history, Vischer analyzes farce, wit, and humor in detail as independent categories. Vischer also abolishes the Hegelian triad of styles—symbolic, classical, and romantic—and argues for a conflict between two main principles, plastic and pictorial—a conflict that opposes a concrete, individualizing, realistic style to the classical tradition.[35]

The volume on poetics is sadly disappointing. It is almost a compendium of all the commonplaces of German idealistic aesthetics. The interpenetration of idea and image, content and form, the need for a totality that yields a "world picture" in every single image, the union of imagery and music, representation and mood, figuration and rhythm are all lucidly expounded and defended.[36] But then Vischer settles down to a conventional exposition of genre theory. It is the usual triad of epic, lyric, and drama, with epic regarding the past, lyric the present, and drama the future.[37] The chapters on the epic are completely dependent on the views of Wilhelm von Humboldt and A. W. Schlegel. Epic is objective, detached, continuous, etc. The lyric is treated more originally not because of the usual characterization as subjective, or being "punctual" in time, but because of the ingenious classification of its subgenres: the "upsurge toward the object" in the hymn or the dithyramb; the "pure dissolution of the object" achieved by song; and the "slow and growing detachment from the object" in contemplative, reflective forms such as the elegy.[38] The drama is considered the highest form. Tragedy is discussed in Hegelian terms as the conflict and reconciliation of ethical forces—though Vischer admits inferior types. He recognizes that in tragedy the guiltless may perish, and he defends the innocence of Desdemona, Cordelia, and Ophelia fervently against the pious sticklers for "poetic justice." [39] The comic is "the act of pure freedom of consciousness." Comedy is the highest genre, because it grants the greatest degree of freedom to subjectivity. "It contains the sublime and the tragic." [40] Comedy, however, teeters on the brink of prose, of rationality, of rhetoric. Vischer cannot share Hegel's prediction of the imminent demise of art, but he shares his contemporaries' sense of its decline. He even endorses Gervinus' argument that the age of poetry has at least temporarily ended, and he sharply criticizes the Young Germany group and the political poets of the time (particularly Herwegh) as inharmonious, corrosive, divided men who could not and did not produce genuine poetry.[41] He has nothing but contempt for Heine and objects to the fashionable nihilism of Hebbel's *Maria Magdalena,* though he admires the play as a psychological study.[42] Temperamentally, Vischer is a cheerful optimist, even a Philistine. In politics (where he began as a radical democrat and ended as an admirer of Bismarck) and in literature he seeks the golden mean, the right balance, common sense, and sense of humor. No wonder that he abandons his early Hegelianism and shares in the trend toward positivism and moderate realism.

Vischer, in later years (1866 and 1873) published an extensive criticism of his own *Aesthetik,* a recantation and self-defense of rare intellectual courage. He abandons the general structure and method of the *Aesthetik,* rejects the Hegelian "movement of concepts," and accepts the Kantian view that the beautiful arises only in the act of intuition and that "natural beauty" cannot be discussed independ-

ently of the imagination.[43] On the other hand, in these two dissertations and in an earlier paper, "Über das Verhältnis von Inhalt und
Form in der Kunst" (1858),[44] he strongly and acutely defends the
union of form and content, the form "full of content," which "has
expression"; and he attacks the new formalist Herbartian aesthetics,
particularly that of Robert Zimmermann, for its "baroque combination of mysticism and mathematics." For Vischer "pure form" does
not exist as an aesthetic fact, since "form does not adhere to the
matter but rises from it." Form is nothing but the "form of the content, the outer of the inner." [45] He recognizes that he and his fellow
Hegelians had minimized legitimate problems of structure and
outer form,[46] but he cannot agree to a theory that divorces form
from meaning and ignores the crucial role of symbol in art.

Vischer's last paper, "Das Symbol" (1887), marks the furthest
stage of his development toward a psychological and empirical
aesthetic, while he still clings to what he considers the essence of the
idealist position. He carefully analyzes the different meanings of
the term "symbol." A symbol is more than a fusion of image and
meaning (as bread and wine in the Eucharist become identical with
the body of Christ). Nor is it the same as "myth," which must be
believed in as reality. Rather, Vischer argues, our modern poetic
belief in myth should be called symbolical. Beyond this first meaning of symbol in religion, he admits a second stage as symbolic: the
animation of nature by the poet. Symbol in this second sense of
animism or anthropomorphism is inspired "by the truth of all
truths that the universe, nature, and spirit must be one at their
root." It is an act of "empathy" which Vischer now analyzes in
purely psychological terms. He distinguishes different stages—a
purely sensuous empathy, a motor empathy, and a final stage of
identification. Vischer looks for evidence of the last stage in dreams
induced by physical stimuli, in physiognomy, and in the language of
gestures. Empathy, he argues, is not merely association added to the
formal relationships that constitute pure beauty. Rather, even
mathematical and logical beauty is assimilable to empathy. There
are not two principles in art—"harmonics" and "mimics"—but only
one: imaginative empathy. A third use of the word "symbol," as
consciously contrived symbolism, as the poetic representation of
what is universally significant and typical, seems to Vischer danger-
ously near to allegory, which he never ceased to condemn in *Faust II*

and in Dante. Symbolism is the basis of all art; but in Vischer it means primarily empathy, animation of nature, anthropomorphism, and thus supports a pantheistic metaphysics. He quotes Fichte: "Art popularizes the transcendental point of view." [47]

Vischer is an extraordinarily representative figure, since he may almost serve as an illustration of the change from Hegelianism to psychologism. His *Aesthetik* will always remain the great compendium of the period, and his later revisions and polemics on the problem of form and content and on the symbol discuss issues that are still with us. De Sanctis, who disliked the man, nevertheless learned something from Vischer, the critic. Ernst Cassirer and Susanne K. Langer are often very close to Vischer in their conception of symbolism and felt form.

A reaction against Hegelianism can also be observed in many of Vischer's contemporaries. In most cases they simply abandoned aesthetics and theory and turned to straight literary history. But Theodor Wilhelm Danzel (1818–50) may be singled out as an exception, because of his unusual theoretical awareness and the clarity of his new aesthetic position, which on some points anticipates Croce. An early pamphlet, *Über die Aesthetik der Hegelschen Philosophie* (1844), criticizes Hegel's confusion of art and religion and the intellectualism that does not see that "every work of art is an individual and a genuinely concrete one." In Hegel the work of art is "only a specific form of the expression and representation of truth." Danzel complains of the Hegelians that their "philosophizing about art consists in breaking up the form and repeating, at the occasion of a work of art, well-known matters of the philosophy of religion and law in its content." [48]

In a review of Ulrici's *Shakespeare*, Danzel rejects the whole assumption that Shakespeare or any other poet held a systematic world view. The idea is "an unhappy expression which condemned a whole age to the Sisyphean labor of reducing the matter [i.e. a work of art] to the thinking of understanding and reason. The idea of a work of art is nothing but what is envisioned in it. It is not represented in the work of art but is the work of art itself. The idea of art can never be expressed in concepts and words. I can never communicate its content in any other way except by putting it whole, just as it is, before the eyes." Its elements are "intuition and mood," communicable only by experience; it follows from this that in a work of art "there is nothing essential or unessential." A work of art for which we could state the fundamental idea would be no genuine work of art. It is even more absurd to think that an idea could be a member of a system, since there is nothing into which it could be fitted. If there were anything more general than the work of art, it could be only the "mood" of the artist which gives "style" to his works. But this is only "a subjective generality, a subjective unity." [49] Criticism can "interpret to the intuition a work in all its individuality." Danzel feels that a comparison with sources may help to show what the author achieved and argues that a "true artistic history of poetry" must finally arise which would be "a history not only of external forms but of the inner conceptions of the subject by different poets." It would point up differences of style and finally trace a "course of evolution." [50] "Without looking right or left," a future literary history will have to present the "metamorphoses of poetic production purely from the poetry itself." [51] Danzel can thus criticize the then flourishing literary history as mere cultural history. He complains that literary history in Germany had skipped the intermediary stage between old-fashioned erudite compilations and philosophical and political histories of the kind written by Gervinus. A simple, pragmatic presentation of materials is lacking. What is needed, Danzel argues, are monographs on the influences from abroad upon German literature (which is part of world literature and therefore cannot be treated independently) and studies in the history of criticism and aesthetics. [52]

Danzel heeded his own advice. In a closely reasoned dissertation, "Über den gegenwärtigen Zustand der Philosophie der Kunst und ihre nächste Aufgabe" (1844–45), he traced the history of German aesthetics, with emphasis on Kant, Schiller, Schelling, and Solger. In other papers he analyzed very acutely some of Moses Mendelssohn's, Goethe's, and Schiller's aesthetic ideas. [53] He then produced an edition of Gottsched's correspondence and began a large-scale monograph on Lessing, of which he finished only one volume before his early death. [54] It was the first thoroughly documented "life and times" of a standard German author: a detailed biography in its historical setting, a minute chronological study of even the most ephemeral writings of Lessing with constant regard to their sources, ideas, and style. Danzel unfortunately did not quite master his materials and could not solve many of the problems he raised. He surrendered his dream of becoming the "Winckelmann of the history of poetry" [55]—the distant ideal of an artistic history of literature hardly realized even today—and settled down to "research," the accumulation of an immense storehouse of facts, sources, parallels, and influences which became, as the century progressed, more and more the staple of literary study in Germany.

FRIEDRICH HEBBEL

Friedrich Hebbel (1813–63) achieved great prominence in Germany, especially at the turn of the century. He was widely performed, newly edited, extensively studied, and hailed as a precursor of Ibsen and as the greatest dramatist of the 19th century. Something of Hebbel's fame then reached abroad, but one has the impression that it remained essentially local, and that even in Germany interest in Hebbel (outside the universities) had died down. Still, his theory of tragedy deserves attention in our context. It has been debated endlessly in Germany in relation to the plays and to its sources. Hegel, Schelling, Solger, G. H. Schubert, and Rötscher have been named and emphasized variously by different investigators.

Hebbel himself vigorously denied that he was a Hegelian. He did not read the *Lectures on Aesthetics* until 1842, in Copenhagen, and often expressed impatience with abstract philosophy, dialectics, and what he considered the false optimism and monism of the Hegelian system.[1] Nevertheless, whatever his exact knowledge of Hegel's texts may have been, in aesthetic and dramatic theory Hebbel is a Hegelian. He recognized this himself concerning the crucial point of tragic guilt.[2] In later years he moved even closer to the Hegelian concept of tragedy, possibly under the influence of Rötscher, whose essay on Goethe's *Wahlverwandtschaften* he had read in 1842 and with whom he started corresponding in 1847. Through reviews and lengthy epistolary discussions, Rötscher seems to have influenced Hebbel's views of reconciliation and the place of history in tragedy toward Hegelian orthodoxy.[3] Felix Bamberg was another Hegelian with whom Hebbel had frequent contacts (after 1843). Hebbel knew Ruge and Mundt, though he came to disapprove of them, and he respected Friedrich Theodor Vischer, who was one of the first critics to discuss him seriously.[4] Thus the atmosphere Hebbel breathed was thoroughly impregnated with Hegelianism. The complimentary references to Solger [5] do not contradict this conclusion, and for our particular question other influences can be discounted. We must as usual distinguish between our concern with Hebbel's theories and the different question of his metaphysics, or the relation between his theories and his practice. Does this or that drama conform to his theories? Or does it contradict them, exceed them, escape them, or contain, implicitly, a different concept of tragedy? All these questions are outside a history of criticism.

Hebbel's diaries and letters contain many pronouncements that sound extremely romantic in their formulas for personal involvement and for the role of the unconscious in creation. Hebbel calls poetry "a hemorrhage; the poet gets rid of his blood and it disappears into the sand of the world." [6] He compares writing poetry to sleepwalking, identifies poetry with dreaming,[7] and notes down his wife's and his own most incoherent dreams with the pedantry of a confirmed Freudian. Creation, like procreation, is best done in the dark.[8] Writing is a necessity or compulsion: "Its first receptive stage lies deep under consciousness and sometimes goes back into the darkest distance of childhood." In composing, Hebbel heard melodies with his inner ear. Themes came to him by chance. He was like "a boy who catches a bird which happens to be sitting there, and looks at it closely only when he has it in his hand." [9]

This is the side of Hebbel that often sounds like a desperate self-assurance that he is, in truth, an inspired poet and not a debater of problems on the stage. The work of art, Hebbel often repeats, is a mysterious, ambiguous, in a certain sense unfathomable "symbol." [10] He would like to avoid the misunderstanding of the idea as a mere abstract concept and even appeals from Hegel to Raphael's Neoplatonic "idea." Still, poetry and philosophy have an identical task. Poetry is "realized philosophy," but it must be a philosophy grown out of life.[11] Art, he insists, is both universal and individual; the poet must "seize the exterior, the visible, the limited, the finite, if he wants to represent the interior, the invisible, the unlimited, the infinite." [12] Language in drama must be pictorial, graphic; this is the only criterion of good art that never fails.[13]

These are all insights inherited from the immediate tradition. Hebbel expresses his most intimate concerns only when he discusses the theory of tragedy in two clumsily written treatises, "Mein Wort über das Drama" (1843) and the preface to his tragedy *Maria Mag-dalena* (1844), to which the more concise and often clearer entries in his diaries form an illuminating commentary and supplement. The only theme of tragedy is the relation of man to the idea or, in modern terms, to the order of the world—the relation of the indi-vidual to the totality. Tragedy represents a true insight into the nature of the world; it depicts the defeat of the individual by the universe. Hebbel's original twist to this old view is that the individ-ual is not punished for his revolt or *hubris* or lack of measure, but that he perishes simply because he is an individual. "The guilt is an original guilt, not to be divorced from the concept of man. It hardly falls within consciousness. It is given with life itself." [14] It is some-thing like original sin without a definite fall and without any hope of redemption, the guiltlessly guilty *principium individuationis*. Thus it does not matter whether the tragic protagonist is engaged in a good or a bad enterprise, whether he is innocent or guilty, suffers passively or revolts heroically. Hebbel, however, prefers the death of the good as a tragic theme. He answers the Danish Hegelian Heiberg (and Hegel) that Antigone is innocent: she merely violated an "untenable law which only formally represents the idea of the state." [15] Similarly, his Agnes Bernauer will be the innocent victim of a cruel though necessary reason of state. For Hebbel tragedy seems to have ceased to be a *theodicée:* instead, it demonstrates depressingly, horrifyingly, that man, being man, is doomed to per-dition and is doomed whatever he does. There is no great difference between action and suffering, since "all action dissolves into suffer-ing confronted with fate, i.e. the will of the world." [16] Man lives in an abyss: and if he rises from it, an unknown hand always pushes him back into it.[17] Tragedy reconciles us with our fate. Man's education is finished when he "comprehends his individual relation to the universe in its necessity." [18] His so-called free will "amounts to his not knowing his dependence on the general laws." Man's will is merely the willing of the necessary: submission to the inevitable.[19] Tragedy will be successful insofar as its action is absolutely neces-sary. Hebbel's ideal would be to create characters who all have the right on their side, and "whose fate arises from the fact that they are these men and not any other." [20] "It is foolish to ask of the poet what even God himself does not offer: reconciliation and the solu-tion of discords. But we can ask of the poet that he give us the discords themselves and not stand between the accidental and the necessary. He is permitted to let every character perish, but he must show at the same time that the ruin is unavoidable, that, like death, it is posited by birth itself." [21] There is no poetic justice, either in life or in art. "There is only one necessity—that the world exists; it is all the same how individuals fare in the world." [22] A pessimistic determinism seems pushed as far as possible: tragedy appears again as a schooling in stoicism, in resignation, in submission to the inscrutable mystery.

Possibly under the pressure of the prevailing Hegelian concepts, Hebbel moves sometimes toward considerations that contradict this basic conception by opening dim vistas of a hypothetical world order, governed by a "moral center," and even of a cosmic drama of a God seeking his own salvation. There is no reconciliation within a tragedy, only a reconciliation which always "falls outside the circle of the specific drama." It is a "reconciliation in itself," [23] in the interest of totality, not of the individual hero. It is not at all necessary that the individual should become conscious of the reconciliation (though it is better that he should). Hebbel offers the curious, hardly consoling simile of a river: "Life is a great stream, individualities are drops; but tragic individualities are pieces of ice that must be melted and which rub each other and repel each other to make this possible." [24] Man, one may interpolate, is an ice jam in the stream of the world, which will continue to flow placidly after the thaw. In tragedy the guilt is "canceled," presumably by the death of the hero, but the "inner ground of guilt remains unrevealed." [25] Sometimes, in entries in his diary, Hebbel even suggests a cosmic tragedy in which the world is "the great wound of God" or "God's fall," man "the Procrustean bed of the Godhead," and creation even the "corset of the Godhead." [26] "A God is buried in the world and wants to rise from it and break through it everywhere, in love, in every noble deed." [27] But these last speculative motifs, which derive from ancient mystical ideas, do not clearly enter into Hebbel's theory of tragedy. [28]

Ordinarily Hebbel's reflections concern much more immediate issues, particularly the relation of tragedy to history and the present. At moments he speaks as if tragedy were identical with history and calls art "the highest historiography." [29] Tragedy occurs mainly in the crises of history: his Judith and Holofernes are not merely woman and man but also Hebraism pitted against Paganism. In *Herodes und Mariamne* two ages of man are contrasted: Herodes represents the Hebrew community and Mariamne prophesies the Christian "rebirth of individuality." [30] Hebbel, however, dislikes and disparages the historical drama of his age—the antiquarian, patriotic plays which try to evoke the glories of the German past.[31] The historical crises reflected in Hebbel's plays allow him, rather, to focus on universal conflicts: the battle between the sexes (which he seems first to have formulated in such terms), the conflict between the state and the individual, and between man and society. In defending *Maria Magdalena* Hebbel could even be taken for an upholder of bourgeois tragedy. But he does not worry about social questions as such, poverty, or the conflict between classes in the affairs of the heart; [32] he sustains the view that universal problems will arise on any social level. He can thus defend contemporaneity as if he were a Young German: he even defines his aim in life as an effort to "represent the present state of the world as it is and how it became that way." [33] In the preface to *Genoveva* (1842), a play based on a medieval theme that had been handled before by the arch-romantic Tieck, Hebbel pleads that "every drama is alive only insofar as it expresses the time from which it sprung, i.e. expresses its highest and deepest interests." [34] Drama is "timely" in a deeper sense than that of the daily journal. He even calls his dramas "artistic sacrifices to the age" and is constantly concerned with the conflict between drama and theater. This conflict frustrated his hope of a new national drama that would be both great poetry and effective stagecraft.[35] The poet is not only a historian and a mirror of his time but also a prophet or (in an expression which in the age of radio and television has almost lost its old zoological association) "the antenna of the time." [36]

All these possibly contradictory assertions and claims are reconciled in the concept of the poet's representativeness, which allows him to be alternately a true interpreter of the past, a spokesman of his time, and a herald of a new age. "Art is the conscience of humanity." [37] The poet has a vision of true reality. But Hebbel's universe is dark and mysterious, contradictory and impenetrable. "Modern fate is the silhouette of God, the Incomprehensible, Unseizable." [38] Hegelian optimism is broken, but Hebbel does not want man to deny the will to life, as Schopenhauer did, nor does he

consider the world a disorderly chaos, as his contemporary Georg
Büchner did. Rather he preserves a strong ethical core: a dour stoic
pride, a residue of Kantianism that relates man to a higher law even
in the ruin of his individual life and lifts him above it.[39]

ARNOLD RUGE (1802–1880)

The tensions among the pupils and followers of Hegel had
become apparent even during Hegel's lifetime. But the actual split
into right and left wings was proclaimed only in 1837 by David
Friedrich Strauss, the author of *Das Leben Jesu* (1835). In 1838
Arnold Ruge, with Theodor Echtermeyer, founded a new periodical, *Die Hallischen Jahrbücher für deutsche Wissenschaft und
Kunst* (suppressed in 1841), which became the rallying ground of
the Hegelians of the left. The disagreements between the two wings
were largely political and religious: the left Hegelians were fervent
liberals and radicals and were sharply critical of traditional Protestant orthodoxy. In literary criticism Ruge was their most vocal
spokesman; he developed the peculiar combination of Hegelian
historicism with radical politics, of relativism with a complete trust
in progress. History is conceived as a long process toward the establishment of freedom. Literature is both a reflection of this process
and a tool for its achievement. On the one hand, the poet cannot
help being "the son of his age," subject to the "genius of his century."[1] On the other hand, every poet has also the obligation of
changing his time. He is both a passive mirror of society, reflecting
its conditions, and a reformer and even revolutionary, who should
sense the direction of history and move with it toward the bright
future. In praising the poems of Georg Herwegh, a political poet
if there ever was one, Ruge simply identifies revolutionary and
creative. "Revolutionary: does that not mean poetical, *novarum
rerum studiosus,* creative? Is not every new poetry the overthrow of
an old and obsolete world of the spirit?" Every poem is "fighting
poetry." "The essence of poetry is democratic," in the sense that the
poet wants "to rule *all* hearts."[2]

But we would be mistaken if we concluded that Ruge simply
recommends political and social poetry that favors his cause. He was
highly critical of the political poets of his time. In many essays he
elaborated a whole scheme of German literary history as a struggle

between spirit and soul, *Geist* and *Gemüt*. All his sympathies are on
the side of the "spirit," conceived as rational in the Hegelian sense,
while *Gemüt* he denounces as romantic, mystical, irrational, and
thus reactionary. Ruge's historical scheme begins with a praise of
the Enlightenment, of Lessing, Schiller, and Kant, because "enlightenment asserts the truth of science, the reality of virtue and
freedom, and finally the existence of the ideal through art." [3] But
Ruge is no ordinary defender of 18th-century rationalism: he sees its
limitations and is acutely aware of what today would be called the
alienation of the artist from society, and the falsity of the unhistorical, abstract cosmopolitanism and aestheticism of the German
classics. He quotes from Schiller: "In body we shall remain citizens
of our time, as it can't be otherwise, but in spirit it is the duty and
privilege of the philosopher and the poet to belong to no nation
and to no time but to be, in the most real sense, a contemporary of
all times," and comments ruefully, "Poor poet of German timeless-
ness! But so it was and so it is. He who does not experience his age,
cannot be its contemporary." [4] Yet Ruge accepted German classical
aesthetics and the idea of the autonomy of art. He praises Schiller's
Letters on Aesthetic Education for their discovery of an absolutely
free aesthetic world. But he thinks that German literature can
advance beyond the classics and their inner freedom when a richer
reality brings about a richer ideal world,[5] or, to put it more bluntly,
when a free Germany will allow a more vital, more real art. Though
full of admiration for both Goethe and Schiller, Ruge deplores their
emphasis on self-realization, on individual culture. Goethe is chided
for his political aloofness. The humanism of the German classics
remained a private affair. "Only a free state produces a poet who
idealizes true reality and produces an ideal which the world can
realize." [6]

On this road toward a union of the ideal and the real, romanticism appears to Ruge as a formidable obstacle, a dangerous enemy
of reason. "Romanticism is a declaration of war by the spirit of
caprice against the free lawful spirit of our age." [7] Romanticism to
Ruge is irresponsibility, fancy, indulgence in speculation, in dreaming, in egocentric wish-fulfillment. It is "the world turned topsy-
turvy." "It puts nature above spirit; head below and legs above;
the unreasonable, even the antirational, such as the plant, and the
animal above the rule of the rational; nature and paradise above the

goal of spirit and culture." [8] What the romantics lack is "spirit and its concept. Their poetry is unpoetic, their freedom insolence, their philosophy irony and mystification." [9] Ruge disparages also the worship of the folk song, which seems to him a sign of despair at the poetry of one's own age.[10] He criticizes Novalis for his association of lust, religion, and cruelty and for his cult of night and death.[11] Neither the Schlegels nor Tieck nor the Younger Romantics find favor in his eyes. Only Heine (whom he knew in Paris) appeals to him, but Heine also is suspected of irresponsibility or romantic caprice. "Has not Heine lost the right to speak seriously? Who believes him anymore?" Heine's poetry is "coquettish": he does not want to surrender to his feelings. "The whole world of truth and the whole reality is lost to him." Ruge admires Heine's antiromantic wit but comes to the conclusion that "it *seems* to be spirit, but is despair at spirit itself." [12] He believes that Heine was a sincere liberal but a desperate lover of freedom, who damaged the cause by his despair and his corrosive wit. Ruge drew up an amusing catechism of romanticism:

A true romanticist believes:

(1) In the genius of Goethe, the absolute perfection of Shakespeare, the depth of Dante, in the Spaniard Calderón, and in some Greek poets. All these are "poets." Schiller and Körner are, however, nonpoets.

(2) This definition remains mysterious. . . . Shakespeare, Dante, Calderón, Goethe, Hans Sachs, F. Schlegel, Holberg, Heinrich von Kleist, Manzoni are poets. Voltaire, on the other hand, Schiller, Körner, Walter Scott, and Wieland might be nice people on other accounts, but they lack the one thing, they are not poets. One does not know why.

(3) Further, the romanticist believes in the Middle Ages, in Roman Catholicism, in medieval art, and Pre-Raphaelite painting.

(4) He believes in the poetry of superstition, in folk poetry in contrast to artificial poetry, in folk songs and chapbooks according to the saying, "the best cannot be expressed in words."

(5) He believes in the style of A. W. Schlegel and in the cosmic humor of Tieck in *Puss in Boots*.

(6) He yearns for Italy and despises everybody who does not praise it.

(7) He educates his children on fairy tales and stories about marvels.

(8) He likes folk festivals and plays, and sighs for the poetry of travel.

(9) His every third word is "deep" or "mystic."

(10) He hates the Enlightenment and the French . . . Words such as "utility" or "taste" are considered vulgar.

(11) He despises the art of gardening and loves the natural growth of the solitude of the forest.

(12) He believes in the end of the world. It has already come about in dramatic poetry, since Shakespeare and Holberg are dead. In no other sphere does he believe in the spirit of freedom, but he does believe in the devil and in ghosts.[13]

In looking over this catalogue, which Ruge insists is partly drawn from observation of a social type, one is struck by the fact that Ruge himself would not have seriously disputed the first two items of this humorous creed. He certainly would not have defended any of the nonpoets (with the exception of Schiller). His antiromanticism is concerned with the mastering of the irrational, the *Gemüt,* by reason. He hopes for a union of poetry and politics in the spirit of philosophy and under the flag of freedom. He is not a realist in any of the later senses: he is perfectly willing to admit all and any devices and conventions in literature. At times he speaks of classicism as his ideal. But he finally concludes that all absolutism is mistaken, or rather that "we reach the absolute and freedom only in history." [14] Ruge more than any of his contemporaries deifies the spirit of time, and, in practice, even public opinion. Like Marx after him, he is a historicist who believes only in historical truth; but he is also, illogically, a utopian for whom the course of history is the irresistible wave of the future, inevitable progress the reason of time. The poet is spokesman and prophet of progress: he cannot help being both.

MARX AND ENGELS

The literary theories and opinions of Karl Marx (1818–83) and Friedrich Engels (1820–95) still exercise an enormous influence. The most casual pronouncements of their early reviews or late

letters have been collected and reprinted in huge editions in the
Communist world. These pronouncements have become the object
of intensive study and have been treated by Marxist critics in the
same way that canonical texts are interpreted and elaborated by
theologians. Marx and Engels were not literary critics by profession;
they became fitfully interested in belles-lettres when moved by
specific situations in their long political careers. Yet the chronology
of their literary opinions has been neglected and the ideas of the
two men have not been clearly distinguished. Their views of literature were not the consequences of their theories of economic
materialism; their source is rather in the world of Young Germany
and the Hegelians of the left, particularly Arnold Ruge.

Marx began his career as a student of literature. In Bonn, in
1835–36, he took courses on Homer and Propertius under A. W.
Schlegel. In Berlin, in 1837, he read Lessing's *Laoköon* and made
long excerpts from Winckelmann and Solger's *Erwin*. In 1842 he
studied C. F. Ruhmor's *Italienische Forschungen* in preparation
for an article, never written, on the relations of religion and art.
Marx was steeped in the German aesthetics of the classical period.
As late as 1857, taking elaborate notes from Vischer's *Aesthetik*, he
prepared another abortive article on aesthetics for C. A. Dana's
New American Cyclopaedia. Still, these aesthetic interests led to
nothing in particular. Marx preserved a taste for Homer, Shakespeare, and the German classics; he praised Dickens and George
Sand for their social sympathies, but he wrote no formal literary
criticism unless we include an attack (1844) on a Hegelian interpretation of Eugene Sue's *Les Mystères de Paris*. Marx there argues
convincingly against the absurd allegorical interpretation of one
Szeliga (the pseudonym of Franz Zychlin von Zychlinski), but discusses the contents of the novel simply as social reality. He reflects,
for instance, on the role of the Parisian *concièrge* as a government
spy, or ridicules the economics of Sue's fictional bank for the poor.[1]
Marx' important theoretical pronouncements occur only after the
establishment of his close collaboration with Engels.

Early in his life Engels was a practicing literary critic in the style
of Young Germany. In 1839 Gutzkow published Engels' reports on
life and letters in his native Barmen-Elberfeld as "Briefe aus dem
Wuppertal." The nineteen-year-old critic had obviously read Heine
and Wienbarg and followed Gutzkow closely in his literary opin-

ions. But Engels soon afterward broke away from Gutzkow's reins. He discovered Börne and in a review of "Die deutschen Volksbücher" (1839) used Börne's blunt method of judging even old German chapbooks from the point of view of political liberalism: Griseldis is an image of the degradation of women; the tales of Helena and Octavianus ascribe superstitious value to royal blood.[2] But this allegiance was also of short duration. Soon Engels read Ruge and embraced Hegelianism: he reviewed Gutzkow's play *Richard Savage* (1840) severely and condemned Alexander Jung's *Vorlesungen* (1842) for their eulogy of Young Germany. But all this early critical activity was soon completely forgotten; it was rediscovered only in the 20th century.[3]

Engels moved to England late in 1842 and became more and more absorbed in the situation of the working classes there. Carefully dropping the parts on Abbot Samson which could be considered romantic medievalism, he translated Carlyle's *Past and Present* for its attack on the "condition of England." [4] In 1844 Engels met Marx in Paris and their close collaboration began. Literature, understandably enough, was not in the foreground of their interests. In a context of polemics against a dissident socialist group, Engels did write a sharp review of a naive book on Goethe, Karl Grün's *Goethe vom menschlichen Standpunkt* (1846), which attempted to make Goethe appear liberal and even radical. Engels, remembering his early reading of Wienbarg, follows Wienbarg's line of calling Goethe contradictory: "now colossal, now petty; now a haughty, scorning genius, who looks down upon the world, now a considerate, contented, narrow Philistine," a great artist but a small man.[5] Both Marx and Engels admired Heine as a writer, but they came to the conclusion that he was "a common dog *politice*" and ridiculed his return to religion.[6]

In the forties the economic and philosophical writings of Marx and Engels in collaboration contained a few fateful pronouncements on the relations of literature to society. In *Die deutsche Ideologie* (1845–46) there is the first declaration of the economic determination of all culture. But it is still vague and even contradictory. Marx and Engels sometimes speak of the dependence in biological terms: cultural life is, at first, "the efflux of man's material behavior." Immediately afterward they deny that ideology has any history or development and assert that thinking and the product of thinking change with material production and communication. "It is not consciousness that determines life, but life that determines consciousness." [7] This is Hegelianism turned upside down or rather, as Marx and Engels would insist, put on its feet. Yet it is "life" in general, not economic production, that they then consider the impetus of historical change. The process of history, they argue, will lead to the new classless society, which will abolish the division of labor and hence the results of that division, the specialization of man. Therefore the artist or poet will disappear as a full-time expert. "In a communist society there will not be any painters, but at the most men who, among other things, also paint" (men apparently like Churchill and Eisenhower). This idyllic view (totally belied by history, and particularly the history of painting with full-time professionals such as Titian, Rembrandt, Rubens, or Cézanne as its masters) implies a kind of humanism which comes out also in Engels' much later praise of the great universal men of the Renaissance: Leonardo, Dürer, Machiavelli, "men not yet enslaved by the division of labor." [8] An escape from the determinism and relativity of history seems to be provided. Extreme historicism breaks down with Marx and Engels because they wish to anchor their dreams in something permanent and universal, a future golden age, a utopia.

In the *Communist Manifesto* (1847–48) there is only one rhetorical question conceivably referring to literature: "Does it require deep intuition to comprehend that man's ideas, views, and conceptions, in one word, man's consciousness, changes with every transformation in the conditions of his material life, in his social relations and in his social existence?" [9] If one interprets the word "with" freely, no complete economic determinism is yet proclaimed: the intellectual life of man changes *with* the transformations of economic order. A parallelism, an analogy is taught—not one-sided dependence.

Marx, writing alone, returned to the question in the "Einführung zur Kritik der politischen Ökonomie" (1857), a manuscript which he abandoned and which was published, in an obscure review, in 1903.[10] Marx surprisingly insists on the "unequal relation between the development of material production and the production of art" and raises the question of the exemption of art from historical relativity by the example of Greek art, which to him, as to most

Germans of the time, seemed of eternal timeless beauty. "In art it is well-known that certain periods of highest development stand in no direct relation with the general development of society, nor with the material basis and the skeleton structure of its organization. Witness the example of the Greeks as compared with the modern nations or even Shakespeare." "The difficulty," Marx admits, "is not grasping the idea that Greek art and epic are connected with certain forms of social developments. It rather lies in understanding why they still provide us with a source of aesthetic enjoyment and prevail in certain respects as the norm and unattainable models." Marx can only answer lamely that the charm of Greek art is the charm of childhood. "The Greeks were normal children. The charm their art has for us does not conflict with the primitive character of the social order from which it has sprung." [11] Historical relativism is saved by a dubious theory of the childhood of mankind and its persistent appeal. Marx himself apparently felt that he had not solved the question and broke off. When he wrote the "Vorwort" to the *Kritik der politischen Ökonomie* (published in 1859; it must be distinguished from the unprinted "Einführung"), he pronounced in general terms the theory of rigid economic determinism. "The modes of material life determine the social, political, and intellectual life processes in general." [12] The problem of timeless beauty was shelved.

In the same year Marx and Engels engaged in an epistolary debate with Ferdinand Lassalle (1825–64) which brought out more concretely what they expected from literature. Lassalle had sent his historical tragedy *Franz von Sickingen* to Marx; and Marx, in a letter of criticism recommended more "Shakspearisieren" than "Schillern," punning on Schiller's name, and disparaged the "transformation of individuals into mere mouthpieces of the time-spirit." He also criticized the choice of the hero, who, to Marx' thinking, was "a knight and hence a representative of a dying class," a "miserable fellow," and not a tragic hero.[13] In an even longer letter to Lassalle, Engels develops these two points, amidst some praise for individual scenes of the play. Lassalle's concept of drama seems to Engels "somewhat too abstract, not realistic enough." He misses a "Falstaffian background." The historical conflict should have been built on "a tragic collision between the historically necessary demand and its practically impossible realization." [14] The objections are made in terms of Hegelian aesthetics. Characters must be concrete universals, individual and representative; tragedy must be a conflict of equal historical forces. Lassalle, in a lengthy reply, quite rightly urged that the objections of his critics amount to his having written "a *Franz von Sickingen* rather than a *Thomas Münzer* or another tragedy from the Peasants' War." He sees also that Marx and Engels confuse fiction and reality, since what they say about the historical Sickingen does not apply to Lassalle's Sickingen in the play. Lassalle complains also that their concept of tragedy leaves no room for human freedom, hence for dramatic action. [15] Lassalle assumes Schiller's concept of tragedy; Marx and Engels believe in Hegel's necessary suprapersonal conflicts. Marx and Engels were right in condemning the play as a stillborn closet drama and in preferring Shakespeare to Schiller; yet it is hard to see why this exchange of letters should have become such a focal document in Marxist aesthetics. Marx and Engels merely say that Lassalle should have been a good poet and a better historian, should have written like Shakespeare, and should have understood the social conflicts within the German Reformation correctly.

After Marx' death Engels became a kind of oracle for letter writers and answered questions also on literary subjects. Only these letters lend support to modern Marxist theories of realism. The first of the letters, to Minna Kautsky (November 26, 1885), expresses dislike for overt propaganda in literature. The message (*Tendenz*) must arise from the situation and action. The concrete universal is recalled in the new guise of a "'type' who is at the same time a specific individual, a 'this' as old Hegel expresses himself." [16] An English letter to Miss Margaret Harkness (1888), commenting on her novel *The City Girl*, complains that "it is not quite realistic enough. Reality, to my mind, implies, besides truth to detail, the truthful reproduction of typical circumstances." Then Engels repeats his view that "the more the opinions of the author remain hidden, the better for the work of art." He gives the example of Balzac, whom he admires as "a far greater master of realism than all the Zolas *passés, présents et à venir.*" Engels knew that Balzac was politically a Legitimist. "His great work is a constant elegy on the irretrievable decay of good society; his sympathies are all with the class doomed to extinction. But for all that, his satire is never keener, his irony never bitterer than when he sets in motion the very men

and women with whom he sympathizes most deeply—the nobles."
Balzac was "compelled to go against his own class sympathies and
political prejudices" but "he saw the real men of the future where
for the time being, they alone were to be found—that I consider one
of the greatest triumphs of Realism, and one of the grandest features
in old Balzac." Engels' one illustration—Balzac's supposed admiration for the heroes of the Rue du Cloître-Saint-Merri, the abortive
uprising of June 5, 1832—is, however, unconvincing. In the relevant story "Un grand Homme de province à Paris" (1839), Balzac
draws a sharp distinction between his hero, Michel Chrestien, with
his symbolic name, and the revolutionaries whom he condemned.[17]
Still, Engels' letter formulates the theory of realism concerned with
"types" rather strikingly and suggests the possibility of a conflict
between an author's intention and performance, overt opinion and
latent involvement. In the eighties, needless to say, these views
were not new: their formulation by Taine, Zola, and Dobrolyubov
in the sixties had spread widely. Zola, in particular, had stressed
the conflict between Balzac's political opinions and his novelistic
practice in very similar terms.[18]

Several of Engels' letters written in the nineties express a definite
retreat from the straight economic determinism of the early theories.
In a letter to Joseph Bloch (September 21, 1890) Engels admits an
interaction between the superstructure and the economic base; he
even doubts that economic change is alone decisive in historical
change. Unforeseeable accidents, inner connections of things so
remote that they are impossible to prove, are admitted.[19] A last
letter, to Hans Starkenburg (January 25, 1894), again emphasizes
an interaction of forces: "The geographical base, the milieu sur-
rounding the social form from outside" is important, too. "Race
itself is an economic factor." "The further the particular sphere
which we are investigating is removed from the economic sphere
and approaches the sphere of pure abstract ideology, the more shall
we find it exhibiting accidents in its developments, the more will
its curve run in a zigzag." [20] A measure of freedom, in the sense of
looseness of connection, seems the final conclusion. Engels has
moved away from rigid economic determinism: he freely uses
Taine's triad of race, milieu, and moment.

The body of pronouncements on literature by Marx and Engels
is scattered, casual, and far from conclusive. It does not amount to

a theory of literature or even to a theory of the relations between literature and society. But the pronouncements are not thereby incoherent. They are held together by their general philosophy of history and show a comprehensible evolution—from early involvement in the polemical situation of the Germany of the thirties and forties, through a stage of rigid economic determinism, to a more mellow and tolerant attitude in the framework of late realism and naturalism. We cannot speak of a Marxist criticism of literature even in the three writers who late in the 19th century proclaimed themselves Marxists and wrote on literary subjects. Franz Mehring (1846–1919) in Germany and Georgi Plekhanov (1857–1918) in Russia tried to combine economic determinism with Darwinian evolutionism and many remnants of idealistic aesthetics. George Bernard Shaw (1856–1950) was a Marxist critic for a brief time, in his own peculiar way. In the 20th century Marxists have formulated a unified literary theory, which often appeals arbitrarily to one or the other stage of Marx' and Engels' evolution. But its roots are in the German situation of the thirties and forties. Present-day Marxist literary theory still shows traces of the strange medley of radical ideology, Hegelian dialectics, economic determinism, and realist typology found in the occasional pronouncements of its spiritual fathers.

RUSSIAN CRITICISM has a special interest for the student of criticism, not only because it throws a vivid light on the great Russian literature of the 19th century, but also because it was a kind of laboratory in which the most radical solutions to age-old problems were tried out. Most of these developments came late in the 19th and early in the 20th century. Some critics sought for the essence of literature in its philosophical and religious ideas, concentrating largely on the interpretation of Dostoevsky. In Dostoevsky's great antipode, Lev Tolstoy, we have a moralistic critic of the purest water and the boldest severity. Only early in the 20th century was the opposite extreme, formalism, worked out by a group of gifted students of literature, but their position had been prepared for in the 19th century by the work of the comparatist Alexander Veselovsky and the linguist Alexander Potebnya. Throughout the earlier part of the 19th century, however, a generally historical and sociological approach to literature was prevalent in Russia. In its Marxist version it has become the official Soviet creed and has made a profound impact everywhere. It was anticipated, in its political and social preoccupations, by the whole line of "radical" critics that began with Vissarion Belinsky in the thirties and continued with his three followers in the sixties, Nikolay Chernyshevsky, Nikolay Dobrolyubov, and Dmitri Pisarev. They represent in general the liberal and revolutionary opposition to Tsarism: but also socially conservative critics, such as Apollon Grigoriev, were basically concerned with an interpretation of literature as history or as the essence of the national mind.

The definition of these opposed positions, the drawing of sharp battle lines, was the result of the upheavals of the later 19th century. The early stages of Russian criticism, not remarkable in themselves, are rather dim echoes of French and German developments however important they were for Russian literary history.

For our purposes it seems sufficient to glance at the 18th century, when the first modern Russian poets introduced the teachings of French neoclassicism. Characteristically, the first modern Russian poet, Antiokh Kantemir (1709-44) complained, in 1739, that there is no Russian word for the French "critique," [1] and Vasily Tredyakovsky (1703-69), the second important figure in the history of Russian poetry, translated Boileau's *Art poétique* into Russian verse (1752). The greatest literary figure of the middle of the century, Mikhail Lomonosov (1711-65), a scientist and poet of sublime odes, elaborated the ancient theory of the three levels of style for the use of the Russian language: the high style was to draw on the Old Slavic vocabulary and the middle style on both Old Slavic and spoken Russian, while the low style was confined to Russian words.[2] Lomonosov saw a peculiar advantage in this recourse to two languages which allowed him to define the hierarchy of genres also stylistically. The aim of poetry with all these court poets was primarily didactic, patriotic, civic. The ode praising the victories of Russian arms was the highest genre; satire, though low, had its great function as a scourge of vice.

Slowly during the second half of the 18th century a shift from rigid French neoclassicism toward a more liberal "taste" was accomplished. A wider reading public and periodicals in the style of the *Spectator* came into being. Taste rather than the rules became the standard. As everywhere, the beginnings of historical interest can be traced: Nikolay Novikov (1744-1818) compiled *A Historical Dictionary of Russian Authors* (1772) which even mentioned a few writers before Peter the Great and tried to list as many nonaristocratic authors as possible.[3] But actual reviewing as an institution came very late to Russia: the great historian Nikolay Karamzin (1766-1826), who founded and edited the review *Vestnik Evropy* (The Messenger of Europe, 1802), declared in his program that "criticizing new Russian books is not a real necessity of our literature." [4] Criticism should praise and encourage, not judge: aesthetics is a doctrine of taste, and taste is ultimately mysterious. Karamzin knew German 18th-century writers such as Sulzer and even Platner.[5] The theoretical allegiance to French classicism weakened and with the first preromantic poet, Vasily Zhukovsky (1783-1852), who translated Gray, Bürger, Goethe, and Schiller, we are transplanted into the atmosphere of English and German ideas about poetry as feeling and imagination. Zhukovsky is one of the first Russians who attempt to characterize their predecessors: he wrote studies of the fable writer Krylov and of Kantemir's satires.[6]

But things became lively in Russian criticism only when the classic-romantic debate was introduced. Prince Pyotr Vyazemsky (1792–1878) expounded romanticism largely as freedom from rules. He wanted a literature that would be both popular and national, express the character and opinions of the nation, be free from the tyranny of rules, and have local color.[7] It was only logical that he should write an enthusiastic foreword to Pushkin's *Prisoner from the Caucasus* (1823).

Still, Alexander Pushkin (1799–1837), who emerged as by far the greatest poet of his time, was not far from wrong when he complained that "we have no criticism. . . . We have not a single commentary, not a single book of criticism." [8] He himself remained a practicing poet and engaged in criticism only occasionally, though it is possible to collect a wealth of literary opinions from his letters and though he wrote a few critical articles and left many more drafts, notes, and excerpts that testify to his avid thirst for literary knowledge. Pushkin was hardly a theorist, but one can in general describe his conception of the poet and the function of poetry. It is somewhat contradictory at first glance. It oscillates between assertions of the complete independence of the poet from his public and grand claims for the poet's guardianship over his people and his immortality descending through the ages. On the one hand, Pushkin expressed his contempt for the mob and chafed under censorship and the Tsar's supervision. He protests that the poet "is not obliged to give account to anybody." He can choose "the most inconspicuous subject." The aim of art "is not moral teaching but the depiction of the ideal." [9] In a letter to Zhukovsky, who wanted to know the purpose of the *Gypsies,* Pushkin answered, "The aim of poetry is poetry." [10] The introductory sketch to the *Egyptian Nights* (1835) obviously agrees with the topic of the improvisation: "the poet himself chooses the subject of his verse; the crowd has no right to command his inspiration." [11] On the other hand, the poet, as several of his most famous poems testify ("The Prophet," "The Poet"), is also a prophet and a priest: he is an inspired singer and thus, in the most exalted sense, the teacher of his nation and of

humanity. We need recall only the splendid version of Horace's
Exegi monumentum to realize how nobly Pushkin regarded his
mission. Clearly, fierce independence is the common denominator
of the two conceptions. Pushkin could hardly conceive of the poet
as an idle singer of an idle day, but neither could he think of him
as a mouthpiece of authority or the servant of the immediate com-
munal need. He rejected both aestheticism and didacticism.

In the literary debate of his time Pushkin sided with the romanticists, though his own art was steeped in the French 18th-century
tradition. Chénier, Parny, Voltaire were important models, and he
preserved a fondness for Boileau.[12] But then he "lost his wits" over
Byron, he glorified Shakespeare and Scott as the genuine poets and
great romantics.[13] He had his reservations toward the rising French
romantic school, though he showed interest in Stendhal and the
poetry of the young Sainte-Beuve.[14] He knew, however, little of the
German romantics. His was a clearly defined taste: a taste for what
preserved a continuity with the past in the romantic writers, with a
suspicion for the extravagant, the formless, and the grotesque. Pushkin lives up to his own definition of taste as "a feeling for symmetry
and harmony."[15] This is why he condemned Radishchev's work as
"mediocre," written in a "barbaric style." He has an "uneducated
contempt for the past, a weak-minded admiration for his own age,
a blind prejudice in favor of the new, and only superficial, limited
knowledge."[16] Pushkin had his reservations even against Belinsky,
the rising critic who was to exalt him to the pinnacle of Russian
literature. "If he would combine with the independence of his
opinions and his astuteness more learning, more reading, more
respect for the tradition, and more caution, if in short, he had more
maturity, we might have in him a really remarkable critic."[17]
Pushkin did not live to see him achieve this maturity.

VISSARION BELINSKY (1811–1848)

The first Russian critic of more than local importance was Vissarion Belinsky. As a matter of fact he is the most important critic
in the whole history of Russian literature; he has no serious rival in
scope or influence. He defined, as only a great critic can, the position
of Russian writers of his time. Pushkin, Gogol, and Lermontov owe
him their pre-eminence, in good part at least. He discerned the early
promise of Dostoevsky, Turgenev, Goncharov, and Nekrasov. His

courage and insight in rejecting the second-rate novelists of his time, his ruthless weeding out of the minor poets, his break with the 18th-century Russian "classics," his cool reception of the rediscovered Old Russian literature determined literary opinion for a century. Today, outside of Russia, where he is canonized almost as a saint, we may deplore the shortcomings and injustices of some of his views. We might disagree with his low ranking of Russian folklore, his underestimation of Russian 18th-century literature, his disparagement of some of the remarkable poets around Pushkin, his excessive praise for such contemporary celebrities as Walter Scott, George Sand, James Fenimore Cooper, and Béranger.[1] But we cannot doubt his eminence as a practical critic and his role in Russian literary and social history.

Belinsky's position as a theorist of literature in a general history of criticism seems to me, however, far less eminent. On questions of theory he must be considered a follower of German romantic criticism, of the whole body of aesthetic thought elaborated by Herder, Goethe, Schiller, the Schlegels, Schelling, and Hegel. He is not an adherent of any single one of these authors, however. He does not share, in all its consequences, the exact view of any one of them. For instance, he cannot be described as a strict Hegelian, since he does not share Hegel's view of the imminent demise of art and has no sympathy for his nostalgic exaltation of the Greeks and Greek sculpture as the highest summit of art. Nor can one distinguish neat periods in Belinsky's critical development: there was no definitely Fichtean, Schellingian, Hegelian, or Feuerbachian period in his criticism. From the very beginning of his writing, from the *Literary Reveries* (1834) to the last annual survey of Russian literature (1847), Belinsky uses the same categories, concepts, and procedures, the same basic theoretical idiom whatever his shifting emphasis and whatever his political convictions. Only in the last five years of his life can one discern a definite change. And even this change occurs in the same tradition and runs exactly parallel to the change that the followers of German speculative thought went through both in Germany and in other countries. Belinsky's evolution is, in this respect, roughly similar to that of Arnold Ruge, De Sanctis, Carlyle, or even Taine, who all absorbed the romantic conceptions and later modified them in favor of what they considered a closer approach to empirical reality, to facts, to science, to national and social needs of the time. I cannot see on what grounds Belinsky, at least in his critical thought, can be described as a "materialist" or even a "realist" in the sense in which the French began to use the term as a literary slogan after 1857.

The problem of the exact sources of Belinsky's fundamental conceptions seems difficult to solve, for it is often impossible to distinguish between his German sources with precision. The problem, moreover, has been obscured by constant assertions that he knew no German whatever. This ignorance of German must be taken with a grain of salt, however; as a student Belinsky gave German lessons; he owned a German set of Goethe and tells about working through Goethe's *Wilhelm Meister* with a dictionary.[2] Yet one need not assume a direct acquaintance with the original German texts to see that he had easy access to their ideas. There were Russian translations of several basic and secondary texts. Belinsky owned and annotated Friedrich Schlegel's *Geschichte der alten und neuen Literatur* in Russian translation;[3] he read Bachmann's *Kunstwissenschaft,* a Kantian treatise; he read an account of Ast, a follower of Schelling, and he knew and was—for a time—enthusiastic about Heinrich Theodor Rötscher, a rather second-rate Hegelian.[4] Besides, Russian writings of that time were full of echoes of German ideas. Belinsky's most direct "teacher" was Nadezhdin, who knew Schelling and the Schlegels well. A friend, Mikhaili Katkov, lent him his notes on Hegel's aesthetics.[5] To these we must add the oral sources: his friends Stankevich and Bakunin were enthusiastic Hegelians. In short, the atmosphere was fairly charged with these ideas.[6]

If only because he wrote most often on Russian topics, Belinsky is not verbally close to German sources. He comes closer when he works on a project of a "Theoretical and Critical Course of Russian Literature" (1841), of which only fragments were published and mostly long after his death.[7] Whenever Belinsky is forced by his scheme to work out aesthetic generalities at the highest level, or when he tries to develop a coherent theory of genres, he falls back on German sources and German formulas. He is also closely dependent on them whenever he surveys world history, or when he pronounces on classical antiquity, the Middle Ages, or the Orient, topics with which he could not have had any firsthand acquaintance. Among all the Germans Belinsky follows Rötscher most closely, especially a paper "Das Verhältnis der Philosophie der Kunst und

der Kritik zum einzelnen Kunstwerk" (1837).[8] His interpretation
of Faust's descent to the Mothers is closely dependent on Rötscher,
and his character sketch of Hamlet (1838) is quite Hegelian in
terminology and conception.[9]

We shall trace the development of Belinsky's ideas by looking at
his most famous articles. The first well-known series, *Literary
Reveries* (1834), proclaims that literature should be the expression
of the national spirit, the symbol of the inner life of a nation, the
physiognomy of a nation.[10] This was a concept already familiar in
Russia, imported from Germany: Friedrich Schlegel's *History of
Ancient and Modern Literature* opens with a similar declaration.[11]
The whole conception is central to romantic literary historiography
and belongs to the whole ideology of romantic nationalism. Belinsky, starting with this concept, gives a negative point to his survey
of older Russian literature: the Russians hitherto do not have a
literature that truly expresses the national spirit. Up till Pushkin at
least, Russian literature has been imitative of Western European
literature, has been bookish, derivative, artificial. It has produced
great isolated talents, but no continuous literary tradition. Everywhere the contrast of "art" and "nature" which runs through
German discussions since Herder is implied or restated in highly
romantic terms. "Literature," says Belinsky, "is not created; it
creates itself like language and customs, independently of the will
and knowledge of people." [12] But while Herder in a similar situation, in reaction against the Frenchified neoclassical literature of
Germany, recommended a return to the distant past, to folklore and
myth, Belinsky assumes a skeptical attitude toward Old Russian
literature and Slavic folklore in general. Later, mostly around the
year 1841, he learned to admire some of its qualities and even wrote
appreciative reviews of the *byliny*, the Igor lay and folk songs.[13]
But Belinsky never wanted to set up folk poetry as a model for
present-day literature. Rather, most often, he describes oral literature in a derogatory way—as archaic, primitive, obsolete, artistically uncouth and clumsy. He thought Lermontov's "Lay of the
Merchant Kalashnikov" worth all the old *byliny* put together.[14]
This largely (though not completely) negative attitude toward folklore and Old Russian literature must, in part, be ascribed to the
polemical situation of the time when the Slavophiles and conserv-
atives in general were exalting the old literature as the great source

of national pride and the true model of modern Russian literature. But Belinsky also held genuinely aesthetic and historical convictions on the limitations of folk poetry. He felt strongly its involvement in the serf civilization from which he wanted Russia to emerge into the light of freedom. Belinsky was not alone in this point of view. In Germany the Schlegels took exactly the same position. Though greatly interested in the *Nibelungen,* they rejected the attempts of the Grimms and other Teutonizers to cut off Germany from the Western tradition and argued that folk poetry belongs to an irrecoverable past.[15]

Still, Belinsky concedes the success of what today would be called local color realism. The Russians, he says, understand nationality to be "the reproduction of scenes from Russian life." They can produce these and do it well. But that does not mean that they have developed a peculiar Russian national spirit, one that would manifest itself in any kind of subject matter and would have the power to assimilate it. The Russians could not produce anything as national as the Frenchified Greeks of classical French tragedy or the Germanized Iphigenia of Goethe. Pushkin's "Prisoner of Caucasus," he argues, is merely picturesque; it could have been written by a foreigner.[16] Still, he recognizes something truly national in *Eugene Onegin* and *Boris Godunov,* without, however, trying to define this quality. Belinsky constantly emphasizes this difference between folklore and nationality. He argues against two things: against the bookish derivative aristocratic literature of the 18th century and against the popular folklore and local color nationalism of the Russian romanticists.

His own ideal of literature is, from the very beginning of his writings, suggested by the terms national, genuine, natural, and real. But what is meant by "naturalness" and "reality"? Surely not anything, at least in these early writings, that even remotely resembles later 19th-century realism. Belinsky speaks of French romanticism as a "return to naturalness," [17] obviously thinking of the overthrow of what seems to him the artificial classicism of the French.

In the next important article after *Reveries,* "On the Russian Short Story and the Stories of Gogol" (1836), Belinsky takes up Friedrich Schlegel's distinction between ideal and real poetry,[18] exalting Shakespeare and Scott as the two great representatives of "real" poetry. Shakespeare, he says, "reconciled poetry with real life" and Scott, "the second Shakespeare, achieved the union with life." [19] Truth, reality, means here "essential truth," inner reality, the truth of imagination. There is no limitation set on the poet's themes and devices. Belinsky praises Caliban in Shakespeare's *Tempest* and is in raptures over the dream in Gogol's *Nevsky Prospekt*.[20] He exalts the "objective" poet who reproduces and mirrors the universe in all its totality and, comparatively, disparages the subjective poet, just as the Schlegels had exalted Goethe against Schiller and had put Shakespeare at the pinnacle of fame as the impartial godlike creator. Belinsky echoes these views: Shakespeare is the new Proteus; he has no ideals, no sympathy. He is the unconscious poet-thinker, presenting a passionless mirror of reality.[21] Creation should be purposeless with purpose, unconscious with consciousness, says Belinsky, repeating the paradoxical formulas of Kant and Schelling. The poet cannot create on demand, by his individual will. Creation is a free activity, meaning free of calculation or reasoning, even "visionary, somnambulic." [22] Belinsky praises Gogol's story "The Old World Landowners" for *not* being copied from reality, but "gained by feeling in the moment of poetic discovery." [23] A primary task of the artist is to create types, figures, which, though concrete individuals, will still have universal significance. Hamlet, Othello, Shylock, and Faust are Belinsky's foreign examples; to these he adds the main characters from Griboedov's *Woe from Wit* and Gogol's lieutenant Pirogov, in *Nevsky Prospekt*, who seems to him, oddly enough, "a type of types," a symbol, a "mystical myth." [24] The Schlegels and Schelling had praised Hamlet, Don Quixote, and Faust in such terms, and so had Charles Nodier, in France.[25] Belinsky stayed with the problems raised by these two articles all his life.

Belinsky developed his critical system (if we can speak of one) in two directions. First, he saw the work of art with increasing emphasis as a completely self-contained whole, a unity of form and content, a "sensuous expression of the Idea," in Hegel's phrase. At the same time he saw it increasingly in a temporal context, relentlessly pushed forward by the stream of history. The historical point of view is implied in the concept of literature as the expression of society. But only in his articles on Lermontov (1841) was he to embrace what I should call the mystique of time.

For a while the historical point of view recedes. In the article on

"Menzel as a Critic of Goethe" (1840) Belinsky attacks contemporaneity, the slogan prominent with the French and Italians of *être
de son temps*. "The contents of art," he now asserts, "are not the
problems of the day, but those of the ages, not the interests of a
country, but of the world, not the fate of parties but of mankind."[26]
Art, they say, should serve society. "If you insist, it does so by
expressing its self-knowledge, but it does exist for itself, has an aim
in itself." [27] Art is social, yet it serves society by serving itself.[28] The
relation between art and morality is similarly solved by the proclamation on that "what is artistic is also moral." Belinsky recognizes
that the writer may violate the moral conventions of his society, but
he cannot violate morality itself.[29] Similarly, art and truth, art and
reality are identified. Art is truth, yet a different kind of truth. As
the next article, that on Griboedov's *Woe from Wit* (1840), states:
"Art is truth in representation, not in abstract thought." The poet
"thinks in images." [30]

Belinsky's concept of reality, at this time at least, is still quite
remote from materialism or even empiricism. Reality, he says
expressly, is the spiritual world, the world of ideas. Everything particular, contingent, irrational is unreal. "Man drinks, eats, dresses—
this is the world of phantoms, but man feels, thinks, knows himself
to be the organ, the vessel of spirit, a finite particle in the general
and infinite—and this is the world of reality." [31] Modern poetry is
the poetry of reality, the poetry of life.[32] This is Belinsky's formula,
which refers to the essential spiritual reality and, in practice, to the
works of the writers he most admires: Shakespeare, Goethe, Scott,
Byron, Cooper abroad; Pushkin and Gogol at home. He always
emphasizes that the poet must create something universal and
typical in which everything contingent is left out.[33] The work of art
forms a self-contained whole, a world, a totality.

At this point in his development, Belinsky uses the category of
wholeness and coherence as a standard of judgment constantly and
with great effect. In the analysis of Gogol's *Inspector General* he
shows how Gogol's comedy is closely organized, forming a totality,
revolving around one central idea and one central figure. "The
Inspector is the source from which everything flows and to which
everything returns." [34] The whole play is "more than a mirror of
reality, it is more like reality than reality itself: it is an artistic
reality." [35] Gogol's comedy is then contrasted with Griboedov's *Woe*

from Wit, much to the disadvantage of the latter. *Woe from Wit* is a mere series of pictures. It is not a real comedy but a satire whose aim is to ridicule a specific local society. In Belinsky's view satire is not art at all, because you cannot be angry and creative at the same time.[36] Griboedov lacks objectivity: the play ends with lyrical outbursts of subjective anger. It should be called not *Woe from Wit* but *Woe from Stubbornness.*[37]

This general point of view is preserved through the next articles, though Belinsky introduces almost casually ideas that later became destructive of the standard of artistic objectivity. The two articles on Lermontov (1840–41) repeat the view that a work of art is an organic whole, a self-enclosed world. There are no beauties and faults in a work of art: whoever grasps the whole sees only the one beauty. Where there is organization there is life, and where there is life there is spirit.[38] He expounds at length the idea that a work of art grows like a plant, an analogy that had been a favorite with the Germans since Herder.[39]

The review of Lermontov's *Poems* (1841) asserts the poet's instinctive creativeness and the superior reality of poetry. It is even extravagant on the latter point. Reality, often dark and ugly, appears illuminated and harmonized in the poet's vision.[40] Belinsky picks up the Kantian distinction between understanding and reason in order to exalt the poet's higher reason. Art purifies reality.[41] Naturalism is expressly disparaged: the hero of a novel need not be shown having dinner each day. "One can very naturally describe a drinking party, an execution, the death of a drunkard who fell into a cesspool—but such descriptions lack a rational idea and aim." [42] Only rational reality exists for the artist: he transforms ordinary reality by his ideals. Poetry, Belinsky declaims rapturously, is the quintessence of life, the poet is the organ of universal life; he lives everything, becomes everything.[43] It is ludicrous to ask him to serve current needs. He does not imitate nature, but rather competes with her: his creations come from the same source by the same process. Art is higher than nature as every conscious and free act is higher than an unconscious and unwilled one.[44] These pages represent a complete repertory of German romantic phrases, with a definite touch of Schelling at a time when Belinsky is supposed to have been in his Hegelian period. The work of art is an organism, art is its own aim, but art is also an insight into higher reality, a kind of

knowledge but nonrational knowledge. Art is a parallel and analogue of nature; the poet is both inspired and highly self-conscious,
completely free. The paradoxes of German dialectical idealism
could not be restated more fully and bluntly.

Strangely enough, in the very same articles Belinsky declares what
in itself is not yet contradictory to this position but contains the
germ of its repudiation. Incidentally and without apparently seeing
all the consequences, he introduces the view that a work of art is the
result of the historical process. He even shifts responsibility for a
work of art away from the artist and his creativity to the age and
makes the poet completely dependent on the temporal constellation.
Speculating on the sequence of literary genres in the manner of the
Germans, he assumes a necessary order of development from the
lyric through the epic to the drama, not only in history but in the
development of every single poet. Lermontov must come to write
tragedies, Pushkin, if he had lived, would have become a great
novelist. "Every national art has its historical development, which
determines the character and kind of activity of the poet." [45] "The
greater the poet—the more he belongs to the community in which
he was born—the closer the development, tendency, and character
of his talent will be to the historical evolution of society." [46] But this
evolution, contrary to the ideal proclaimed only a few pages before,
is now conceived as a progress toward reflection and subjectivity.
The assumption is made (though never argued) that the progress of
society and literature must be toward reflection and subjectivity,
contemporaneity and immediate relevance. Today objective poetry
is hardly possible. Belinsky expressly recants his article on "Menzel
as a Critic of Goethe" by deploring Goethe's lack of historical and
social interests, his satisfied acceptance of reality. That is why the
less artistic but more humane poetry of Schiller has found greater
resonance than Goethe's.[47] Subjectivity and contemporaneity are
now accepted, at least as a historical necessity. Belinsky still tries to
reconcile this new situation with his dominant theories. A great
poet speaking of himself speaks of the general, speaks of humanity.[48]
A Russian poet expressing a historical moment of Russian society
becomes truly national, becomes one with the people.[49] Somewhat
tortuously, all these arguments are put forward to justify Lermontov's poetry of despair and revolt.

Still, the evolution in the direction of a defense of subjective, contemporaneous poetry was by no means complete. The chapters Belinsky prepared for a book on poetics in 1841 show hardly any traces of the new views. "The Division of Poetry into Genres" is only a rather jumbled rehearsal of the ideas of German critics. We hear even of the "poetry of poetry," a term beloved by Friedrich Schlegel and Jean Paul.[50] We get the Schlegels' view of the sculpturesque character of Greek tragedy, objective, eternally beautiful; [51] and we arrive at a glorification of Scott, the Homer of Christian Europe.[52] Didactic poetry is excluded from genuine poetry.[53] A theory of tragedy is outlined in orthodox Hegelian terms: *Antigone* demonstrates the triumph of the eternal and general over the individual and particular.[54] Belinsky is even more violent than the most nationalistic Germans in his rejection of French literature: the French have no poetry; their drama belongs rather to a history of fashions than of art.[55] We are told that "the nature of poetry was consciously developed only by German thought." [56]

The next piece, "The Idea of Art," is completely Hegelian, though the famous phrase (used by Belinsky before) that "art is thinking in images" can, in this form, be found also in August Wilhelm Schlegel and in a little known German aesthetician, Trahndorff.[57] Belinsky expounds the Hegelian view of history, that mankind passes through three stages: myth, art, and thought. The essay concludes with a translation of Rötscher's farfetched interpretation of Faust's descent to the Mothers.

The essay "On the General Meaning of the Word Literature" is much more original, as it tries to draw distinctions between the current Russian terms in view of a history of Russian literature. Belinsky distinguishes oral literature (*slovesnost*) from manuscript literature before the introduction of printing (*pisemnost*), and both of them from modern printed literature (*literatura*). But modern printed literature does not embrace all books. Literature is only what expresses a historically developing national spirit.[58] The national spirit excludes everything contingent. It is the dialectical movement of the Idea. Even aberrations from sound taste, if they are general, are considered as expressing the spirit of a time and nation. French tragedy under Louis XIV and French romanticism are Belinsky's examples of typical bad taste.[59] Everything turns on the peculiarity of a national literature: its basic view of the world. Belinsky retracts the conclusion of *Literary Reveries* that there is no genuinely Russian literature, but he still insists that it is purely local; important historically, not aesthetically; a mere promise for the future.[60] The next piece of the series, "A General View of Popular Poetry," asserts that nationality is the alpha and omega of the aesthetics of our time; that each nation has its own logic; that a nation's literature should express its personality; that all nations should ultimately form one ideal personality—humanity.[61] Romantic nationalism leading to humanism is restated here fervently.

In the articles on Gogol's *Dead Souls* (1842) a change in Belinsky's taste can be observed and with it a new shift of emphasis in theory, though at first this is only slight and verbal. Gogol is hailed as being the first who looked boldly and straight at Russian reality.[62] Belinsky defends a naturalistic detail in *Dead Souls* that had elicited much horrified comment: the little scene in which a sentry kills a louse on his collar. Gogol seems to Belinsky a more significant writer than Pushkin, because he is more social, more in the spirit of his time.[63] The emphasis on nationality is strong. Gogol contributes to national self-knowledge; he cannot be "higher than his era and his country." [64] He is purely local and thus incomprehensible outside of Russia. Belinsky does not think of Gogol only as a naturalistic painter of Russian reality. He even denies that *Dead Souls* is a satire and emphasizes its subjectivity, its high lyrical pathos.[65] He asserts that poetry is an expression of reality, but expression means an idealization of the appearances of reality, a bringing-out of their general significance.[66]

An article commenting on a "Speech on Criticism" (1842) by Alexander Nikitenko develops Belinsky's theoretical position at this intermediate stage. Reality, he proclaims, is the watchword of the contemporary world; our age rejects "art for art's sake." [67] The great writers of the time are Scott, Cooper, and a new star, George Sand, the first poetic glory of the contemporary world.[68] But Belinsky's outlook has not yet become completely relativistic and historistic. He still recognizes that art, while subject to the process of historical evolution, is concerned also with the eternal truths of existence, and that in criticism there is first an aesthetic judgment, which decides whether a work of art is worthy of the attention of historical criticism.[69] At this time, Belinsky sees no conflict between historical and aesthetic criticism, for each requires the other and cannot exist without it; [70] nor does he see any conflict between aesthetic and social demands on a writer. He declares somewhat blandly that it is easy to reconcile art with service to the community. The poet must be a citizen, a son of his society and age; he must fuse his desires with that of his society. For this he needs sympathy, love, a sound practical feeling for truth.[71] The serious conflicts between society and art of the next hundred years are not foreseen, even as a possibility.

Belinsky's theory of criticism remains unchanged for a while longer, still focused on the concept of organicity. A review of Baratynsky's poems (1842) attacks the older atomistic criticism of faults and exalts the new criticism that judges a work of art as a whole, discovers its idea, and shows the close union of content and form. The critic should trace the mind of the poet in his works; he should discern the leading idea, the dominant mood; he should discover and clarify the poet's inner vision, his *pathos*.[72] An article on Derzhavin (1842) begins with a new proclamation that art belongs to the sphere of absolute knowledge and has its own eternal laws.[73] Thus the conversion to a relativistic point of view was not yet complete.

A curious passage that praises "prose" as having killed "romanticism" in Pushkin's development illustrates how deceptive Belinsky's phrasing can be and how false it would be to infer from this a conversion to realism at that time. One might think that "prose" here means something like realism; surely it must mean abandoning verse in favor of prose. But *Mozart and Salieri, The Covetous Knight, Galub,* and *The Stone Guest,* all in verse, are declared to be "pure prose." Prose, Belinsky says, means "richness of inner poetic content, masculine maturity and strength of mind." [74] The "prose" period of Russian literature, praised by Belinsky, is simply all Russian literature since about 1829—that is, all literature that is not sentimental or romantic in the narrow sense in which Belinsky used the term. But "prose" is not realism: it is "the real fact put through the imagination of the poet, heightened by the light of a universal meaning, as a portrait on which the man represented may be more like himself than on a daguerrotype." [75]

It is in the first article of a long series of papers devoted to the works of Pushkin (1843) that Belinsky embraced the mystique of time and progress completely. He still agrees that the aim of criticism is to distinguish between the eternal and the temporal, the

artistic and the historical, but he now assigns this task not to the
critic or to aesthetics but to the "historical movement of society
itself." The more alive a phenomenon, the more will the knowledge
of it depend on the movement of society itself.[76] This view is used
to buttress the main argument of the articles; Pushkin belongs to a
bygone and superseded stage of Russian literature and society.
That is why the public became indifferent to Pushkin after his first
successes. "Meanwhile time progressed, and with it progressed life,
giving birth to new events, giving new facts to knowledge and lifting
it on the road of development." Lermontov thus satisfies a superior
time, a time superior in its demands and characters to that expressed
by the poetry of Pushkin. The assumption is that of an automatic
fated progress, a higher and higher rising of the wave of the future.
Even critical opinion can form itself only by time and from time.
Belinsky admits, or rather boasts, that he could not have taken this
position toward Pushkin before. He himself has changed with the
times and does not envy "finished natures." [77] Again he recants the
argument of the *Literary Reveries*. Russia, he now says, has a literature, a vital organic development, with a history. Again he surveys
older Russian literature without seriously modifying his severe
judgment about the figures of the 18th and early 19th century,
though seeing them now as links in a chain, or rather as stepping-
stones leading up to the temple of contemporary Russian poetry.
Their failures are excused on the ground that they could not help
being what they were, as they lived in an age that cramped and
hampered their development. Derzhavin is pronounced a born poet,
a great talent, though he did not produce and could not have produced a single perfect work of art, because of the historical situation
of the time. The social life of the age could not yield rich materials
for him.[78] Sentimentalism is considered to have been a useful step
toward an understanding of poetry. Karamzin, though disparaged
by absolute standards, is declared to have achieved something
genuinely great. He is an example of a man who lived in vital relation with his age, while other men perished in their struggle with
the spirit of the time.[79] Similarly, romanticism, which Belinsky
defines narrowly as subjectivism, was a historical necessity. But man
has another world than that of the heart: he must deal with the
world of history and social activity.[80] Responsibility for art is thus
put on society. The materials readymade for the poet's use by society

have become the determinants of his work. On the one hand, there
is nature producing talents without asking whether they are needed
or not. On the other hand, there is society, which must produce a
poetic reality to make poetry possible.[81] Rather naively, Belinsky
declaims about the Greeks who saw beautiful men at every step in the
streets, and the Italians of the Middle Ages who had Madonna-like
women as models for their painting. "Without beautiful models
there is no painting," says Belinsky and analogizes about poetry.
Pushkin "appeared in a time when it was for the first time possible
to have poetry in Russia." [82] This type of pronouncement may seem
merely a comfortable hindsight, an irrefutable but meaningless
assertion that things could not have been different. But it also
implies not only trust in the stream of history but praise for Russian
life and its awakening toward freedom. The growth of a genuine
Russian society after the shock of the Napoleonic invasion made
genuine poetry possible.

In his discussion of Pushkin's development Belinsky does not
actually pursue very far the idea of a complete dependence of the
poet on the social situation and the materials offered by society.
Rather he attempts to define the prevailing mood, the general
pathos of Pushkin's poetry, which he finds in a "light, clear, consoling sadness." [83] He repeats his romantic formulas about organic
form and asserts the need of one pathos, one spirit, which should
permeate all the works of a writer.[84] In the later articles he again
tries to define this general spirit of Pushkin's work, but succeeds less
well than before. Pushkin is first of all an artist who could take anything and make it beautiful.[85] He is a meditative rather than a
reflective or philosophical poet.[86] He looks at everything with love
and good will; he does not reject or curse anything.[87] He is a national
Russian, but one cannot define this quality.[88] Belinsky reflects
unfavorably on Pushkin's aristocratic pride, his contempt for the
crowd, his trust in supernatural inspiration and in the apartness of
the poet. He can conclude that Pushkin belongs to a bygone age. "A
large part of his works has lost interest: it lacks answers to the urgent,
painful problems of the present day." [89] The audience, in Pushkin's
later years, rightly asked for more moral and philosophical questions in poetry.[90]

The articles surveying Pushkin's writings, one by one, apply this
general point of view. Pushkin is, like Goethe, the poet of a vanished

age, an age of pure artistry. The discussion of the individual works brings out both the best and the worst in Belinsky's methods and displays his extreme unevenness as a critic: his incalculable sudden flashes of insight next to lapses into mere didacticism and moralizing. Thus Pushkin's *Gypsies* is used as a peg on which to hang a lecture about jealousy as a vice not worthy of a well-educated man. Othello, to Belinsky's mind, is possible only in the barbarous age in which Shakespeare lived.[91] *Poltava* is used to demonstrate the theory that an epic poem is impossible in this age; *Poltava* fails by a standard of genre criticism. It is not a proper epic—in the sense that it depicts a truly national event—it only tries to be one. The private loves of Mazeppa and Maria disturb the focus.[92] *Onegin,* highly praised as a historical poem, is considered dated, old-fashioned. "But it is not the poet's fault that everything in Russia moves so quickly. If the poem did not seem obsolete, that would only show that an imaginary society was depicted in it. But would it be worth talking about such a poem?"[93] A definite local and temporal color is here considered to be a sign of obsolescence. At the same time, Belinsky asserts the inevitability of such obsolescence by saying "that genius is never ahead of its time, but always divines its content and meaning."[94] He commits one of his worst critical blunders in his characterization of Tatyana as a "moral embryo," and "Egyptian statue, immobile, heavy, fettered."[95] In the name of a romantic religion of passion and a romantic criticism of conventional marriage à la George Sand, Tatyana is lectured for her final refusal of Onegin.[96] As so frequently, Belinsky confuses fiction and life and ignores the requirements of a plot and thus of his old standards of wholeness and coherence in order to have a pretext for a sermon on the backwardness of Russian womanhood.

Belinsky returns to literary criticism when he discusses *Boris Godunov* (1845). He argues that it is not a drama but an epic poem in dialogue form; it contains neither passions nor conflicts nor events. Godunov is a melodramatic villain tortured by bad conscience. He is honest and mean, a hero and a coward all at once, in short, a mass of contradictions. Every scene is independent; the play lacks totality (*l'ensemble*), Godunov's character is a mosaic of unrelated traits.[97] Insofar as it is judgment by a theory of genres and standards of organicity and coherence, this is genuine criticism. But Belinsky soon spoils it by ignoring the distinction between poetry

and history. He absolves Pushkin of the responsibility of failing to
write a proper drama of Russian history, laying the blame not on
the conditions of the stage in Pushkin's day but rather on the time
of Boris Godunov himself. Russian history, he argues, had then a
quietistic character. There were no developing personalities; the
family was everything.[98] Godunov left no trace behind him in
history; he was a talented man who wrongly considered himself a
genius, an upstart possessing neither ideas nor principles.[99] Belinsky, with great assurance, pronounces on the psychology of these
dim historical persons: for instance, the fine scene between the
Pretender and Maria, his Polish love, is criticized on the ground that
love for a woman was not in the character of the historical Dmitri.[100]
But how could Belinsky or anybody else be certain of this? And even
if it were attested by historical evidence, what could it matter to
Pushkin? He could have devised a fictional character to feel passion
for a woman if he had wanted it that way. It is worth looking at such
a detail of Belinsky's criticism to see the sudden shift from romantic
critical standards to a reliance on outside, inartistic, preartistic
reality in history or society. Belinsky deteriorated, to my mind, as a
critic the more he succumbed to his propensity to worship "time"
and "progress," to his inclination to regard "reality" and "society"
as fixed elements outside a writer's work which were to be erected
into "laws," in practice, into rigid yardsticks for art.

This shift led to a loosening of Belinsky's former firm grasp of the
principle of organicity. In the article "Thoughts and Remarks on
Russian Literature" (1846) he breaks up the unity of form and content by declaring that a Russian poet, however great his talent, can
"compete with a European poet only in form, but not in the content
of his poetry." The poet receives his content from the life of his
nation. Its importance depends on the historical position of his
nation's life and not on the poet himself and his talent.[101] The
unpronounced implication is that Russian life is miserable today
and thus its literature must be poor. Let us change Russian life and
the literature will be great. A frequently quoted passage prophesy-
ing Russia's greatness a hundred years later asserts a fervent faith in
progress, both social and literary.[102]

Belinsky gets into great difficulties when he tries to apply this
idea to foreign literatures: he must now praise French literature,
for he admires the French as the authors of the Great Revolution

and the July revolution and hence as the standard-bearers of contemporary progress. He has to recognize that French literature reflects its social and historical life much more closely than German. But his fixed taste revolts against the implications of his theory: he has long ago declared French classical tragedy to be non-art; he has expressed his profound contempt for the sensational literature of the French romantics. He now saves his theory by a most awkward maneuver. Corneille's tragedies, he says, are "theoretically ugly," but they do contain the inner power and pathos that inspired Mirabeau. Not a single comedy of Molière's can withstand aesthetic criticism: each is contrived rather than created. One must, however, admit that the French have a vital theater.[103] Belinsky thus introduces a distinction between good art and bad art that still may be socially more beneficent. He seems to imply that we should prefer bad art if it has a good social effect. But this is not said in so many words, and Belinsky falls back on his trust in time. "Of all critics the greatest, the one fullest of genius, the most infallible is time." [104] He does not see that time means, after all, only the aggregate judgments of critics (including himself) and readers.

The last two annual surveys of Russian literature, those for 1846 and 1847, formulate his final doctrines most memorably. He now uses the term "natural school" [105] for Russian literature since Gogol and emphasizes naturalistic standards of lifelikeness. Against the current criticism that the naturalists depict only the negative side of Russian life, he holds out the hope that with the improvement of Russian society it will be possible to show also its positive sides.[106] He definitely rejects the fantastic as an artistic device when he criticizes Dostoevsky's *Double*. "It can have its place only in lunatic asylums, not in literature. It is the business of doctors and not of poets." [107] He even goes so far as to demand the "closest possible resemblance of the persons described with their models in real life." [108] Gogol is praised for concentrating all his attention on the crowd, the mass, the ordinary people.[109] The inundation of literature by peasant types is defended. The peasant is a human being; we pity him. The Redeemer has come for all men; and literature, as the expression of society, "facilitated the appearance in society of this movement for the emancipation of the serfs rather than merely reflected it: literature anticipated it rather than merely succeeded in keeping abreast of it." [110] Belinsky seems to give up his former view of literature as a reflection of society, which it can never transcend or outstrip. He seems to assign it a role of leadership, even of anticipatory divination. The strength of modern art, he finds, is in nobly undertaking to serve the interests of society.[111] Naturalism is praised as a movement toward reality, averse to the fantastic and ghostly.[112] Again, he asserts his oddly phrased confidence in progress: "One can go only forward, never back." Development is improvement, success, progress.[113]

In these two articles Belinsky is preoccupied with the rising social novel. He had welcomed Dostoevsky's *Poor People* as a novel of social protest, but was disappointed with the fantastic *Double* and the puzzling and obscure *Landlady*.[114] He has much to say in praise of realistic novels, stories and sketches by Grigorovich, Veltman, Dal', and others. He praises Herzen's novel *Who Is to Blame?* for the profundity of its thought.[115] Along with his whole age, he grossly overpraises George Sand and even Eugène Sue, though he sees the shortcomings of the latter.[116] He has come to look at Goethe with the eyes of his recent German critics: as a representative German, alienated from society, indifferent to society and history, a mere artist, as Pushkin too had come to seem.[117]

One can understand how these last pronouncements have largely determined the image of Belinsky in the eyes of posterity. Soviet criticism and the whole tradition of radical thought in Russia since Chernyshevsky finds here the earliest local justification of its general point of view. But the image is grossly simplified. It ignores the bulk of Belinsky's earlier writings, which we have described above, and it ignores the many reservations even in these last two articles. Such passages in the latter writings may be viewed merely as survivals of his older views: I should prefer to regard them as evidence that Belinsky had not lost his basic sensibility and taste, his grasp of the nature of art, or even his original insight into the relations of literature and reality, literature and society.

Belinsky did not become simply the propounder of a naturalistic art that would serve a specific social or didactic purpose, such as the emancipation of the serfs, or more generally the freeing of Russia from autocracy. In his attack on the doctrine of art for art's sake he recognizes that "art must be first art and only afterwards can it be the expression of the spirit and drift of the society of a given age." He rejects what seems to him both bad extremes: art for art's sake and didacticism. He argues that pure art is a dreamy abstraction that has never existed anywhere.[118] "To deny art the right of serving public interests means debasing it, not raising it, for that would mean depriving it of its most vital force, that is, the Idea, and would make it an object of sybaritic pleasure, a plaything of lazy idlers." [119] Belinsky, one sees, does not argue against the existence of a realm of aesthetics, against the autonomy of art as understood by Kant and Schiller. They never would have doubted its great role in world history and would have never thought of it as purely sensual pleasure. What Belinsky is arguing against is rather an ornamental, hedonistic view of art as it may have been propounded by Gautier or simply, instinctively, and crudely by defenders of the pleasures of poetry, music, dancing, and painting in Russia. Belinsky understood very well the danger of didacticism. It is merely instructive: cold, dry, and dead. "With whatever beautiful ideas a poem is filled and however much it deals with contemporary problems, if it has no poetry in it, it can contain neither beautiful ideas nor any problems." [120] "Purpose" must be located in the heart, not in the head alone. Over and over again, and even in his very last article, Belinsky emphasizes the difference between art and science or philosophy. The poet speaks in images and pictures, shows things and does not prove them.[121] Belinsky by no means thinks of "naturalism" merely in terms of accuracy or even of insight into social realities. He sees that in a work of art, "reality must have passed through imagination," that imagination must create "something whole, complete, unified, and self-contained." [122] In the old manner of his dialectics he even admits the role of personality in art. While objectivity, "the ability to present the facts of reality without relation to oneself, is but another expression of the poet's nature," he still admits that the poet is mirrored in his work as a man, as a character, as a personality. Even Shakespeare, even Scott manifest themselves.[123] We must always have in mind Belinsky's historical position before the victory of 19th-century realism and naturalism. What he is arguing against is pseudoclassicism, still a force in Russia, and romanticism, which Belinsky thinks of as conservative medievalism and folklore worship or as fantastic and gruesome claptrap. Within the fold of realism he includes writers as diverse in their procedures and techniques as Shakespeare, Scott, Cooper, George Sand, and Dickens. In Russia the "natural school" means Gogol and any writer who seems to

Belinsky to have created something substantial, "real," important, natural. He praises the rather humble beginnings of local color realism, "physiological" sketches of Petersburg, peasant stories, and so on, and he is interested in novels that raise and debate social questions. But he has not lost his critical sense. Thus Herzen's *Who Is to Blame?*, a book that appealed to his ideology very strongly, is still said not to be a work of art, not a real novel, but rather a document.[124] Herzen is called a philosopher and not a poet.[125] One usually hears of Belinsky's rejection of Pushkin's fairy tales and Dostoevsky's *Double* as instances of his prejudice against nonrealistic art, but one should remember that he also praised *The Bronze Horseman, The Stone Guest,* and even *Rusalka* almost unreservedly, and that his objections to the *Double* are not conceived merely in realistic terms. He criticized the *Double,* not unreasonably after all, for Dostoevsky's inability to master the overflow of his great powers, to define and limit the artistic development of the idea. Belinsky recognizes "profound conceptions" and a "great creative power" in the story.[126] He prophesies a continuous development and growth for Dostoevsky, foreseeing something of his future greatness, in spite of occasional jibes at and outbursts of disillusionment with a man whom he once regarded as an ally.[127]

Belinsky, no doubt, overrated the accuracy and social import of Gogol's art, and he was bitterly disappointed with *Select Passages from a Correspondence with Friends.* But one cannot say that he did not see the other elements in Gogol. In a review of the second edition of *Dead Souls,* which he still calls the "greatest work of Russian literature," he voices his strong dislike for Gogol's prophetic tone and bombastic lyricism.[128] As early as 1836 he had expressed his contempt for Gogol's intellect by dismissing the essays interspersed in his *Arabesques.*[129] The famous open letter understandably tries to widen the gulf between the early admired Gogol and the despised new book. "If this book did not bear your name, would anyone have thought that this turgid and squalid bombast was the work of the author of *The Inspector General* and *Dead Souls?*"[130] This was good polemics but hardly real criticism. At the moment of rage and disillusionment, discovering in Gogol a "proponent of the knout, apostle of ignorance, champion of obscurantism,"[131] Belinsky could only reject the religious zealot or hypocrite who was hurting the cause of freedom and progress. For him this was no time for literary criticism.

We must conclude that Belinsky was a critic soaked in the views of the German theorists, firm in his hold on their central doctrine: art is concrete, sensuous knowledge, the work of art is an organic whole. The artist must be seen as an unconscious-conscious creator on the analogy of nature. Art is the expression of a nation and an age; it is "characteristic" of that nation and age and should be so. In the last years of his life, however, Belinsky experienced a change, undoubtedly caused by his increasing dissatisfaction with Russian conditions: it was a turn toward political radicalism. It may have had something to do with a religious crisis that led to the abandonment of his old faith. It is closely parallel to the development of many of his contemporaries, especially the Young Hegelians. With them, just as with Belinsky, the "spirit" of Hegel lost its meaning of a force penetrating into the mysteries of the universe. It was replaced by the "spirit of the time," by the idea that man's mind is merely an expression of social and historical reality. Arnold Ruge proclaimed the power of time to be the absolute master in history: he exalted history, which he strangely identified with public opinion, to the heights of the absolute.[132] Similarly, Belinsky proclaimed reality his God and embraced a mystique of time, a blind trust in progress.

Increasingly, Belinsky encouraged realism in the sense of describing Russian social reality with realistic techniques, and he called for clear expression of social purpose, which would help in organizing a public opinion hostile to the regime. In judging Belinsky we must remember that, as Chernyshevsky pointed out long ago, literary criticism in Russia was a vehicle of much general discussion on politics, society, morals, and the like largely by virtue of the fact that censorship was less severe in what was ostensibly book reviewing. Belinsky was a general critic of society who used every opportunity to talk about the emancipation of the serfs, the superstitions and prejudices of the Russian caste system, the dignity of the human individual, the status of woman, and the question of nationality. He thereby quite consciously adulterated his literary criticism with matter only remotely connected with the subject at hand.

His criticism is frequently vitiated by the style required in magazine writing at that time: diffuse description, repetition, digression, and too much quotation, incessant polemics with enemies who have since receded into obscurity, elementary explanation for a public requiring general education and enlightenment—in short, rhetorical overemphasis aiming at immediate, startling effects. In this respect Belinsky compares unfavorably with a contemporary such as Sainte-Beuve, who could be concise and subtle, sophisticated and refined, as he addressed a very different audience. Belinsky is rather similar in his diffuseness and digressiveness to such English magazine writers as De Quincey, Wilson, or Macaulay. But he has a kind of impressive massiveness, a pathos of devotion to his country's literature and to the progress of its society, that cannot be easily matched in the West. Considering the conditions under which he labored, the temptations to which he was exposed as a public figure, and the violence of his volatile temperament, one must admire his generally firm hold on the nature of art, the high standards he applied and upheld, the vigor and penetration of many of his criticisms, and the power of characterization he displayed.

Belinsky had one very important historical function in Russia: he transmitted the doctrines of German idealism to the tradition of Russian criticism. He was the authority for the critics of the fifties and sixties, though they tried to ignore or minimize the idealistic elements in their master. Later Marxist critics, Mikhailovsky and Plekhanov as well as Lenin, could appeal to Belinsky: in him certainly they found the view that literature evolves automatically with society—the mystique of time—which came to them also from Marx and Engels, as all three have a common source in the Germans. Belinsky set a mark on Russian criticism that even today has not been completely obliterated.

BIBLIOGRAPHIES AND NOTES

THERE IS NO satisfactory history of French criticism, but there are the chapters in the third volume of George Saintsbury's *A History of Criticism and Literary Taste in Europe* (3 vols. Edinburgh, 1900–04), the short sketches of Ferdinand Brunetière, *L'Évolution de la critique depuis la Renaissance jusqu'à nos jours* (Paris, 1900), and of Philippe van Tieghem, *Petite Histoire des grandes doctrines littéraires en France* (Paris, 1946), as well as the old book by Alfred Michiels, *Histoire des idées littéraires en France au XIXe siècle et de leurs origines dans les siècles antérieures* (4th ed., 2 vols. Paris, 1863), and the collection of essays by Irving Babbitt, *The Masters of Modern French Criticism* (Boston, 1912). On aesthetics there is a mediocre book by T. M. Mustoxidi, *Histoire de l'esthétique française: 1700–1900* (Paris, 1920).

Albert Cassagne, *La Théorie de l'art pour l'art en France chez les derniers romantiques et les premiers réalistes,* Paris, 1906; reprinted 1959.

H. A. Needham, *Le Développement de l'esthétique sociologique en France et en Angleterre au XIXe siècle,* Paris, 1926; Mediocre.

H. J. Hunt, *Le Socialisme et le romantisme en France,* Oxford, 1935; excellent.

A. E. Carter, *The Idea of Decadence in French Literature, 1830–1900,* Toronto, Canada, 1958.

Margaret Gilman, *The Idea of Poetry in France, from Houdar de la Motte to Baudelaire,* Cambridge, Mass., 1958; excellent.

On German influences: André Monchoux, *L'Allemagne devant les lettres françaises de 1814 à 1835* (Paris, 1953), with bibliography.

On Barante: "Sainte-Beuve" in *Portraits contemporains* (1843), Vol. 4. Georg Brandes in *Main Currents,* Vol. 1, has a chapter on Barante.

On Sismondi: Carlo Pellegrini, *Il Sismondi e la storia delle letterature dell'Europa meridionale,* Geneva, 1926; Jean-R. de Salis, *Sismondi, 1773–1842: La Vie et l'œuvre d'un cosmopolite philosophe,* Paris, 1932, and *Sismondi, 1773–1842: Lettres et documents inédits suivis d'une liste des sources et d'une bibliographie,* Paris, 1932; Sainte-Beuve, *Nouveaux Lundis,* Vol. 6 (1863).

On Fauriel: J. B. Galley, *Claude Fauriel* (Paris, 1909), biographical; Sainte-Beuve, *Portraits contemporains,* Vol. 4 (1845).

On Ampère there is no adequate monograph. The best essays are: Sainte-Beuve, *Portraits littéraires,* 2 (1844), *Portraits contemporains, 3* (1846), and *Nouveaux Lundis, 13* (1868); Heinz Haufe, *J. J. Ampère (1800–64), ein Kritiker der Frühromantik,* Dresden, 1935.

On Villemain: G. Vauthier, *Villemain 1790–1870* (Paris, 1913), biographical; Sainte-Beuve, *Portraits contemporains,* 2 (1836); *Causeries du lundi 1* (1849), *6* (1852); J. Barbey d'Aurevilly, *Les Critiques,* Paris, 1888; Ernest George Atkin, "Villemain and French Classicism," in *Studies by Members of the Department of Romance Languages* (of the University of Wisconsin), (Madison, Wis., 1924), pp. 126–51.

On Chasles: J. Barbey d'Aurevilly, *Les Critiques,* Paris, 1888; E. Margaret Phillips, *Philarète Chasles, Critique et historien de la littérature anglaise,* Paris, 1933; A. Levin, ed., *The Legacy of Philarète Chasles,* Vol. 1, *Selected Essays on Nineteenth Century French Literature* (Chapel Hill, N.C., 1957), introductory comment; two more volumes to appear.

On Planche: Sainte-Beuve, *Nouveaux Lundis, 5,* 67 ff.; *Causeries du lundi, 11,* 482; *Mes Poisons* (Paris, 1926), p. 31; Maurice Regard, *L'Adversaire des romantiques: Gustave Planche* (2 vols. Paris, 1955), is exhaustive; bibliography.

On Saint-Marc Girardin: Laurence W. Wylie, *Saint-Marc Girardin Bourgeois,* Syracuse, N.Y., 1947; bibliography. Also Sainte-Beuve, *Causeries du lundi, 1* (1849); Nisard in *Études de critique littéraire* (1858); and De Sanctis in *Saggi critici, 1* (1856).

On Nisard: E. Equey, *Désiré Nisard et son œuvre,* Berne, 1902; diss., thin. Also Sainte-Beuve in *Portraits contemporains, 3* (1836), and *Causeries du lundi, 15* (1867); Edmond Scherer in *Études, 1* (1863); Barbey d'Aurevilly, *Les Critiques,* 1888; and Edward Dowden, in *New Studies in Literature,* London, 1895.

On Vinet: E. Scherer, *Alexandre Vinet: Notice sur sa vie et ses écrits* (Paris, 1853), little on criticism; Louis Molines, *Étude sur Alexandre Vinet, critique littéraire,* Paris, 1890; Ernest Seillière, *Christianisme et romantisme: Alexandre Vinet, historien de la pensée française,* Paris, 1925; Edwin Borschberg, *Alexandre Vinet als Literaturhistoriker,* Zurich, 1940. François Jost, *Alexandre Vinet, interprète de Pascal,* Lausanne, 1950. See also Sainte-Beuve in *Portraits contemporains, 3* (1837); *Portraits littéraires, 3* (1847); Scherer in *Études, 1* (1863); Jean Bonnerot, "État présent des études sur Vinet," in *Revue d'histoire littéraire de la France, 56* (1956), 385–91; François Jost, "Alexandre Vinet en face de Blaise Pascal," in *Essais de littérature comparée, 2* vols. Fribourg, 1964, *1,* 169–200.

On Magnin: no modern study; Sainte-Beuve, in *Nouveaux Lundis*, 5 (1863), 440–78, and in *Portraits contemporains*, 3 (1843), 387–414.

On Leroux, besides Hunt: Félix P. Thomas, *Pierre Leroux, sa vie, son œuvre, sa doctrine*, Paris, 1904; David Owen Evans, *Le Socialisme romantique: Pierre Leroux et ses contemporains*, Paris, 1949.

On Cousin: Frederic Will, *Intelligible Beauty in Aesthetic Thought from Winckelmann to Victor Cousin*, Tübingen, 1958.

On Gautier, besides Cassagne: Sainte-Beuve's review of *Les Grotesques* in *Portraits contemporains*, 5 (1844), and remarks in *Nouveaux Lundis*, 6 (1863), esp. 295 ff.; Helen E. Patch, *The Dramatic Criticism of Théophile Gautier* (Bryn Mawr, Pa., 1922), with list of hundreds of articles. M. C. Spencer, "The Problem of Ghost-Writing in the Critical Work of Théophile Gautier," in *Symposium, 17* (1963), 101–13, must be taken into account. Also René Jasinski, *Les Années romantiques de Th. Gautier*, Paris, 1929; Georges Matoré, ed., *La Préface de Mademoiselle de Maupin* (Paris, 1946), with a useful introduction.

NOTES: FRENCH CRITICISM BEFORE 1850

1. In *Législation primitive* (Paris, 1829), 2, 223. "La littérature est l'expression de la société" (originally in *Mercure de France*, 1802). In an article "Du Style et de la littérature" (1806) in *Mélanges littéraires, politiques et philosophiques* (3d. ed. Paris, 1852), pp. 169–206, De Bonald develops the idea interestingly as a parallel to Buffon's "le style est l'homme même," saying it should be "Le style est l'expression de l'homme." It follows that literature is to society as the style is to man, and that one can define literature as "the style of society." Every society has its style as every people has its language. De Bonald defines society as "the form of political and religious constitution."

2. 4th ed. 1824, p. 38: "symptômes de la maladie générale"; p. 214: "un esprit universel de la nation"; p. 215: "Les livres n'ont pas seulement reçu l'influence du public; ils ont, pour ainsi dire, été écrits sous sa dictée."

3. *Ibid.*, p. 5: "Devenue un organe de l'opinion, un élément de la constitution politique. Faute d'institutions regulières, la littérature en était une."

4. *Ibid.*, pp. 182, 184, 282.

5. Guizot wrote many articles for *Le Publiciste*. He praises A. W. Schlegel for his knowledge of antiquity and concept of fate (August 29, 1808). For details see Charles H. Pouthas, *La Jeunesse de Guizot* (Paris, 1936), pp. 232–33. *Vie des poètes français du siècle de Louis XIV* (Paris, 1813), was reissued by Guizot as *Corneille et son temps*, Paris, 1852.

6. "Études sur Shakespeare" in *Œuvres complètes de Shakespeare, Traduction de M. Guizot* (new ed. Paris, 1860), V. *1*, 1: "La littérature n'echappe point aux révolutions de l'esprit humain; elle est contrainte de le suivre dans sa marche"; p. 127: "Le système classique est né de la vie et des mœurs de son temps; ce temps est passé"; p. 59: "Asile des mœurs comme des libertés germaines"; p. 128: "Il sera large et libre, mais non sans principes et sans lois."

7. Friedrich Schlegel's *Histoire de la littérature ancienne et moderne* appeared in 1829, translated by William Duckett (1804–63). Duckett was a schoolmate of Planche at the Collège de Bourbon and became editor of *Chronique de Paris*. See M. Regard, *Planche, 1*, 23, 29, 176, 193, 230. Cf. Marcel Françon, "Note Balzacienne: William Duckett," in *Symposium, 13* (1959), 102–05.

8. For Sismondi on A. W. Schlegel see *Lettres inédites de Sismondi, de Bonstetten ... à la Comtesse d'Albany*, ed. S.-R. Taillandier (Paris, 1863), pp. 168, 278; Benjamin Constant, "Journal intime," in *Œuvres complètes*, Pléiade ed., p. 310. On Bouterwek see Pellegrini, pp. 93 ff. Sismondi freely acknowledges his indebtedness; see *Littérature du Midi, 1*, 13 n.

9. *De la littérature du Midi de l'Europe,* 4 vols., Paris, 1813; *1*, iii, 10; *4*, 260–61, 562.

10. *Ibid., 1*, ii: "L'influence réciproque de l'histoire politique et religieuse des peuples sur leur littérature, et de leur littérature sur leur caractère."

11. *Ibid., 4*, 557: "A reproduit la littérature classique des Grecs et des Romains." *1*, 343: "Elle demeure fort en arrière sous le rapport de la sensibilité, de l'enthousiasme, de la chaleur, de la profondeur et de la vérité des sentiments." *4*, 557: "... ce mélange d'amour, de chevalerie et de religion."

12. *Ibid., 2*, 69: "La rêverie sans but est plus conforme à l'essence de la poésie, qui ne doit jamais être un moyen, mais qui est à elle-même son propre objet." Cf. *1*, 361, 382 ff.; *2*, 257–58, 434 ff.

13. *Ibid., 3*, 340 ff.; *4*, 105 ff.

14. *Ibid., 3*, 99, 470–71: "Un traité fort obscur."

15. Stendhal, *Rome, Naples et Florence*, ed. Daniel Muller (Paris, 1919), *2*, 260: "Sismondi est travaillé par deux systèmes opposés: admirera-t-il Racine ou Shakespeare? Dans ces perplexités, il ne nous dit pas de quel parti est son cœur; peut-être n'est-il d'aucun parti."

16. See Edmond Eggli and Pierre Martino, *Le Débat romantique en France: 1813–1830.* Vol. *1*, 1813–16 (Paris, 1933), pp. 43 ff.

17. *Chants, 1*, xxv: "L'expression directe et vraie du caractère et de l'esprit national ... qui vit ... dans le peuple lui-même, et de toute la

vie du peuple. . . . À la fois et la véritable histoire nationale de la Grèce moderne, et le tableau le plus fidèle des mœurs de ses habitants." Page ci: "Une continuation, une altération lente et graduelle de l'ancienne poésie, et spécialement de l'ancienne poésie populaire des Grecs." Page cxxvi: "C'est précisément ce défaut d'art ou cet emploi imparfait d'art, c'est cette espèce de contraste ou de disproportion entre la simplicité du moyen et la plénitude de l'effet, qui font le charme principal d'une telle composition. . . . Elle participe . . . au caractère et au privilège des œuvres de la nature."

18. See Frédéric Ozanam, "M. Fauriel et son enseignement" in *Œuvres complètes* (Paris, 1872), *8*, 107–68, esp. p. 126; André Mazon, "Claude Fauriel et les poèmes prétendus anciens de Russie et de Bohême," in *Revue des Études slaves*, 21 (1944), 121–44.

19. *Histoire de la poésie provençale* (Paris, 1846), *1*, v–vi: "Toutes les littératures . . . participent . . . à la marche générale par laquelle l'humanité s'élève progressivement d'une condition à une autre, de l'enfance à la jeunesse, de la jeunesse à la maturité." ". . . cette tendance générale se croise ou se combine toujours avec des tendances particulières ou secondaires . . . Le climat, le sol, l'état social, la croyance religieuse, les relations de commerce, les résultats des guerres et des conquêtes" ". . . une physionomie locale, un caractère d'individualité."

20. *Ibid.*, *1*, 16–17, 26–27, 40, 44, 399; 2, 144, 445 ff., on Wolfram; *2*, 371: "L'extension, la modification, le raffinement systématique d'une littérature antérieure, plus grossière, plus naturelle et plus populaire." *2*, 370: "Une hypothèse contraire à la marche ordinaire de l'esprit humain."

21. *Dante et les origines de la langue et de la littérature italiennes*, ed. J. Mohl (2 vols., Paris, 1854), *1*, 373, 405. Page 463: "la plus froide, la plus factice et la plus fausse de toutes les formes poétiques." Page 461: ". . . un noble aveu de ses torts envers la mémoire de Béatrix." Pages 430, 437, 489, 501, 534.

22. Renan, *Nouveaux Cahiers de jeunesse* (Paris, 1907), pp. 293–94: "M. Fauriel a réellement créé en France la littérature comparée, et la science des origines littéraires, le point de vue d'envisager la littérature comme une science historique, bien supérieur sans doute à la fade critique littéraire et mesquine de La Harpe, Geoffroy, Petitot et même de Marmontel et Voltaire." Claude-Bernard Petitot (1772–1825) was an editor of Racine, Molière, a 23-volume *Répertoire du Théâtre*, etc., hardly a literary critic.

23. *Littérature, Voyages et Poésies* (Paris, 1858), *1*, 173 (originally in *Globe*, April 29, May 20, 1826): "Chacun de ces ouvrages correspond à quelque disposition de son âme ou de son esprit; il faut y chercher

l'histoire des sentiments et des événements qui ont rempli son existence."
Page 180: "Le point de vue historique ... ne cherchant que Goethe dans
ses œuvres."

24. In *Von Kunst und Altertum*, Vols. 5 and 6. See *Werke*, J.-A. *38*,
23–38. Ampère called on Goethe, April 27, 1827, and was three times at
dinner, May 3, 4, and 6. Eckermann, May 3, 1827. See *Gespräche*, ed.
Houben, pp. 497–98, 502.

25. *Littérature, Voyages*, pp. 204 ff., 220 ff., 225 ff., 257 ff., 311 f.

26. *Mélanges d'histoire littéraire et de littérature* (2 vols. Paris, 1867),
1, 1–50. Page 3: "C'est de l'histoire comparative des arts et de la littérature chez tous les peuples que doit sortir la philosophie de la littérature
et des arts." Page 33: "C'est le temps où le véritable individu est la race,
la tribu. Le poète est la voix de cet individu collectif et rien de plus."
Page 42: "Cette critique est féconde ... pleine de respect pour le génie
et de sévérité pour l'erreur, admire volontiers et condamne avec
indépendance."

27. *Nouveaux Lundis, 13*, 224: "Je suis à certains égards un élève
d'Ampère."

28. *Histoire littéraire de la France avant Charlemagne*. 2d ed. 2 vols.
Paris, 1867. *1*, 4: "Plonger dans ces ténèbres créatrices ... dans ce chaos
fécond qui enfantera un monde." Page 14: "... à la voie romaine, au
sol romain." See also "Les Renaissances," in *Mélanges, 1*, 437–67.

29. *Histoire littéraire, 2*, 238: "Elle exprime souvant ce qui est caché
... elle est une confidente qui nous révèle ce qu'on a pensé, ce qu'on a
senti en secret, ce qui a été latent, comprimé; elle est comme ces échos
qui répètent au loin des mots prononcés tout bas. Elle manifeste parfois
non la domination d'un fait, mais une réaction contre ce fait. Elle
exprime des désirs, des vœux, un certain idéal qui est au fond des âmes.
De plus, elle n'est pas toujours la voix du moment même où elle se
produit; elle est parfois le retentissement de ce qui a été, le dernier
soupir de ce qui meurt, le premier cri de ce qui vivra."

30. See *Mélanges*, Vol. 1. Apparently there still exist full shorthand
notes of Ampère's lectures, which would make a complete history of
French literature up to the 18th century.

31. *Rome et Dante*, Paris, 1848. Page iii: "Comparer l'art à la réalité
qui l'a inspiré, et l'expliquer par elle." Page 213: "Il est bon de voir ce
qu'il a vu, de vivre ou il a vécu."

32. Brunetière, *Évolution*, pp. 195 ff. Chasles in *Mémoirs* (Paris,
1877), 2, 171–75: "Le véritable initiateur ... il a fondé l'histoire littéraire en France."

33. In *Discours et Mélanges littéraires*, 3d ed. 1825; *Études de littérature ancienne et étrangère*, new ed. Paris, 1877.

34. *Tableau de la littérature au XVIIIe siècle*, new ed. 4 vols. Paris, 1873. See *1, 2*.

35. "De la littérature en France durant les quinze années de la Restauration" in *Choix d'études sur la littérature contemporaine* (Paris, 1857), p. 336: "Un appendice de l'histoire sociale." Cf. p. 321.

36. *Tableau, 1*, 251: "La marque du temps, l'esprit de ces dernières années du règne de Louis XIV." *1*, iv: "Le contre-coup du génie français au dehors, dans plusieurs productions célèbres d'Angleterre et d'Italie." *1, 2*: "Nous montrerons par un tableau comparé ce que l'esprit français avait reçu des littératures étrangères, et ce qu'il leur rendit." *1*, 19: "Le feu croisé."

37. *Tableau de la littérature au moyen âge* (new ed. 2 vols. 1875), *1*, 32: "Nous aimons tout ce qui est beau, ingénieux, nouveau, n'importe quelle soit l'école. Nous croyons même qu'il ne faut vouloir être d'aucune école, pas même de celle du génie." *1*, 103; 31: "Son type le plus expressif et le plus heureux." *1*, 314: "Le monument le plus complet de l'imagination et des croyances d'un peuple." *1*, 316–18, 218: "Quand on peut discuter, avec une justesse d'érudit, ce qui convient à chaque époque, on n'est pas soi-même sous la séduction de ses propres paroles; on n'est pas trompé, on ne trompe pas." *2*, 203: "Quel que soit l'heureux génie d'un écrivain de ce vieux temps, il reste toujours quelque chose de gothique et d'étrange." *2*, 209: "la vraie poésie ... elle ne fut jamais contemporaine que du bon goût." *2*, 245: "... subtilement naturelle, laborieusement téméraire ... un dégoût savant."

38. *Études de littérature ancienne et étrangère*, p. 274: "C'est aux Anglais qu'appartient Shakspeare, et qu'il doit rester." *Tableau de la littérature au XVIIIe siècle, 3*, 308: "Voilà Shakespeare éminemment classique; il se rencontre avec Euripide."

39. In *Choix d'études sur la littérature contemporaine*, Paris, 1857.

40. *Études sur l'antiquité*, Paris, 1847; *Études sur le XVIIIe siècle en Angleterre*, 2 vols. 1846; *Études sur la littérature et les mœurs de l'Angleterre au XIXe siècle*, 1850; *Études sur Shakespeare, Marie Stuart et l'Arétin*, 1852; *Études sur la littérature et les mœurs des Anglo-Américains au XIXe siècle*, 1851; *Études sur l'Allemagne ancienne et moderne*, 2 vols. 1854; *Études sur l'Espagne et sur les influences de la littérature espagnole en France et en Italie*, 1847.

41. *Études sur l'antiquité*, p. 9: "Bayle le protestant touche à Montaigne le catholique; le gibelin Dante, aux servants d'amours provençaux; Molière donne la main à Térence."—From "De l'esprit et de la critique littéraire" (1834), in *The Legacy of Philarète Chasles*, ed. A. Levin, Chapel Hill, 1957. Page 5: "Un labyrinthe sans lumière."

42. *Études sur l'Allemagne, 2*, xii–xiii: "L'harmonie des variétés dans

les œuvres de l'esprit; le *Welt-Literatur* dont parlait Goethe; c'est-à-dire la conciliation des points de vue opposés." *Études sur l'antiquité,* p. 11.

43. "De l'esprit" in *Legacy*, p. 3: "La seule contrée où la Critique a reposé sur de larges bases, où le génie des nationalités ait été compté pour quelque chose, où l'on ait compris l'immense variété de la nature humaine et l'influence de cette variété sur les arts, où l'on ait accepté la pensée de chaque peuple soumise à toutes ses modifications politiques et sociales, et admiré tour à tour les mille formes que le *beau* et l'*idéal* peuvent revêtir dans leur passage à travers l'histoire."

44. *Études sur le XVIIIᵉ siècle en Angleterre.* 2 vols. Paris, 1846. 2, 279: "Le premier des critiques modernes ... qui a pénétré le plus avant dans l'étude de la vieille langue et des auteurs anglais du XVIᵉ siècle." *Journal des Débats,* 14 September 1836, quoted by Phillips, p. 127: "L'esprit le plus vaste serait celui qui concilierait tout."

45. In *Revue de Paris*, 1830, reprinted in *Legacy*, pp. 29–38: "Les ressorts employés jusqu'ici par elle, il les a violemment comprimés; il ne l'a point changée, il l'a multipliée par elle-même."

46. In *Journal des Débats*, 24 August 1850, in *Legacy*, p. 156.

47. *Études sur l'antiquité,* "Euripide et Racine," pp. 245–68.

48. *L'Angleterre au XVIᵉ siècle* (Paris, 1879), pp. 146–47: "Un poète sceptique, observateur calme et souvent cruel, frère de Montaigne, ému d'une pitié un peu ironique pour les hommes."

49. "Études sur Jean Paul" in *Caractères et paysages* (Paris, 1833), pp. 43–128. *Études sur l'Allemagne: ancienne et moderne* (Paris, 1854) contains long extracts from *Siebenkäs, Schmelzle* and a good characterization of his style (pp. 302–07). —On Heine, see *Études sur l'Allemagne* (Vol. 2, 1861), pp. 265–80. —On Melville, *Études sur la littérature et les mœurs des Anglo-Américains au XIXᵉ siècle* (Paris, 1851), pp. 185–235. —"Hoelderlin: le fou de la révolution" in *Études sur l'Allemagne* (Vol. 2, 1861), pp. 355–62.

50. *Mémoires,* 2 vols. Paris, 1876–77. 2, 251: "La plus profonde foi dans la causalité." —Review of Taine's *Histoire de la littérature anglaise,* in *Journal des Débats*, 28 April 1867, in *Legacy*, p. 220: "Cette essence de l'âme est la liberté et la liberté, c'est la vie."

51. *Mémoires,* Vol. 2, 250: "... traître par principe." "Le Don Juan fascinateur du harem intellectuel."

52. *Portraits littéraires,* 3d ed. 2 vols. Paris, 1853. *1,* 157–59: "L'étonnement." "La pierre et l'étoffe sont les principaux, je devrais dire les seuls acteurs de ce livre." *Nouveaux Portraits littéraires,* 2 vols. Paris, 1854. *1,* 274, 285: "Un puéril entassement de scènes impossibles. ... un acte de folie."

53. *Portraits littéraires*, 2, 173: "... se réfugier derrière Shakspeare et Milton pour respirer plus à l'aise l'odeur de l'encens qu'il a lui-même allumé."

54. "De la critique française" in *Portraits littéraires*, 2, 301–24.

55. *Nouveaux Portraits*, *1*, 401: "J'admets la sincérité dans le blâme comme dans la louange, et je vois tout simplement, dans cette mobilité de jugement, une maladie morale."

56. On the English articles and the plagiarism, see Michiels, *op. cit.*, 2, 348 ff. and Regard, *1*, 90 ff.

57. See *Portraits littéraires*, *1*, 1–32, 33–57, 61–72.

58. *Cours de littérature dramatique* (new ed. 5 vols. Paris, n.d.), *1*, 17: "Chaque sentiment a son histoire; et cette histoire est curieuse, parce qu'elle est, pour ainsi dire, un abrégé de l'histoire de l'humanité. Quoique les sentiments du cœur humain ne changent pas, cependant ils ressentent aussi l'effet des révolutions religieuses et politiques qui se font dans le monde."

59. *Ibid.*, *1*, 79 ff., 120 ff., 143 ff., 187 ff., esp. 164–65.

60. See Wiley, *Saint-Marc Girardin;* and Sainte-Beuve in *CL*, *1* (1849), the very first causerie. De Sanctis in two articles, "Saint-Marc Girardin" and "Triboulet," in *Saggi critici*, Vol. 1.

61. Reprinted in *Études de critique littéraire*, Paris, 1858, and in *Essais sur l'école romantique*, Paris, 1891.

62. The first edition is very rare. The later reissues (1848, etc.) tone down the polemical passages very considerably.

63. *Études*, 4th ed. Paris, 1878. Esp. "Conclusion," 2, 381 ff. and on three types of poets, 2, 366.

64. *Essais sur l'école romantique*, pp. 235–36: "Langue, qui pour vouloir tout peindre, substitue des images aux réalités, des couleurs aux pensées; langue bariolée, éblouissante, qu'on voit avec les yeux du corps; une palette versée sur une toile, mais non pas un tableau."

65. "La critique dans M. Saint-Marc Girardin" in *Études de critique littéraire*, pp. 148–49. —*Histoire de la littérature française*, 17th ed. 4 vols. Paris, n.d., *4*, 540: "Chacun à son goût ... Une science exacte."

66. *Ibid.*, *3*, 210: "C'est cette ressemblance nécessaire des styles, dans la différence des sujets ou du génie particulier des grands écrivains, qui fait la beauté de notre littérature: c'est l'unité de la langue dans la diversité des écrits. Je défierais le critique le plus exercé, s'il ne sait pas l'endroit de mémoire, de reconnaître à qui appartient une pensée exprimée en perfection."

67. *Ibid.*, *4*, 128 ff., 160 ff., 321 ff., 415 ff. "Pertes," "gains."

68. *Ibid.*, *1*, 361 ff. 3, 70 ff. Cf. *Essais sur l'école romantique*, p. 136, for an early passage (1831) on the role of the artist.

69. In *Chrestomathie française*, Lausanne, 1870. Vol. 3, an introductory "Discours sur la littérature française," refers to both Schlegels; e.g. p. 21 n., and to Bouterwek, p. 23 n.; quotes Jean Paul, pp. 24 n., 95 n.; Goethe, pp. 27 n., 32 n., 62 n.; Friedrich Schlegel on Bossuet, Racine, and Rousseau, pp. 37 n., 50 n., all in German. On Goethe, *Études sur la littérature française au XIXᵉ siècle*, 3 vols. Lausanne, 1911. *1*, 154.

70. *Ibid., 1*, 153, 379.

71. *Ibid., 2*, 296: "Sa vocation n'est pas de savoir, mais de voir. Sa faculté à lui, c'est l'intuition."

72. *Des Pensées de Pascal* (Paris, 1843), was the epoch-making report on the manuscript of the *Pensées*. Vinet's review in *Études sur Blaise Pascal* (Lausanne, 1936), pp. 68–114.

73. *Études, 2*, 119: "La reproduction incessamment nouvelle et surprenante d'un mystère qui ne change point." ". . . la révélation la plus complète et la plus profonde que l'homme puisse recevoir."

74. *Ibid., 2*, 3–5.

75. *Ibid., 3*, 356–57: "La poésie, en général, ne définit pas les objets: elle les montre, elle leur donne une forme . . . Ce que nous demandons au poète, ce n'est pas l'idée d'un objet, c'est cet objet lui-même, concret, complex, vivant."

76. *Études, 2*, 75: "La poésie ne vivra jamais d'idées pures et de généralités . . . le lecteur y cherchera toujours un individu, afin de s'y trouver soi-même."

77. *Ibid., 3*, 14: "Au fond de l'âme . . . C'est du dedans, non du dehors, qu'elles colorent la diction; ce n'est pas un fard, c'est un incarnat."

78. *Ibid., 1*, 446: "La poésie matérialisait tout."

79. *Ibid., 2*, 263: "Les fables d'Orphée et d'Amphion sont la vérité même: elles nous reportent au point de jonction du bon et du beau, du réel et de l'idéal, et, l'on pourrait dire, à la vraie raison de la poésie."

80. *Ibid., 1*, 322: "Tout ce qui est assemblé du dehors . . . tout ce qui, au lieu de croître comme une plante, a été construit comme un édifice, ne peut avoir, poétiquement, aucune vérité."

81. *Ibid., 2*, 193: "Il se souvient encore d'une première vision, il se souviendra un jour de s'être souvenu."

82. *Les Origines du théâtre moderne* (Paris, 1838), pp. xi–xii, xxvii–xxviii: "C'est rétablir un des anneaux brisés de la perfectibilité humaine."

83. Besides the edition of Hroswitha and the book on the puppets, there is a long series of articles on the old French theater in *Journal des Savants*, 1846–58, culminating in a study of *Patelin* (1855–56).

84. In 1827. Reprinted from *Le Globe* in Vol. 2 of *Causeries et Méditations historiques et littéraires,* 2 vols. Paris, 1843.

85. *Causeries,* Vol. 1. "Qu'est-ce que l'esthétique, et qu'est-ce qu'une poétique" (pp. 61–88), and particularly "Ahasvérus, mystère, par Edgar Quinet, et de la nature du génie poétique" (pp. 89–158). Also in Edgar Quinet, *Œuvres complètes* (1858), 7, esp. p. 94.

86. *Origines,* pp. 2–3: "Non d'après les différences artificielles de la forme, mais d'après la nature des cordes intérieures que chacun d'eux fait vibrer dans le cerveau du poète et dans l'âme des auditeurs."

87. *Causeries, 1,* 93: "Sa vocation est de déchiffrer les grands caractères que le doigt de l'Éternel a imprimés sur toutes choses, et de traduire en vibrations poétiques la secrète musique que le monde exhale du sein de tous les éléments et de toutes les créatures."

88. *Ibid., 1,* 313: "La poésie, qu'on peut appeler la demiscience et mieux peut-être la prescience, fait jaillir à travers le rayonnement de ses symboles et l'éclair de ses métaphores une foule de vérités anticipées dont la science trouvera plus tard la démonstration." "Toute expression vraiment poétique est la révélation d'un nouveau rapport découvert entre le monde physique et le monde moral."

89. *Ibid., 1,* 219: "Il doit nous ouvrir, à tous moments, la perspective de l'infini."

90. *Ibid., 1,* 141–42, 144–45, 153–56. 157: "Celle-ci ne reflète pas seulement les images ou les sensations reçues; elle en crée qui sont à elle, c'est-à-dire que des rapports qu'elle découvre entre deux images ou entre deux idées, elle tire une troisième image ou une troisième idée, expression de ce rapport, et qui est son propre ouvrage. C'est en ce sens que la poésie est créatrice."

91. *Ibid., 1,* 313: "S'ensuit-il que l'initiative sociale et religieuse appartienne de nos jours aux poètes, et qu'ils doivent aborder de front les problèmes métaphysiques et sociaux?" Page 315: "Il y a plus d'invention, plus de création, plus d'originalité réelles dans quelques pages écrites sous la dictée du cœur et de l'imagination, que dans les vagues lieux communs d'avenir dont le poète a cru devoir trop souvent... masquer le vide de sa pensée."

92. See Hunt, p. 11 and Marguerite Thibert, *Le Rôle social de l'art d'après les saint-simoniens,* Paris, 1927.

93. Hunt, p. 35: "L'artiste seul ... par la puissance de cette sympathie qui lui fait embrasser Dieu et la société, est digne de diriger l'humanité."

94. Hunt, p. 71: "L'artiste est le *verbe* du Prêtre."

95. In *Le Globe,* 29 March and 8 April 1829. Reprinted in *Œuvres complètes,* Paris, 1851. Vol. 1, 324, as "De la poésie du style." "... des

expressions vagues et indéterminées à l'expression propre, des métaphores et des allegories à des comparaisons d'idées." "Parler par symboles, allégoriser" "... la grande innovation, en fait de style, depuis
cinquante ans."

96. *Revue Encyclopédique*, Vol. 52, October 1831. "Aux Philosophes.
De la poésie de notre époque." Pages 407–08: "Là poésie est cette aile
mystérieuse qui plane à volonté dans le monde entier de l'âme, dans
cette sphère infinie dont une partie est couleurs, une autre sons, une
autre mouvement, une autre jugement, etc. mais qui toutes vibrent en
même temps suivant certaines lois, en sorte qu'une vibration dans une
région communique à une autre région, et que le privilège de l'art est
de sentir et d'exprimer ces rapports, profondément cachés dans l'unité
même de la vie. Car de ces vibrations harmoniques des diverses régions
de l'âme il résulte un *accord*, et cet accord c'est la vie; et quand cet
accord est exprimé, c'est l'art; or, c'est accord exprimé, c'est le symbole;
et la forme de son expression, c'est le rhythme, qui participe lui-même
du symbole: voilà pourquoi l'art est l'expression de la vie, le retentissement de vie, et la vie elle-même." In text, translation from Gilman,
p. 223.

97. "Allégorie" in *Encyclopédie nouvelle, ou Dictionnaire philosophique*, Paris, 1835–41. *1*, 527: "Métaphore, symbole, mythe, ne sont que
des allégories à divers degrés."

98. From *Le Globe*, as above, note 95. *Œuvres, 1*, 330–31: "Une
forme intermédiaire entre la comparaison et l'allégorie proprement
dites, plus rapide que la comparaison et moins obscure que l'allégorie.
C'est un véritable emblème ... la métaphore d'une idée."

99. *Revue encyclopédique*, p. 647: "Le fond noir et profond du cœur
humain dans notre époque."

100. "Considérations sur Werther et en général sur la poésie de notre
époque" in *Werther par Goethe*, Paris, 1845. Page 24: "Symbole du
chaos où nous agitons, et d'ou sortira un monde." Pages 289, 41. Page
45: "Le salut de la destinée individuelle lié à celui de la destinée universelle."

101. Paulin Limayrac, "La Poésie symboliste et socialiste," *Revue
des Deux Mondes*, new ser. 14 (1844), 682: "La Poésie symboliste n'a
pas d'avenir en France, et le socialisme, en l'accaparant, lui a porté un
rude coup."

102. Sainte-Beuve, *Correspondance générale. 7*, 143–44, letter to Hor-
tense Allart, October 1847: "Un dieu et un révélateur." Cf. *Les Cahiers*
(Paris, 1876), p. 105: "Il est devenu dieu, et je suis devenu bibliothécaire."

103. Contrary to the usual views, not only government censorship and

control but a definitely directed literature was the aim of both the revolutionary and Napoleonic regimes and the Bourbon Restoration. The theory was supplied by De Bonald. See, e.g., Sainte-Beuve, *Causeries du lundi, 4,* 428 ff. and B. Munteano, "Une Théorie de la littérature dirigée sous la révolution et l'empire," in *Actes du quatrième congrès international d'histoire littéraire moderne* (Paris, 1948), pp. 191–203.

104. *La Préface de Mademoiselle de Maupin,* ed. G. Matoré (Paris, 1946), pp. 16–17, 25, 26, 30, 31: "A quoi sert la beauté des femmes? Pourvu qu'une femme soit ... en état de recevoir l'homme et de faire des enfants, elle sera toujours assez bonne pour des économistes. A quoi bon la musique? à quoi bon la peinture? ... Il n'y a de vraiment beau que ce qui ne peut servir à rien: tout ce qui est utile est laid." Page 32: "Je renoncerai très joyeusement à mes droits de Français et de citoyen, pour voir un tableau authentique de Raphaël, ou une belle femme nue." Page 35: "A-t-on inventé un seul péché capital de plus?"

105. B. Constant, *Journaux intimes,* 11 February 1804. *Œuvres,* Pléiade ed., p. 266: "L'art pour l'art, et sans but." Robinson had just written articles on Kant for an obscure English periodical, *The Monthly Register.* I discovered and described the manuscript of the last unpublished article on Kant's aesthetics in my *Kant in England* (Princeton, 1931), pp. 157–58.

106. *Cours de philosophie professé à la Faculté des Lettres pendant l'année 1818 par M. V. Cousin* (Paris, 1836), p. 224: "Il faut de la religion pour la religion, de la morale pour la morale, comme de l'art pour l'art."

107. *Cours d'esthétique,* ed. Ph. Damiron (Paris, 1843), pp. 24 ff. Quatrième leçon: "Différence de l'utile et du beau."

108. *Cours,* p. 298: "Engagé sous les formes sensibles."

109. *L'Artiste,* December 14, 1856. Page 4: "La concupiscence des yeux, *concupiscentia oculorum*—ce péché est notre péché."

110. Preface to *Albertus* (1832). *Poésies complètes,* ed. R. Jasinski, Paris, 1932. *1,* 81–2: "L'art, c'est la liberté, le luxe, l'efflorescence, c'est l'épanouissement de l'âme dans l'oisiveté."

111. "La Divine Epopée, par Alexandre Soumet," in *Revue des Deux Mondes,* 4th ser., *26* (April 1841), 121: "Le soin exquis de l'exécution. Le mot poète veut dire littéralement *faiseur;* tout ce qui n'est bien fait n'existe pas." Page 126: "Le vers est une matière étincelante et dure comme le marbre de Carrara."

112. *Les Grotesques,* new ed. Paris, 1904. Page 267: "L'air aussi est de pierre ... les petits ruisseaux qui tombent des rochers ont l'air de stalactites plutôt que d'eaux molles et pénétrables, le feuillage des arbres semble fait avec du fer blanc."

113. *Ibid.*, pp. 336, 105. Page 154: "L'école des versificateurs-gram-mairiens." Page 156: "Esprit juste, mais étroit, critique passionné et ignorant." Page 261: "Une clarté de verre, une limpidité d'eau filtrée, une exactitude géométrique." Page 98: "Une véritable grand poète... qui a commencé le mouvement romantique." Page 122: "Il n'a pas l'elévation et la mélancolie de Théophile."

114. *Histoire du romantisme suivie... d'une étude sur la poésie française 1830–1868* (Paris, 1929), pp. 82, 61 ff., 115 ff.

115. *Fusains et eaux-fortes*, Paris, 1907. Page 306: "Maturité complète, la civilisation extrême, le couronnement des choses." "Un frisson nouveau."

116. *Histoire du romantisme.* Page 300: "Sur les confins extrêmes du romantisme..." Page 301: "... manque d'ingénuité et de candeur." Pages 305–06. Page 301: "Le poète n'a aucune indulgence pour les vices, les dépravations et les monstruosités qu'il retrace avec le sang-froid d'un peintre de musée anatomique. Il les renie comme des infrac-tions au rhythme universel; car, en dépit de ces excentricités, il aime l'ordre et la *norme.* Impitoyable pour les autres, il se juge non moins sévèrement lui-même."

117. *Portraits et souvenirs littéraires*, Paris, 1892. Page 167: "Natur-ellement maniéré." Pages 172, 183–84, 206.

BIBLIOGRAPHY: SAINTE-BEUVE

The writings of Sainte-Beuve are quoted from the old editions fre-quently reprinted: *Premiers Lundis* (3 vols. Paris, 1874–76), as *Pre Lu; Portraits littéraires* (3 vols. Paris, 1862–64), as *Po Li; Portraits contem-porains* (5 vols. Paris, 1869–71), as *Pc; Portraits de femmes* (Paris, 1879), as *PF; Port Royal* (7 vols. Paris, 1867–71), as *Po Ro;* for *Chateaubriand et son groupe littéraire* (2 vols. Paris, 1861), I used the annotated edition by Maurice Allem, 1949, as *Cha; Causeries du lundi* (16 vols. Paris, 1857–72), as *CL; Nouveaux Lundis* (13 vols. Paris, 1863–70), as *NL; Étude sur Virgile*, Paris, 1870; *Chroniques parisiennes*, ed. J. Troubat, Paris, 1876; *Les Cahiers*, ed. J. Troubat, Paris, 1876; *Mes Poisons, Cahiers intimes,* ed. V. Giraud, Paris, 1926; Part of the original text of the Lausanne lectures was published as *Port Royal: Le Cours de Lausanne,* ed. Jean Pommier, Paris, 1937. Sainte-Beuve's letters up to and including 1864 in *Correspondance générale,* ed. Jean Bonnerot, 13 vols. Paris, 1935–63.

Jean Bonnerot, *Bibliographie de l'œuvre de Sainte-Beuve* (3 parts in 4 vols. Paris, 1937–52), is most valuable. The third volume in two parts contains a chronological list of all his writings and a list of his readings.

The best life is André Billy, *Sainte-Beuve, sa vie et son temps,* 2 vols. Paris, 1952. Shorter biographies are those of Maurice Allem, *Portrait de Sainte-Beuve* (Paris, 1954) and of Harold Nicolson, *Sainte-Beuve* (London, 1957), derivative from Billy. Lewis Freeman Mott, *Sainte-Beuve,* New York, 1925; factual.

Gustave Michaut, *Sainte-Beuve avant Les Lundis* (Paris, 1903), is a full descriptive account of Sainte-Beuve's earlier writings. A. G. Lehmann, *Sainte-Beuve. A Portrait of the Critic 1804–1842* (Oxford, 1962), is a fine intellectual biography. Carlo Bo, *Delle Immagini giovanili di Sainte-Beuve* (Florence, 1938), contributes little.

Marcel Proust, *Contre Sainte-Beuve* (Paris, 1954, written 1908–10); curious.

Lander MacClintock, *Sainte-Beuve's Critical Theory and Practice after 1849* (Chicago, 1920), is a useful thesis. William Frederick Giese, *Sainte-Beuve, A Literary Portrait* (Madison, Wisc., 1931), is an enthusiastic description of his views.

Maxime Leroy, *La Pensée de Sainte-Beuve* (Paris, 1940), concerns religion and politics and hardly touches literary criticism. Gustave Michaut, *Études sur Sainte-Beuve* (Paris, 1905), discusses special points: the relation to Michiels, to Chateaubriand, etc. André Bellessort, *Sainte-Beuve et le XIXe siècle* (Paris, 1927), is a good, general account, somewhat popular in nature.

The following articles seemed to me most interesting or helpful:

Irving Babbitt, in *Masters of French Criticism* (Boston, 1912), pp. 97–188; still the best essay in English.

Gabriel Brunet, "Regard sur Sainte-Beuve," in *Évocations littéraires* (Paris, 1930), pp. 183–248; highly critical.

W. H. Frohock, "The Critic and the Cult of Art: Sainte-Beuve and the Esthetic Movement," *Romanic Review, 32* (1941), 379–88. Cf. Edna Fredrick, "The Critic and the Cult of Art: Further Observations," *ibid., 33* (1942), 385–87.

Remy de Gourmont, "Sainte-Beuve, créateur de valeurs," in *Promenades philosophiques* (9th ed. Paris, 1913), pp. 33–44; first published 1904.

Jean Hytier, "Balzac et Sainte-Beuve: une haine littéraire," *Rivista de estudios franceses, 6* (1951), 47–88.

A. G. Lehmann, "Sainte-Beuve, critique de la littérature anglaise," *Revue de littérature comparée, 18* (1954), 419–39.

Henri Peyre, many unfavorable comments in *Writers and Their Critics* (Ithaca, N.Y., 1944); index.

E. M. Phillips, "The Present State of Sainte-Beuve Studies," *French Studies, 5* (1951), 101–25, for many more references.

Martin Turnell, "Literary Criticism in France," "Sainte-Beuve," in *Scrutiny, 8* (1939), 177–82; reprinted in R. W. Stallman, *Critiques and Essays in Criticism* (New York, 1949), pp. 421–34.

Carl A. Viggiani, "Sainte-Beuve (1824–30), Critic and Creator," *Romanic Review, 44* (1953), 263–72.

Emile Zola, "Sainte-Beuve," in *Documents littéraires, Œuvres complètes,* ed. Maurice Le Blond (Paris, 1928), pp. 209–54; first published 1881.

NOTES: SAINTE-BEUVE

1. Marcel Proust, *Contre Sainte-Beuve,* Paris, 1954. Page 142: "Ce monde unique, fermé, sans communication avec le dehors qu'est l'âme du poète ..." Page 143: "L'abîme qui sépare l'écrivain de l'homme du monde ... le moi de l'écrivain ne se montre que dans ses livres."

2. *Reperusals and Recollections* (London, 1936), p. 30.

3. *NL, 3,* 13–16: "Tel arbre, tel fruit." "Familles d'esprits."

4. *Ibid.,* p. 32: "Haines de race." "Comment voulez-vous obliger Boileau à goûter Quinault; et Fontenelle à estimer grandement Boileau? et Joseph de Maistre ou Montalembert à aimer Voltaire?"

5. *CL, 3,* 51–52.

6. *NL, 3,* 17: "J'entrevois des liens, des rapports, et un esprit plus étendu, plus lumineux, et resté fin dans le détail, pourra découvrir un jour les grandes divisions naturelles qui répondent aux familles d'esprits."

7. *Po Ro, 1,* 55.

8. *NL, 9,* 70–71: "... il y aura toujours une certaine partie inexpliquée, inexplicable, celle en quoi consiste le don individuel du génie ... on aura toujours une place très suffisante ... où loger ce principal ressort, ce moteur inconnu, le centre et le foyer de l'inspiration supérieure ou de la volonté, la monade inexprimable."

9. *NL, 8,* 66 ff., esp. 70, 86, 88, 93. Page 86: "... il n'est qu'une âme, une forme particulière d'esprit pour faire tel ou tel chef-d'œuvre." Page 88: "... un dernier point et comme une dernière citadelle irréductible." Page 93: "Non, le poëte n'est pas une chose si simple, ce n'est pas une résultante ni même un simple foyer réflecteur; il a son miroir à lui, sa *monade* individuelle unique."

10. *NL, 3,* 18 ff. Cf. *Cahiers,* p. 70.

11. *NL, 8,* 71.

12. *NL, 3,* 28: "Que pensait-il en religion? Comment était-il affecté du spectacle de la nature? Comment se comportait-il sur l'article des

femmes? Était-il riche, était-il pauvre? Quelle était sa manière journalière de vivre? ... Enfin, quel était son vice ou son faible?"

13. *NL, 1*, 213: "Était-elle jolie? A-t-elle aimé? Quel a été le motif déterminant de sa conversion?"

14. *NL, 3*, 18: "Un bon naturaliste dans ce champ si vaste des esprits."

15. *NL, 6*, 400: "Le libre examen, qui n'épargne pas même les religions et les dieux, ne saurait être interdit à l'égard des poëtes."

16. *NL, 6*, 419: "... ce besoin ... de regarder dedans et derrière les cœurs ..."

17. *Cha, 1*, 95: "le monarque qu'il était *un homme*."

18. *PC, 1*, 136: "... un petit appendice à l'appui de La Rochefoucauld ..."

19. *NL, 6*, 400: "... de s'imposer ainsi tout sculpté, façonné de ses propres mains ..."

20. *Cha, 1*, 83–84, 201 n.: "Quelle arrangement et quelle pose jusque dans la mort!" *2*, 58.

21. *NL, 2*, 17: "... il faut faire les portraits le plus ressemblants possible, le plus étudiés et réellement vivants, y mettre les verrues, les signes au visage, tout ce qui caractérise une physionomie au naturel, et faire partout sentir le nu et les chairs sous les draperies, sous le pli même et le faste du manteau."

22. Letter to Ernest Bersot, 9 May 1863: "Glisser le scalpel et indiquer le défaut de la cuirasse? de montre les points de suture entre le talent et l'âme? ..." "l'âme la plus sordide, le plus méchant singe qui existe." In *Correspondance* (2 vols., Paris, 1877–78), *1*, 316.

23. *Po Li, 2*, 116, 115, 118.

24. *Mes Poisons*, p. 49: " 'C'est un homme, me disait M. Molé, qui calcule tout ce qu'il dit, jusques au *bonjour*.' Et it était comme cela dès l'âge de seize ans; mais moi, je croyais d'abord à ses paroles. —Je ne crois pas qu'il y ait d'homme à qui il coûte moins de mentir."

25. *NL, 5*, 253: "... le siècle du charlatanisme littéraire, humanitaire, éclectique, néo-catholique et autre ..."

26. *NL, 10*, 149: "... sa lyre et son âme, sa vie et son œuvre sont une même chose."

27. *Po Li, 1*, 30: "... les biographes s'étaient imaginé, je ne sais pourquoi, que l'histoire d'un écrivain était tout entière dans ses écrits, et leur critique superficielle ne poussait pas jusqu'à l'homme au fond du poëte."

28. *Pre Lu, 2*, 298–99: "L'écrivain est toujours assez facile à juger, mais l'homme ne l'est pas également." "... qu'un homme est difficile à connaître. ... Dès qu'on cherche l'hommé dans l'écrivain, le lien du

moral au talent, on ne saurait étudier de trop près, de trop bonne heure, tandis et à mesure que l'objet vit."

29. Pensées XX, in back of *Vie, poésies et pensées de Joseph Delorme*, p. 141: "L'artiste, comme s'il était doué d'un sens à part, s'occupe paisiblement à sentir sous ce monde apparent l'autre monde tout intérieur qu'ignorent la plupart . . . Il assiste au jeu invisible des forces, et sympathise avec elles comme avec des âmes; il a reçu en naissant la clef des symboles et l'intelligence des figures."

30. *NL, 4,* 363: "L'art aussi est un monde. . . . Le philosophe, le moraliste, le sage, le chrétien y peuvent profiter: le poëte qui, par ses conceptions puissantes, fait rivalité au monde et dont le secret est de le réfléchir dans un miroir magique immense, se sent déconcerté, découragé; il s'arrête de désespoir à mi-chemin, s'il y a trouvé son calvaire."

31. *Cha, 1,* 135: "La vraie raison peut-être pour laquelle on n'a jamais tiré ce masque de Chateaubriand, c'est que lui-même avait sa sincérité et qu'il n'a jamais trop dissimulé que ce fût un masque,—un masque noble."

32. *Ibid.,* 148: "Sa sincérité, je ne dis pas de fidèle (cet ordre supérieur et intime nous échappe), mais sa sincérité d'artiste et d'écrivain."

33. *NL, 6,* 338: "La nature à travers un léger travestissement. . . . 'Le masque nous a rendus vrais.'"

34. *CL, 13,* 277: "homme d'esprit, sagace, fin, perçant et excitant."

35. *NL, 3,* 110–11. ". . . je ne puis en mon âme et conscience consentir à un tel jugement, et je ne pense pas qu'aucun de ceux qui ont connu le personnage y souscrive. . . . Je conçois qu'un homme qui laisse des ouvrages achevés, des monuments peu accueillis d'abord et peu compris de ses contemporains . . . soit proclamé homme de génie sur sa tombe, tandis qu'il ne passait de son vivant que pour un original distingué."

36. *Pre Lu, 2,* 299–300: ". . . les hommes, les œuvres secondaires m'intéressent singulièrement en bien des circonstances. C'est pour moi véritablement affaire d'équité."

37. *Tableau,* Paris, 1876. *1,* 149, 256. There is a full study of the difference between the two versions in G. Michaut, *Études sur Sainte-Beuve,* Paris, 1905.

38. E.g. *Tableau, 1,* 106, 134, on Hardy, p. 402.

39. Cf. *Po Ro, 3,* 94, 323, 326–27, 343.

40. *Po Ro, 6,* 245: "un investigateur, un observateur sincère, attentif et scrupuleux. . . . de voir les choses et les hommes comme ils sont, et de les exprimer comme on les voit, de décrire autour de soi, en serviteur de la science, les variétés de l'espèce, les diverses formes de l'organisation humaine, étrangement modifiée au moral dans la société et dans le dédale artificiel des doctrines." Page 243: "le mystère de ces âmes

pieuses, de ces existences intérieures, y recueillir la poésie intime et profonde qui s'en exhalait."

41. See Antoine Adam, *Histoire de la littérature française au XVIIe siècle*, Vol. 2, L'Époque de Pascal, pp. 178–79. L'Abbé Bremond, *Histoire littéraire du sentiment religieux*, and J. Laporte, *La Doctrine de la grâce chez Arnauld* (Paris, 1922), give different interpretations of Port Royal.

42. *Po Ro, 1, 146.*

43. *Ibid.,* 147 ff.; 2, 53; 3, 272 ff.; 2, 395 ff.; 6, 83 ff.

44. *Po Ro, 1,* 147 ff. Page 240: "l'euphuïsme... et le gongorisme de la dévotion."

45. *Po Ro, 3,* 120; 6, 118 ff.

46. *Po Ro, 2,* 386. Page 409: "l'homme naturel"; pp. 425–26: "La méthode... peut se qualifier à bon droit perfide." Cf. p. 397.

47. *Po Ro, 3,* 451: "... Archimède en pleurs au pied de la Croix."

48. *Po Ro, 3,* 414 ff.

49. *PC, 5,* 215: "Sa foi fut antérieure à son doute."

50. *Po Ro, 3,* 53, 102 n., 103, 121.

51. *Po Ro, 3,* 400–01, 414, cf. 105 n.

52. *CL, 1,* 317–18: "Sa philosophie de l'histoire... n'en est pas moins beaucoup trop logique pour être vraie." Cf. Albert Sorel, "Sainte-Beuve et les historiens" in *Études de littérature et d'histoire* (Paris, 1901), pp. 59–72.

53. *Cha, 1,* 19: "... connaître les hommes n'est pas assez quand il s'agit des œuvres; et tout en s'appliquant à bien caractériser les productions de l'esprit comme l'expression d'un temps et d'un ordre de société, on ne saurait négliger d'y saisir ce qui n'est pas de la vie passagère, ce qui tient à la flamme immortelle et sacrée, au génie même des Lettres."

54. *Cha, 1,* 35–36 n.: "Avant tout reproduire le mouvement, l'unité et l'ensemble d'une époque littéraire..." Page 35: "... à ce qui a influé, à ce qui compte."

55. *NL, 4,* 296: "une nécropole... la succession et le jeu des écoles et des groupes, les noms et la physionomie des vrais chefs, à marquer les caractères et les degrés des principaux talents, le mérite des œuvres vraiment saillantes et dignes de mémoire..."

56. *Pre Lu, 3,* 142 ff. A review of Crépet's *Les Poètes français,* 1861.

57. *Cha, 1,* 36: "... dans l'histoire littéraire, là où les soldats comptent moins, et où les chefs sont presque tout."

58. *Cha, 1,* 14: "la cigale obligée de chanter dans la gueule du lion."

59. *CL, 2,* 145: "Un Epicurien qui a l'imagination catholique."

60. *Cha, 1,* 23; 2, 91. *1,* 206: "Il a transporté le centre de la prose de Rome à Byzance, et quelquefois par delà Byzance, de Rome à Antioche

ou à Laodicée. C'est de lui que date dans la prose française le style bas-empire."

61. *PF,* 381: "Il est doux de comprendre tout ce qui a vécu." Cf. *CL,* 5, 39: "Il y a lieu de peindre, dans un temps, tout ce qui a vécu, brillé, fleuri à son heure . . ."

62. *CL, 15,* 67–68: ". . . j'aime tout ce qui est de l'homme quand l'homme est distingué et supérieur; je me laisse et me laisserai toujours prendre à la curiosité de la vie, et à ce chef-d'œuvre de la vie,—un grand et puissant esprit; avant de la juger, je ne pense qu'à la comprendre et qu'à en jouir quand je suis en présence d'une haut et brillante personnalité."

63. *Mes Poisons,* p. 10: "je me détache de moi . . ."

64. *NL, 2,* 1–2: "Mon désir serait de le faire dans un parfait esprit d'impartialité; car cette impartialité, cette neutralité même . . . devient, je l'avoue, un de mes derniers plaisirs intellectuels. Si c'est un dilettantisme, je confesse que j'en suis atteint."

65. *NL, 5,* 391: "je me pique peut-être de n'être rien en particulier et que je m'aime mieux apparemment sous cette forme brisée, multiple et fuyante que sous toute autre."

66. *Cha, 1,* 19.

67. *Ibid.,* p. 264: "Une généreuse indifférence."

68. *PL, 1,* 367: ". . . qu'on soit fanatique ou même trop convaincu, ou épris d'une autre passion quelconque." Page 369: "Cette indifférence du fond, il faut bien le dire, cette tolérance prompte, facile, aiguisée de plaisir, est une des conditions essentielles du génie critique." Pages 370–71: "au revers du génie créateur et poétique, du génie philosophique avec système; il prend tout en considération, fait tout valoir. . . . Le génie critique n'a rien de trop digne, ni de prude, ni de préoccupé. . . . Il ne reste pas dans son centre . . . il ne craint pas de se mésallier. . . ." Page 377: "cette faculté critique et discursive, relâchée et accommodante. Le métier de critique est comme un voyage perpétuel avec toutes sortes de personnes et en toutes sortes de pays, par curiosité."

69. *Mes Poisons,* p. 10: "La critique littéraire, celle même que je fais, hélas! est à peu près incompatible avec la pratique chrétienne. Juger, toujours juger autrui! ou bien reproduire autrui, se transformer en lui, comme je fais souvent: opération au fond toute païenne, métamorphoses d'Ovide."

70. *NL, 1,* 9: "L'auteur . . . ne comprend que sa propre manière d'être et sa propre individualité; par cela même il nous avertit qu'il n'est pas un critique." Page 10: "J'ai souvent pensé que le mieux pour le critique qui voudrait se réserver le plus de largeur de vues, ce serait de n'avoir aucune faculté d'artiste, de peur de porter ensuite dans ses divers jugements la secrète prédilection d'un père et d'un auteur intéressé."

71. *CL, 1,* 278: "L'art de la critique... consiste à savoir lire judicieusement les auteurs, et à apprendre aux autres à les lire de même."

72. *Po Li, 3,* 546: "Le critique n'est qu'un homme *qui sait lire, et qui apprend à lire aux autres.*"

73. *Cha, 1,* 189: "Savoir bien lire un livre en le jugeant chemin faisant, et sans cesser de le goûter, c'est presque tout l'art du critique. Cet art consiste encore à comparer, et à bien prendre ses points de comparaison: ainsi, a côté *d'Atala* lire *Paul et Virginie* et *Manon Lescaut;*— à côté de *René* lire *Oberman* et *le Lépreux;* —à côté des *Martyrs* lire *l'Odyssée, Télémaque* et Milton. Faites cela, et laissez-vous faire. Le jugement résultera tout naturellement en vous et se formera de votre impression même."

74. *PC, 5,* 342: "Après créer et enfanter des œuvres de génie, il reste encore quelque chose de digne et de beau, c'est de les sentir et de les faire admirer. L'enthousiasme, la *muse* du critique doit être là."

75. *PC, 1,* 416: "Car, loin de nous de penser que le devoir et l'office de la critique consistent uniquement à venir après les grands artistes, à suivre leurs traces lumineuses, à recueillir, à ranger, à inventorier leur héritage, à orner leur monument de tout ce qui peut le faire valoir et l'éclairer! Cette critique-là sans doute a droit à nos respects; elle est grave, savante, définitive; elle explique, elle pénètre, elle fixe et consacre des admirations confuses, des beautés en partie voilées, des conceptions difficiles à atteindre, et aussi la lettre des textes quand il y a lieu." Page 417: "... elle doit s'attacher à eux de préférence... faire honte à la médiocrité qui les coudoie, crier *place* autour d'eux comme le héraut d'armes, marcher devant leur char comme l'écuyer." See Heine's witty ridicule, quoted below, p. 335.

76. *CL, 1,* 373: "Le *secrétaire* du public..." *4,* 515: "Un bibliothécaire de confiance."

77. *Po Li, 3,* 546: "La critique, telle que je l'entends et telle que je voudrais la pratiquer, est une *invention* et une *création* perpetuelle."

78. Letter to J.-G. Chaudes-Aigues, June 7–8, 1838. *Correspondance générale, 2,* 384: "Une dépendance de la partie élégiaque et romanesque."

79. *PF,* p. 411: "exhaler avec détour une certaine poésie cachée."

80. *PC, 3,* 399: "... sous prétexte de peindre quelqu'un, c'est souvent un profil de lui-même qu'il cherche à saisir."

81. *PC, 2,* 486–87.

82. *PC, 3,* 362: "la pénètre, comme ferait un aromate secret." Pages 363–64: "... l'esprit poètique, intime, précis, et en tant qu'il touche aux racines mêmes, existe plus peut-être que dans d'autres manières bien autrement brillantes et spécieuses ..."

83. *Cha, 2,* 93: "Si, dans une œuvre nouvelle, l'originalité réelle suffit

à racheter les défauts? de quel ordre est l'ouvrage? de quelle portée et de quelle *volée* est l'auteur?"

84. *Ibid.*, p. 95: "Le vrai critique devance le publique, le dirige et le guide."

85. *PC, 5,* 265.

86. *Ibid.*, pp. 268–69: "La haine d'un sot livre . . . ce sens juste et vif."

87. *CL, 1,* 382: "ils vous diront tout, excepté un jugement. . . . Ils n'oseront se commettre jusqu'à dire: Ceci est bon, ceci est mauvais."

88. *CL, 15,* 356: "de maintenir la tradition et de conserver le goût."

89. *CL, 15,* 376: "Le degrés de l'art, les étages de l'esprit."

90. *CL, 12,* 191: "La vraie critique . . . consiste plus que jamais à étudier chaque être, c'est-à-dire chaque auteur, chaque talent, selon les conditions de sa nature, à en faire une vive et fidèle description, à charge toutefois de le classer ensuite et de le mettre à sa place dans l'ordre de l'Art." Cf. *NL, 3,* 300.

91. *CL, 6,* 511–12: "Saluons et reconnaissons aujourd'hui la noble et forte harmonie du grand siècle. Sans Boileau, et sans Louis XIV qui reconnaissait Boileau comme son Contrôleur-Général du Parnasse, que serait-il arrivé? Les plus grands talents eux-mêmes auraient-ils rendu également tout ce qui forme désormais leur plus solide héritage de gloire? Racine, je le crains, aurait fait plus souvent des *Bérénice;* La Fontaine moins de Fables et plus de Contes; Molière lui-même aurait donné davantage dans les Scapins, et n'aurait peut-être pas atteint aux hauteurs sévères du *Misanthrope.* En un mot, chacun de ses beaux génies aurait abondé dans ses défauts. Boileau, c'est-à-dire le bon sens du poëte critique, autorisé et doublé de celui d'un grand roi, les contint tous et les contraignit, par sa présence respectée, à leurs meilleures et à leurs plus graves œuvres." Cf. a similar, earlier (1844) passage: *Po Li, 1,* 115–16.

92. *CL, 6,* 512.

93. *CL, 2,* 456–57.

94. *NL, 4,* 72.

95. *NL, 9,* 86–87: "Épicurisme du goût, à jamais perdu, religion dernière ce ceux même qui n'avaient plus que celle-là, dernier honneur et dernière vertu des Hamilton et des Pétrone, comme je te comprends, comme je te regrette, même en te combattant, même en t'abjurant."

96. *Po Ro, 2,* 89: "Il ne paraît jamais plus noble, plus complet, plus véritablement délicat et élevé, qu'au sein d'une nature saintement morale; mais il se voit souvent très développé chez des natures bien différentes. Une certaine corruption agréable (est-il permis de le confesser?) n'y messied pas, et en raffine même extrêmement plusieurs parties rares."

97. *NL, 2, 27; CL, 3,* 391: "la pudeur de l'esprit."

98. *NL, 1,* 12: "de plus fin et de plus instinctif."

99. *CL, 1,* 283: "l'amour du simple, du sensé, de l'élevé, de ce qui est grand ..."

100. *NL, 9,* 277: "Eugénie de Guérin craignait l'excès; elle n'appuie pas, elle ne *tâche* pas: elle avait du goût."

101. *CL, 3,* 40: "L'idée de *classique* implique en soi quelque chose qui a suite et consistance, qui fait ensemble et tradition, qui se compose, se transmet et qui dure."

102. *Pre Lu, 2,* 226, on Mickiewicz, 1833: "une sorte de Bohémien vagabond et presque de Juif errant ..."

103. *CL, 3,* 53: "Car il faut choisir, et la première condition du goût ... est de ne pas voyager sans cesse, mais de s'asseoir une fois et de se fixer. Rien ne blase et n'éteint plus le goût que les voyages sans fin ..."

104. *CL, 15,* 373–78. Page 373: "Le professeur n'est pas le critique. Le critique ... est une sentinelle toujours en éveille, sur le qui-vive. ... il doit peu s'écarter des lieux consacrés qu'il a charge de montrer et de desservir." Page 376: "On est fier de simples trouvailles curieuses (quand elles le sont), qui n'exigent aucune méditation, aucun effort d'esprit, mais seulement la peine d'aller et de ramasser. ... On dirait que l'ère des scholiastes et commentateurs se rouvre et recommence. On est aussi honoré, considéré pour cela, et bien plus, que si l'on avait tenté un beau roman, un beau poëme, les chemins de la vraie invention, les routes élevées de la pensée. ... encourageons toute recherche laborieuse, mais laissons en tout la maîtrise au talent, à la méditation, au jugement, à la raison, au goût." Page 378: "... on en viendrait en tout à préférer les matériaux à l'œuvre, l'échafaudage au monument."

105. *NL, 5,* 471: "Par nature et par goût, je n'aurais jamais été de ceux qui ont défriché le Moyen-Age ... l'enthousiasme excessif des uns, la complaisance un peu minutieuse des autres ..."

106. *NL, 3,* 384: "[Ils] n'avaient pas et n'ont pas en eux tous les terme voulus de comparaison." Page 396: "Quiconque ... a lu Sophocle dans le texte est à jamais préservé de ces éclipses ou de ces aberrations du goût."

107. *CL, 15,* 358: "nous avons à embrasser, à comprendre, à ne jamais déserter l'héritage de ces maîtres et de ces pères illustres, héritage qui, depuis Homère jusqu'au dernier des classiques d'hier ... forme le plus clair et le plus solide de notre fonds intellectuel." Page 362: "Le sentiment d'un certain beau conforme à notre race, à notre éducation, à notre civilisation, voilà ce dont il ne faut jamais se départir ... leur héritage pour nous et leurs bienfaits se confondent." Pages 367–68: "... les plus grands des hommes ne sont jamais extravagants, ridicules,

grotesques, fastueux, jactancieux, cyniques, *messéants* en permanence.
... la tradition nous le dit, et la conscience de notre propre nature
civilisée nous le dit encore plus haut, la raison toujours doit présider et
préside en définitive, même entre ces favoris et ces élus de l'imagination ..."

108. *CL, 15,* 369; *NL, 3,* 265: "Goethe, le plus grand des critiques
modernes et de tous les temps ..."

109. *CL, 15,* 369–70: "les littératures ... contentes d'être de leur
nation, de leur temps, du régime où elles naissent et fleurissent ... les
littératures qui sont et qui se sentent chez elles, dans leur voie, non
déclassées, non troublantes n'ayant pas pour principe le *malaise,* qui
n'a jamais été un principe de beauté." Page 370: "La littérature classique
ne se plaint pas, ne gémit pas, ne s'ennuie pas." Pages 370–71: "Le
classique ... a cela ... d'aimer sa patrie, son temps, de ne voir rien de
plus désirable ni de plus beau."

110. *CL, 6,* 397 ff.

111. *CL, 15,* 371: "Hamlet, Werther, Childe Harold, les Renés purs,
sont des malades pour chanter et souffrir, pour jouer de leur mal ... la
maladie pour la maladie."

112. *CL, 1,* 18–19: "La jeunesse ... est devenue positive; elle ne rêve
plus ..."

113. *CL, 15,* 372: "... on se retrouverait à l'unisson; la lutte, la
maladie morale cesseraient, et la littérature d'elle-même redeviendrait
classique par les grandes lignes et par le fond (c'est l'essentiel). ... Nous
recommencerions peut-être à avoir des monuments."

114. *CL, 15,* 381: "Ils ne pensent pas en effet, pour le moment, au
même objet, aux mêmes ouvrages de l'auteur en question, aux mêmes
endroits de ses œuvres; que c'est qu'ils ne l'ont pas tout entier présent,
qu'ils ne le *comprennent* pas actuellement tout entier. Une attention
et une connaissance plus étendues rapprocheraient les jugements dissi-
dents et les remettraient d'accord."

115. *NL, 3,* 378: "Relisez un chant d'Homère, une scène de Sophocle,
un chœur d'Euripide, un livre de Virgile! grandeur ou flamme du
sentiment, éclat de l'expression et, s'il se peut, harmonie de composition
et d'ensemble ..."

116. Cf. *Cahiers de notes grecques,* ed. Ruth Mulhauser (Chapel Hill,
N.C., 1955), badly edited. See review by F. M. Combellack in *Comparative Literature, 8* (1956), 351–54.

117. *Virgile,* p. 23: "un prêtre de Virgile. ... cette école française
admiratrice de l'antiquité dans le sens de Fontanes, de Chateaubriand,
de Delille lui-même ..." Page 24: "De Virgile, d'Horace, d'Ovide, de
Lucain jusqu'à nous, la pente est unie, la perspective est droite et

ininterrompue ... C'est uniquement par le majestueux et triomphal aqueduc romain que sont arrivées jusqu'à nous bien des fontaines de la Grèce." Page 25: "... une religion plus discrète qui tient à l'amour du beau, du naturel, du fin et du délicat dans la poésie."

118. *Ibid.*, pp. 89, 92, 94, 99, 102: "... l'unité de ton et de couleur, de l'harmonie et de la convenance des parties entre elles, de la proportion, de ce goût soutenu, qui est ici un des signes du génie, parce qu'il tient au fond comme à la fleur de l'âme, et qu'on me laissera appeler une suprême délicatesse ..."

119. *Ibid.*, pp. 433, 434, 440. Page 433: "un bréviaire de goût, de poésie, de sagesse pratique et mondaine." Page 440: "un ange, une âme."

120. *Pre Lu, 3,* 72–133.

121. *CL, 11,* 198 ff., esp. 208: "L'expression de l'histoire de son temps."

122. *CL, 14,* 282, 284, 296, 282: "Deux ou trois perles dans son fumier."

123. *CL, 12,* 63: "Un acte de goût." Page 69: "Un poëte assez facile, et plutôt trop facile."

124. *NL, 13,* 310.

125. *CL, 12,* 65.

126. *CL, 12,* 173 ff.; 176, 179.

127. *Pre Lu, 3,* 143.

128. *CL, 8,* 73: "En tout, Malherbe, même dans sa maigreur et son peu d'étoffe, est toujours digne et a des moments d'une élégance parfaite et ravissante." Cf. *NL, 13,* 360.

129. *Po Ro, 3,* 274: "Shakspeare, le plus grand (dans l'ordre poétique) des hommes purement naturels." On Shakespeare see also *PC, 5,* 331; *Pre Lu, 1,* 330.

130. *Po Li, 1,* 22: "un code poétique abrégé"; page 15: "Boileau, selon nous, est un esprit sensé et fin, poli et mordant, peu fécond; d'une agréable brusquerie; religieux observateur du vrai goût; bon écrivain en vers ..."

131. *Po Li, 1,* 95. Page 92: "des sentiments personnels, tendres, passionnés, fervents."

132. *Pre Lu, 2,* 207: "Moi-même, hélas! ... n'ai-je pas prétendu quelque part qu'il était bien plus propre à l'élégie, au lyrique, qu'au dramatique ..."

133. *Po Li, 1,* 130: "Un poëte lyrique, c'est une âme à nu qui passe et chante au milieu du monde ..." Page 131: "un monde à part, un monde poétique de sentiments et d'idées ..." Page 133: "... ce fut le moins lyrique de tous les hommes à la moins lyrique de toutes les époques."

134. *Po Li, 2,* 97, 98. Page 97: "ni l'art ni le style poétique."

135. *Po Li, 1,* 174: "Chénier est le révélateur d'une poésie d'avenir, et il apporte au monde une lyre nouvelle ..."

136. *CL, 9,* 535: "On passait subitement d'une Poésie sèche, maigre, pauvre ... à une Poésie large, vraiment intérieure, abondante, élevée et toute divine."

137. *PC, 1,* 295–300.

138. *Ibid.,* pp. 308–48.

139. *Ibid.,* pp. 349–74.

140. *CL, 1,* 20–34, 63–78.

141. *CL, 4,* 389–407, with disparaging comment on *Histoire des Girondins.*

142. *CL, 7,* 533: "Lamartine vise habituellement à l'ange, et La Fontaine, s'il semble élever les bêtes jusqu'à l'homme, n'oublie jamais non plus que l'homme n'est que le premier des animaux." Page 535: "noble, volontiers sublime, étherée et harmonieuse, mais vague ..."

143. *PC, 1,* 378; also *CL, 11,* 462.

144. *Pre Lu, 1,* 179, 187.

145. *Mes Poisons,* pp. 46–47: "Hugo dramatique, c'est Caliban qui pose pour Shakespeare."

146. *PC, 2,* 536–42, cf. 70.

147. *Chroniques parisiennes,* p. 245 (1844): "Cette poésie-là me paraît comme de l'albâtre assez artistement travaillé, mais pâle, sans couleur; la vie et le sang n'y circulent pas." Also in *Correspondance générale, 5,* Part II, 644, letter to J. Olivier, 5 August 1844.

148. *NL, 6,* 398 ff., 440: "un déclin très bien soutenu ..."

149. *CL, 2,* 306.

150. *PC, 3,* 321.

151. *PC, 2,* 202 ff.

152. *CL, 13,* 364 ff.

153. *PC, 5,* 119.

154. *PC, 2,* 523: "Un art exagéré chez qui la forme surmonte, écrase si étrangement le fond."

155. See, e.g., *NL, 1,* 205.

156. *NL, 6,* 265 ff.

157. *CL, 14,* 74, 79, 72, 78. Page 72: "un grand romantique, et en ce sens qu'il avait remonté à l'inspiration directe de la beauté grecque, et aussi en cet autre sens qu'il avait ouvert, par *René,* une veine toute neuve de rêve et d'émotion poétique." Page 78: "... songeons un peu à ce qu'a été la poésie lyrique moderne, en Angleterre, de Kirke White à Keats et à Tennyson en passant par Byron et les Lakistes, —en Allemagne, de Bürger à Uhland et à Rückert en passant par Goethe, —et demandons-nous quelle figure nous ferions, nous et notre littérature,

dans cette comparaison avec tant de richesses étrangères modernes, si nous n'avions pas eu notre poésie, cette même école poétique tant raillée. . . . Supposez-la absente, quelle lacune!"

158. *CL, 9, 330*: "Venu à ce genre de composition que par la critique, et d'après certaines idées antérieures et préconçues."

159. *CL, 9, 305, 334, 337*; p. 335: "une spirituelle mascarade italienne."

160. *CL, 13, 276–77.*

161. *NL, 3, 109 ff.* Page 118: "Il découronne par trop l'imagination humaine. Par aversion pour le clinquant, il fait trop fi des richesses de la parole et des magnificences légitimes qu'en tirent la passion, la fantaisie ou l'éloquence."

162. *PC, 2, 327–57.*

163. *Ibid.*, p. 346 n.: ". . . quand j'ai lu ces choses-là, il me semble toujours que j'ai besoin de me laver les mains et de brosser mon habit." For Ampère, see *Mes Poisons*, p. 110.

164. *Ibid.*, p. 469: "maréchaux de France . . . qui s'évalue à *deux millions*, si j'ai bien compris."

165. *Po Ro, 1, 549 ff.*, 558–59.

166. See *NL, 3, 19.*

167. *CL, 2, 443–63.*

168. *Ibid.*, particularly pp. 443, 449, 456, 459, 461–62. Page 443: "peut-être le plus original, le plus approprié, et le plus pénétrant." Page 459: "Cela ne se passe point ainsi dans la vie." Page 461: "un plus grand, plus sûr et plus ferme écrivain . . . elle ne tâtonne jamais dans l'expression . . . peut-être l'égal de M. de Balzac en invention, en fécondité et en composition." Page 462: "ne sait pas autant écrire que Balzac."

169. Quoted by Billy, 2, 38. A letter to Benoît Jouvin, September 1866.

170. *CL, 13, 346 ff.* Page 347: "Un livre composé, médité, où tout se tient, où rien n'est laissé au hasard de la plume." Page 360: "Sa méthode qui consiste à tout décrire et à insister sur tout ce qui se rencontre . . . Un livre, après tout, n'est pas et ne saurait jamais être la réalité même." Page 363: "Fils et frère de médecins distingués, M. Gustave Flaubert tient la plume comme d'autres le scalpel. Anatomistes et physiologistes, je vous retrouve partout!"

171. *NL, 4, 73 ff.* Page 77: "Mais les nerfs humains ne sont pas des cordages, et, quand ils en ont trop, quand ils ont été trop broyés et torturés, ils ne sentent plus rien."

172. *Ibid.*, pp. 90, 95. Page 90: "mangeurs de choses immondes."

173. *CL, 9, 527–29*: "vous vous êtes dit, j'imagine: 'Eh bien! j'en trouverai encore de la poésie, et j'en trouverai là où nul ne s'était avisé de la cueillir et de l'exprimer.' Et vous avez pris l'enfer, vous vous êtes

fait diable." "Vous vous défiez trop de la passion; c'est chez vous une théorie. Vous accordez trop à l'esprit, à la combinaison ... n'ayez jamais peur d'être trop commun ..."

174. *CL, 15,* 350–51.

175. Letter to Baudelaire, 1860, quoted by Billy, *2,* 107: "Ce livre très spirituel, très ingénieux, très raffiné."

176. *NL, 1,* 400–01: "M. Baudelaire a trouvé moyen de se bâtir ... un kiosque bizarre ... et mystérieux, où on lit de l'Edgar Poë, où l'on récite des sonnets exquis, où l'on s'enivre avec le haschich pour en raisonner après, où l'on prend de l'opium et mille drogues abominables dans des tasses d'une porcelaine achevée. Ce singulier kiosque, fait en marqueterie, d'une originalité concertée et composite, qui, depuis quelque temps, attire les regards à la pointe extrême du Kamtchatka romantique, j'appelle cela *la folie Baudelaire.*" Page 402: "... un candidat poli, respectueux, exemplaire, d'un gentil garçon, fin de langage et tout à fait classique dans les formes."

177. Billy *2,* 116. For other comment, cf. Proust, *Contra Sainte-Beuve.*

178. See Georges Roth, "Ce que Sainte-Beuve a su d'anglais," *Revue Germanique, 12* (1921), 378–81; and A. C. Lehmann, *Sainte-Beuve,* in bibliography.

179. *CL, 2,* 226–46.

180. *CL, 11,* 139 ff., 195: "L'union de la poésie de la famille et du foyer avec celle de la nature."

181. *CL, 8,* 431 ff.

182. *NL, 8,* 126 ff.

183. *NL, 10,* 447–48.

184. *NL, 9,* 85: *"faire le siège* d'un écrivain ..."

185. *PC, 1,* 162–63; *Po Ro, 3,* 251: "à brûle-pourpoint."

186. *NL, 1,* 3 ff.

187. *Cha, 1,* 172 ff., 252: "image 'verticale.' "

188. *NL, 7,* 199 ff.

189. *PL, 1,* 156.

BIBLIOGRAPHY: ITALIAN CRITICISM

Giuseppe Borgese, *Storia della critica romantica in Italia* (Naples, 1905; reprinted Florence, 1949), is the only book that discusses all these authors, but its perspective seems to me quite distorted. There is much useful comment in Walter Binni, ed., *I Classici italiani nella storia della critica,* 2 vols. Florence, 1954–55. See also Aldo Vallone, *La Critica dantesca nell'ottocento*, Florence, 1958; and Mario Puppo, *Poetica e cultura del romanticismo*, Rome, 1962.

Scalvini is quoted from *Foscolo, Manzoni, Goethe* (quoted as *FMG*), Turin, 1948. On S.: Mario Marcazzan, "Ugo Foscolo nella critica di Giovita Scalvini," in *Romanticismo critico e coscienza storica*, Florence, 1947; and Puppo, pp. 139–71.

Gioberti is quoted from Edizione Nazionale. Vols. 2 and 3: *Del Primato morale e civile degli Italiani*, ed. Ugo Redanó, Milan, 1938–39; Vol. 11: *Del Bello*, ed. Enrico Castelli, Milan, 1939; other passages from *Scritti Scelti*, ed. Augusto Guzzo, Turin, 1954, on Gioberti: see Carmelo Sgroi, *L'Estetica e la critica letteraria di V. Gioberti*, Florence, 1921; Carlo Calcaterra, "Gli studi dantesche di V. Gioberti," in *Dante e il Piemonte* (Turin, 1922), pp. 39–256.

Tommaseo has to be quoted from original editions. *Opere*, ed. A. Borlenghi, Naples, 1958, contains little criticism; *Commento alla Divina Commedia*, ed. U. Cosmo, 3 vols. Turin, 1920. On Tommaseo: Paolo Prunas, *La Critica, l'arte e l'idea sociale di Niccolò Tommaseo*, Florence, 1901; Fausto Montanari, "L'Estetica e la critica di Niccolò Tommaseo," *Giornale storico della letteratura italiana*, 98 (1931), 1–72; Ettore Caccia, *Tommaseo critico e Dante*, Florence, 1956; Croce comments in *Conversazioni critiche*, (Bari, 1950), *1*, 63–67. See Petre Ciureanu, "Un'amicizia italiana: Sainte-Beuve e Tommaseo," in *Revue de littérature comparée*, 28 (1954), 444–57.

Mazzini is quoted from Edizione nazionale: *Scritti letterari, editi e inediti*, 5 vols. Imola, 1906–19. There also the French and English versions of many articles. On M. see De Sanctis, *La Letteratura italiana nel secolo XIX*, 2 (Bari, 1953), 363–79; and Borgese. G. Guadagnini, "La Fonte delle teorie romantiche mazziniane," *Giornale storico della letteratura italiana*, *89* (1927), 37–110, sees Madame de Staël as M.'s main source.

On Emiliani Giudici see Getto, and Antonio Russi, "Paolo E. G. e la storia letteraria dell'età romantica," *Convivium*, *11* (1939), 402–09.

On Settembrini see Bonaventura Zumbini, in *Studi di letteratura italiana*, Florence, 1894.

Tenca is quoted from *Giornalismo e letteratura nell'ottocento*, ed. G. Scalia, Bologna, 1959; a fuller selection, *Prose e poesie scelte*, ed. Tullo Massarani, 2 vols. Milan, 1888; on Tenca Borgese, Carlo Muscetta, introduction to De Sanctis, *La Scuola cattolico-liberale* (Torino, 1953), pp. xxx–xli, and Scalia's introduction; see Umberto Bosco, "Giusti, Tenca, Carducci," *Giornale storico della letteratura italiana*, *134* (1957), 535–47. Reprinted in *Realismo romantico* (Rome, 1959), pp. 111–26.

NOTES: ITALIAN CRITICISM

1. *Scritti,* ed. Niccolò Tommaseo, Florence, 1860. Mario Marcazzan was the first to study the manuscripts preserved in Brescia and to edit *Foscolo, Manzoni, Goethe,* Turin, 1948.

2. The essay on *Ortis,* written in 1817, was not printed until 1871, as preface to an edition of Foscolo's novel. *FMG,* pp. 432–33: "una grande fragranza di poesia: ma è fragranza artificiale . . . una miniera di piccoli poemetti."

3. *FMG,* p. 210: "forma interna"; page 212: "l'idea, l'anima." Page 221: "Nel suo libro è non so che di austero, quasi direi d'uniforme, d'insistente senza alcuna tregua mai verso un unico obbietto: non ti senti spaziare libero per entro la gran varietà del mondo morale: t'accorgi spesso di non essere sotto la gran volta del firmamento che cuopre tutte le multiformi esistenze, ma bensì d'essere sotto quella del tempio che cuopre i fedeli e l'altare."

4. *FMG,* p. 383: "L'arte non deve somigliare all'universo governato della necessità, ma deve ritrarre l'uomo, la vita dell'umanità. La libertà è il fondamento dell'arte. L'arte esce dalla vita e dee uscire alla vita"; page 370: "L'arte dev'essere volta al miglioramento degli uomini."

5. *FMG,* p. 270: "Nell'arte l'idea esce dagli occulti seni dell'infinito, senza perdere nullameno in tutto la sua universalità." Page 233, symbol vs. allegory. Pages 307–08: "Coll'aumentare di questi aumentano i giudizi."

6. *Scritti scelti,* pp. 175–79: "La fantasia degli spettatori è il vero e unico teatro." Cf. Susanne K. Langer, *Feeling and Form,* New York, 1953.

7. Edizione Nazionale, *Del Bello,* p. 158: "Dante non avrebbe potuto essere il massimo poeta e scrittore se non fosse stato eziandio filosofo e teologo insigne." Page 159: "Se l'inferno per un certo rispetto serve al poeta di velo allegorico per dipingere e sferzare la corrotta patria, divenuta quasi un inferno dei vivi, l'ingegno del magnanimo esule s'innalza a più vasto concepimento e ravvisa nella scena del mondo un' ombra delle verità superiori, considerando l'ordine delle cose imma- nenti come il tipo delle successive. Il qual concetto, che spazia e signor- eggia per tutta la Divina Commedia, costituisce il vincolo delle tre cantiche, l'unità e l'armonia di tutto il poema."

8. Printed in *Opere di V. Gioberti,* 27, Naples, 1866. Carlo Calca- terra, "Gli Studi danteschi di V. Gioberti," in *Dante e il Piemonte* (Turin, 1922), pp. 39–256, studied these notes carefully and makes large claims for them. But they do not differ substantially from the later comments.

9. *Del Bello*, p. 172: "Catolicissimo."

10. *Scritti scelti*, p. 628: "Il vate della metafisica e della divina scienza"; page 623: "La Genesi universale delle lettere e arti cristiane, in quanto tutti i germi tipici dell'estetica moderna, vi si trovano racchiusi e inizialmente esplicati."

11. *Ibid.*, pp. 634 ff. Page 639: "ironia dolce."

12. *Ibid.*, p. 645: "Col Tasso ammutì la tromba dell'Italiana poesia ... finché morì, cantando, si può dir fra la scene, sulla labbra delle virtuose e dei soprani, e sotto la penna d'un canonico, scrittore di epitalami aulici, d'ariette teatrali, e poeta cesareo."

13. *Ibid.*, p. 377.

14. *Del Primato*, Ed. Naz., 2, 324: "Le opere del Leopardi sono animate da una malinconia profonda, da una tranquilla e logica disperazione, che apparisce al lettore, non come un morbo del cuore, ma come una necessità della spirito, e il sunto di tutto un sistema."

15. *Scritti scelti*, p. 484: "Il Rousseau della poesia, e il creatore della critica"; page 488: "Ha fatto fare, a parer mio, de' gran passi alla Critica e a tutta l'Estetica, anzi ha quasi interamente rinnovellata la faccia di quelle scienze."

16. E.g. *Storia civile nella letteraria*, Rome, 1872, reprints *Studi critici*, Venice, 1843. *Ispirazione ed arte*, Florence, 1858, also uses *Studi critici* and *Bellezza educatrice*, Venice, 1838, etc. More in Prunas, pp. 75–80.

17. *Antologia*, October 1831, p. 10: "un artista scettico ... sarebbe il più inefficace, il più disperato, il più misero degli artisti."

18. *Ispirazione ed arte*, Florence, 1858. Page 430: "Elegantemente disperato, prolissamente dolente e dottamente annoiato di questa misera vita." Letter to Gino Capponi, September 1833, in *Carteggio inedito dal 1833 al 1874*, ed. P. Lungo and P. Prunas (Bologna, 1911–32), *1*, 20: "Il n'y a pas de Dieu, parce que je suis bossu; je suis bossu parce qu'il n'y a pas de Dieu." The letter is a parody of Fénelon's *Télémaque*.

19. A letter to U. F. Prato-Guasti, 1847. Quoted by Prunas, p. 127: "Una menzogna dolorosa, un commedia amara, una satira virulente del suo tempo e delle opere sue." *Studi filosofici* (Venice, 1840), 2, 255: "Senza religione non è poesia."

20. Review of *I Promessi sposi*, in *Antologia*, October 1827. In reprint of review in *Ispirazione ed Arte*, Florence, 1858, some modifications. Most liberal in Appendix to *Duca d'Atene* (Florence, 1858), pp. 231–32: "L'immaginario ed il finto."

21. *Dizionario estetico* (Venice, 1840), *3*, 170: "Poeta credente, perchè grande, e popolare perchè credente."

22. Detailed examination by Ettore Caccia, *Tommaseo critico e Dante*.

23. *Opere*, ed. A. Borlenghi, Ricciardi, Naples, 1958. Pages 834–38:

"Le interiezioni sono più poetiche delle epopee: . . . unica poesia di noi mortali è la lirica." "Il verso è calcolo; il calcolo è canto, e fa cantare; l'aritmetica è una poesia rinforzata . . . la poesia senza calcolo è vaporosa, vacua, od atea o kantiana." "La poésie c'est le nuage doré . . . la poésie est dans le cœur, dans la gorge, dans les bras, dans la voix, sur les lèvres, dans le sourire, dans les yeux, sur le front . . . La poésie c'est l'action . . . c'est le Verbe." See Croce's comment in *Conversazioni critiche* (Bari, 1950), *1*, 63–67.

24. *Dizionario estetico* (2 vols., Milan, 1852), 2, 146: "Il dubbio mesto e severo e passionato dell'inglese divino . . . il dubbio gelido e derisore di questo cortigiano . . . l'attore dall'uomo."

25. Cf. the drastic comments noted in Ciureanu, an article strangely entitled "Un'amicizia italiana."

26. On Vico, see "G. Vico e i suo secolo" in *Storia civile nella letteratura*, Rome, 1872. There also the essays on Gozzi and Chiari.

27. *Nuova proposta di correzioni e aggiunte al Dizionario italiano* (Venice, 1841), p. 1: "Quand' io vedo una verità metafisica o storica confermata da un fatto filologico, questo dico, è il suggello del vero."

28. Some key essays: *Scritti letterari*, Vol. *1* (1906): "D'una letteratura europea" (1829), "Saggio sopra alcune tendenze della letteratura Europea nel XIX secolo" (1829), "Pensieri. Ai poeti del secolo XIX" (1832); Vol. 2 (1910): "De l'Art en Italie" (1835), "Prefazione d'un periodico letterario" (*l'Italiano*, 1836), "Storia letteraria" (1836), "Della Fatalità considerata com' elemento drammatico" (1836), "Victor Hugo" (1836), "Di Victor Hugo e dell'*Angelo Tiranno di Padova*" (1838), "Italian Literature since 1830" (1838); Vol. 3 (1913): "Hugo's *Les Voix Intérieures*" (1838), "The Present State of French Literature" (1838); Vol. 4 (1915): "De l'état actuel de la littérature" (1837), "Poésie-art" (1837), "*The French Revolution*" (1840), "Byron and Goethe" (1841); Vol. 5 (1919): "On the Works of Thomas Carlyle" (1843), "Dante Alighieri" (1844).

29. *Scritti*, 2, 254: "Egli particolarizza, segrega, concentra, invece d'universalizzarla, la vita." 2, 257: "Tutto è definito, determinato, materializzato." 2, 258: "teorica rovinosa, mortale all'Arte . . . negazione della vita e dell'unità universale."

30. *Ibid., 3*, 375, 400, English original.

31. *Ibid.,* p. 254, in English.

32. "Della Fatalità considerata com' elemento drammatico" (1836), *ibid.,* 2, 169–200.

33. A review of the Italian translation of Friedrich Schlegel's *Geschichte* (1828), *ibid., 1,* 113–25.

34. *Ibid.,* p. 172: "Un frammento d'Eschilo dissotterato."

35. *Ibid.*, p. 189: "Né mai l'espiazione può fruttare al altri che all'individuo, né mai innalzarsi alla maestá del sacrificio ... Non intento, non progresso commune. Solitudine in vita; solitudine in morte." *2, 198*: "L'accordo tra l'individuo e il pensiero sociale, tra la libertà e la legge dell'universo."

36. On Alfieri, *ibid.*, *1*, 258–60; on Leopardi, *ibid.*, *2*, 314. Mazzini wrote the "lettera apologetica" as Preface to his edition of Foscolo's *Scritti politici* (1844), reprinted in *5*, 159–82. On Foscolo see *Scritti letterari*, *2*, 295 ff. On Manzoni, *Scritti*, *1*, 31–41.

37. *Scritti letterari*, *5*, 195, 214, in English.

38. *Ibid.*, *4*, 425; *5*, 85, 91, in English.

39. *Ibid.*, *2*, 69, on Mickiewicz. *1*, 377–86, review of Bowring's *Cheskian Anthology* (1833).

40. *Storia* (Florence, 1845), *1*, 54: "La fusione della dottrina politica e della letteraria che noi desiderammo negli storici tutti della nostra letteratura." This "Discorso preliminare" was suppressed in the 2d ed. *Storia della letteratura italiana*, 2 vols., Florence, 1855.

41. *Lezioni di letteratura italiana*, ed. Valentino Piccoli (3 vols. Turin, 1927), *1*, 17: "La lotta della Chiesa col potere civile, con l'arte, con la scienza, con la libertà, con la religione stessa." Page 21: "La letteratura fu ghibellina, cercò molte aspirazioni nel Paganesimo, si sollevò contra l'autorità della Chiesa, non volle ubbidire ma ragionare, ed infine riuscì allo scetticismo."

42. *Ibid.*, *1*, 70: "Frate cane, frate lupo, frate sole, e suor luna."

43. *Ibid.*, *1*, 114: "Il sorgere della ragione contro l'autorità." Cf. p. 172.

44. *Ibid.*, pp. 202 ff., on *Africa*; *2*, 257 ff., on *Adone*; *3*, 153–56, on Goldoni; *3*, 236 ff., on *Grazie*.

45. *Giornalismo e letteratura nell'ottocento*, p. 96: "un valente italiano" ... "ristabilire l'armonia tra gli scrittori e la moltitudine." Page 83: "La poesia deve esprimere il sentimento generale di un'epoca." Page 85: "formola letteraria." Page 89: "Le lettere risorsero spontanee e feconde insieme colle civili instituzioni." Page 90: "L'arte è una ed immutabile nella sua essenza, e ... i tempi possono bensì modificarla nelle sue manifestazioni, ma non isnaturarla, né falsarla."

46. *Ibid.*, pp. 288 ff., on *Conciliatore;* 156 ff., on Manzoni; 191 ff., on Pellico; 101 ff., on Grossi. The article on Foscolo in *Prose e poesie scelte*, ed. Tullo Massarani (2 vols. Milan, 1888), *1*, 197–270.

47. "Della letteratura slava" (1847) and "Dell'Avvenire dei popoli slavi" (1852), in *Prose*, Vol. 2. The sources of information seem German. Zhukovsky misspelled or misprinted Inkowsky, etc.

48. The essay on Prati in *Giornalismo*, 129–45. Essays on Nicolini

and Torti in *Prose,* Vol. 1. Much of Tenca's criticism is still buried in the files of the *Rivista europea (1845–47)* and *Crepuscolo* (after 1850).

49. *Giornalismo,* p. 243: "desumere dalle vicende esterne della nazione quelle cause di grandezza e di decadimento letterario ... Questo materialismo storico, questa diffidenza dei grandi destini della letteratura." Page 273: "ravvicinare, armonizzare gl'intelletti." Page 233: "Stromento attivo di sviluppo estetico."

BIBLIOGRAPHY: ENGLISH CRITICISM

Besides George Saintsbury's *History of Criticism* and William K. Wimsatt and Cleanth Brooks, *Literary Criticism: A Short History* (New York, 1957), M. H. Abrams, *The Mirror and the Lamp: Romantic Theory and the Critical Tradition* (New York, 1953) discusses several writers of the time (Carlyle, Mill, etc.) perceptively. Ian Jack, *English Literature 1815–1832* (Oxford, 1963) pays attention to criticism and has a valuable chapter, "Interest in Foreign Literature and in Earlier English Literature."

There are general reflections in Jerome H. Buckley, *The Victorian Temper: A Study in Literary Culture* (Cambridge, Mass., 1952), Walter E. Houghton, *The Victorian Frame of Mind* (New Haven, 1957), and John Holloway, *The Victorian Sage* (London, 1953).

We have no history of English literary scholarship or historiography for this period. There are some hints in Gerard O'Leary, *English Literary History and Bibliography* (London, 1928), an unpretentious bibliographical handbook, and in Stephen Potter, *The Muse in Chains* (London, 1937), a glib attack on the teaching of literature which culminates in praise of "King Saintsbury."

On ballad study, see Sigurd B. Hustvedt, *Ballad Books and Ballad Men,* Cambridge, Mass., 1930.

On romances, see Arthur Johnston, *Enchanted Ground: The Study of Medieval Romance in the Eighteenth Century* (London, 1964), which has something on the early 19th century, too.

On Hallam an excellent anonymous article in *Edinburgh Review,* 72 (October 1840), 194. The author was Herman Merivale (1806–74). (Information by Walter Houghton.) See the good remarks in Emerson's *Journal,* Vol. *8,* p. 461 (1854).

NOTES: INTRODUCTORY

1. These were essays in *The Examiner* (January–May 1831), republished with an introductory essay by Frederick A. von Hayek (Chicago, 1942), pp. 6, 21.

2. See C. R. Decker, *The Victorian Conscience* (New York, 1952), for reaction to Balzac, Flaubert, Zola, and Baudelaire in England.

3. Cf., e.g., Ruskin's letter to Furnivall, 9 June 1854: "Until people are ready to receive all I say about art as 'unquestionable' . . . I don't consider myself to have any reputation at all worth caring about." *Works*, ed. Cook-Wedderburn, *36*, 169.

4. Harrison Ross Steeves, *Learned Societies and English Literary Scholarship*, New York, 1913.

5. Ed. Henry Southern, 14 vols. 1820–26; second series, 1827–28. See Saintsbury, *3*, 283–86 for an excessively favorable account. His list of contributors is incorrect; there is no evidence for Hartley Coleridge's collaboration. Charles Wentworth Dilke (1789–1864) wrote most of the papers on Elizabethan drama and James Crossley (1800–83) those on 17th-century prose.

6. Besides Potter, for details see C. H. Firth, *The School of English Language and Literature: A Contribution to the History of Oxford Studies*, Oxford, 1909; and R. W. Chambers, *Philologists at University College*, London, 1927.

7. See Eleanor F. Adams, *Old English Scholarship from 1566–1800*, New Haven, 1917.

8. See Bruce Dickins, "John Mitchell Kemble and Old English Scholarship" in *Proceedings of the British Academy*, 25 (1939), pp. 51–84; and Marvin C. Dilkey and H. Schneider, "John M. Kemble and the Brothers Grimm," *Journal of English and Germanic Philology*, 40 (1941), 461–73.

9. *Ancient English Metrical Romanceës* (London, 1802), *1*, xxxiii. See Bertrand H. Bronson, *Joseph Ritson, Scholar-at-Arms*, 2 vols. Berkeley, Calif., 1938. Bronson overrates him extravagantly; see my review in *Philological Quarterly*, *20* (1941), 184–87.

10. *Specimens of Early English Metrical Romances*, 3 vols. London, 1805.

11. W. J. Thoms proposed the term "folklore" in the *Athenaeum*, 22 August, 1846.

12. See Hustvedt, *Ballad Books and Ballad Men*.

13. Reprinted in W. C. Hazlitt's ed. of Warton's *History* (London, 1871), *1*, 32–33, 92. Price knows the Grimms, Görres, and Creuzer.

14. Many reprints of Elizabethan poetical miscellanies were edited by Sir Samuel Edgerton Brydges and Thomas Park. On Brydges, a curious enthusiast, see Mary Catherine Woodworth, *The Literary Career of Sir Samuel Edgerton Brydges*, Oxford, 1935. *Ancient Critical Essays upon English Poets and Poësy*, ed. J. Haslewood (2 vols. London, 1811–15). Reprints Puttenham, Webbe, etc.

15. On Marlowe, see C. F. Tucker Brooke, "The Reputation of Chris-

topher Marlowe," *Transactions of the Connecticut Academy of Arts and Sciences*, 25 (1922), 347–408. —Robert Greene, ed. A. Dyce, 1831. —Middleton, ed. A. Dyce, 1840. —Ford, ed. Henry Weber, 1811, and W. Gifford, 1827. —Webster, ed. A. Dyce, 1830. —Ben Jonson, ed. W. Gifford, 1816. —Beaumont and Fletcher, ed. H. Weber, 1812; George Darley, 1840; and A. Dyce, 1843–46. —Massinger, ed. W. Gifford, 1805.

16. See A. H. Nethercot, "The Reputation of the 'Metaphysical Poets' during the age of Johnson and the 'Romantic Revival,'" *Studies in Philology*, 22 (1925), 81–132; Austin Warren, "Crashaw's Reputation in the 19th Century," *PMLA*, 51 (1936), 769–85; Kathleen Tillotson, "Donne's Poetry in the 19th Century (1800–72)," in *Elizabethan and Jacobean Studies Presented to F. P. Wilson* (Oxford, 1959), pp. 307–26; Joseph E. Duncan, *The Revival of Metaphysical Poetry*, Minneapolis, 1959.

17. *Works. Including His Life and Correspondence*, 4 vols., London, 1836. Much on Browne's reputation is in O. Leroy, *Le Chevalier Thomas Browne*, Paris, 1931.

18. See Louisa Stuart Costello, *Specimens of the Early Poetry of France from the Time of the Troubadours and Trouvères to the Reign of Henri Quatre*, London, 1835; Edgar Taylor, *Lays of the Minnesinger, or German Troubadours*, London, 1825; Taylor also translated Wace's *Chronicle* (London, 1837) with good reproductions of the Bayeux Tapestry, and the Grimms' *Fairy Tales* as *German Popular Stories* (2 vols. 1823–26), with elaborate notes.

19. Cary's translation was preceded by Henry Boyd's very poor version, 3 vols. 1802. Cary's *Inferno* was published in 2 vols. 1805–06; the whole *Divine Comedy* in 2 vols. 1814. On Cary, see R. W. King, *The Translator of Dante*, London, 1925.

20. William Herbert, *Select Icelandic Poetry*, 2 vols. London, 1804–06; Henry Weber and R. Jamieson, *Illustrations of Northern Antiquities*, Edinburgh, 1814; George Borrow, *Romantic Ballads*, 1826.

21. Sir John Bowring, *Specimens of the Russian Poets*, 1820; —*Servian Popular Poetry*, 1827; —*Specimens of the Polish Poets*, 1827; —*Poetry of the Magyars*, 1830; —*Cheskian Anthology*, 1832; etc.

22. Sir William Jones' translation of Kalidasa's *Sakuntala* dates back to 1789. Horace H. Wilson (1786–1860) published *Select Specimens of the Theatre of the Hindus*, Calcutta, 3 vols. 1826–27; and Edward William Lane produced a translation of the *Arabian Nights* from the Arabic (*The Thousand and One Nights*, 3 vols. London, 1839–41).

23. Chambers calls the book "a textbook for those lectures on English literature, which are now given in so many institutions for mechanics and others." Still he claims it to be "the only History of English Litera-

ture which has as yet been given to the world" (preface). *The Cyclo-paedia of English Literature,* largely an anthology, appeared first in 2 vols., in 1844.

24. I quote the London, 1876 reprint, in 4 vols: *1*, 67, 164; *4*, 331.

25. *Ibid.*, *3*, 243, 290; *4*, 229; *3*, 315, 264.

26. *Ibid.*, *3*, 241–42, 255–56, 289; *2*, 227; *3*, 343.

27. *Ibid.*, *3*, 226, 349.

28. Vol. *1*, xi–xiii.

29. 1815 ed., Vol. 2, 157–58.

BIBLIOGRAPHY: CARLYLE

I quote the Centenary Edition (30 vols. London, 1896–99) as *Works*, the *Essays* (5 vols.) as *E, Heroes and Hero-worship* as *HH, Past and Present* as *PP, German Romance* as *GR.* Also:

> *Lectures on the History of Literature,* ed. J. R. Greene (New York, 1892), as *LHL.*
>
> *Carlyle's Unfinished History of German Literature,* ed. Hill Shine (Lexington, Ky., 1951), as *HGL.*
>
> *Two Note Books,* ed. C. E. Norton (New York, 1898), as *TN.*
>
> *Reminiscences,* ed. C. E. Norton (London, 1932), as *Rem.*
>
> *Collectanea,* ed. S. A. Jones (Canton, Pa., 1953), contains an early review of *Faust* (1822).

The ample correspondence, especially with Emerson, J. S. Mill, and J. Sterling contains many literary opinions reported also by interviewers such as Sir Charles Gavan Duffy (*Conversations with Carlyle,* New York, 1892) or F. Espinasse (*Literary Recollections,* New York, 1893).

Comment is endless though there is little on the literary criticism. F. W. Roe, *Thomas Carlyle as a Critic of Literature* (New York, 1910), is useful though perverse in its conclusions.

On relations to Germans:

> C. F. Harrold, *Carlyle and German Thought: 1819–1834* (New Haven, 1934), is best.
>
> Cf. Werner Leopold, *Die religiöse Wurzel von Carlyles literarischer Wirksamkeit dargestellt an seinem Aufsatz "State of German Literature"* (1827), Halle, 1922. A superior German thesis.
>
> There is a good section in Jean-Marie Carré, *Goethe en Angleterre* (Paris, 1920), pp. 101–87.

On some details see:

> B. H. Lehman, *Carlyle's Theory of the Hero,* Durham, N.C., 1928.
>
> Hill Shine, *Carlyle's Fusion of Poetry, History and Religion by 1834,* Chapel Hill, N.C., 1938.

Hill Shine, *Carlyle and the Saint-Simonians,* Baltimore, 1941.

Hill Shine, *Carlyle's Early Reading to 1834,* University of Kentucky Libraries, Occasional Contributions, No. 57, Lexington, Ky., 1953. Lists 3184 items.

Louis Merwin Young, *Thomas Carlyle and the Art of History,* Philadelphia, 1939.

There is an excellent chapter on Carlyle's rhetoric and terms in John Holloway, *The Victorian Sage,* London, 1953.

Many more references and discussions of related questions in my older writings:

1. "Carlyle and German Romanticism," in *Xenia Pragensia* (Prague, 1929), pp. 375–403.

2. A section in my *Kant in England* (Princeton, 1931), pp. 183–202.

3. "Carlyle and the Philosophy of History," *Philological Quarterly,* 23 (1944), 55–76, largely a review of Hill Shine and Mrs. Young. (Nos. 1 and 3 reprinted in my *Confrontations,* Princeton, 1965.)

NOTES: CARLYLE

1. Cf., e.g., *Life of John Sterling,* p. 192.

2. Cf. his attitude toward the Irish, on the Polish question, toward the Czechs, and especially toward Negroes, e.g. in the affair of Governor Eyre. See also his approval of the Opium War (*PP,* p. 267).

3. The manuscript of the *History of German Literature,* now in the Yale University Library, was edited by Hill Shine, Lexington, Ky., 1951. Only the introductory sections have any critical value. It seems odd that Saintsbury (*History of Criticism, 3,* 497 n.) should single out the two medieval essays as the best.

4. Frohwalt Küchler, *Carlyle und Schiller* (Halle, 1902), and "Carlyle und Schiller" *Anglia, 26* (1903), 1–93, 393–446, examines the relationship minutely, e.g. the use of Doering's biography.

5. *E, 2,* 198.

6. *Collectanea,* 78, 88.

7. See *Early Letters,* ed. C. E. Norton (London, 1886), pp. 283–84, 286 ("Goethe the greatest genius and the greatest ass"), 307–08, 312, and the preface to *Wilhelm Meister, 1,* 10. Cf. C. T. Carr, "Carlyle's Translations from the German," *Modern Language Review, 42* (1947), 223–32; and O. Marx, *Carlyle's Translation of Wilhelm Meister,* Baltimore, 1925.

8. *Wilhelm Meister, 1,* 6, 8.

9. *Ibid.,* p. 28.

10. *E, 1,* 173, 195.

11. *E, 1,* 244.

12. *E, 2,* 438.

13. *E, 2,* 449.

14. Goethe to Eckermann, 25 July 1827, *Gespräche,* ed. Houben, 508: "den geistigen und sittlichen Kern."

15. *E, 1,* 12, 19.

16. *GR, 2,* 121.

17. *E, 1,* 17. Carlyle seems to draw on Jean Paul's own discussion of humor in *Vorschule der Aesthetik,* ed. Wustmann, p. 173.

18. *GR, 2,* 127–27.

19. *E, 2,* 100, 123.

20. *GR, 1,* 261.

21. Some references to Schlegels, e.g. in *Schiller,* 36, 169, or *Wilhelm Meister, 1,* 7, in *E, 1,* 24, 77, 144, 351. In *E, 1,* 80, Carlyle wrongly ascribes a passage from Friedrich to August Wilhelm.

22. Actually Friedrich Schlegel's "Zeitgeist" is the disturber of eternity, identical with Satan. See *Werke* (2d ed. 1846), *15,* 88–92.

23. *GR, 1,* 264.

24. Letter July 12, 1843, in Froude, *Life in London, 1,* 258. For a fuller discussion of Carlyle's relation to Tieck (they met in 1852) see E. Zeydel, *Ludwig Tieck and England,* Princeton, 1931.

25. *TN,* p. 140. See C. F. Harrold, "Carlyle and Novalis," *Studies in Philology,* 27 (1930), 47–63.

26. *E, 2,* 43, 52.

27. *GR, 2,* 19. Cf. *Dichtung und Wahrheit,* in *Werke,* J.-A., *23,* 60–61.

28. *E, 1,* 366. It will surprise any reader of the violently pro-Habsburg *Ottokar* to hear Carlyle say that Grillparzer "seems to be an Austrian" (*E, 1,* 361).

29. See the books by Hill Shine and Mrs. Young and my article, "Carlyle and the Philosophy of History," cited in bibliography.

30. Cf. *E, 2,* 76; and *1,* 353.

31. *E, 1,* 39; and 2, 50.

32. *E, 3,* 46; *3,* 57; Froude, *Life in London, 1,* 231; *HH,* 57.

33. *E, 1,* 253.

34. *E, 1,* 54; 2, 337, 369.

35. *GR, 1,* 4.

36. *E, 1,* 290, 288.

37. *E, 2,* 341–42.

38. *HGL,* pp. 6–9.

39. *E, 1,* 351.

40. *E, 1,* 51–52.

41. *E, 1,* 53.

42. *E, 3,* 178; *1,* 314; *2,* 377.

43. *E, 2,* 437.

44. *E, 1,* 255.

45. *E, 3,* 227–28.

46. *E, 1,* 245.

47. *E, 3,* 78. Cf. *E, 1,* 27, where Carlyle complains that Franz Horn talks too often of "representing the Infinite in the Finite."

48. *E, 1,* 277–78, 208, 284.

49. *E, 1,* 253.

50. *HH,* p. 90; *Meister, 1,* 26.

51. *E, 2,* 377; *3,* 51.

52. Letter to J. Sterling, 9 June 1837, in *Letters to Mill,* p. 203.

53. *Sartor,* pp. 175, 179.

54. *E, 3,* 250–51.

55. *HH,* p. 97.

56. *HH,* p. 83; *LHL,* p. 10; *HH,* p. 90; *LHL,* p. 22.

57. *E, 3,* 49.

58. *E, 3,* 54–56.

59. *PP,* p. 46.

60. *Letters to Mill,* 13 June 1833, p. 57.

61. *E, 3,* 100, 56.

62. *Sartor,* pp. 221–22; *Latter-day Pamphlets,* pp. 81–82: "A new astonishing Phallus-Worship, with universal Balzac-Sand melodies and litanies in treble and in bass." The manuscript of an unfinished article attacking George Sand is in the possession of Professor Frederick W. Hilles of Yale University.

63. Sir Charles G. Duffy, *Conversations with Carlyle* (New York, 1892), pp. 75–76. Carlyle's objection to Dickens is mainly ideological: "His theory of life was entirely wrong. He thought men ought to be buttered up, and the world made soft and accommodating to them, and all sorts of fellows have turkey for their Christmas dinner." Carlyle preferred Thackeray as "he has more reality in him, and would cut up into a dozen Dickenses."

64. *Latter-Day,* p. 322.

65. Advice to both Brownings, to Tennyson, Emerson, etc. (*Correspondence, 2,* 152). Theory condemned in *LHL,* p. 188. Carlyle argues that there is no theory except of the planets. "All theory becomes more and more confessedly inadequate, untrue, unsatisfactory, almost a kind of mockery to me!" (Letter to Emerson, 26 September 1840, in *Correspondence, 1,* 330.) Cf. a letter of 28 August 1841: "It is many years since I ceased reading German or any other metaphysics and gradually

came to discern that I had happily got done with that matter altogether
. . . Metaphysics is but a kind of disease. We shall never know 'what we
are' " (in Espinasse, *Literary Recollections*, 58–60). Cf. "The study of
metaphysics, I say, had only the result . . . at last, to deliver me altogether
out of metaphysics" (*LHL*, p. 214). Carlyle voiced early an aversion to
aesthetics. See *TN*, p. 41, complaining of Schiller's and Goethe's *"palabra*
about the nature of the fine arts. Did Shakespeare know ought of the
aesthetic? did Homer?" Cf. "Goethe-and-Schiller's *Kunst* has far
more brotherhood with Pusey-and-Newman's *Shovelhattery,* and other
the like deplorable phenomena, than it is in the least aware of" (to
Emerson, 2 March 1847, *Correspondence*, 2, 153).

66. *E, 5, 25; 3, 79.*
67. *E, 5, 25; LHL*, pp. 21–22; *E, 5, 26; Latter-Day*, pp. 322–26.
68. *E, 4, 26.*
69. Letter to Sterling, 21 November 1842, *Letters to Mill*, pp. 263–64.
70. *E, 4, 49*; cf. also *E, 3, 10, 234, 40.*
71. *LHL*, p. 52.
72. *E, 3, 75.*
73. *E, 4, 40.*
74. *E, 1, 290–91; E, 3, 45; E, 2, 100.*
75. Sterling, pp. 55, 57; Journal, 26 May 1835, in Froude, *Life in
London, 1, 38.*
76. Duffy, *Conversations*, p. 58. Cf. *Rem.*, p. 251; *Rem.*, p. 357; To
Emerson, 13 May 1835, *Correspondence, 1, 72; Rem.*, p. 359. Cf. *Letters
to Mill*, p. 112; *Letters 1826–36*, p. 505. Note that Wordsworth alluded
to Carlyle in a sonnet "Portentous change, when History . . ." (in *Poetical
Works.*, ed. De Selincourt, *4*, 130) as "Power's blind Idolator."
77. *Rem.*, p. 65. Cf. *Two Notebooks*, pp. 217–18.
78. To Emerson, 1 April, 1840, *Correspondence, 1*, 303–04. Froude,
Life in London, 2, 42.
79. To Mill, 18 April 1833, *Letters to Mill*, p. 48.
80. *Rem.*, p. 358. Cf. Journal, 26 May 1835, in Froude, *Life in London,
1*, 38, and Espinasse, 69–79.
81. *E, 1, 313, 283.*
82. *E, 1, 283–84.*
83. On the planned essay on Thomas Moore's *Life of Byron*, see
Selections from the Correspondence of Macvey Napier (London, 1879),
p. 96. Main passages in "Wotton Reinfred," *Last Words of Thomas
Carlyle* (London, 1892), p. 95. In essay on Goethe, *1*, 218, on Burns *E, 1*,
269, 315–16, on Scott *4, 53.* More favorable views in early letters.
84. *E, 4, 59.*
85. *Sartor*, 153.

86. *E, 1,* 193 n.
87. *E, 4,* 38.
88. *E, 4,* 35, 72, 73.
89. *E, 4,* 36, 55, 54.
90. *E, 4,* 33, 75, 77.
91. *E, 3,* 31.
92. Letter to Browning 8 March 1853, *Letters to Mill,* 292.
93. *E, 1,* 277.
94. Journal 1848, quoted in D. A. Wilson, *Carlyle at his Zenith* (London, 1927), p. 15.
95. *LHL,* pp. 176, 179.
96. *LHL,* p. 177; *E, 3,* 134; *LHL,* p. 183.
97. *LHL,* p. 181; *HH,* p. 178.
98. *HH,* pp. 182-3.
99. *E, 3,* 70, 75, 69-70.
100. *E, 3,* 120.
101. *HH,* pp. 184-86.
102. *E, 1,* 405, 410-11, 414, 426.
103. *E, 1,* 446, 452, 461.
104. *E, 3,* 185, 201, 244-45. Goethe made a partial translation of *Essai sur la peinture* (1795) interspersed with critical comments (see *Werke,* J.-A., *33,* 205-61, 318).

BIBLIOGRAPHY: DE QUINCEY

I quote *The Collected Writings,* ed. D. Masson (14 vols. London, 1896), as M. Also *The Posthumous Works,* ed. Alexander H. Japp (2 vols. London, 1891), as Japp. Edward Sackville West, *Thomas De Quincey, His Life and Work* (title of English edition: *A Flame in Sunlight*) (New Haven, 1936), contains a brief survey of the criticism.

Sigmund K. Proctor, *Thomas De Quincey's Theory of Literature* (Ann Arbor, 1943), makes extravagant claims for De Quincey's greatness.

John E. Jordan, *Thomas De Quincey, Literary Critic: His Method and Achievement* (Berkeley, 1952), is the best detailed analysis.

John E. Jordan, *De Quincey to Wordsworth: A Biography of a Relationship,* Berkeley, Calif., 1962.

Among essays, see Leslie Stephen's severe account in *Hours in a Library,* Vol. 1, London, 1874; Saintsbury's in *Essays in English Literature (1780-1860),* London, 1890; the pamphlet by J. H. Fowler, *De Quincey as Literary Critic,* English Association, 1922; the chapter in A. E. Powell, *The Romantic Theory of Poetry,* London, 1926; my "De

Quincey's Status in the History of Ideas," *Philological Quarterly, 23* (1944), 248–72, an extended review of Proctor's book, reprinted in *Confrontations,* Princeton, 1965; John E. Jordan, "De Quincey on Wordsworth's Theory of Diction," *PMLA, 68* (1953), 764–78. J. Hillis Miller, *The Disappearance of God* (Cambridge, Mass., 1963), contains a remarkable chapter on De Quincey, pp. 17–80.

NOTES: DE QUINCEY

1. Stephen, *Hours in a Library,* London, 1899. *1,* 260.
2. Japp, 2, 17.
3. M, 2, 142–47, 226–28. Cf. Japp, 2, 32–34.
4. M, *13,* 195–96. A passage in "The Spanish Military Nun."
5. Japp, 2, 210, 26.
6. M, *10,* 48 n.
7. Japp, 2, 210.
8. M, *11,* 325. For a full discussion see Jordan, *PMLA* (1953), cited in the Bibliography above.
9. M, *11,* 294 (1845).
10. M, *11,* 88–89.
11. M, *10,* 48 n.
12. Howe, ed., *Complete Works, 18,* 8. "Science depends on the discursive or *extensive*—art on the intuitive and *intensive* power of the mind . . . In fact, we judge of science by the number of effects produced —of art by the energy which produces them. The one is knowledge— the other power." An article in the *Morning Chronicle,* 1814. First pointed out by Elisabeth Schneider, *The Aesthetics of William Hazlitt* (Philadelphia, 1933), p. 45 n.
13. See M, *11,* 156–221, and *4,* 380–94. On Herder's "Kraft" see this *History, 1,* 186.
14. M, *10,* 48.
15. M, *4,* 308.
16. M, *11,* 55–56, cf. *5,* 106; *10,* 45 n.
17. M, *10,* 108–09 n.; *5,* 231–32.
18. M, *10,* 227, 229–30.
19. M, *10,* 260.
20. M, *10,* 94, 100, 104.
21. M, *11,* 17.
22. M, *5,* 231.
23. M, *5,* 234–35.
24. M, *10,* 164.
25. Proctor, p. 261.

26. M, *10*, 105.

27. Proctor, p. 167. More in my essay in *Philological Quarterly, 23* (1944), 248–72. Reprinted in *Confrontations*, Princeton, 1965.

28. M, *2*, 73–74. De Quincey frequently disparaged the Schlegels: M, *4*, 428; *8*, 92; *10*, 42–44, 350; *11*, 50, 227.

29. M, *11*, 267, 270.

30. Lessing, "Wie die Alten den Tod gebildet" (1769); Herder, "Wie die Alten den Tod gebildet" (1786); Schiller's poem, "Die Götter Griechenlands" (1788), etc.

31. M, *8*, 210, 213, 227, etc.; *6*, 141.

32. M, *10*, 302.

33. M, *10*, 309, 313, 333; *8*, 46.

34. M, *10*, 359.

35. M, *10*, 194–95. See this *History, 1*, 221, and above, pp. 98–9.

36. M, *11*, 143.

37. M, *11*, 61.

38. From "First Epistle of Second Book of Horace," lines 263–64. De Quincey perversely takes Pope to refer to the conquest of France by Henry V at Agincourt in 1415 instead of to the victories of Marlborough. M, *11*, 137 ff., cf. 96–97.

39. M, *10*, 342.

40. M, *11*, 12 ff., 19 ff.; *4*, 104–17; *1*, 344; *4*, 297; *De Quincey and His Friends*, ed. James Hogg (London, 1895), *1*, 92, on Crabbe.

41. M, *11*, 119.

42. M, *11*, 34.

43. M, *11*, 68–69, 83–84.

44. M, *11*, 111, 72, 131.

45. M, *11*, 33, 95, 122, 68.

46. For recent conceptions of Pope's art see, e.g., Austin Warren, "Alexander Pope," in *A Rage for Order* (Chicago, 1948), pp. 37–51; Maynard Mack, "Wit and Poetry and Pope," in *Pope and His Contemporaries: Essays Presented to George Sherburn* (Oxford, 1949), pp. 20–40; William K. Wimsatt, "Rhetoric and Poems: The Example of Pope," in *English Institute Essays, 1948* (New York, 1949), pp. 179–207.

47. M, *10*, 274; *5*, 231; *8*, 93.

48. A collection of De Quincey's anti-French pronouncements is given in Leslie Stephen's essay, pp. 264–65. Since then some late manuscript notes for a more sympathetic treatment of French drama have been discovered: see "De Quincey on French Drama" in *More Books, 14* (1939), 347–52.

49. M, *11*, 222–58, a review of Carlyle's translation in *London Magazine* (August 1824). The first part, which attacks Carlyle's translation

and makes the most extravagant statements about Goethe's immorality, dullness, etc., is not reprinted in M.

50. M, *4*, 418; 437.

51. M, *2*, 225.

52. M, *11*, 259–72 (1821).

53. It is thus impossible to agree with Clarence D. Thorpe (appendix to Proctor's book, p. 297) that De Quincey's work on German literature has an importance exceeding that of Carlyle's.

54. M, *4*, 54.

55. M, *10*, 393–94.

56. M, *11*, 389 ,392–93.

57. M, *11*, 459 (1847).

58. M, *11*, 374–76.

59. M, *2*, 236–39, 242, 283.

60. M, *11*, 306.

61. M, *11*, 317–19. The quotation is from "Written in March While Resting on the Bridge at the Foot of Brother's Water," in *Poetical Works* (ed. Selincourt), *2*, 220.

62. M, *11*, 301, 303, 315.

63. M, *10*, 436. The principle is used also for *Lear* (M, *10*, 49) and *Paradise Lost* (M, *10*, 403–04).

BIBLIOGRAPHY: HUNT

Hunt has to be quoted from the 19th-century editions, since there are no modern collections except *Leigh Hunt's Dramatic Criticism 1808–1831,* ed. L. H. and C. W. Houtchens, New York, 1949, and *Leigh Hunt's Literary Criticism,* ed. L. H. and C. W. Houtchens, New York, 1956. The latter is not an anthology but a collection of inferior unreprinted articles, some not even literary criticism.

I quote *Imagination and Fancy* (3d ed. London, 1846) as *IF*.

Edmund Blunden, *Leigh Hunt's "Examiner" Examined* (London, 1928), reprints some of Hunt's early reviews.

Edmund Blunden, *Leigh Hunt and his Circle* (London, 1930), is the best life.

The huge monograph (2 vols., 295 and 647 pp. octavo) by Louis Landré, *Leigh Hunt* (Paris, 1935–36), contains a full survey of Hunt's criticism and literary opinions, friendships, and quarrels.

See—besides Saintsbury, Abrams, and Alba Warren—G. Saintsbury, "Leigh Hunt," in *Essays in English Literature, 1780–1860* (London, 1890), pp. 201–33.

Erika Fischer, *Leigh Hunt und die italienische Literatur,* diss., Freiburg im Breisgau; Quakenbrück, 1936. A compilation.

Jeffrey Fleece, "Leigh Hunt's Shakespearean Criticism," in *Essays in Honor of Walter Clyde Curry* (Nashville, Tennessee, 1954), pp. 181–96.

Clarence Dewitt Thorpe, "An Essay in Evaluation," in *Leigh Hunt's Literary Criticism,* pp. 3–73. Full of extravagant praise.

Carolyn W. and Lawrence H. Houtchens, "Leigh Hunt," *The English Romantic Poets and Essayists. A Review of Research and Criticism,* ed. C. W. and L. H. Houtchens (New York, 1957), pp. 262–98. Very useful.

NOTES: HUNT

1. *The Book of the Sonnet* (2 vols. Boston, 1867), *1*, 87 n.

2. *Examiner,* 1819. Reprinted in Blunden, *Leigh Hunt's "Examiner" Examined,* p. 220.

3. Hunt wrote three articles on Hazlitt's critical works: on "Characters of Shakespear's Plays" (1817), reprinted in *Leigh Hunt's Dramatic Criticism 1808–1831,* ed. L. H. and C. W. Houtchens (New York, 1949), pp. 167–79, and notes 317–21; "Lectures on the English Comic Poets," in *Examiner,* April 18, 1819, and "Lectures on the Literature of the Age of Elizabeth," in *Examiner,* March 19, 1820. The complex relationship of Hunt and Hazlitt is traced in Landré, *Leigh Hunt.*

4. *IF,* pp. v, 277, 295, 29–30, 31–32, 2, 32.

5. *Wit and Humour* (London, 1846), pp. 9, 12.

6. *IF,* pp. 32–33, 62.

7. *The Feast of the Poets* (London 1814), line 18. This is a verse satire in the style of the 17th-century "Sessions of the Poets," which Hunt rewrote several times and supplied with long polemical notes.

8. *The Book of the Sonnet, 1,* 4.

9. "Lamia" II, line 237. Blunden, *Leigh Hunt's "Examiner" Examined,* p. 147. There is a similar passage in *Men, Women and Books* (London, 1847), pp. 4–5.

10. *Literary Criticism,* ed. L. H. and C. W. Houtchens, p. 387. *IF,* p. 316.

11. Blunden, *"Examiner" Examined,* p. 210.

12. *IF,* p. 63.

13. London, 1849, *1,* 8, 12.

14. See esp. *Lord Byron and Some of His Contemporaries,* London, 1828. The sections on Byron are used but toned down in the *Autobiography* (1850). Barnette Miller, *Leigh Hunt's Relations with Byron, Shelley and Keats* (New York, 1910) is completely superseded by Landré.

Much of this belongs to a history of political warfare rather than criticism.

15. *Stories from the Italian Poets* (2 vols. London, 1846), *1*, x, 60. Cf. *The Book of the Sonnet, 1*, 17.

16. *IF*, pp. 237, 239.

17. *Wit and Humour*, pp. 308–09, 330.

18. *The Feast of the Poets*, p. 90; —Letter to John Forster (1847) in Luther A. Brewer, *My Leigh Hunt Library: The Holograph Letters* (Iowa City, Ia., 1938), p. 246.

19. *A Jar of Honey from Mount Hybla*, London, 1848; *Stories from the Italian Poets*, 2 vols. London, 1846; *The Book of the Sonnet*.

20. *IF*, pp. 74, 105, 103–35. An earlier version (1833) in *Literary Criticism*, pp. 420–45. "The greatest painter" is on p. 445.

21. Hunt's early reviews of Keats, beginning with praise of the Chapman sonnet, December 1, 1816, in Blunden, pp. 127–58. See Hyder E. Rollins, *The Keats Circle: Letters and Papers, 1816–1878*, Cambridge, Mass., 1948, and J. R. McGillivray, "On the Development of Keats' Reputation," in *Keats: A Bibliography and Reference Guide*, Toronto, 1949.

22. See Walter Graham, "Shelley's Debt to Leigh Hunt and the *Examiner*," *PMLA, 40* (1925), 185–92. Payson G. Gates, "Leigh Hunt's Review of Shelley's Posthumous Poems" in *The Papers of the Bibliographical Society of America, 42* (1948), 1–40, prints a manuscript destined for *The Westminster Review* in 1825 but rejected at the advice of T. L. Peacock.

23. *IF*, p. 277.

24. Reprinted in *Literary Criticism*, pp. 344–71, 509–27.

25. *The Book of the Sonnet, 1*, 88. A letter quoted in Landré, 2, 196.

26. *Wit and Humour*, p. 69.

27. *Ibid.*, pp. 260, 280–81; and see "Pope, in some lights in which he is not usually regarded" in *Men, Women, and Books*, London, 1870 (original ed. 1847), pp. 203–14.

28. *IF*, pp. 220, 222.

29. *Dramatic Criticism*, p. 168.

30. *Ibid.*, pp. 15, 20, 78–83, 103, 201. *Examiner*, Sept. 25, 1808; April 5, 1818.

31. *True Sun*, 9 August 1833, quoted by Landré, 2, 165. See also *Literary Criticism*, pp. 585–604, for preface to *Stories in Verse*, London, 1855.

32. *A Jar of Honey*, p. 108.

33. Cf., e.g., *IF*, p. 286, on Coleridge's "Love": "I can hardly say a

word upon this poem for very admiration," or *Jar of Honey*, p. 114.

34. *IF*, pp. 303, 334, on stanza 15 of "St. Agnes' Eve."

35. *Essays in English Literature 1790–1860* (London, 1890), p. 222.

36. Clarence D. Thorpe, "An Essay in Evaluation" in *Leigh Hunt's Literary Criticism*, ed. L. H. and C. W. Houtchens, p. 14.

BIBLIOGRAPHY: MACAULAY

I quote *Critical and Historical Essays* (6 vols. Boston, 1900) as *E*, and *Biographies and Poems, ibid.*, as *B*. Letters and journals are quoted from the standard *The Life and Letters of Lord Macaulay*, by his nephew, George Otto Trevelyan, 2 vols. London, 1876. Further extracts from the Journal in Richmond Croom Beatty, *Lord Macaulay*, Norman, Oklahoma, 1938.

There are three useful articles on the criticism: Stanley T. Williams, "Macaulay's Reading and Literary Criticism," *Philological Quarterly, 3* (1924), 119–31, a list; P. L. Carver, "The Sources of Macaulay's *Essay on Milton*," *Review of English Studies, 6* (1930), 49–62, on Hazlitt; and Frederick L. Jones, "Macaulay's Theory of Poetry in *Milton*," *Modern Language Quarterly, 13* (1952), 356–62, on Peacock as a source.

NOTES: MACAULAY

1. *Estetica* (8th ed. Bari, 1945), p. 411.

2. Trevelyan, 2, 7–8.

3. *E, 4*, 121, 110, 89, 114.

4. *E, 1*, 191–92.

5. See this *History, 1*, 130 ff., and 2, 127, 226 f. Cf. the articles by Carver and Jones quoted in the Bibliography above.

6. *E, 1*, 3, 86.

7. *E, 1*, 190, 91.

8. *E, 1*, 90, 88, 89.

9. *E, 1*, 196, 198, 199, 200.

10. *E, 1*, 205–06. On Defoe cf. *1, 3*; and Trevelyan 2, 454–55.

11. *E, 1*, 105–06.

12. *E, 1*, 149.

13. *E, 1*, 10, 13, 14, 19, 15.

14. *E, 1*, 101–02.

15. *E, 2*, 354; *6*, 68; *B*, 79; *E, 2*, 353.

16. Trevelyan, *1*, 335 (letter, October 21, 1833).

17. *E, 1*, 214, 226. Trevelyan, *1*, 120.

18. *E, 5,* 62, 57.

19. *E, 6,* 130 ff., 139, 143, 145.

20. *B,* 44, 45–46.

21. *E, 6,* 53–54.

22. *E, 2,* 331, 334, 333.

23. *E, 2,* 210, 211; *1,* 203.

24. *E, 2,* 217.

25. *E, 2,* 227, 225.

26. Trevelyan, *2,* 9.

27. Trevelyan, *2,* 150. December 13, 1843. On Jeffrey, see this *History,* 2, 111 ff.

28. Beatty, p. 331. April 2, 1850. Beatty, p. 332. September 30, 1858.

29. Beatty, p. 339, without date.

30. Trevelyan, *2,* 379. August 12, 1854. "Read Northanger Abbey: worth all Dickens and Pliny together."

31. Beatty, p. 340. September 16, 1859.

32. Trevelyan, *2,* 279. July 28, 1850.

33. On love of Richardson, see Trevelyan, *1,* 131, 377; on Jane Austen, 2, 293, 379. *Marginal Notes by Lord Macaulay,* selected and arranged by Sir George Otto Trevelyan (London, 1907), contains rather commonplace marginalia on Shakespeare, Plato, Cicero, etc. For the astonishing reading list of almost all classical authors during his stay in India, see Trevelyan, *1,* 371, 431, 436.

34. *E, 6,* 50.

35. *E, 2,* 209; *1,* 163.

36. Examples of ranking in Trevelyan, *1,* 371–72, 474; *2,* 198, 205, 434, etc.

37. *E, 2,* 352.

BIBLIOGRAPHY: MILL

I quote *Dissertations and Discussions* (2d ed. 3 vols. London, 1867) as *DD; Early Essays,* ed. J. W. M. Gibbs (London, 1897), as *EE.* Also *Autobiography,* ed. J. J. Coss, New York, 1924; and *The Letters,* ed. Hugh S. R. Elliott, 2 vols. New York, 1910.

There is a *Bibliography of the Published Writings of John Stuart Mill,* ed. Ney MacMinn, J. R. Hainds, and J. M. McCrimmon, Evanston, Illinois, 1945.

For comment on the criticism see Abrams, Alba Warren, and the essay by Walter J. Ong, "J. S. Mill's Pariah Poet," *Philological Quarterly, 29* (1950), 333–44, which surely overstates the view that the poet is an outcast, a pariah, and remains "absurd" in Mill's conception. John M. Robson," J. S. Mill's Theory of Poetry," *University of Toronto Quarterly, 29* (1960), 420–38.

NOTES: MILL

1. *The Works*, ed. J. Bowring, 11 vols. Edinburgh, 1843. See Vol. 8, Table v; 2, 2531, and Mill's *DD, 1,* 389.

2. *Autobiography*, p. 104.

3. *Inaugural Address Delivered to the University of St. Andrews, Feb. 1, 1867* (London, 1867), p. 86.

4. *DD, 1,* 353.

5. *DD, 1,* 69–70.

6. *DD, 1,* 75–76, 68.

7. *DD, 1,* 71–72.

8. *DD, 1,* 83, 84, 85, 93, 80. Mill combined the two early articles under a new and more modest title, "Thoughts on Poetry and Its Varieties" when he republished them in *DD*, in 1859.

9. See the essay by Ong quoted in the Bibliography above.

10. Letter to J. Sterling, 20–22 October, 1831. *Letters, 1,* 11–12.

11. This must be said against Alba Warren, who in his chapter makes Mill a follower of Carlyle.

12. *DD, 1,* 326–27.

13. *DD, 1,* 354.

14. In *Westminster Review, 29* (1838), 313.

15. To Carlyle, 5 July 1833. *Letters, 1,* 54–55. See also letter of 17 July 1832, *Letters, 1,* 35.

16. *EE*, 279.

17. *EE*, 315, and *DD*, 2, 129.

18. *EE*, 265–66.

19. Diary, 11 April 1854, in *Letters*, 2, 385–86.

BIBLIOGRAPHY: RUSKIN

I quote *The Works* of John Ruskin, Library Edition, ed. Sir E. T. Cook and A. D. O. Wedderburn (39 vols. London, 1902–12), as W. The last volume contains an excellent analytical index of topics and terms.

Ruskin as Literary Critic, ed. A. H. R. Ball, Cambridge, 1928; a useful selection.

On Ruskin see: R. Wilenski, *John Ruskin,* London, 1933; and John D. Rosenberg, *The Darkening Glass: A Portrait of Ruskin's Genius,* New

York, 1961. Both these books, though concerned with the writings, are preoccupied with the personality and its pathology.

On aesthetics see: Henry Ladd, *The Victorian Morality of Art: An Analysis of Ruskin's Esthetic,* New York, 1932; and Sister Mary Dorothea Goetz, *A Study of Ruskin's Concept of the Imagination,* Washington, D.C., 1947; useful. There is a good chapter in Graham Hough, *The Last Romantics,* London, 1947.

NOTES: RUSKIN

1. W, *3,* 273. Cf. p. 265.

2. Letter to C. E. Norton, 28 January 1866. W, *36,* 501.

3. W, *34,* 377.

4. W, *12,* 373; *20,* 76–77; *12,* 122 n.

5. W, *11,* 187; *5,* 276.

6. W, *3,* 81 n.

7. W, *19,* 588; *36,* 193.

8. W, *7,* 429–30. Ruskin edited and revised a translation of *Ulric the Farm Servant,* Orpington, 1888. See W, *32,* 343–45, for his preface.

9. W, *19,* 584, and *18,* 53 ff.

10. W, *19,* 211–12.

11. W, *18,* 72.

12. W, *5,* 277–78.

13. *Fors Clavigera,* Letter 79, July 1877. W, *29,* 160.

14. W, *4,* 186.

15. W, *7,* XL–XLI (1858).

16. *Fors Clavigera,* Letter 76 (1877). W, *29,* 91.

17. Cf. W, *12,* 507: "I owe more to Carlyle than to any other living writer." Also *28,* 22; *35,* 15, 77; *37,* 15, etc.

18. See Appendix II to vol. 3 of *Modern Painters,* W, *5,* 427–30, and "Romanist Modern Art," W, *9,* 436–40, attacking Pugin. Cf. Hough, *The Last Romantics,* pp. 86–90.

19. W, *5,* 427–30.

20. W, *4,* 215. Cf. *ibid.,* p. 121 n.

21. W, *3,* 623–24.

22. Cf., e.g., W, *11,* 201–02; *20,* 165; *28,* 446–47.

23. W, *3,* 488.

24. W, *3,* 466.

25. W, *11,* 48 and n.

26. W, *3,* 157, 343.

27. W, *4,* 47–48.

28. W, *4*, 57, 52. The first passage was dropped in all editions after the first.

29. W, *4*, 190.

30. W, *4*, 144.

31. W, *4*, 288.

32. See "On the Pleasures of Fancy" (1884), W, *33*, 482–83.

33. W, *4*, 228.

34. W, *5*, 112.

35. Graham Hough, *The Last Romantics*, p. 37.

36. W, *16*, 276–77; W, *5*, 140 ff.

37. W, *3*, 509–10.

38. W, *3*, 268–69.

39. W, *3*, 514–15.

40. W, *4*, 269–71.

41. W, *4*, 278.

42. W, *5*, 25.

43. W, *4*, 295.

44. W, *5*, 133; *11*, 175.

45. W, *4*, 255.

46. W, *5*, 115.

47. W, *17*, 258–60.

48. W, *19*, 300.

49. W, *18*, 350.

50. W, *18*, 346–47, 352.

51. W, *5*, 204.

52. W, *5*, 204, 206–07. Reference is to *Inferno*, *3*, 112.

53. W, *5*, 216–17, 211.

54. See the note to the passage in A. Pope, *Pastoral Poetry and An Essay on Criticism*, ed. E. Audra and Aubrey Williams (London, 1961), pp. 77–78 n.

55. W, *18*, 124. The quotation is from Wordsworth's "Three Years She Grew in Sun and Shower."

56. *Pathetic Fallacy in the Nineteenth Century*, Berkeley, 1942.

57. W, *20*, 46.

58. E.g. W, *13*, 545; *19*, 250; *20*, 78, 83, 295, 298–99, or *18*, 173, 437, 439–40; and *9*, 14; *19*, 390; *24*, 203–04.

59. W, *10*, 196.

60. W, *5*, 321.

61. W, *20*, 212.

62. See his *Autobiography* (New York, 1943), pp. 33, 53, and comment in John D. Rosenberg, *The Darkening Glass*, pp. 71 ff.

63. Marcel Proust, *Pastiches et mélanges* (Paris, 1933), p. 195:

"L'Univers reçut tout d'un coup à mes yeux un prix infini." *A un ami* (Paris, 1948), p. 149: "Cela n'empêche pas les ouvrages de Ruskin d'être souvent stupides, maniaques, crispants, faux, irritants, mais s'est toujours estimable et toujours grand." More on Proust and Ruskin in Walter A. Straus, *Proust and Literature* (Cambridge, Mass., 1957), pp. 177–86, and the bibliography.

64. W, *15*, 27 n.

BIBLIOGRAPHY: AMERICAN CRITICISM

There are several general histories of American criticism, none very satisfactory.

Norman Foerster, *American Criticism* (Boston, 1928), is a series of searching essays on Poe, Emerson, Lowell, and Whitman, with a final affirmation of the New Humanist point of view.

George E. De Mille, *Literary Criticism in America* (New York, 1931), ranges from Poe to Stuart Sherman; colorless.

Bernard Smith, *Forces in American Criticism* (New York, 1939), has a Marxist point of view, intermittently perceptive.

Floyd Stovall, ed., *The Development of American Literary Criticism* (Chapel Hill, 1955), is a composite volume, with contributions of very unequal value.

John Paul Pritchard, *Criticism in America* (Norman, Oklahoma, 1956), is a bad, scrappy compilation. See also his earlier *Return to the Fountains* (Durham, N.C., 1942), on classical sources.

Robert E. Spiller, ed., et al., *Literary History of the United States* (3 vols. New York, 1948), contains chapters on criticism and much information in Vol. 3, the Bibliography.

Clarence Arthur Brown, ed., *The Achievement of American Criticism* (New York, 1954), is an excellent historical anthology, with introductions and bibliographies.

On the early period before the Civil War, see William Charvat, *Origins of American Critical Thought*, Philadelphia, 1936; Benjamin T. Spencer, *Quest for Nationality: An American Literary Campaign*, Syracuse, N.Y., 1957; and J. P. Pritchard, *Literary Wise Men of Gotham: Criticism in New York 1815–1860*, Baton Rouge, La., 1963.

NOTES: INTRODUCTORY

1. Smith, *Forces in American Criticism*, p. 217.

2. *Edinburgh Review,* January 1820. A review of Scybert's *Annals of the United States.*

3. Brown, *The Achievement of American Criticism,* pp. 143–44.

4. *Ibid.,* p. xxi, from *Kavanagh.*

5. Before 1835 there were 31 American editions of Kames' *Elements of Criticism,* 53 of Blair's *Lectures,* and 9 of Alison's *Essays on Taste.* See Charvat, *Origins of American Critical Thought,* pp. 30–31.

6. In New York, 1826, published only in 1884; see Brown, p. 111 n.

7. *Ibid.,* p. 112, 115, 116.

8. 1832; in Brown, pp. 219 ff.

BIBLIOGRAPHY: POE

I quote as *W The Complete Works,* ed. James A. Harrison (17 vols. New York, 1902), the so-called Virginia Edition, and by far the most complete. *The Letters* are quoted from the edition of John Ward Ostrom, 2 vols. Cambridge, Mass., 1948.

Comment is endless, the best, most critical, being: Norman Foerster, *American Criticism* (Boston, 1925), pp. 1–51; and Yvor Winters, *In Defense of Reason* (Denver, Colo., 1947), pp. 234–61. Before in *Maule's Curse,* Norfolk, Conn., 1938.

Further comments:

Allen Tate, "The Angelic Imagination: Poe as God," in *The Forlorn Demon* (Chicago, 1953), pp. 56–78. Also in *The Man of Letters in the Modern World* (New York, 1955), pp. 113–31.

Joseph Chiari, *Symbolisme from Poe to Mallarmé* (London, 1956), esp. pp. 97–116.

Charles Feidelson, Jr., *Symbolism and American Literature* (Chicago, 1953), pp. 36–39, 248–49.

Margaret Alterton and Hardin Craig, preface to *E. A. Poe, Representative Selections* (Cincinnati, 1935), an attempt to reduce Poe's theories to a rational system.

N. Bryllion Fagin, *The Histrionic Mr. Poe* (Baltimore, 1949), has a chapter on drama criticism.

Edward H. Davidson, *Poe: A Critical Study* (Cambridge, Mass., 1957), esp. pp. 43–75.

Vincent Buranelli, *Edgar Allan Poe* (New York, 1961), pp. 54–63, 110–27.

Sidney P. Moss, *Poe's Literary Battles* (Durham, N.C., 1963). A detailed study vindicating Poe.

For sources:

Margaret Alterton, *The Origins of Poe's Critical Theory,* Iowa City, 1925.

Marvin Laser, "The Growth and Structure of Poe's Concept of

Beauty," *ELH*, *15* (1948), 69–84, suggests the influence of Shelley's *Defence of Poetry* after its printing in 1840.

Floyd Stovall, "Poe's Debt to Coleridge," *University of Texas Studies in English*, *10* (1930), 70–127.

Albert J. Lubell, "Poe and A. W. Schlegel," *Journal of English and Germanic Philology*, *52* (1953), 1–12.

Henry A. Pochmann, *German Culture in America* (Madison, Wis., 1957), pp. 405–08.

Other articles: Nelson F. Adkins, " 'Chapter on American Cribbage': Poe and Plagiarism," in *The Papers of the Bibliographical Society of America*, *42* (1948), 169–210; and George Kelly, "Poe's Theory of Unity," *Philological Quarterly*, *37* (1958), 34–44.

NOTES: POE

1. Cf. *W*, *10*, 100, 196, or *11*, 158.

2. *W*, *12*, 8.

3. *W*, *12*, 4.

4. *W*, *16*, 120.

5. *W*, *12*, 140.

6. *W*, *11*, 89.

7. E.g. "The Germans lived during the whole of the middle ages in utter ignorance of the art of writing," *W*, *16*, 115; *14*, 71.

8. *W*, *14*, 289.

9. *W*, *11*, 266.

10. *W*, *11*, 177; *10*, 137.

11. *W*, *15*, 260.

12. *W*, *13*, 171.

13. See Pochmann, *German Culture in America*, pp. 383–86, for comment.

14. *W*, *11*, 38–64.

15. *W*, *12*, 118, on Mrs. Mowatt's *Fashion*.

16. See review of Willis' *Tortesa* and Longfellow's *Spanish Student*, *W*, *13*, 33 ff.

17. *W*, *11*, 2.

18. E.g. *W*, *14*, 282; *11*, 41.

19. Cf. *W*, *14*, 74, or *11*, 1–2.

20. *W*, *11*, 2.

21. *W*, *14*, 272; *11*, 70.

22. *W*, *14*, 271–2; cf. *11*, 258.

23. *W*, *14*, 272; *11*, 70.

24. *W*, *13*, 131.

25. *W, 16,* 164.

26. *W, 11,* 148–49.

27. *W, 11,* 68.

28. *W, 11,* 71.

29. *W, 13,* 112–13.

30. *W, 14,* 273.

31. *W, 4,* 203–04.

32. This term has overtones derived from its use in phrenology. See Edward Hungerford, "Poe and Phrenology," *American Literature,* 2 (1930), 209–31.

33. *W, 14,* 273–74.

34. *In Defense of Reason,* p. 241.

35. *W, 8,* 283.

36. *W, 14,* 274.

37. *W, 10,* 159–60.

38. *W, 14,* 291.

39. *W, 14,* 198.

40. *W, 14,* 201.

41. Probably suggested by the lavish praise in A. W. Schlegel, *Über dramatische Kunst und Litteratur* (Heidelberg, 1817), *3,* 344–45.

42. *W, 10,* 66.

43. *W, 8,* 299.

44. *W, 14,* 275; cf. *11,* 75.

45. To J. R. Lowell, 2 July 1844; in *Letters,* ed. Ostrom, *1,* 257–58.

46. *W, 14,* 275; cf. *11,* 75.

47. There is, however, one isolated passage in the "Colloquy of Monos and Una" which refers to "analogy" as speaking in "proof-tones to imagination alone," *W, 4,* 202.

48. See *W, 14,* 187, or *16,* 197.

49. *W, 14,* 187.

50. See *Les Premiers Traits de l'érudition universelle,* Leyden, 1767. Bielfeld reproduces Voltaire's article on imagination (1765) in the *Encyclopédie,* and echoes Batteux and Condillac.

51. *W, 8,* 283.

52. *W, 12,* 38–39.

53. *W, 12,* 27, and *15,* 13–14.

54. *W, 8,* 295–96.

55. *W, 12,* 39–40.

56. See Stovall on Coleridge, and Lubell and Pochmann on Schlegel.

57. *W, 16,* 313.

58. See Alterton-Craig, introduction, esp. pp. xxxi, xxxiii, xlviii, lii.

59. *W, 4,* 150.

60. *W, 11,* 148.

61. *W, 14,* 73.

62. *W, 14,* 195.

63. Preface to "La Genèse d'un poëme" (1859), a translation of Poe's "Philosophy of Composition," in *Œuvres complètes,* ed. J. Crépet (Paris, 1922–53), *9,* 153–54: "S'est-il fait, par une vanité étrange et amusante, beaucoup moins inspiré qu'il ne l'était naturellement? A-t-il diminué la faculté gratuite qui était en lui pour fair la part plus belle à la volonté? Je serais assez porté à la croire ... Après tout, un peu de charlatanerie est toujours permis au génie, et même ne lui messied pas."

64. *W, 14,* 194–95.

65. See the convincing articles by W. K. Wimsatt, Jr., "Poe and the Chess Automaton," *American Literature, 11* (1939), 138–51; "What Poe Knew of Cryptography," *PMLA, 58* (1943), 754–79; "Poe and the Mystery of Mary Rogers," *PMLA, 56* (1941), 230–48. For the opposite view see Denis Marion, *La Méthode intellectuelle d'Edgar Poe,* Paris, 1952.

66. See Aldous Huxley, *Vulgarity in Literature,* London, 1930.

67. *W, 14,* 266.

68. *W, 14,* 266.

69. *W, 14,* 196.

70. *W, 14,* 267.

71. *W, 14,* 196.

72. *W, 13,* 153.

73. *W, 13,* 153; *11,* 108.

74. *W, 11,* 108; cf. *14,* 188.

75. See this *History,* 2, 49.

76. E.g. *W, 16,* 57; *10,* 37.

77. *W, 14,* 193.

78. *W, 13,* 45; *14,* 188; *10,* 117.

79. *W, 16,* 10.

80. *W, 11,* 75; *11,* 24; *14,* 275.

81. See W. L. Werner, "Poe's Theories and Practice in Poetic Technique," *American Literature, 2* (1930), 157–65. Hervey Allen, *Israfel* (2 vols. New York, 1926), 2, 763, quotes an auditor at Poe's lecture at Lowell, Mass., on 16 July 1848 on Poe's stressing the regular beat, "measuring the movement as if he were scanning it." See Gay Wilson Allen, *American Prosody* (New York, 1935), pp. 57–61, for an analysis of "The Rationale of Verse."

BIBLIOGRAPHY: EMERSON

I quote:

Complete Works, the Centenary Edition (12 vols. Boston, 1903) as *W.*

Journals, 1820–1872 (10 vols. Boston, 1909), as *J.*

The Letters, ed. Ralph L. Rusk (6 vols. New York, 1939), as *L.*

The Correspondence of Thomas Carlyle and Ralph Waldo Emerson, 1834–1872 (2 vols. Boston, 1894), as *Cor.*

Parnassus, ed. R. W. Emerson, Boston, 1875.

The Uncollected Writings: Essays, Addresses, Poems, Reviews and Letters, ed. C. C. Biglow (Boston, 1912), as *UW.*

James Elliot Cabot, *A Memoir of R. W. Emerson,* 2 vols. Boston, 1887.

The huge literature is analyzed well in F. I. Carpenter, *Emerson Handbook,* New York, 1953; and in Floyd Stovall's chapter *of Eight American Authors. A Review of Research and Criticism,* ed. F. Stovall (New York, 1956), pp. 47–99. There the many distinguished essays devoted to Emerson are listed: e.g. those by Matthew Arnold, Leslie Stephen, Henry James, George Santayana, and W. C. Brownell. Missing is E. R. Curtius' in *Kritische Essays zur europäischen Literatur,* Bern, 1950.

Among recent general studies, Sherman Paul, *Emerson's Angle of Vision* (Cambridge, Mass., 1952), and Stephen E. Whicher, *Freedom and Fate: An Inner Life of R. W. Emerson* (Philadelphia, 1953), are outstanding.

Vivian C. Hopkins, *Spires of Form: A Study of Emerson's Aesthetic Theory* (Cambridge, Mass., 1951), is the best book on the topic.

Emerson Grant Sutcliffe, *Emerson's Theories of Literary Expression* (Urbana, Ill., 1923), is still useful.

The chapter in Norman Foerster's *American Criticism* (Boston, 1928), emphasizes his classical sympathies.

Donald MacRae, "Emerson and the Arts," *Art Bulletin, 20* (1938), 78–95, has perceptive remarks on aesthetics.

F. O. Matthiessen, *American Renaissance* (New York, 1941), contains a fine chapter mainly concerned with Emerson's language.

Charles Feidelson, Jr., *Symbolism and American Literature* (Chicago, 1953), devotes several pages to brilliant reflections on Emerson's symbolism.

R. P. Adams, "Emerson and the Organic Metaphor," *PMLA, 69* (1954), 117–30, argues an important point well.

On sources, see:

my "Emerson and German Philosophy," *New England Quarterly, 16* (1943), 41–62 (reprinted in *Confrontations,* Princeton, 1965) still seems sound in its conclusions.

More in Henry A. Pochmann, *German Culture in America,* Madison, Wisc., 1957; and in Stanley M. Vogel, *German Literary Influences on the American Transcendentalists,* New Haven, 1955.

Kenneth W. Cameron, *Emerson the Essayist: An Outline of His Philosophical Development through 1836 with Special Emphasis on the Sources and Interpretation of Nature,* 2 vols. Raleigh, N.C., 1945.

John Smith Harrison, *The Teachers of Emerson* (New York, 1910), concerns the Neoplatonists.

Vivian C. Hopkins, "The Influence of Goethe on Emerson's Aesthetic Theory," *Philological Quarterly, 27* (1948), 325–44; and the same author's "Emerson and Cudworth: Plastic Nature and Transcendental Art," *American Literature, 23* (1951), 80–98.

NOTES: EMERSON

1. *W 3,* 38.

2. 21 July 1855; see *L, 4,* 520. Whitman published the letter in the *New York Daily Tribune,* 10 October 1855. Emerson later retreated somewhat from his first spontaneous enthusiasm. Cf., e.g., "Our wild Whitman, with real inspiration but choked by Titanic abdomen," in *L, 5,* 87 (1857).

3. *Essays in Literary Criticism,* ed. I. Singer (New York, 1956), p. 224.

4. *W, 2,* 57.

5. *W, 12,* 12.

6. *L, 2,* 167 (8 October 1838).

7. *Cor, 1,* 161 (10 May 1838) and *1,* 325 (30 August 1840).

8. *J, 8,* 463 (1854).

9. Austin Warren, *New England Saints* (Ann Arbor, Mich., 1956), p. 46.

10. Traced particularly well in Whicher, *Freedom and Fate.* The attempt by Pochmann, *German Culture,* to make Emerson's Neoplatonism only a passing interlude between a Kantian and a scientific phase in his thinking seems to me quite unconvincing.

11. *W, 3,* 196.

12. *W, 1,* 24, and *12,* 217–18. Note that this is a translation from K. P. Moritz, as quoted in Goethe, *Werke,* J.-A., *33,* 61.

13. *W, 6,* 305.

14. *W, 8*, 40, 43.

15. *W, 7*, 182; "The Problem" in *W, 9*, 7.

16. *W, 3*, 9–10.

17. *W, 1*, 24; *W, 2*, 354.

18. "The Rhodora," *W, 9*, 38; *W, 4*, 56.

19. *Parnassus*, preface, p. lv.

20. *W, 1*, 55.

21. *W, 8*, 17, 20–21.

22. *W, 8*, 38.

23. *W, 7*, 52; cf. *J, 3*, 395–96 (1834), and *J, 7*, 173–74 (1846).

24. *W, 8*, 23.

25. *W, 3*, 20.

26. *W, 1*, 32.

27. *W, 3*, 20; cf. Plotinus, *Select Works*, tr. Thomas Taylor, London, 1817.

28. *W, 3*, 34–35.

29. *W, 3*, 34; *W, 4*, 121.

30. *W, 12*, 300–02.

31. *W, 8*, 15.

32. *J, 6*, 18 (1841).

33. *W, 6*, 304.

34. *W, 12*, 129.

35. *W, 12*, 283.

36. *W, 1*, 111.

37. *W, 8*, 34–35, 37.

38. *W, 2*, 82–83.

39. *W, 2*, 356.

40. *W, 6*, 255.

41. *J, 9*, 207 (1859).

42. *J, 5*, 227 (1839).

43. *W, 2*, 358.

44. *W, 12*, 278. Emerson misquotes Bacon (*Advancement of Learning*, Bk. 11, iv, 2): "It doth raise and erect the mind, by submitting the shows of things to the desires of the mind; whereas reason doth buckle and bow the mind into the nature of things." Emerson, by suppressing the second half and adding the sentence about the ideal world, makes Bacon sound much more Platonic than the text warrants.

45. *W, 8*, 57; *J, 2*, 401 (1831).

46. *W, 7*, 50.

47. *W, 1*, 29.

48. *W, 3*, 21–22.

49. *W, 1*, 30.

50. *W, 12*, 366. Repeated in *Parnassus*, p. lv.

51. *W, 8*, 13.

52. *W*, 2, 108; cf. *W*, 2, 352.

53. *W*, 7, 52–53; cf. Goethe, *Werke*, J.-A., 27, 108; *33*, 108, quoted in this *History, 1*, 208.

54. *W, 12*, 303–04; also *J, 4*, 90 (1836); *J*, 5, 434 (1840); and cf. *J, 9*, 24–25 (1856), which refers to Sainte-Beuve's essay. The article "Shakespeare und kein Ende" (*Werke*, J.-A., *37*, 41–42) seems the most obvious source. See this *History, 1*, 220.

55. *J, 10*, 267, 278 (1868–69).

56. *W, 3*, 18–19.

57. *W, 12*, 408, 410, 413.

58. Henry James, *Literary Remains* (Boston, 1885), p. 293; J. R. Lowell, *Letters*, ed. C. E. Norton (New York, 1894), 2, 175 (1876).

59. *W, 12*, 276.

60. *W*, 7, 48–49.

61. *W*, 2, 133; *W, 12*, 71.

62. *UW*, 138–39.

63. *W*, 7, 38.

64. *UW*, 21; *W, 8*, 30–31.

65. *W*, 2, 17.

66. *J, 3*, 309 (1834).

67. *J, 5*, 487 (1840); *J, 5*, 520–22 (1841); *W, 8*, 196.

68. *J, 8*, 541 (1855); *J, 6*, 243 (1842).

69. *W, 8*, 274 ff., 296.

70. *W, 12*, 72; *W, 3*, 232; also *J, 5*, 102 (1838).

71. *W*, 2, 357–58.

72. *J, 5*, 129–30 (1838).

73. *J, 6*, 275 (1842).

74. *W*, 2, 356, 362; *J, 5*, 398 (1840); *W*, 2, 365.

75. *W, 1*, 35.

76. *J, 5*, 295 (1839).

77. *J, 5*, 283 (1839).

78. *W, 3*, 25.

79. *W, 8*, 56.

80. *W, 3*, 47.

81. *W, 3*, 8.

82. See Nelson F. Adkins, "Emerson and the Bardic Tradition," *PMLA, 63* (1948) 662–77.

83. *J, 5*, 399 (1840).

84. See, e.g., *J, 2*, 233–34; *W*, 7, 193–94; *W, 12*, 341; *J, 5*, 112. Cf., e.g., Vivian Hopkins, *Spires of Form*, p. 244, n. 95.

85. Ed. Chesley J. Mathews, in *Harvard Library Bulletin, 11* (1957), 208–44, 346–62.

86. See Charles Lowell Young, *Emerson's Montaigne* (New York, 1941), esp. pp. 10 ff. Emerson cared for Montaigne as a person and moralist but hardly came to grips with his skepticism. He never even refers to the "Apology of Raimond Sebond." "The grand old sloven" in *J, 3, 538* (1835).

87. This is an anthology, a publishing venture, which was, in part, the work of Emerson's daughter, Edith, and thus must be judged rather as a huge commonplace book with many concessions to contemporary taste. Emerson's introduction is of interest.

88. See *W, 2,* 245 ff. "Heroism," and p. 256. Also epigraph to "Self-Reliance" (*W, 2,* 43) and *W, 8,* 55, 328. For Emerson's reading in Beaumont and Fletcher, see, e.g., *J, 5,* 85 ff. (1839).

89. *J, 7,* 163 (1846); *J, 5,* 347 (1839). *Parnassus,* p. lx.

90. *L, 6,* 19 (1868); *W, 12,* 319.

91. *W, 5,* 298; *W, 8,* 66; *J, 2,* 107–09 (1826), *Parnassus,* p. viii; cf. J. B. Moore, "Emerson and Wordsworth," *PMLA, 41* (1926), 179–92.

92. *J, 9,* 336–37 (1861).

93. *J, 4,* 436 (1838); *5,* 261 (1839).

94. *J, 8,* 462 (1854). A more temperate passage: *J, 8,* 29–30 (1849).

95. See, e.g., *L, 1,* 264 (1829); *J, 2,* 253–54 (1828), 415–16 (1831); *J, 5,* 5 (1838). See also Cabot, *Memoir, 2,* 751, and the selections in *Parnassus,* pp. iv, vi.

96. *W, 4,* 217–18; *W, 11,* 448.

97. *W, 11,* 451; *W, 4,* 191, 197, 212–13, 215; *J, 10,* 27 (1864).

98. *W, 8,* 69; *W, 12,* 325–26; *W, 4,* 284, also 287.

99. *W, 3,* 242; *W, 4,* 274. Cf. Frederick B. Wahr, *Emerson and Goethe* (Ann Arbor, 1915), for more details.

100. See the article by Vivian Hopkins, "The Influence of Goethe," in the Bibliography above.

101. See my article on "Emerson and German Philosophy" for fuller discussion of question of sources. Emerson knew something of Schelling's aesthetics through knowing Coleridge's paraphrase of his Munich Academy address (see this *History,* 2, 75, 152); and in 1845 he read or tried to read Cabot's translation of Schelling's "Vom Wesen der menschlichen Freiheit" (see *L, 3,* 293, 298–99, 303–04, 343).

BIBLIOGRAPHY: THE OTHER TRANSCENDENTALISTS

Thoreau is quoted from *Writings,* Riverside Edition, 10 vols. Cambridge, Mass., 1894), as *W,* and from the *Journal,* 14 vols. Boston, 1906. Jones Very's *Essays and Poems* (Boston, 1839) is used. Margaret Fuller is quoted from *The Writings,* selected and edited by

Mason Wade (New York, 1941), as *TW*, with bibliography of the articles. When this edition fails, I quote the selections: *Art, Literature and the Drama* and *Life Without and Life Within* (Boston, 1874), ed. Arthur B. Fuller (also called Vols. 5 and 6 of *Works*).

On Thoreau, see Matthiessen and Feidelson, and Fred W. Lorch, "Thoreau and the Organic Theory of Poetry,"*PMLA, 53* (1938), 286–302.

On Jones Very, see William I. Bartlett, *Jones Very: Emerson's 'Brave Saint,'* Durham, N.C., 1942.

On Margaret Fuller, see Pochmann and

> Frederick A. Braun, *Margaret Fuller and Goethe,* New York, 1910.
>
> Helen N. McMaster, "Margaret Fuller as a Literary Critic," *University of Buffalo Studies, 7,* (1928), No. 3.
>
> Arthur R. Schultz, "Margaret Fuller: Transcendentalist Interpreter of American Literature," in *Monatshefte für deutschen Unterricht, 34* (1942), 169–82.
>
> F. O. Matthiessen, "Margaret Fuller as Critic," in *The Responsibilities of the Critic* (New York, 1952), pp. 145–47.

NOTES: THE OTHER TRANSCENDENTALISTS

1. *Journal, 1,* 94.
2. *Ibid., 9,* 99.
3. *Ibid., 13,* 56.
4. *Ibid., 7,* 386–87.
5. *Ibid., 8,* 441, and *1,* 329.
6. *Miscellanies, W, 10,* 100, 102, 111, 113, 124.
7. *Journal, 9,* 86.
8. *W, 2,* 164.
9. *A Week on the Concord and Merrimack Rivers, W, 1,* 453.
10. Yvor Winters, in *Maule's Curse* (Norfolk, Conn., 1938), since included in *In Defense of Reason* (Denver, Colo., 1947), pp. 262 ff. Winters' praise of the essays, p. 269. Also Abrams, *The Mirror and the Lamp* (New York, 1953), pp. 247–48.
11. See *Poems,* ed. W. P. Andrews (Boston, 1883), p. 20.
12. *Essays and Poems,* p. 37.
13. *Ibid.,* pp. 47, 70, 60, 91.
14. Quoted in Perry Miller, *The Transcendentalists* (New York, 1950), p. 339.
15. *Ibid.*
16. *TW,* p. 225.
17. *Art, Literature and the Drama,* pp. 23–24.
18. *TW,* p. 360.

19. *Ibid.*, pp. 363, 390, 393.

20. Letter in T. W. Higginson, *Margaret Fuller Ossoli* (Boston, 1884), p. 90; and Emerson's letters, esp. *L*, 2, 352–53, 24 October 1840).

21. *TW*, p. 374.

22. *Ibid.*, pp. 397, 400. See Poe, *Works*, Virginia Edition, *15*, 79; *17*, 290, 333. Poe called her an "ill-tempered," "detestable old maid."

23. *TW*, pp. 383, 366.

24. *Life Without and Life Within*, pp. 153–57, 127–40; *Art, Literature, and the Drama*, 198.

25. *Ibid.*, pp. 207–21.

26. *TW*, pp. 312–46, esp. pp. 337–38, 332–33.

27. *Ibid.*, pp. 301–11, esp. pp. 303, 310.

28. *Ibid.*, pp. 351–52, *Life Without and Life Within*, pp. 131–33.

29. On Goethe see esp. the preface to Eckermann, *TW*, p. 232 (1839); and the paper in *The Dial* (1841), *TW*, p. 242. Full list in Pochmann, p. 764, n. 307.

30. "Menzel's View of Goethe" (1841) in *Life Without and Life Within*, pp. 13–22.

31. *TW*, pp. 246–47, 262–64, 264 ff.

32. *Ibid.*, p. 252.

33. *Ibid.*, pp. 244, 248, 259.

34. *Ibid.*, pp. 242, 238.

BIBLIOGRAPHY: GERMAN CRITICISM

Volume 4 of Bruno Markwardt, *Geschichte der deutschen Poetik* (4 vols. Berlin, 1959), is the fullest treatment. Though very learned, it suffers from schematic categorizing and complete provinciality. There is a slight sketch by S. Lempicki, "Literarische Kritik," in Merker-Stammler, *Reallexikon der deutschen Literaturgeschichte* (4 vols. Berlin, 1925–31), 2, 145–58. For an anthology with a Marxist slant see *Meisterwerke deutscher Literaturkritik*, ed. Hans Mayer, Vol. 2, *Von Heine bis Mehring*, Berlin, 1956.

There is a convenient reprint of the attacks on Goethe in Michael Holzmann, *Aus dem Lager der Goethe-gegner*, Berlin, 1904. A reprint of early reviews and a full bibliography of Goethe criticism up to 1832 is in Oscar Fambach, *Goethe und seine Kritiker*, Düsseldorf, 1955.

Instructive are books on intellectual trends: Erich Rothacker, *Einleitung in die Geisteswissenschaften*, 2d ed. Tübingen, 1930; and Karl Löwith, *Von Hegel bis Nietzsche*, Zurich, 1941. Trans. David E. Green, New York, 1964.

Grillparzer:
   I quote *Sämtliche Werke,* ed. Moritz Necker (16 vols. Leipzig, 1903), as *SW.*
Comment on Grillparzer:
   Fritz Strich, *Franz Grillparzer's Ästhetik* (Berlin, 1905), is still best.
   Josef Nadler, *Franz Grillparzer* (Vaduz, Lichtenstein, 1948), contains a survey of his views.
   Arturo Farinelli, *Grillparzer und Lope de Vega* (Berlin, 1894), is largely a source study.
   Werner Milch, "Grillparzers literarische Kritik," in *Kleine Schriften* (Heidelberg, 1957), pp. 38–46.
Uhland:
   I quote *Gesammelte Werke,* ed. Hermann Fischer (6 vols. Stuttgart, 1892), as *GW.*
   On Uhland, see Hermann Schneider, *Uhland, Leben, Dichtung, Forschung,* Berlin, 1920.
Eichendorff:
   I quote *Geschichte der poetischen Literatur Deutschlands,* ed. W. Kosch, Kempten, 1906.
Comment on Eichendorff:
   R. Schindler, *Eichendorff als Literarhistoriker,* Mulhouse, 1926; Zurich dissertation.
   Otto Keller, *Eichendorffs Kritik der Romantik,* Zurich, 1954.
   H. E. Hass, "Eichendorff als Literaturhistoriker," in *Jahrbuch für Ästhetik und allgemeine Kunstwissenschaft,* ed. H. Lützeler, 2 (1954), 103–77.
Carus:
   I quote C. G. Carus, *Goethe,* ed. Ernst Merian-Genast, Zurich, 1948; good introduction by the editor.
Menzel:
   E. Jenal, *Menzel als Dichter, Literaturhistoriker und Kritiker* (Berlin, 1937), attempts a rehabilitation.
Börne:
   I quote *Gesammelte Schriften* (12 vols. Hamburg, 1862), as *GS.*

NOTES: GERMAN CRITICISM

   1. See Saintsbury, *History of Criticism, 3,* 569–73, who produces him as a "surprise" of his German chapter.
   2. See Farinelli, and *SW, 13,* 10–11, 20.
   3. *SW, 14,* 38: "Alles, was kommt, musste so kommen; der Willkür, der Stimmung, dem Genie, der Laune ist kein Spielraum gelassen, bis aufs Blut wird alles erklärt."

4. *SW, 14,* 42: "Die Fortschritte der Kunst sind von den Talenten abhängig, und nicht von den Weltbegebenheiten. Goethe wäre derselbe grosse Dichter geworden, wenn es auch nie einen Friedrich den Grossen gab, und die französiche Revolution, die doch drastisch genug war, hat keinen einzigen Poeten hervorgebracht."

5. *SW, 14,* 45: "Ein Genie ist immer eine Art Wunder und kann durchaus nicht natürlich erklärt werden."

6. *SW, 14,* 40: "Unter die Reisebeschreibungen klassifizieren."

7. *SW, 14,* 41.

8. *SW, 16,* 109; *15,* 189–90: "Wer *etwas* weiss und kann, der schreibt *etwas* und nicht über etwas. . . . Das kritische Talent ist ein Ausfluss des hervorbringenden. Wer selbst etwas machen kann, kann auch das beurteilen was andere gemacht haben."

9. *SW, 15,* 135, 131. Strich, p. 8, quotes a saying from 1859 on Bouterwek: "der beste Asthetiker und einzig verlässliche Führer im Reiche der Theorie." Much more on sources in Strich.

10. *SW, 15,* 127, 129, 136, 156. Page 159: "nicht allegorisch, aber gewissenmassen symbolisch."

11. *SW, 15,* 176, 179 ff. Page 181 "Dunkle Ahnung." Page 185: "Personifikation der Naturnotwendigkeit. . . . Ein Welttropus." Cf. also draft of preface to *Die Ahnfrau* (1817), and other notes in *SW, 3,* 14–20.

12. *SW, 15,* 175. *12,* 95: "Gefühl der Notwendigkeit." "Die innere Form des Dramas." *12,* 66: "Gegenwart." *12,* 111: "Die Inkongruenzen der Natur zur Geltung und Wirklichkeit bringen." Cf. *15,* 186. *SW, 12,* 135: "Durch seine blosse Existenz Glauben erzwingt." On gesture, see Strich, pp. 98 ff.

13. *SW, 13,* 50; *15,* 178. On *Ottokar,* see *SW, 12,* 93–95, 102.

14. *SW, 15,* 150; also *12,* 89. *15,* 151: "Der Komplex der Mittel, seine Gedanken lebendig auf den Zuhörer übergehen zu lassen." Cf. *14,* 64.

15. *SW, 14,* 10, 18, 32, 40, 80, etc. On Corneille, *14,* 189–90.

16. *SW, 14,* 81 ff. On Werner, *14,* 87.

17. *SW, 14,* 94–95, 118; *12,* 140. "Ein lumpiger Patron."

18. A conversation with Otto Prechtler, in Nadler, p. 371: "Der Mann weiss alles. Er weiss zum Beispiel, wie unser Herrgott entstanden ist, ich aber weiss das nicht, und so kann ich mit ihm nicht sprechen."

19. *SW, 14,* 136.

20. *GW, 4,* 41. Originally in Fouqué's *Musen,* 1812.

21. *GW, 6,* 13: "Er hat die Gegenwart ergriffen."

22. *GW, 4,* 135–37: "Den Gang dieser Entwicklung."

23. *GW, 4,* 137: "organisch." Page 147: "Ein poetischer Kern."

24. *GW, 1,* 448. See letter to C. Lachmann, 20 July 1827, quoted in Mary Thorp, *The Study of the Nibelungenlied* (Oxford, 1940), p. 35.

25. The discussion of the romantics reproduces the earlier version in *Über die ethische und religiöse Bedeutung der neueren romantischen Poesie in Deutschland*, Leipzig, 1847.

26. *Geschichte*, p. 364: "wesentlich Katholischer . . . als die meisten seiner Katholizisierenden Zeitgenossen."

27. *Zur Geschichte des Dramas* (Leipzig, 1854), pp. 57–58.

28. *Geschichte*, pp. 56, 297.

29. *Zur Geschichte des Dramas*, pp. 67–68.

30. On Goethe criticism, see my bibliography above, p. 330. Schubarth wrote *Zur Beurtheilung Goethes*, Breslau, 1818; and the expanded *Zur Beurtheilung Goethes in Beziehung auf verwandte Literatur und Kunst*, 2 vols. Breslau, 1820. He visited Goethe and corresponded with him. On him, see Hans Titze, quoted below, p. 344.

31. Carus' *Psyche. Zur Entwicklungsgeschichte der Seele* (Pforzheim, 1846), was greatly admired by Dostoevsky, who seems to have drawn from Carus his theoretical conception of the Unconscious. See G. Gibian, "C. G. Carus' *Psyche* and Dostoevsky," *American Slavic Review, 14* (1955), 371–82.

32. *Goethe*, p. 176: "Eine Pflanze, eine Palme, einen Adler, einen Löwen."

33. *Ibid.*, pp. 221, 229, 231, 245: "Mehr *beendet* als *vollendet*."

34. Johann Friedrich Wilhelm Pustkuchen's fake continuation of *Wilhelm Meisters Wanderjahre* (1821) was apparently the signal for the campaign.

35. *Die deutsche Literatur* (2 vols. Stuttgart, 1828), *1*, 22: "Innerlichkeit, Sinnigkeit, Beschaulichkeit."

36. *Ibid., 2*, 214: "Hetäre." Note that the section on Goethe repeats an earlier article in the *Europäische Blätter* (1824) and that the new edition of *Deutsche Literatur* (1836) is even more virulent.

37. See below, p. 249.

38. *GS, 4*, 6. Preface to *Dramaturgische Blätter*, 1829.

39. *GS, 4*, 8: "Ich sah im Schauspiele das Spiegelbild des Lebens, und wenn mir das Bild nicht gefiel, schlug ich, und wenn es mich anwiderte, zerschlug ich den Spiegel. Kindischer Zorn! In den Scherben sah ich das Bild hundertmal. Ich war bald dahinter gekommen, dass die Deutschen kein Theater haben, und einen Tag später, dass sie keines haben *können*. Das erstere war mir gleichgültig—man kann ein sehr edles, ein sehr glückliches Volk sein, ohne gutes Schauspiel—aber das Andere betrübte mich."

40. *GS, 5*, 116; *4*, 316.

41. *GS, 1*, 313. Page 320: "Der Dichter der Niedergebornen, der Sänger der Armen. . . . der Jeremias seines gefangenen Volkes."

42. See Holzmann, and *GS, 6*, 209–31.

BIBLIOGRAPHY: HEINE

I quote *Sämtliche Werke*, ed. Oskar Walzel (10 vols. Leipzig, 1912–15, with additional Register-Band), as *W*.

Also: *Briefe, Erste Gesamtausgabe*, ed. Friedrich Hirth, 6 vols. Mainz, 1950–51.

The best general book is Otokar Fischer, *Heine* (2 vols. Prague, 1923–24), in Czech and unfortunately never translated.

On the criticism, see Arne Novák, *Menzel, Börne, Heine a počátkové mladoněmecké kritiky* (Menzel, Börne, Heine and the Beginnings of Young German Criticism), Prague, 1906, also in Czech, with emphasis on Heine's polemics.

Walter Leich, "Heines Kunstphilosophie," *Zeitschrift für Aesthetik*, *17* (1924), 411–15; on art criticism.

Alfred Mayerhofer, *Heinrich Heines Literaturkritik*, Munich, 1929; a compilation.

On special topics:

Georg Mücke, *Heinrich Heines Beziehungen zum deutschen Mittel-alter*, Berlin, 1908. Heine is criticized as a lazy student of *Germanistik*.

Fritz Friedlaender, *Heine und Goethe*, Berlin, 1932.

Friedrich Hirth, *Heinrich Heine und seine französischen Freunde*, Mainz, 1949. Extremely erratic in its judgments.

Georg Lukács, "Heinrich Heine als nationaler Dichter," in *Deutsche Realisten des 19. Jahrhunderts* (Bern, 1951), pp. 89–146; Marxist.

Kurt Weinberg, *Henri Heine: "Romantique défroqué," héraut du symbolisme français*, New Haven, 1954. The title thesis seems overstated.

NOTES: HEINE

1. *W, 10,* 166: "Die mühseligen Errungenschaften so vieler Jahrhun-derte, die Frucht der edelsten Arbeiten unsrer Vorgänger." Cf. preface to the French edition of *Lutezia* (1855, quoted from *Lutèce*, Paris, 1892, p. xii), Heine's last piece of writing: "Ils [the Communists] détruiront mes bois des lauriers et y planteront des pommes de terre . . . le prolé-tariat vainqueur menace mes vers, qui périrent avec tout l'ancien monde romantique." But Heine sympathizes with their demands for social justice and their hatred of the Teutomans.

2. *W, 10,* 147: "Unsre Zuchthäuser, unsre Bordelle, unsre Kasernen."

3. *Ibid.*: "Kant als Sorbet von Vanille, Fichte als Pistache, Schelling als Arlequin."

4. *W, 9,* 481: "Ein Haufen Würmer . . . die der heilige Fischer zu Rom sehr gut zu benutzen weiss, um damit Seelen zu ködern."

5. *W, 9,* 33: "Der grösste Schriftsteller, den das neue Frankreich hervorgebracht." There seems to me no evidence whatever for an affair between Heine and George Sand, as confidently asserted by Hirth, p. 85, 185 ff. Heine's letter (August 17, 1838) complaining of his enslavement to Mathilde, and George Sand's sympathizing but distant reply, are conclusive. See *Briefe, 2,* 272–73, and *5,* 259.

6. *W, 10,* 44: "Der grösste ihrer jetzt lebenden Dichter in Versen (jedenfalls der grösste nach Béranger)," *Ein Wintermärchen,* Kaput V: "ein Gassenjunge." On comedies, *W, 8,* 293–94.

7. *W, 9,* 38: "Wie ein Naturforscher irgendeine Tierart oder ein Pathologe eine Krankheit." Balzac dedicated a story, "Un Prince de la Bohème" (1840) to Heine.

8. *W, 9,* 350: "Ein Deutscher, eine gute deutsche Haut."

9. *W, 8,* 290: "Auf das Zierliche und Miniaturmässige gerichtet."

10. *W, 10,* 301: "Dieses gereimte Rülpsen."

11. *W, 9,* 45 ff., 272: "Versifiziertes Sauerkraut." Cf. *W, 8,* 288 ff.

12. *W, 8,* 81: " 'Seht da den Büffel, den Abkömmling eines Büffels, den Stier der Stiere, alle andre sind Ochsen, nur dieser ist der rechte Büffel!' so lief einst St.-Beuve jedesmal vor Victor Hugo einher, wenn dieser mit einem neuen Werke vors Publikum trat, und stiess in die Posaune und lobhudelte den Büffel der Poesie." This passage alone accounts for Sainte-Beuve's later dislike of Heine. We have two perfunctory reviews by Sainte-Beuve (in *Premiers Lundis, 2,* 248–58 [1833] and in *Revue des Deux Mondes* [1 June 1834], 621–23), some allusions, a letter to Charles Berthoud (6 January 1867, reprinted in *Premiers Lundis, 2,* 258–59) complaining of his "epigramms" and violent pronouncements reported by the Goncourts (*Journal,* 23 February 1863 and 20 June 1864, 9 vols. Paris, 1888, *2,* 95, 210).

13. *W, 10,* 265: "Chateaubriand ist ein Polichinell, der seine Marotte den Leuten vorhält: '*Ecco il vero cruce.*' "

14. *W, 10,* 13–14.

15. See Kenneth Haynes, "Heine, Hazlitt, and Mrs. Jameson" in *Modern Language Review, 17* (1922), 42–49, for parallels. For Heine's praise of Hazlitt, in *W, 8,* 170, compare Courier and Börne, *ibid.,* p. 468. Guizot is quoted in *W, 8,* 294–98.

16. *W, 10,* 256; *8,* 80: "Weder der Religion, noch der Politik soll sie als Magd dienen, sie ist selber letzter Zweck, wie die Welt selbst." See also letter to Gutzkow, 23 August 1838 (*Briefe, 2,* 278): "Kunst ist Zweck der Kunst."

17. *W, 7,* 46, and note on p. 447. "Ich stimme daher ganz überein mit jener erhabenen Ansicht . . . eine unabhängige zweite Welt . . . denn

in der Kunst gäbe es keine Zwecke, wie in dem Weltbau selbst, wo nur der Mensch die Begriffe, 'Zweck und Mittel' hineingrübelt: die Kunst, wie die Welt sei ihrer selbst willen da." . . . "Ich kann aber dieser Ansicht nicht unbedingt huldigen."

18. *W, 7, 140:* "Die keinen Unterschied machen wollen zwischen Leben und Schreiben, die nimmermehr die Politik trennen von Wissenschaft, Kunst und Religion, und die zu gleicher Zeit Künstler, Tribune und Apostel sind."

19. *W, 5, 317; 7, 15; 4, 225.*

20. *W, 8,* 110: "Es gehört etwas mehr als eine blosse Meinung dazu, um so einen gotischen Dom aufzurichten."

21. *W, 6,* 57–58: "Das träumende Spiegelbild ihrer Zeit." "In heiliger Harmonie mit ihrer Umgebung; sie trennten nicht ihre Kunst von der Politik des Tages."

22. *W, 10,* 250: "In der Kunst ist die Form alles, der Stoff gilt nichts."

23. *W, 6,* 25: "In der Kunst bin ich Supernaturalist. Ich glaube, dass der Künstler nicht alle seine Typen in der Natur auffinden kann, sondern dass ihm die bedeutendsten Typen, als angeborene Symbolik eingeborner Ideen, gleichsam in der Seele geoffenbart werden." Page 23: "Töne und Worte, Farben und Formen, das Erscheinende überhaupt, sind jedoch nur Symbole der Idee, Symbole, die in dem Gemüte des Künstlers aufsteigen, wenn es der heilige Weltgeist bewegt."

24. *W, 6,* 297–98.

25. *W, 6,* 22.

26. *W, 4,* 395: "Tiefe Naturlaute, wie wir sie im Volksliede, bei Kindern und anderen Dichtern finden . . . den beängstigenden Zwang, den er sich antun muss, um etwas zu sagen, nennt er eine 'grosse Tat in Worten'—so gänzlich unbekannt mit dem Wesen der Poesie, weiss er nicht einmal, dass das Wort nur bei dem Rhetor eine Tat ist, bei dem wahren Dichter aber ein Ereignis."

27. *W, 10,* 58: "Innere Seele"; cf. p. 76.

28. *W, 7,* 358, on Jakob Grimm. Mücke, makes much of Heine's dependence on Rosenkranz's *Geschichte der deutschen Poesie im Mittelalter,* Halle, 1830.

29. Good comment in Barker Fairley, *Heinrich Heine: An Interpretation,* Oxford, 1954.

30. *W, 8,* 352: "Objektive Freiheit." "Die künstlerische Form hielt er für Gemütslosigkeit."

31. *W, 8,* 167.

32. *W, 7,* 13 ff.; cf. 5, 174–75.

33. *W, 8,* 400: "Eine stille Gemeinde . . . wo die Freude des alten

Bilderdienstes, der jauchzende Götterglaube sich fortpflanzte von Geschlecht auf Geschlecht."

34. *W, 7*, 48–49; *4*, 100: "Klares Griechenauge"; *5*, 167, 362–63.

35. *W, 7*, 448: "Das Wesen der Kunst."

36. Letter, 12 October 1825, in *Briefe, 1*, 232–33: "Das Hauptelement der Tragödie."

37. *W, 4*, 87–88: "Keine katholische Harmonie der Gefühle erlügen . . . Jakobinisch unerbittlich, die Gefühle zerschneiden, der Wahrheit wegen."

38. See *Briefe, 1*, 232; *W, 7*, 83–84; *W, 8*, 184: "Jauchzende Bitterkeit, eine weltverhöhnende Ironie"; *W, 7*, 92 ff.; *W, 8*, 129–53; *W, 7*, 81 f., 221, 143–44, 105–06, 125–26, 142 ff., 23, 64–68.

39. *W, 8*, 503: "Meister des Wortes . . . schreiben objektiv, und ihr Charakter verrät sich nicht in ihrem Stil."

40. 10 June, 1823, in *Briefe, 1*, 85.

41. *W, 9*, 374: "Schön, edel, wohlgewachsen und reinlich." Repeated in *W, 10*, 266.

42. *W, 7*, 243: "Subjektiv, lyrisch und reflektierend."

43. *W, 4*, 333: "Die Welt selbst mitten entzwei gerissen ist. Denn da das Herz des Dichters der Mittelpunkt der Welt ist, so musste es wohl jetziger Zeit jämmerlich zerrissen werden." The term *"Zerrissenheit"* became fashionable through a story of Alexander v. Ungern-Sternberg, *Die Zerrissenen* (1832) written after this passage in *Bäder von Lucca* (1830).

44. *W, 6*, 23: "Was will der Künstler? oder gar, was muss der Künstler?"

45. *W, 7*, 23: "In der reproduzierenden Kritik aber, wo die Schönheiten eines Kunstwerks veranschaulicht werden, wo es auf ein feines Herausfühlen der Eigentümlichkeiten ankam . . . da sind die Herren Schlegel dem alten Lessing ganz überlegen."

46. *W, 7*, 71: "Die altenglischen Gedichte . . . geben den Geist ihrer Zeit, und Bürgers Gedichte geben den Geist der unsrigen."

47. *W, 7*, 68: "Herder betrachtete die ganze Menschheit als eine grosse Harfe in der Hand des grossen Meisters, jedes Volk dünkte ihm eine besonders gestimmte Saite dieser Riesenharfe und er begriff die Universal-harmonie ihrer verschiedenen Klänge."

48. Reviews of *"Tassos Tod,* Trauerspiel von W. Smets," and "Michael Beers *Struensee"* date from 1821 and 1828 respectively. See *W, 5,* 177 ff., 325 ff.

49. *W, 7*, 88–89: "Der Leser fühlt sich da wie in einem verzauberten Walde; er hört die unterirdischen Quellen melodisch rauschen; er glaubt manchmal, im Geflüster der Bäume, seinen eigenen Namen zu

vernehmen; die breitblättrigen Schlingpflanzen umstricken manchmal beängstigend seinen Fuss, wildfremde Wunderblumen schauen ihn an mit ihren bunten sehnsüchtigen Augen; unsichtbare Lippen küssen seine Wangen mit neckender Zärtlichkeit; hohe Pilze, wie goldne Glocken, wachsen klingend empor am Fusse der Bäume; grosse schweigende Vögel wiegen sich auf den Zweigen, und nicken herab mit ihren klugen, langen Schnäbeln; alles atmet, alles lauscht, alles ist schauernd erwartungsvoll: —da ertönt plötzlich das weiche Waldhorn, und auf weissem Zelter jagt vorüber ein schönes Frauenbild, mit wehenden Federn auf dem Barett, mit dem Falken auf der Faust."

50. *W*, 7, 58–59.

51. Cf. Karl Kraus, *Heine und die Folgen* (1910, reprinted in *Untergang der Welt durch schwarze Magie,* Vienna, 1922), for Heine as ancestor of *Schmockerei.*

BIBLIOGRAPHY: YOUNG GERMANY

I have not used any of the very incomplete collected editions of Gutzkow and Laube. Comment, e.g., in Georg Brandes, *Main Currents of Nineteenth Century Literature* (see this *History, 4,* 000). Johannes Prölss, *Das junge Deutschland* (Stuttgart, 1892), and H. H. Houben, *Jungdeutscher Sturm und Drang* (Leipzig, 1911), are ample but rarely focused on the literary criticism.

Walter Dietze, *Junges Deutschland und die deutsche Klassik. Zur Ästhetik und Literaturtheorie des Vormärz* (Berlin, 1957), is most instructive in spite of its Marxist slant.

On Wienbarg, see Viktor Schweizer, *Ludolf Wienbarg. Beiträge zu einer jungdeutschen Ästhetik,* Leipzig, 1897.

On Gutzkow, Harry Iben, *Karl Gutzkow als literarischer Kritiker. Die jungdeutsche Periode,* Greifswald, 1928; poor. Also, Klemens Freiburg-Rüter, *Der literarische Kritiker Karl Gutzkow,* Leipzig, 1930; good.

On Laube: Erich Ziemann, *Heinrich Laube als Theaterkritiker,* Emstetten, 1934.

On Mundt: Walter Prinz, *Theodor Mundt als Literarhistoriker,* Halle, 1912; slight.

NOTES: YOUNG GERMANY

1. Full discussion in Johannes Prölss, pp. 611 ff., and in H. H. Houben, pp. 61 ff.

2. See Schweizer, and Werner Storch, *Die ästhetischen Theorien des jungdeutschen Sturm und Drangs* (Bonn, 1927), who shows that Wienbarg followed, among others, Schelling's Oration of 1807 very closely (see this *History*, 2, 75).

3. *Aesthetische Feldzüge* (Hamburg, 1834), pp. 67, 88, 134. Page 280: "Poesie des Lebens."

4. *Ibid.*, pp. 274. Page 268: "Das nach Befreiung ringende Deutschland."

5. *Ibid.*, pp. 285, 288. Page 306: "Einen dunklen Anflug von Gemüth."

6. *Zur neuesten Literatur* (2d ed. Hamburg, 1838), p. 147: "Kühn, grossartig und durchaus genetisch . . . Die Zusammenstellung der philosophischen Revolution Deutschlands mit der politischen Revolution Frankreichs ist der Glanzpunkt seines welthistorischen Witzes."

7. See *Zur Philosophie der Geschichte* (Hamburg, 1836), later called *Philosophie der Tat und des Ereignisses*. In *Gesammelte Werke* (Frankfurt, 1845), *4*, 28–29. On the lyric: in "Vergangenheit und Gegenwart," *Jahrbuch der Literatur* (Hamburg, 1839), pp. 46 ff. "Mit der Lyrik allein ist dem Jahrbundert nicht geholfen . . . Die Lyrik scheint mir interimistisch, unfruchtbar, zukunftlos."

8. Preface to *Die Ritter vom Geiste* (3d ed. Leipzig, 1854), p. ix: "Die ganze Zeit, die ganze Wahrheit, die ganze Wirklichkeit." This is an old idea of Gutzkow's propounded first in *Briefe eines Narren an eine Närrin* (Hamburg, 1832), p. 182.

9. On Büchner see *Beiträge zur Geschichte der neuesten Literatur* (Stuttgart, 1836), *1*, 181–89; and *Götter, Helden, Don Quixote* (Hamburg, 1838), pp. 19–50.

10. *Börnes Leben* (Hamburg, 1840), p. 17. Page 22: "Heine affectiert ein Dichter zu sein aber schreibt wie ein Gamin."

11. *Über Goethe* (Berlin, 1836), pp. 182, 187. Page 38: "Im Häuslichen." Page 91: "Harmlosigkeit."

12. *Ibid.*, p. 230. Page 232: "Zur Weltliteratur gehört alles das würdig ist in fremde Sprachen übersetzt zu werden."

13. *Ibid.*, p. 241: "Nur ein Charakter, der sich der Poesie bemächtigte."

14. *Ibid.*, pp. 253–54. Page 256: "Die Zeit der Tendenz kann beginnen, wenn man über die Zeit des Talentes im Reinen ist."

15. A selection of the theatrical criticism: *Theaterkritiken und dramaturgische Aufsätze*, ed. Alexander Weilen, 2 vols. Berlin, 1906.

16. Originally published as the second part of Friedrich von Schlegel, *Geschichte der alten und neuen Literatur. Bis auf die neueste Zeit fortgeführt von Theodor Mundt*, Berlin, 1842.

17. *Ibid.*, p. 2: "Der Begriff der Literatur als einer zusammenhängenden, nationalen Wissenschaft, ... als eines concreten Bestandtheils der wahren Wirklichkeit des Volksgeistes."

18. *Ibid.*, pp. 30–31, 36, 71. Page 2: "Die Revolution ist der Mythus der neuen Zeit."

19. *Ibid.*, p. 432: "Der wahre Kern und der höchste Reiz."

20. *Ibid.*, p. 75: "Der Bergmann, der sich in seinem eigenen Schacht verloren und dort mitten unter all seinen Reichthümern verschüttet gefunden worden."

21. *Ibid.*, p. 89: "Kaum ein Dichter (hat) das wahre Bedürfnis des modernen Geistes so tief empfunden und erkannt."

22. *Ibid.*, p. 96. Page 156: "Der politische Werther seiner Zeit."

23. *Ibid.*, pp. 273–300, 191 ff.

BIBLIOGRAPHY: GERVINUS

Max Rychner, *Georg Gottfried Gervinus. Ein Kapitel über Literaturgeschichte,* Bern, 1922; good.

Rudolf Unger, "Gervinus und die Anfänge der politischen Literaturgeschichtsschreibung in Deutschland," *Nachrichten von der Gesellschaft der Wissenschaften zu Göttingen,* Philologisch-historische Klasse, Fachgruppe IV, Neue Folge, Band I, No. 5 (Berlin, 1935), pp. 71–94.

See comment in Vittorio Santoli, "Deutsche Literaturgeschichte und Literaturkritik im 19. Jahrhundert," in *Fra Germania e Italia* (Florence, 1962), pp. 252–63.

NOTES: GERVINUS

1. Über Börnes Briefe aus Paris" in *Deutsche Jahrbücher* (1835), reprinted in *Gesammelte kleine historische Schriften* (Karlsruhe, 1838), pp. 383–410. On Börne and Heine see also the section "Die romantische Dichtung und ihre inneren Veränderungen in ihrer Ausbreitung über Europa" in *Geschichte des neunzehnten Jahrhunderts* (Leipzig, 1866), *8,* 180–87.

2. *Geschichte* (Leipzig, 1835–42), *5,* 732: "Jene Blüthe unserer Dichtung ist einmal vorüber, sie ist ins Kraut gewachsen ... grosse Geschichte." Gervinus alludes to Goethe's "Literarischer Sansculottismus" (1795), discussed in this *History, 1,* 219.

3. *Geschichte, 5,* 735: "Der Wettkampf der Kunst ist vollendet; jetzt sollten wir uns das andere Ziel stecken, das noch kein Schütze getroffen

hat, ob uns auch da Apollon den Ruhm gewährt, den er uns dort nicht versagte."

4. Fifth ed. renamed *Geschichte der deutschen Dichtung* (Leipzig, 1871–74), *1*, vii: "Unberechenbare Gefahren."

5. *Geschichte, 1,* 11: "Ich habe mit der ästhetischen Beurtheilung der Sachen nichts zu thun, ich bin kein Poet und kein belletristischer Kritiker. Der ästhetische Beurtheiler zeigt uns eines Gedichtes Entstehung aus sich selbst, sein inneres Wachstum und Vollendung, seinen absoluten Werth, sein Verhältniss zu seiner Gattung und etwa zu der Natur und dem Charakter des Dichters. Der Aesthetiker thut am besten, das Gedicht so wenig als möglich mit anderen und fremden zu vergleichen, dem Historiker ist diese Vergleichung ein Hauptmittel zum Zweck."

6. *Ibid., 3,* "Rücktritt der Dichtung aus dem Volke unter die Gelehrten."

7. *Ibid., 5,* 108: "Die leitenden Momente in den Zeitideen zu finden, die historische Verknüpfung anzudeuten." Page 110: "Ein Symbol dieser Zeit."

8. *Ibid., 5,* 118: "Ein Gedicht, das pflanzlich aus dem Boden, aus der Lage des Volks und der Zeit hervorkeimte und dessen Entfaltung von dem Anbau dieses Boden völlig abhängig ist."

9. *Ibid.:* "stand an dieser Stelle notwendig still, weil das Vaterland hier selber still stand, das die Kluft zwischen dem empfindenden, dem denkenden Leben und dem activen noch heute nicht überschritten hat."

10. *Ibid., 5,* 120: "Ohne einen wesentlichen Fortschritt in dem grossen Leben der Nation."

11. *Ibid., 5,* 487: "Es hat Alles seine Zeit und Bedingung, und so hat die Tragödie nie eine grosse Epoche gehabt, ohne dass die Lage der wirklichen Welt für den Tragöden eine Schule dargeboten hätte." Page 488: "Unser Trauerspiel irrte rathlose umher, bis die französischen Zustände orientirten." This last word is changed to "zurechtwiesen" in the 5th edition.

12. *Ibid., 5,* 489: "Wenn unsere heutige Jugend erst sorgen wollte, *Geschichte zu machen,* dann würde sie sich für das Geschäft der poetischen Mache ein besseres Glück versprechen dürfen."

13. *Ibid., 4,* viii. From 1 Henry IV, III. 1. 128–29. Gervinus adds ll. 1. 261–62 and ll. 3. 93–94.

14. I always quote the 1st edition, the text of which remained unchanged through all editions in these passages. The 5th ed. (1871–74) diverges most, as Karl Bartsch brought it up to date. Still, the critically interesting parts remained virtually untouched.

15. *Geschichte 5,* 657, 674 ff., 684–85.

16. See the interesting autobiography, *G. G. Gervinus Leben. Von ihm selbst* (1st ed. 1860; Leipzig, 1893), pp. 71 ff.

17. *Geschichte* (5th ed.), *5*, 678: "In der Romantik ging unsere Dichtung in Fäulniss über; sie ward aber der Dünger einer neuen Saat, aus der die Wissenschaften der Literaturgeschichte, Plastik, Geschichte, Mythologie, Sprachforschung aufwuchsen." Not in 1st and 2d eds.

18. *Geschichte* (1st ed.), *5*, 614: "eine ganz neue Wissenschaft, die Literaturgeschichte, angeregt mehr als selbst geschaffen."

19. *Ibid., 1*, 2: "Statt einem forschendem Werke der Gelehrsamkeit ein darstellendes Kunstwerk." Cf. *1*, 15.

20. *Ibid., 5*, 609, 611, 614, 621 ff.

21. *Ibid., 1*, 11.

22. *Ibid., 1*, 289, 322. Modified in 2d (1840) and subsequent editions. *1*, 311, 314, 316, or 5th ed. *1*, 483, 486, 488.

23. *Ibid., 1*, 271–73.

24. *Ibid., 4*, 406: "Zwischen Nord und Süd, swischen Niederland und Griechenland, zwischen Natur und Ideal." Page 413: "Das eigentümlichste und deutscheste, was unsere neuere Poesie geschaffen hat."

25. On Forster in Vol. 7 of *Georg Forsters sämtliche Schriften,* 9 vols. Leipzig, 1843. Reprinted in Hans Mayer, ed., *Meisterwerke, 2*, 283–360. On Voss, *Geschichte, 5*, 56–57.

26. *Ibid., 4*, 505: "Am Rande der durchlebten Erfahrung und zum Abschluss fertig, zur Bewältigung geschickt, ehe er zu Werke schritt." Page 506: "Auf der gefährlichen Scheide von Gefühl und Reflexion, von Instinct und Bewusstsein." Page 508: "Jene Gabe, die Dinge innerlichst zu geniessen und doch in objective Ferne zu stellen."

27. *Ibid., 5*, 78: "Von Regellosigkeit zur Ordnung und Klarheit, von nordischer Barbarei zur südlichen Cultur."

28. *Ibid., 5*, 471–72: "Das einzige (Gedicht) vielleicht, was die sämtlichen Jahrhunderte einem wiedererstandenen Griechen ohne Commentare und ohne Verlegenheit bieten dürften."

29. *Ibid., 5*, 496, 498. Page 704: "Peinliche Duldsamkeit."

30. *Ibid., 4*, 575, 396–97, 709.

31. *Ibid., 5*, 399.

32. *Ibid., 5*, 106: "Von Lücken, Rätseln und Widersprüchen voll."

33. *Ibid., 5*, 718: "Orphische Periode ... nur psychologische Merkwürdigkeit." Page 714: "körperlos, nebelhaft." Page 720: "unsäglich geringfügig."

34. *Ibid., 5*, 722. Page 724: "Die Entstehung, die Art, die Deutung dieses Gedichts hat das Widerliche für uns, was Dante's und Tasso's Commentare zu ihren eigenen Dichtungen. . . ." "Es wird beseitigt blei-

ben wie Miltons wiedergewonnenes Paradies und Klopstocks erzwungene Dramen."

35. *Ibid.*, *5*, 102, 467. Page 98: "Die reinste Blüthe der modernen Sittigung."

36. *Ibid.*, *5*, 369, 492, 495, 502, 506–07, 512.

37. *Ibid.*, *5*, 511 ff., 442.

38. *Ibid.*, *5*, 146.

39. *Ibid.*, *5*, 486: "Er gibt den reinen Zusammenhang der Handlung und Katastrophe auf, der bei Shakespeare und Göthe immer ganz tadellos ist."

40. *Ibid.*, *5*, 475–76.

41. *Ibid.*, *5*, 493 ff.

42. *Ibid.*, *5*, 700: "Flieht das Objective."

43. *Ibid.*, 5th ed., *5*, 717: "Lyrische Gedichte sind eigentlich wie die Kindheit eines Poeten, und sie können nie an sich interessieren, wenn es der Dichter nicht weiter gebracht." Not in 1st and 2d editions.

44. *Ibid.*, 1st ed., *5*, 650: "Die Fäden, die der Dichter behaglich von dem Rocken der Zeit und die, die er angestrengt wie die Spinne aus seinem Innern herausspinnt."

45. *Ibid.*, *4*, 356: "Er zittert vor dem Blutbade, den dieser letzte Satz, Handlungen seien der eigentliche Vorwurf der Poesie, unter den Dichtern anrichten würde."

46. *Ibid.*, *1*, 10.

47. *Shakespeare* (4 vols. Leipzig, 1849–50), *4*, 315: "Jene höhere Ordnung . . . die ewige Gerechtigkeit in den menschlichen Dingen . . . den Finger Gottes."

48. *Ibid.*, *4*, 396: "Cordelia stirbt in der Glorie einer verklärten Retterin, Lear in Versöhnung, Gloster lächelnd, Kent mit Freudigkeit."

49. *Ibid.*, *2*, 410–11, 230. Page 219: "Die Personification . . . der thierischen sinnlichen Natur."

50. *Ibid.*, *4*, 84. Page 105: "Zwischen politischer Pflicht und unsittlicher Leidenschaft."

51. *Ibid.*, *3*, 413. Page 464: "Eine dichterische *Theodicée.*"

52. *Ibid.*, *1*, 30, 54; *2*, 191; *4*, 271 ff., 297.

53. *Ibid.*, *2*, 60; *3*, 454.

54. *Ibid.*, e.g. *4*, 363.

55. *Ibid.*, *3*, 250; *4*, 151.

56. *Ibid.*, *3*, 260, 356.

57. *Ibid.*, *3*, 316: "Die blosses Verkörperung der inneren Versuchung."

58. *Ibid.*, *3*, 398–99, 237; *1*, 43; *3*, 297–98.

59. *Ibid., 3,* 286 ff. *4,* 421: "Freidenkend"; *1,* 4: "Lehrer von unbe-streitbarer Autorität"; *4,* 418: "Die Bresche des Fortschritts offen hält."

BIBLIOGRAPHY: THE HEGELIANS

I know of no general study, but see Hans Titze, *Die philosophische Periode der deutschen Faustforschung (1817–1839),* Greifswald, 1916; and Hans Jürg Lüthi, *Das deutsche Hamletbild seit Goethe,* Bern, 1951.

On Rötscher: Robert Klein, *Heinrich Theodor Rötschers Leben und Werke,* Berlin, 1919; and Walter Schnyder, quoted below under Hebbel.

On Rosenkranz there is good comment in B. Bosanquet's *A History of Aesthetic* (London, 1892), pp. 401–09.

Eugen Japtok, *Karl Rosenkranz als Literaturkritiker* (Freiburg im Breisgau, 1964), reviews the early criticism.

On Vischer:

O. Hesnard, *F. T. Vischer,* Paris, 1921; early life and account of the *Aesthetik;* undistinguished.

Hermann Glockner, *F. T. Vischer und das neunzehnte Jahrhundert,* Berlin, 1931; excellent, sympathetic.

Ewald Volhard, *Zwischen Hegel und Nietzsche. Der Ästhetiker F. T. Vischer,* Frankfurt a.M., 1934; critical.

Hannalene Kipper, *Die Literaturkritik F. T. Vischers,* Giesen, 1941; slight.

Benedetto Croce, "Ricordo di un vecchio critico tedesco: F. T. Vischer," in *Goethe* (4th ed. 2 vols. Bari, 1946), *2,* 132–47; excellent on Vischer's *Faust* criticism.

Georg Lukács, "Karl Marx und F. T. Vischer," in *Beiträge zur Geschichte der Ästhetik* (Berlin, 1954), pp. 217–85; Marxist, very inter-esting.

Fritz Schlawe, *F. T. Vischer als Literaturhistoriker,* Diss., Tübingen, 1953. Also, Schlawe, *F. T. Vischer,* Stuttgart, 1959; a good biography.

Willi Oelmüller, *F. T. Vischer und das Problem der nachhegelschen Ästhetik,* Stuttgart, 1959.

On Danzel: the life by Otto Jahn prefixed to *Gesammelte Aufsätze,* Leipzig, 1855.

Croce, *Estetica,* p. 377, quotes Danzel with approval and refers to him frequently.

Hans Mayer, ed., *Meisterwerke deutscher Literaturkritik* (Berlin, 1956), *2,* 361–407; reprints two articles.

NOTES: THE HEGELIANS

1. Leipzig, 1824, *1*, 142: "Der Weg, den Faust geht, ist aber der notwendige Weg, den der Gedanke gehen muss, denn dieser geht im Laufe seiner Entwicklung durch alle Weisen des Zwiespalts und Unterschieds zwischen Mensch und Gott, zwischen Subjekt und Objekt, zwischen Einzelnen und Allgemeinen, zwischen Diesseits und Jenseits."

2. Halle, 1825. See Erich Seemann, *Ein Beitrag zur Entstehungsgeschichte von Goethes Faust II: Goethe und Hinrichs*, Hannover, 1938. Yale Diss.

3. *Ibid.*, p. 233: "In dem freien Geständniss, dass er gefehlt habe."

4. "Der Hamlet des Ducis und der des Shakespeare" in *Vermischte Schriften* (Berlin, 1834), 2, 269–98.

5. See *Über Princip und Methode der Hegelschen Philosophie* (Halle, 1841), *Das Grundprincip der Philosophie* (2 vols. Leipzig, 1845–46), and many later writings.

6. Berlin, 1835, *1*, 23. Title of chapter: "Entwickelung der verschiedenen Zweige der Kunst in ihrer nothwendigen Idee." The two vols. discuss only the epic and the lyric.

7. *Geschichte der hellenischen Dichtkunst*, Halle, 1839, p. 162: "Das unmittelbare Walten der göttlichen Gerechtigkeit und der sittlichen Nothwendigkeit."

8. *Ibid.*, pp. 187, 197, 205, 219, 227, 233. Page 186: "In einer ideellen Ordnung." Page 236: "Der leitenden Hand Gottes sich entwinden, selbst absoluter Herr, selbst Gott."

9. *Ibid.*, pp. 194, 200, 211. Page 237: "Ihre glänzenden Träume von sinnlicher Lust und weltlicher Glückseligkeit."

10. See above, p. 224.

11. See *Die Kunst der dramatischen Darstellung*, 3 vols. Berlin, 1841–46; *Dramaturgische und ästhetische Abhandlungen*, Leipzig, 1864. A list with extracts of theatrical reviews in Klein, pp. 98–221.

12. Berlin, 1837–42, *1*, 3–72, "Das Verhältniss der Philosophie der Kunst und der Kritik zum einzelnen Kunstwerk."

13. *Ibid.*, *1*, iv: "Die grossen Kunstwerke in ihrer innern Vernünftigkeit, ihrer Einheit von Gedanke und Darstellung zu begreifen." *1*, vii: "Einsicht in die Nothwendigkeit des Organismus." *1*, 22: "Wie gewinnt denn der frei angeschaute Gedanke überhaupt *Form* und *Umgränzung? Wie gewinnt also überhaupt das Unendliche endliche Gestalt?*"

14. *Ibid.*, *4*, 124. Page 102: "Dialektik des abstrakten Rechts." *4*, 117: "Dieser in Antonio bewusstlos wirkenden Widerspruch seiner idealen

Natur mit den Interessen und Zwecken seiner merkantilischen Thätigkeit."

15. *Ibid., 4*, 42: "Der Zufall trägt also nur dazu bei, das Unabwendbare zu offenbaren."

16. *Ibid., 1*, 131–32. Page 79: "Der furchtbare Wahn, das Wort an die Stelle der That, die Rede an die Stelle der Gesinnung zu setzen."

17. *Ibid., 1*, 88: "Durch das Übermass des Leidens entsündigt und zu Gestalten welche das Unglück geheiligt."

18. Halle, 1830, pp. vii, 7, 276, 434, 497, 508, etc.

19. See this *History*, Vol 4.

20. Königsberg, 1847, p. 111: "Von der *Cultur* zur *Natur* und von dieser zum *Ideal*, vom Ideal endlich zur *Idee*."

21. Indications are in Jean Paul and Solger but Christian Hermann Weisse (1801–66), in his *System der Aesthetik als Wissenschaft von der Idee des Schönen* (Leipzig, 1830), and Arnold Ruge, *Neue Vorschule der Aesthetik* (Halle, 1837), discussed the concept explicitly.

22. Königsberg, 1853, p. iv.

23. *Ibid.*, pp. xiii–iv: "Formlosigkeit, die Amorphie, die Asymmetrie, die Disharmonie, die Incorrectheit, die Defiguration oder die Verbildung, das Gemeine, das Kleinliche, das Schwächliche, das Niedrige, das Widrige, das Plumpe, das Todte und Leere, das Scheussliche, das Abgeschmackte, das Ekelhafte, das Böse, das Verbrecherische, das Gespenstische, das Diabolische."

24. *Ibid.*, pp. 217 ff. Page 220: "Dem Gewöhnlichen, dem Zufälligen und Willkürlichen durch die Ausserordentlichkeit der Form eine Bedeutung zu geben." See also pp. 386 ff.

25. *Ibid.*, p. 94: "Der grelle Contrast kann ... schön werden. ...Synthese heterogener Gegensätze." Page 42: "Die Kunst (muss) auch das Hässliche idealisiren, d. h. nach den allgemeinen Gesetzen des Schönen ... behandeln."

26. See *Kritische Gänge*, 2 vols. Tübingen, 1844; *Neue Folge*, 6 vols. Stuttgart, 1861–73; *Altes und Neues*, 3 vols. Stuttgart, 1881–82; *Neue Folge*, Stuttgart, 1889; *Goethes Faust*, 3d ed. Stuttgart, 1921; *Shakespeare-Vorträge*, 6 vols. Stuttgart, 1899.

27. *Goethes Faust*, p. 55: "absurd, affektiert, steif, widerwärtig, lächerlich."

28. *Kritische Gänge*, Neue Folge, *3*, 137: "Positive Kritik."

29. For these, see *Kritische Gänge*, Neue Folge, Vol. 2, and *Shakespeare-Vorträge*, lectures from the seventies and eighties edited by his son, Robert Vischer, from notes taken by students. The whole first volume is occupied by *Hamlet*, translated and commented upon scene by scene.

30. *Kritische Gänge,* Neue Folge, 2, 65–156, esp. pp. 90, 121, 129, 131. Page 115: "Ein solcher verhärteter Stotterer des Handelns."

31. "Shakspeare in seinem Verhältniss zur deutschen Poesie, insbesondere zur politischen" (1844), reprinted in *Kritische Gänge,* Neue Folge, 2, 1–62. The preface of 1860 states some reservations against the early conceptions. On reconciliation of Schiller and Shakespeare, see *Aesthetik,* 5, 1416–19.

32. *Aesthetik,* 6 vols. Reutlingen-Stuttgart, 1846–57. Vischer presented "Plan zu einer neuen Gliederung der Aesthetik" (1843), reprinted in *Kritische Gänge* (Tübingen, 1844), 2, 343–96.

33. *Aesthetik, 1,* 94: "Zufälligkeit." Cf. *Kritische Gänge,* 2, 376.

34. *Aesthetik, 1,* 141: "Eine Verewigung des Individuums." Page 334: "Eine negative Stellung zur Idee ... sich der Durchdringung mit der Idee widersetzt." Page 400: "Geist der Immanenz."

35. *Ibid.,* 5, 1211–15.

36. *Ibid.,* 5, 1216, 1243. Page 1166: "In jedem Bilde ein Weltbild."

37. *Ibid.,* 5, 1260.

38. *Ibid.,* 5, 1330: "Punctualität"; p. 1342: "Eine Lyrik des Aufschwungs zum Gegenstande" ... "des reinen Aufgehens des letzteren ins Subjecte ... der beginnenden und wachsenden Ablösung aus ihm in der Betrachtung."

39. *Ibid.,* 5, 1406 ff., 1423, 1429; and discussions of varieties of the tragic in *1,* 300 ff. On women characters, see *Kritische Gänge,* Neue Folge, 2, xi, xxl, 14 ff., 20. On Ophelia, see also *Shakespeare-Vorträge, 1,* 471–72.

40. *Aesthetik,* 5, 1443–44: "Act der reinen Freiheit des Selbstbewusstseins." Page 1445: "Die Komödie enthält das Erhabene, das Tragische in sich."

41. *Kritische Gänge, 2,* 315: "Mit unserem Dichten ist es nichts, es ist jetzt die Zeit zum Trachten." Reviews of Herwegh, *ibid.,* 282 ff., 316 ff. Also in *Kritische Gänge,* Neue Folge, *4,* 166.

42. See "Zum neueren Drama. Hebbel," in *Altes und Neues* (Stuttgart, 1889), pp. 1–26, esp. 16 ff.

43. "Kritik meiner Aesthetik," in *Kritische Gänge,* Neue Folge, *5,* 1–156, and *6,* 1–132, esp. *6,* 110: "Begriffsbewegung," and 5, 6.

44. Zurich, 1858. Accessible only in a reprint of *Kritische Gänge,* ed. Robert Vischer (Berlin, 1920), *4,* 198–221.

45. *Kritische Gänge,* Neue Folge, *5,* 85: "Inhaltsvolle Form"; p. 86: "Die Form hat wesentlich Ausdruck"; *6,* 21: "Eine barocke Verbindung von Mystik und Mathematik"; *6,* 15: "Die Form hängt nicht am Stoff, sondern geht aus ihm hervor"; *6,* 16: "Form des Inhaltes, das Äussere des Inneren."

46. Cf. preface to *Kritische Gänge*, Neue Folge, 2, iv, vi, where Vischer draws attention to his analysis of the composition of *Lear* in *Aesthetik*, *3*, 44–49.

47. *Altes und Neues.* Neue Folge, 1889, pp. 296, 297, 299, 304, 307. Page 310: "Die Wahrheit aller Wahrheiten, dass das Weltall, Natur und Geist in der Wurzel Eines sein muss." Page 320: "Zuempfindung, Nachempfindung, Einempfindung." Page 336: "Harmonik und Mimik." Pages 337, 341: "Die Kunst macht den transcendentalen Standpunkt zum gemeinen." From *Das System der Sittenlehre* (1798), in J. G. Fichte, *Sämtliche Werke* (8 vols. Berlin, 1845–46), *4*, 353. Vischer quotes incorrectly. Fichte says: "Gesichtspunkt zu dem gemeinen."

48. Hamburg, 1844, p. 22. Page 42: "Ein Einzelnes, und zwar ein wahrhaft concretes." Page 52: "Die Kunst nur eine bestimmte Form der Äusserung und Darstellung des Wahren." Page 62: "Das Philosophiren über die Kunst besteht dann darin, dass man die Form zerbricht, und nun, bei Gelegenheit des Kunstwerks, über den Inhalt das aus Religions- und Rechtsphilosophie anderweitig Bekannte wiederholt."

49. "Shakspeare und noch immer kein Ende" in *Gesammelte Aufsätze*, ed. Otto Jahn (Leipzig, 1855), pp. 203–26 (reprinted also in H. Mayer, ed., *Meisterwerke deutscher Literaturkritik*, 2, 370–407). Pages 216, 218: "Unseliger Ausdruck, der ein ganzes Zeitalter zur Sisyphus-arbeit einer Zurückführung der Sache auf das Denken des Verstandes und der Vernunft verdammt hat. Der Gedanke eines Kunstwerks ist nichts Anderes als das ... Erschaute, welches nicht in dem Kunstwerke dargestellt, sondern das Kunstwerk selbst ist. Der Kunstgedanke kann niemals durch Begriffe und Worte ausgedrückt werden.... Nie kann ich seinen Inhalt anders mittheilen als dadurch, dass ich es eben ganz wie es ist vor Augen stelle ... Anschauung und Stimmung ... gar kein Wesentliches und Unwesentliches." Page 219: "Ein subjectives Allgemeine, nur eine subjective Einheit."

50. *Ibid.*, p. 225: "Das Werk in seiner ganzen Eigentümlichkeit für die Anschauung vermitteln." Page 226: "Eine wahre Kunstgeschichte der Poesie, in welcher nicht nur die äusseren Formen, sondern auch die innere Auffassung des Stoffs bei den verschiedenen Dichtern ... Entwicklungsgang."

51. "Über die Behandlung der Geschichte der neueren deutschen Literatur," in *Gesammelte Aufsätze*, pp. 197–202. Reprinted in H. Mayer, ed., *Meisterwerke*, 2, 361–69, p. 202: "Ohne links und rechts zu sehen, die Metamorphosen der poetischen Production rein aus dieser selbst."

52. *Ibid.*, pp. 197, 200, 202.

53. *Ibid.*, pp. 1–84; pp. 85–98: "Moses Mendelssohn." Pages 118–45:

"Goethe und die Weimarschen Kunstfreunde in ihrem Verhältniss zu Winckelmann." Pages 227–44: "Schillers Briefwechsel mit Körner."

54. *Gottsched und seine Zeit. Auszüge aus seinem Briefwechsel,* Leipzig, 1848. *—Gotthold Ephraim Lessing. Sein Leben und seine Werke,* Leipzig, 1850. The volume goes to 1774. A second, final, volume, by G. E. Guhrauer, was published in 1854.

55. *Gesammelte Aufsätze,* p. 226: "Der Winckelmann der Geschichte der Poesie wird noch erwartet."

BIBLIOGRAPHY: HEBBEL

I quote Friedrich Hebbel, *Sämtliche Werke,* Historisch-kritische Ausgabe, ed. R. M. Werner, 24 vols. Berlin, 1901–07. Of these: *Werke,* 12 vols., as *W; Tagebücher,* 4 vols., as *T;* and *Briefe,* 8 vols., as *B.*

Among the books on his theory, see:

Arno Scheunert, *Der Pantragismus als System der Weltanschauung und Ästhetik Friedrich Hebbels,* Hamburg, 1903, 2d ed. 1930.

Arthur Kutscher, *Friedrich Hebbel als Kritiker des Dramas,* Berlin, 1907.

Benno von Wiese, *Die deutsche Tragödie von Lessing bis Hebbel* (Hamburg, 1948, 4th ed. 1958), contains three important chapters on Hebbel.

Joachim Müller, *Das Weltbild Friedrich Hebbels* (Halle, 1955), has a good chapter, "Die Kunst und das Drama."

On sources, see:

Hermann Glockner, "Hebbel und Hegel," *Preussische Jahrbücher, 188* (1922), 63–86.

Ludwig Marcuse, "Der Hegelianer Hebbel—gegen Hegel," *Monatshefte, 39* (1947), 506–14.

Walter Schnyder, *Hebbel und Rötscher unter besonderer Berücksichtigung der beiderseitigen Beziehungen zu Hegel,* Berlin, 1923.

In English, Edna Purdie, *Friedrich Hebbel, A Study of his Life and Work* (Oxford, 1932), devotes a few perfunctory pages to his "Conception of Tragedy" (pp. 255–69).

NOTES: HEBBEL

1. On Hegel, see, e.g., *W, 11,* 406; *B, 2,* 143 (4 December 1842); *B, 2,* 278 (2 July 1843); *B, 4,* 153 (6 March 1849); *B, 4,* 282 (19 April 1851); *B, 5,* 45 (15 September 1852); *B, 6,* 2 (8 January 1857); *B, 6,* 115 (22 February 1858).

2. *T, 2,* 388 (25 March 1844).

3. This is shown convincingly in Schnyder; see bibliography above.

4. On Vischers *T, 3,* 241–42 (6 June 1847), and *B, 6,* 139 (1 June 1858). Vischer wrote an article "Zum neueren Drama—Hebbel" in 1847, reprinted in *Kritische Gänge,* Vol. 6, Munich, 1922.

5. *B, 5,* 327 (23 July 1856). See also *B, 6,* 139 (1 June 1958), and *T, 1,* 215 (2 March 1838).

6. *T, 2,* 63 (3 September 1840): "Poesie ist ein Blutsturz; der Dichter wird sein Blut los und es zerrinnt im Sande der Welt."

7. *B, 5,* 164 (13 June 1854); *B, 5,* 203 (12 December 1854); *T, 3,* 311 (22 August 1848); *T, 3,* 241 (3 June 1847).

8. *T, 4,* 295 (1 May 1863). Also *B, 7,* 341–43; *B, 6,* 348 (16 October 1860).

9. *W, 11,* 406. Page 47: "Das Schaffen dessen erstes Stadium, das empfangende doch tief unter dem Bewusstsein liegt und zuweilen in die dunkelste Ferne der Kindheit zurückfällt." *T, 3,* 311 (22 August 1848); *B, 7,* 302 (23 February 1863): "Er fängt ihn, weil er gerade da sitzt, und sieht sich ihn erst näher an, wenn er ihn in der Hand hat."

10. *T, 2,* 96 (2 February 1841): "Jedes echte Kunstwerk ist ein geheimnissvolles, vieldeutiges, in gewissem Sinne unergründliches Symbol."

11. Letter, 30 July 1862, in *Neue Hebbel-Dokumente,* ed. Kralik and Lemmermayer (Berlin, 1913), p. 161. *W, 11,* 29, 56: "Die realisierte Philosophie." *W, 11,* 38. Cf. *T, 2,* 201 (7 October 1842).

12. *T, 2,* 51 (June 1840); *T, 2,* 95 (2 February 1841); *T, 2,* 106 (25 March 1841): "Der Dichter muss durchaus nach dem Äusseren, dem Sichtbaren, Begränzten, Endlichen greifen, wenn er das Innere, Unsichtbare, Unbegränzte, Unendliche darstellen will."

13. *W, 11,* 70, 72.

14. *W, 11,* 29: "Diese Schuld ist eine uranfängliche, von dem Begriff des Menschen nicht zu trennende und kaum in sein Bewusstsein fallende, sie ist mit dem Leben selbst gesetzt."

15. *W, 11,* 31: "Ein bürgerliches, in sich selbst unhaltbares, und nur der Form nach die Idee des Staats repräsentirendes Gesetz."

16. *W, 11,* 52: "Alles Handeln löst sich dem Schicksal, d.h. dem Weltwillen gegenüber, in ein Leiden auf."

17. *T, 2,* 57 (13 August 1840).

18. *T, 1,* 267 (12 August 1838). *T, 3,* 269 (18 September 1847): "Wenn der Mensch sein individuelles Verhältniss zum Universum in seiner Nothwendigkeit begreift." Also *B, 4,* 102–03 (1 May 1848).

19. *T, 3,* 412 (21 December 1851): "Die sogenannte Freiheit des Menschen läuft darauf hinaus, dass er seine Abhängigkeit von den allgemeinen Gesetzen nicht kennt." Cf. *T, 2,* 155 (2 March 1842).

20. *B, 4,* 129 (14 August 1848): "Deren Schicksal daraus hervorgeht, dass sie eben diese Menschen sind und keine andere."

21. *T, 2,* 269 (29 August 1843): "Es ist thöricht, von dem Dichter zu verlangen, was Gott selbst nicht darbietet, Versöhnung und Ausgleichung der Dissonanzen. Aber allerdings kann man fodern, dass er die Dissonanzen selbst gebe und nicht in der Mitte zwischen dem Zufälligen und dem Nothwendigen stehen bleibe. So darf er jeden Character zu Grunde gehen lassen, aber er muss uns zugleich zeigen, dass der Untergang unvermeidlich, dass er, wie der Tod, mit der Geburt selbst gesetzt ist."

22. *T, 2,* 286 (6 November 1843): "Es giebt nur Eine Nothwendigkeit, die, dass die Welt besteht; wie es den Individuen aber in der Welt ergeht, ist gleichgültig." Cf. *T, 2,* 311 (21 November 1843).

23. *T, 2,* 415 (25 June 1844): "Die Versöhnung fällt immer über den Kreis des speziellen Dramas hinaus." Rötscher, in Hebbel, *Briefwechsel,* ed. Felix Bamberg (Berlin, 1890–92) 2, 300. suggests term "die an sich seiende Versöhnung."

24. *T, 2,* 239 (6 March 1843): "Im Interesse der Gesammtheit, nicht in dem des Einzelnen, des Helden, und es ist gar nicht nöthig, obgleich besser, dass er sich selbst ihrer bewusst wird … Das Leben ist der grosse Strom, die Individualitäten sind die Tropfen, die tragischen aber Eisstücke, die wieder zerschmolzen werden müssen und sich, damit dies möglich sey, an einander abreissen und zerstossen."

25. *W, 11,* 31: "Er lässt daher nicht die Schuld unaufgehoben, wohl aber den innern Grund der Schuld unenthüllt."

26. *T, 2,* 239 (6 March 1843): "Die grosse Wunde Gottes." *T, 2,* 378: "Gottes Sündenfall." *T, 1,* 377 (8 October 1839): "Der Mensch ist das Prokrustesbett der Gottheit." *T, 1,* 391 (28 October 1839): "Die Schöpfung ist die Schnürbrust der Gottheit."

27. *T, 2,* 67 (25 September 1840): "In der Welt ist ein Gott begraben, der auferstehen will und allenthalben durchzubrechen sucht, in der Liebe, in jeder edlen That."

28. Benno von Wiese (see bibliography above) tries to make these mystical ideas the center of Hebbel's theory.

29. *W, 11,* 5: "Die höchste Geschichtsschreibung." Also *W, 11,* 58.

30. *T, 2,* 26–27 (3 April 1840); *W, 8,* 418: "Wiedergeburt der Individualität."

31. *W, 11,* 60–61.

32. *W, 11,* 62.

33. *T, 3,* 186 (30 January 1847): "Meine Lebensaufgabe, den gegenwärtigen Welt-Zustand, wie er ist und ward, darzustellen."

34. *W, 1,* 432: "Ein jedes Drama ist nur so weit lebendig, als es der Zeit, in der es entspringt, d.h. ihren höchsten und wahrsten Interessen, zum Ausdruck dient."

35. *W, 11,* 48: "Zeitgemässig . . . Künstlerische Opfer der Zeit."

36. *W, 11,* 15; *T, 1,* 260 (22 June 1838): "Das Genie ist der Fühlfäden seiner Zeit."

37. *T, 2,* 152 (20 February 1842): "Die Kunst ist das Gewissen der Menschheit."

38. *T, 1,* 224 (10 March 1838): "Das moderne Schicksal ist die Silhouette Gottes, des Unbegreiflichen und Unerfassbaren."

39. *T, 2,* 254 (12 July 1843). See the distichs in *W, 6,* 448: "An den Tragiker."

BIBLIOGRAPHY: RUGE

Ruge is quoted from *Gesammelte Schriften* (10 vols. Mannheim, 1846–48), as *GS.* Especially Vol. 1, "Unsere Classiker und Romantiker seit Lessing, Geschichte der neuesten Poesie und Philosophie"; and Vol. 2: "Über die gegenwärtige Poesie, Kunst und Literatur."

Cf. *Briefwechsel und Tagebuchblätter,* ed. P. Nerrlich, 2 vols. Berlin, 1886.

On Ruge: Douglas A. Joyce, *Arnold Ruge as a Literary Critic,* unpublished Harvard University diss. (1952), which I examined briefly. It should be printed.

See also comment in Löwith, *Von Hegel bis Nietzsche,* Zurich, 1941.

NOTES: RUGE

1. *GS, 3,* 219: "Sohn seiner Zeit"; *GS, 5,* 387: "Genius des Jahrhunderts."

2. *GS, 2,* 270: "Revolutionär, heisst das nicht poetisch, *novarum rerum studiosus,* schöpferisch? . . . Jede neue Poesie, ist sie nicht der Umsturz einer alten und veralteten Geisteswelt?" *GS, 2,* 362: "Jede Poesie ist eine kämpfende." *GS, 2,* 364: "Das Wesen der Poesie ist demokratisch . . . alle Herzen zu beherrschen."

3. *GS, 1,* 9: "Die Aufklärung behauptet die Wahrheit der Wissenschaft, die Wirklichkeit der Tugend und Freiheit, endlich die Existenz des Ideals durch die Kunst."

4. Schiller to F. H. Jacobi (25 January 1795), *Briefe,* ed. Jonas, *4,* 110–11: "Wir wollen dem Leibe nach Bürger unserer Zeit bleiben weil es nicht anders sein kann; sonst aber dem Geiste nach ist es das Vorrecht und die Pflicht des Philosophen, wie des Dichters, zu keinem Volk und

zu keiner Zeit zu gehören, sondern im eigentlichen Sinne der Zeitgenosse aller Zeiten zu sein." *GS, 1*, 44: "Armer Dichter der deutschen Zeitlosig- keit! Aber so war es und so ist es: wer keine Zeit erlebt, kann freilich nicht ihr Genosse sein."

5. *GS, 1*, 176, 90.

6. *GS, 1*, 121: "Nur der freie Staat erzeugt einen Dichter, der die wahre Wirklichkeit idealisiert und ein Ideal hervorbringt, das die Welt ernstlich verwirklicht."

7. *GS, 1*, 301: "Die Romantik ist die Kriegserklärung dieses Geistes der Willkür gegen den freien gesetzlichen Geist unsrer Zeit."

8. *GS, 1*, 324: "Die Romantik ist die verkehrte Welt, sie setzt die Natur über den Geist, den Kopf nach unten und die Beine nach oben, das Unvernünftige, ja das Vernunftlose, wie die Pflanze und das Organ- ische zur Regel des Vernünftigen, die Natur und das Paradies zum Ziel des Geistes und der Cultur."

9. *GS, 1*, 326: "Der Geist und sein Begriff . . . Ihre Poesie unpoetisch, ihre Freiheit Frechheit, ihre Philosophie Ironie und Mystification."

10. *GS, 1*, 388, on Arnim-Brentano, or 441 on "dumme Naturklänge."

11. *GS, 1*, 272.

12. *GS, 2*, 15: "Hat Heine das Recht ernsthaft zu reden, nicht verscherzt? Wer glaubt ihm noch?" *Ibid., 2*, 34: "Die ganze Welt der Wahrheit und die ganze Realität geht ihm verloren." *Ibid., 2*, 52: "Sie scheint Geist zu sein und sie ist nichts, als die Verzweiflung am Geiste selbst."

13. *GS, 1*, 430–31: "Ein ächter Romantiker glaubt: 1) An den genialen Göthe, an die unbedingte Vollkommenheit Shakespeare's, an die Tiefe Dante's, und an Calderon den Spanier, auch an einige Griechen. Diese sind 'Dichter', Schiller und Körner dagegen sind 'Nichtdichter'. 2) Diese Bestimmung bleibt mysteriös . . . Shakespeare, Dante, Calderon, Göthe, Hans Sachs, F. Schlegel, Holberg, Heinrich von Kleist, Manzoni sind Dichter; Voltaire dagegen, Schiller, Körner, Walter Scott und Wieland mögen sonst hübsche Leute sein, aber 'es fehlt ihnen das Eine, *Dichter* sind sie nicht.' Warum, das weiss man nicht. 3) Der Romantiker glaubt ferner an das Mittelalter, an den Katholicismus, an die mittelaltrige Kunst und an die Vor-Raphaelsche Malerei. 4) An die Poesie des Aber- glaubens, an die Volkspoesie im Gegensatz gegen die Kunstpoesie, an Volkslieder und Volksbücher, nach der Melodie: 'Das Beste wird durch Worte nicht deutlich.' 5) An den Styl A. W. Schlegels und an Tieck's Welthumor im Kater. 6) Er sehnt sich nach Italien, und verachtet je- den als geistlos, der es nicht lobt. 7) Er erzieht seine Kinder nach der Wunder- und Märchenschrulle. 8) Die Narrenfeste, Volksspiele, die alte Reisepoesie gehören zu seinen frommen Wünschen. 9) Sein drittes

Wort ist tief und mystisch. 10) Er hasst die Aufklärung und die Franzosen ... Die Wörter, Nutzen und Geschmack in den Mund zu nehmen ist trivial. 11) Er verachtet die Park- und Gartenkunst und liebt den Naturwuchs der 'Waldeinsamkeit.' 12) Er glaubt an den Weltuntergang, und zwar ist derselbe bereits eingetreten, in der dramatischen Poesie, seit Shakespeare und Holberg tot sind ... Er glaubt endlich auch in keiner andern Sphäre an den Freiheitzeugenden Geist, wohl aber an den Teufel und an Spuck."

14. *GS, 3, 405:* "Das Absolute oder die Freiheit erreichen wir nur in der Geschichte."

BIBLIOGRAPHY: MARX-ENGELS

There is a convenient collection, here quoted as *UKL,* Karl Marx–Friedrich Engels, *Über Kunst und Literatur: Eine Sammlung aus ihren Schriften* (ed. Michail Lipschitz, Berlin, 1948), based on a Russian collection (1933) which exists also in a French version: *Sur la littérature et l'art* (with additional texts by Lenin and Stalin), ed. Jean Fréville, Paris 1937. The English collection, Karl Marx–Friedrich Engels, *Literature and Art: Selections from their Writings* (New York, 1947), is only a small selection. More translations in Karl Marx–Friedrich Engels, *Selected Works,* ed. V. V. Adoratsky, 2 vols. New York, 1935.

Comment is endless. Peter Demetz, *Marx, Engels und die Dichter* (Stuttgart, 1959), is the best study of the texts. Originally a Yale dissertation, 1956. Bibliography.

Georg Lukács, *Karl Marx und Friedrich Engels als Literaturhistoriker* (Berlin, 1948), and *Beiträge zur Geschichte der Ästhetik* (Berlin, 1954), contain several studies attempting to interpret the texts as a coherent system of Marxist aesthetics.

Ludwig Marcuse, "Die marxistische Auslegung des Tragischen," *Monatshefte, 46* (1954), 241–48.

NOTES: MARX AND ENGELS

1. *UKL,* 301 ff. 316, 348.
2. *UKL,* 471.
3. See Gustav Mayer, *Friedrich Engels in seiner Frühzeit, 1820–1835,* Berlin, 1920; and *Friedrich Engels,* The Hague, 1934.
4. In "Die Lage Englands" in *Deutsch-französische Jahrbücher* (1844) Demetz shows that Marx and Engels must have derived some of the phraseology of the *Communist Manifesto* from Carlyle. Marx-

Engels reviewed *Latter Day Pamphlets* (1850) most unfavorably (*UKL*, 201–09).

5. *UKL*, 216–29. Pages 218–19: "bald kolossal, bald kleinlich; bald trotziges, spottendes, weltverachtendes Genie, bald rücksichtsvoller, genügsamer, enger Philister."

6. *UKL*, 365: "Ein kommuner Hund *politice*." Engels' letter to Marx of 21 December 1866. Besides Demetz, cf. Ludwig Marcuse, "Heinrich Heine und Marx," *Germanic Review, 30* (1955), 110–24.

7. *UKL*, 4: "Direkter Ausfluss ihres materiellen Verhaltens ... Nicht das Bewusstsein bestimmt das Leben, sondern das Leben bestimmt das Bewusstsein."

8. *UKL*, 90: "In einer kommunistischen Gesellschaft gibt es keine Maler, sondern höchstens Menschen, die unter anderm auch malen." *UKL*, 173: "Noch nicht unter die Teilung der Arbeit geknechtet."

9. *UKL*, 13: "Bedarf es tiefer Einsicht, um zu begreifen, dass mit den Lebensverhältnissen der Menschen, mit ihren gesellschaftlichen Beziehungen, mit ihrem gesellschaftlichen Dasein auch ihre Vorstellungen, Anschauungen und Begriffe, mit einem Worte auch ihr Bewusstsein sich ändert?"

10. By Karl Kautsky in *Die Neue Zeit, 21* (1903), 710–18, 741–45, 772–81.

11. *UKL*, 21–22. "Das unegale Verhältnis der Entwicklung der materiellen Produktion zur künstlerischen ... Bei der Kunst bekannt, dass bestimmte Blütezeiten derselben keineswegs im Verhältnis zur allgemeine Entwicklung der Gesellschaft, also auch der materiellen Grundlage, gleichsam des Knochenbaus ihrer Organisation stehn. Z. B. die Griechen, verglichen mit den Modernen oder auch Shakespeare ... Die Schwierigkeit liegt nicht darin, zu verstehn, dass griechische Kunst und Epos an gewisse gesellschaftliche Entwicklungsformen geknüpft sind. Die Schwierigkeit ist, dass sie für uns noch Kunstgenuss gewähren und in gewisser Beziehung als Norm und unerreichbare Muster gelten ... Normale Kinder waren die Griechen. Der Reiz ihrer Kunst für uns steht nicht im Widerspruch zu der unentwickelten Gesellschaftsstufe, worauf sie wuchs."

12. *UKL*, 3: "Die Produktionsweise des materiellen Lebens bedingt den sozialen, politischen und geistigen Lebensprozess überhaupt."

13. *UKL*, 110–13; letter of 19 April 1859. Page 112: "Das Verwandeln von Individuen in blosse Sprachröhren des Zeitgeistes." Page 111: "Ein *Ritter* und *Repräsentant einer untergehenden Klasse* ... Ein *miserabler* Kerl."

14. *UKL*, 113–16; letter of 18 May 1859: "Etwas zu abstrakt, nicht

realistisch genug ... Falstaffscher Hintergrund ... Tragische Kollision zwischen dem historisch notwendigen Postulat und der praktisch unmöglichen Durchführung."

15. *UKL*, 116–46. Page 140: "Einen *Franz von Sickingen* und nicht einen *Thomas Münzer* oder eine andere Bauernkriegstragödie."

16. *UKL*, 102: "Ein Typus, aber auch zugleich ein bestimmter Einzelmensch, ein 'Dieser', wie der alte Hegel sich ausdrückt."

17. *UKL*, 103–04. See Demetz (pp. 226 ff.) on Balzac's stories.

18. See this *History*, Vol. 4.

19. *UKL*, 6.

20. Not in *UKL*. From *Dokumente des Sozialismus*, ed. Eduard Bernstein (Berlin, 1903), 2, 73–75: "Die geographische Grundlage .. das die Gesellschaftsform nach aussen umgebende Milieu ... Rasse selbst ist ein ökonomischer Faktor ... Je weiter das Gebiet, das wir gerade untersuchen, sich vom Ökonomischen entfernt, und sich dem reinen abstrakt Ideologischen nähert, desto mehr werden wir finden, dass es in seiner Entwicklung Zufälligkeiten aufweist, desto mehr im Zickzack verläuft seine Kurve."

BIBLIOGRAPHY: RUSSIAN CRITICISM

There are several histories of Russian criticism, either obsolete or doctrinaire Marxist:

A. L. Volynsky, *Russkie kritiki. Literaturnye ocherki*, St. Petersburg. 1896.

I. I. Ivanov, *Istoriya russkoi kritiki*, originally, in parts, in *Mir Bozhi*, 1897–1900.

A. Lunacharsky and V. Polyansky, eds., *Ocherki po istorii russkoi kritiki*, 2 vols. Moscow and Leningrad, 1929–31.

B. P. Gorodetsky, A. Lavretsky, and B. S. Meilakh, eds., *Istoriya russkoi kritiki*, 2 vols. Moscow and Leningrad, 1958.

A general history of aesthetics contains some Russian chapters: M. F. Ovsyannikov and Z. V. Smirnova, *Ocherki istorii esteticheskikh uchenii*, Moscow, 1963.

An anthology in Italian is useful: Ettore Lo Gatto, ed., *L'Estetica e la poetica in Russia*, Florence, 1947.

Pushkin's literary opinions are conveniently collected in N. V. Bogoslovsky, ed., *Pushkin o literature*, Moscow, 1934.

1. A. D. Kantemir, *Sochineniya, pisma i izbrannye perevody* (St. Petersburg, 1867), *1*, 167.

2. M. V. Lomonosov, *Polnoe sobranie sochinenii* (Moscow and Leningrad, 1953), *7*, 588–9.

3. *Opyt istoricheskogo slovarya o rossiiskikh pisatelyakh* (1772). Analyzed in Gorodetsky et al., *Istoriya russkoi kritiki*, *1*, 91–4.

4. *Vestnik Evropy*, *6* (1802), 228–9: "Что принадлежит до критики новых русских книг, то мы не считаем ее истинною потребностью нашей литературы."

5. Karamzin, *Sochineniya* (St. Petersburg, 1848), *3*, 645–6; *2*, 122, quoted in Gorodetsky, *1*, 112, 114, 115.

6. Zhukovsky, "O kritike," *Vestnik Evropy*, *48* (1809), 36. Quoted in Gorodetsky, *1*, 167.

7. Preface to Pushkin, "Bakhchisaraisky fontan" (1824), quoted in Gorodetsky, *1*, 208; and *Damsky zhurnal*, Vol. 6, No. 8, p. 77, quoted *ibid.*, *1*, 231.

8. Letter to A. A. Bestuzhev (May–June 1825), in *Pushkin, o literature*, p. 75: "Именно критики у нас и недостает. Мы не имеем ни единого комментария, ни единой критической книги." Cf. *The Letters of Alexander Pushkin*, translated J. T. Shaw (3 vols., Bloomington and Philadelphia, 1963), *1*, 222.

9. Cf. "Iz Pindemonte," "Никому отчета не давать," etc. *Pushkin o literature*, p. 242 n. (1836, "Mnenie M. E. Lobanova . . ."): "Самый ничтожный предмет может быть избран стихотворцем." *Ibid.*, p. 377 (projected preface to Canto VIII and IX of *Evgeny Onegin*, 1830): "Почувствовали, что цель художества есть идеал, а не нравоучение."

10. Letter to V. A. Zhukovsky (May–June 1825), *Pushkin o literature*, p' 74: "Цель поэзии—поэзия." Cf. *Letters*, *1*, 219.

11. *Polnoe sobranie sochinenii* (Moscow 1949), *4*, 251: "Поэт сам избирает предметы для своих песен; толпа не имеет права управлять его вдохновением."

12. Cf. the poem (1833) beginning "Французских рифмачей суровый судия . . ." where he calls himself "поклонник верный твой" (your faithful admirer).

13. On Byron, see Gorodetsky, *1*, 293, quoting Academy ed., *7*, 170: "С ума сходил." *Pushkin o literature*, pp. 115–16, etc. On Shakespeare, see the draft of the preface to *Boris Godunov*, *ibid*., p. 117. On Scott, i.a., *ibid*., pp. 114–15.

14. A letter to E. M. Khitrovo (May 1831): "in ecstasy" (в восторге) about *Rouge et noir. Pushkin o literature*, p. 290. Cf. *Letters, 2*, 488. On Sainte-Beuve, see the long review (1831) of *Vie, poésies et pensées de Joseph Delorme*, in *Pushkin o literature*, pp. 258–68.

15. "Otryvki" (1827) in *Pushkin o literature*, p. 105: "В чувстве соразмерности и сообразности."

16. "Aleksandr Radishchev" (1836). *Pushkin o literature*, p. 365: "Посредственное . . . варварский слог." "Невежественное презрение ко всему прошедшему; слабоумное изумление перед своим веком, слепое пристрастие к новизне; частные, поверхностные сведения." It seems impossible to accept the common Soviet view that Pushkin meant to praise Radishchev.

17. "Pismo k izdateliu" (23 April 1836). *Pushkin o literature*, p. 425: "Если бы с независимостию мнений и остроумием своим соединял он более учености, более начитанности, более уважения к преданию, более осмотрительности,—словом, более зрелости, то мы бы имели в нем критика весьма замечательного."

BIBLIOGRAPHY: BELINSKY

I quote from *Sobranie sochinenii*, ed. F. M. Golovenchenko (3 vols. Moscow, 1948), as *G*. When this fails, from *Polnoe sobranie sochinenii*, ed. S. A. Vengerov, 11 vols. Petersburg, 1900–17. The letters, from *Izbrannye pis'ma*, ed. N. I. Mordovchenko and M. Ya. Polyakov, 2 vols. Moscow, 1955.

As far as possible I have used the anonymous English translation, *Selected Philosophical Works*, Moscow, 1948. This contains *Literary Reveries* and the essays of the last period, but nothing of the middle stage.

There is a small German anthology (142 pp.), *W. Belinskij, der Begründer der modernen Literaturkritik*, ed. Rudolf Dietrich, Berlin, 1948; and a German translation (by A. Kloeckner) of *Hamlet: Deutung und Darstellung*, Berlin, 1952.

Of the immense comment in Russian I have found the following most useful:

A. N. Pypin, *Belinsky: ego zhizn i perepiska*, 2 vols. Petersburg, 1876.

A. L. Volynsky (Akim Flekser), *Russkie kritiki* (Petersburg, 1896), esp. 81 ff.

Iv. Ivanov, *Istoriya russkoi kritiki* (Petersburg, 1900), esp. Part III, pp. 39–333.

Iury Aikhenvald, *Siluety russkikh pisateley* (3d ed. Moscow, 1917), III, 1–14.

G. V. Plekhanov, *V. G. Belinsky. Sbornik statei*, Moscow, 1923.

A. Lavretsky, *Belinsky, Chernyshevsky, Dobrolyubov v borbe za realizm*, Moscow, 1941; and *Estetika Belinskogo*, Moscow, 1959.

P. I. Lebedev-Polyansky, *V. G. Belinsky. Literaturnokriticheskaya deyatelnost*, Moscow and Leningrad, 1945.

In English: Herbert E. Bowman, *Vissarion Belinski, 1811–1848: A Study in the Origins of Social Criticism in Russia*, Cambridge, Mass., 1954; informative.

In Italian: Ignazio Ambrogio, *Belinskij e la teoria del realismo*, Rome, 1963; excellent.

Valuable articles, uncollected writings, bibliographies, and a list of Belinsky's books are in three volumes (*55, 56, 57*) of *Literaturnoe Nasledstvo*, Moscow, 1948–52. The miscellaneous volume of articles edited by N. Brodsky, *Belinsky: istorik i teoretik literatury* (Moscow, 1949), is distinctly inferior.

On Belinsky and Hegel, see:

J. V. Laziczius, "Fr. Hegels Einfluss auf V. Belinskij," *Zeitschrift für slavische Philologie*, 5 (1928), 339–55.

D. Tschiževskij, "Hegel in Russland," in *Hegel bei den Slaven* (Reichenberg, 1934), esp. pp. 207–29.

Boris Jakowenko, *Ein Beitrag zur Geschichte des Hegelianismus in Russland* (Prague, 1934), pp. 46–62.

A. Koyré, "Hegel en Russie," in *Études sur l'histoire de la pensée philosophique en Russie* (Paris, 1950), esp. pp. 145–63.

The Marxist point of view is strongly put by Georg Lukács, "Die internationale Bedeutung der russischen demokratischen Literaturkritik," in *Der russische Realismus in der Weltliteratur* (Berlin, 1949), pp. 13–35.

NOTES: BELINSKY

1. I am less disturbed by Chizhevsky's further evidence of Belinsky's bad judgment (in *Hegel bei den Slaven*, p. 207, repeated by Koyré, *Études*, 147). Belinsky dismisses the second part of *Faust* and the *Divine Comedy* as "dead bad allegories" ("мертвая, пошлая символистика"). He simply echoes the opinion of Fr. T. Vischer

which he read in *Hallische Jahrbücher*. Obviously Belinsky did not have the linguistic equipment to grapple with the second part of *Faust* or the *Divine Comedy*. His violent rejection of French tragedy and Molière is more disturbing but is the kind of polemical injustice common with the greatest critics. Letter to I. I. Panaev (19 August 1839). *Izbrannye Pisma*, *1*, 235–6.

2. The set of Goethe is described in *Literaturnoe Nasledstvo*, *55* (1948), 554. Cf. letter to Botkin (12 August 1838), *Izbrannye Pisma*, *1*, 142.

3. See *Literaturnoe Nasledstvo*, *55* (1948), 512–13, for description. Most later references to the Schlegels are disparaging because of their conservative medievalism and Catholicism, though their eminence is recognized. Cf. esp. *G*, *2*, 660, *3*, 32, 159–60.

4. Gottlieb Ludwig Ernst Bachmann, *Vseobshchee nachertanie teorii iskusstva* (1832), trans. M. V. Khistyakov. See *G*, *1*, 454 and n. 784. Shevyrev translated Ast in *Moskovsky telegraf* (1828), no. 4. Belinsky alludes to Ast, *G*, *1*, 519. See note, *G*, *1*, 787. Rötscher's article "Das Verhältniss der Philosophie der Kunst und der Kritik zum einzelnen Kunstwerk," from *Abhandlungen zur Philosophie der Kunst* (1837), was translated by M. H. Katkov in *Moskovsky nablyudatel* (1838), no. 17. Belinsky reproduces it at length, *G*, *1*, 409–17. He quotes Rötscher on The Descent to the Mothers in *Faust II*, *G*, *2*, 81–82. References to Rötscher *Izbrannye pisma*, *1*, 216, and *2*, 125. But later Belinsky disparaged Rötscher as a Philistine: *Izbrannye pisma*, *2*, 144–5 (March 1841).

5. S. A. Vengerov makes much of Belinsky's early dependence on Nadezhdin and prints Nadezhdin's criticism, *Polnoe sobranie*, *1*, 453–542. On Katkov's interest in Hegel, see *Izbrannye pisma*, *1*, 86, 245.

6. See any description, esp. by Chizhevsky and Koyré.

7. Only the piece "The Division of Poetry into Genres" was published in 1841. "The Idea of Art," "The General Meaning of the Word 'Literature,' " and "A General View of Popular Poetry" only in 1862.

8. See above, n. 4.

9. The question of Belinsky's *Hamlet* interpretation is puzzling. It agrees in all essential features (self-dissolution, etc.) with that of Rötscher in *Die Kunst der dramatischen Darstellung* (Berlin, 1844), Vol. 2. But Belinsky's essay dates from 1838, and I am unable to trace an earlier printing of Rötscher's interpretation. An earlier, highly Hegelian interpretation is that of Eduard Gans, in *Vermischte Schriften*, Berlin, 1834. See Hans J. Lüthi, *Das deutsche Hamletbild seit Goethe*, Bern, 1951.

10. *G*, *1*, 16, 22–3.

11. Cf. *Sämmtliche Werke* (2d ed. Vienna, 1846), *1*, 11: Literature "der Inbegriff aller intellectuellen Fähigkeiten und Hervorbringungen einer Nation." Also *1*, 195. The term "physiognomy" of a nation is common in Herder, *Werke*, ed. Suphan, *13*, 365; *19*, 148.

12. *G*, *1*, 73: "Литературу не создают; она создается так, как создаются, без воли и ведома народа, язык и обычаи."

13. Belinsky reviewed the main folklore collections: those of Sukhanov, Sakharov and Krisha Danilov in four articles (all in Vol. 6 of Vengerov). A full discussion, M. Azadovsky, "Belinsky i russkaya narodnaya poeziya," in *Literaturnoe Nasledstvo*, *55*, 117–50.

14. *G*, *2*, 136, cf. *1*, 667.

15. Cf. this *History*, *2*, p. 23, e.g. F. Schlegel, *Werke*, *2*, 54.

16. *G*, *1*, 79: "Наша народность покуда состоит в верности изображения картин русской жизни."

17. *G*, *1*, 54: "Возвращение к естественности."

18. *G*, *1*, 103.

19. *G*, *1*, 107–8: "Шекспир навсегда помирил и сочетал ее с действительною жизнию . . . Вальтер Скотт . . . был вторым Шекспиром, который докончил соединение искусства с жизнию."

20. *G*, *1*, 141–2.

21. *G*, *1*, 107, 111. Note that Hazlitt calls Shakespeare a "Proteus of the Human intellect," *Works*, ed. Howe, *8*, 42. Schiller and Coleridge emphasized Shakespeare's objectivity. See also M. H. Abrams, *The Mirror and the Lamp* (New York, 1953), 244 ff.

22. *G*, *1*, 127: "Главный отличительный признак творчества состоит в таинственном ясновидении, в поэтическом сомнабуле," p. 129.

23. *G*, *1*, 135: "Угадано чувством в минуту поэтического откровения!"

24. *G*, *1*, 136–7: "Тип из типов . . . мистический миф."

25. Cf. this *History*, *2*, 77. Nodier's "Des types en littérature," in *Rêveries littéraires morales et fantastiques* (Brussels, 1832), pp. 41–58.

26. *G*, *1*, 431: "Не такова истинная поэзия: ее содержание не вопросы дня, а вопросы веков, не интересы страны, а интересы мира, не участь партий, а судьбы человечества."

27. *G*, *1*, 430–1: "Если хотите, оно и служит обществу, выражая его же собственное сознание . . . но оно служит обществу не как что-нибудь для него существующее, а как нечто существующее по себе и для себя, в самом себе имеющее свою цель и свою причину."

28. *G, 1,* 437.

29. *G, 1,* 439: "Что художественно, то уже и нравственно."

30. *G, 1,* 456: "Истина открылась человечеству впервые—в *искусстве,* которое есть *истина в созерцании,* то есть не в отвлеченной мысли . . . Поэт мыслит образами," p. 464.

31. *G, 1,* 469: "Человек пьет, ест, одевается—это мир *призраков,* . . . человек чувствует, мыслит, сознает себя органом, сосудом духа, конечною частичностью общего и бесконечного—это мир *действительности.*"

32. *G, 1,* 466.

33. *G, 1,* 495.

34. *G, 1,* 508: "Лицо ревизора есть источник, из которого всё выходит и в который всё возвращается." Note that "Totalität" is quoted in German, *G, 1,* 501.

35. *G, 1,* 492: "Это больше нежели . . . зеркало действительности, но более походит на действительность, нежели действительность походит сама на себя, ибо всё это—художественная действительность."

36. *G, 1,* 475.

37. *G, 1,* 512: "Это горе,—только не от *ума,* а от *умничанья,*" p. 516.

38. *G, 1,* 559.

39. *G, 1,* 560. On analogy with a plant, much in Abrams, esp. 168 ff., 202 ff.

40. *G, 1,* 631.

41. *G, 1,* 641.

42. *G, 1,* 643: "Можно очень натурально изобразить пытку, казнь, несчастную смерть человека, упавшего в нетрезвом виде в помойную яму,—но все эти изображения будут возмутительны для души, неизящны и безмысленны, ибо в них не будет никакой разумной мысли, никакой разумной цели."

43. *G, 1,* 643, 644, 649.

44. *G, 1,* 649–50.

45. *G, 1,* 557: "У искусства всякого народа есть свое историческое развитие, вследствие которого определяется характер и род деятельности поэта."

46. *G, 1,* 653: "Чем выше поэт, тем больше принадлежит он обществу, среди которого родился, тем теснее связано развитие, направление и даже характер его таланта с историческим развитием общества."

47. *G, 1,* 670. Note that most editions have the reading "tumannaya' (cloudy) instead of "gumannaya" (humane).

48. *G*, *1*, 671.

49. *G*, *1*, 673, 667.

50. *G*, *2*, 12. Cf. Jean Paul's *Vorschule der Aesthetik*. par. 72. The term comes from Friedrich Schlegel's *Athenaeum*, Fragment, No. 247.

51. *G*, *2*, 28.

52. *G*, *2*, 40.

53. *G*, *2*, 49.

54. *G*, *2*, 53.

55. *G*, *2*, 51, 58.

56. *G*, *2*, 33: "Высказал всю сущность поэзии, сознательно' развитую германским мышлением."

57. *G*, *2*, 67: "Искусство есть . . . мышление в образах." Cf. A. W. Schlegel, in 1798: poetry is "bildlich anschauender Gedanken-ausdruck." *Vorlesungen über philosophische Kunstlehre*, ed. A. Wünsche (Leipzig, 1911), p. 35. K. F. E. Trahndorff, *Aesthetik* (Berlin, 1827), p. 85: "Die Poesie . . . denkt Bilder." See also p. 86.

58. *G*, *2*, 95.

59. *G*, *2*, 100.

60. *G*, *2*, 113.

61. *G*, *2*, 121.

62. *G*, *2*, 287.

63. *G*, *2*, 313.

64. *G*, *2*, 291, 300: "Никто не может быть выше века и страны."

65. *G*, *2*, 288–9.

66. *G*, *2*, 313.

67. *G*, *2*, 354: "Решительно отрицает искусство для искусства."

68. *G*, *2*, 356–7.

69. *G*, *2*, 357.

70. *G*, *2*, 361.

71. *G*, *2*, 363.

72. *G*, *2*, 422.

73. *G*, *2*, 481.

74. *G*, *2*, 457: "Чистая, беспримесная проза . . . Мы под 'прозою' разумеем богатство внутреннего поэтического содержания, мужественную зрелость и крепость мысли . . ."

75. *G*, *2*, 460: "Факт действительности . . . проведенный через фантазию поэта, озаренный светом общего значения, *возведенный в перл создания*, и потому более похожий на самого себя, более верный самому себе, нежели самая рабская копия с действительности верна своему оригиналу. Так, на портрете, сделанном великим живописцем, человек более похож на самого себя, чем даже на свое отражение в дагерротипе . . ."

76. *G*, *3*, 174: "Исторического движения общества."

77. *G*, *3*, 178: "Между тем время шло вперед, а с ним шла вперед и жизнь, порождая из себя новые явления, дающие сознанию новые факты и подвигающие его на пути развития . . . Мы не завидуем *готовым натурам* . . ."

78. *G*, *3*, 190–1.

79. *G*, 3, 210.

80. *G*, 3, 266.

81. *G*, 3, 335.

82. *G*, *3*, 335, 337: "Нельзя сделаться великим живописцем, имея какой бы то ни было великий талант, если в годы изучения искусства нет хороших натурщиков . . . Пушкин явился именно в то время, когда только что сделалось возможным явление на Руси поэзии, как искусства."

83. *G*, *3*, 363: "Светлою, ясною и отрадною грустью . . ."

84. *G*, *3*, 378, 380.

85. *G*, *3*, 403.

86. *G*, *3*, 410.

87. *G*, *3*, 405.

88. *G*, *3*, 402.

89. *G*, *3*, 410: "Время опередило поэзию Пушкина и большую часть его произведений лишило того животрепещущего интереса, который возможен только как удовлетворительный ответ на тревожные, болезненные вопросы настоящего."

90. *G*, *3*, 412.

91. *G*, *3*, 457–8.

92. *G*, *3*, 467, 472–3, 476.

93. *G*, *3*, 511: "Разве вина поэта, что в России всё движется так быстро? . . . Если б в 'Онегине' ничто не казалось теперь устаревшим или отсталым от нашего времени,—это было бы явным признаком, что в этой поэме нет истины, что в ней изображено не действительно существовавшее, а воображаемое общество; в таком случае что ж бы это была за поэма и стоило бы говорить о ней?"

94. *G*, *3*, 516: "Гений никогда не упреждает своего времени, но всегда только угадывает его не для всех видимое содержание и смысл."

95. *G*, *3*, 562, 552: "Нравственного эмбриона! . . . Татьяна, как личность, является . . . подобною египетской статуе, неподвижной, тяжелой и связанной."

96. *G*, *3*, 564.

97. *G*, *3*, 567, 587–8.

98. *G*, *3*, 568–9.

99. *G*, *3*, 583–4.

100. *G*, *3*, 594.

101. *G*, *3*, 44: "Русский великий поэт, будучи одарен от природы и равным великому европейскому поэту талантом . . . может соперничетвовать с ним только в *форме*, но не в *содержании* поэзии."

102. Vengerov, *12*, 224 (actually ed. by V. S. Spiridonov, Moscow, 1926).

103. *G*, *3*, 56–7.

104. *G*, *3*, 67: "Из всех критиков самый великий, самый гениальный, самый непогрешительный—время."

105. *G*, *3*, 649: "Так называемую *натуральную школу*." Cf. p. 774, and p. 902 n. referring to Bulgarin's use of the term in *Severnaya Pchela* (1846), No. 22.

106. *G*, *3*, 649.

107. *G*, *3*, 674: "Фантастическое в наше время может иметь место только в домах умалишенных, а не в литературе, и находиться в заведывании врачей, а не поэтов."

108. *G*, *3*, 783: "Близкое сходство изображаемых ею лиц с их образцами в действительности . . ."

109. *G*, *3*, 781.

110. *G*, *3*, 788–9: "В этом отношении литература сделала едва ли не больше: она скорее способствовала возбуждению в обществе такого направления, нежели только отразила его в себе, скорее упредила его, нежели только не отстала от него."

111. *G*, *3*, 797.

112. *G*, *3*, 801.

113. *G*, *3*, 677: "Вперед итти можно, назад—нельзя . . ."

114. *G*, *3*, 68–86 (on *Poor People*), 673–5 (*Double*, and *Mr. Prokharchin*), 836–7 (*The Landlady*). Also letter to Annenkov (15 February 1848), *Izbrannye Pisma*, *2*, 388.

115. *G*, *3*, 809.

116. On George Sand, see, e.g., *G*, *3*, 24, "without doubt the first talent in the whole writing world of our time" ("Жорж Занд, бесспорно, первый талант во всем пишущем мире нашего времени"). On Sue, the review of *Mystères de Paris*, *G*, *2*, 628–46, part of which is highly unfavorable. Still, Belinsky thought Sue had more talent than Balzac, Dumas, Janin, Soulié, etc. (*G*, *3*, 22).

117. On Goethe, note the review of the Russian translation of the *Roman Elegies*, in Vengerov, *6*, 241–72, and three uncollected reviews in *Literaturnoe Nasledstvo*, *55* (1948), 342, 344, 361. There is a long note by V. Zhirmunsky, pp. 345–50.

118. *G*, *3*, 791: "Признавая, что искусство, прежде всего должно

быть искусством, мы тем не менее думаем, что мысль о каком-то чистом, отрешенном искусстве, живущем в своей собственной сфере, не имеющей ничего общего с другими сторонами жизни, есть мысль отвлеченная, мечтательная. Такого искусства никогда и нигде не бывало.''

119. *G, 3*, 797: ''Отнимать у искусства право служить общественным интересам—значит не возвышать, а унижать его, потому что это значит лишать его самой живой силы, то есть мысли, делать его предметом какого-то сибаритского наслаждения, игрушкою праздных ленивцев.''

120. *G, 3*, 789: ''Какими бы прекрасными мыслями ни было наполнено стихотворение, как бы ни сильно отзывалось оно современными вопросами, но если в нем нет поэзии,— в нем не может быть ни прекрасных мыслей и никаких вопросов . . .''

121. *G, 3*, 798.

122. *G, 3*, 790: ''Надобно уметь явления действительности провести через свою фантазию, дать им новую жизнь . . . смысл чего-то единого, полного, целого, замкнутого в самом себе.''

123. *G, 3*, 792. ''Способность изображать явления действительности без всякого отношения к самому себе—есть опять-таки выражение натуры поэта.''

124. *G, 3*, 809.

125. *G, 3*, 813.

126. *G, 3*, 673–4: ''В 'Двойнике' автор обнаружил огромную силу творчества, характер героя принадлежит к числу самых глубоких, смелих и истинных концепций . . .''

127. Dostoevsky's reminiscences in *Diary of a Writer* for January 1877, chap. 2, sec. 3. Disillusionment is expressed most strongly in a letter to Annenkov (15 February, 1848): "Every one of his new works is a new failure. . . . We boasted about the genius Dostoevsky. I, the first critic, made a thrice-double ass of myself" (''Каждое его новое произведение—новое падение. . . . Надулись же вы, друг мой, с Достоевским—гением! . . . Я, первый критик, разыграл тут осла в квадрате''). *Izbrannye Pisma*, 2, 388. Belinsky alludes to *Tempest*, V. 1. 295. Caliban says: "What a thrice-double ass / Was I, to take this drunkard for a god, / And worship this dull fool!"

128. *G, 3*, 684: '' 'Мертвые души' стоят выше всего, что было и есть в русской литературе . . .''

129. *G, 1*, 147.

130. *G, 3*, 713–14: ''Не будь на вашей книге выставлено вашего

имени, и будь из нее выключены те места, где вы говорите о себе как писатель, кто бы подумал, что эта надутая и неопрятная шумиха слов и фраз—произведение автора 'Ревизора' и 'Мертвых душ'?''

131. *G, 3*, 709:''Проповедник кнута, апостол невежества, поборник обскурантизма и мракобесия . . .''

132. See Karl Löwith, *Von Hegel bis Nietzsche* (Zurich, 1941), esp. pp. 97 ff.

CHRONOLOGICAL TABLE
OF WORKS

FRANCE

1809	de Barante:	*De la littérature française au XVIIIe siècle*
1813	Sismondi:	*De la littérature du Midi de l'Europe*
	Madame de Stael:	*De l'Allemagne*
1823	Claude Fauriel:	*Chants populaires de la Grèce moderne*
	Stendhal:	*Racine et Shakespeare*
1827	Hugo:	Preface to *Cromwell*
1828	Philarète Chasles:	*Tableau de la marche et des progrès de la littérature française au XVIe siècle*
	Sainte-Beuve:	*Tableau de la poésie française au XVIe siècle*
1828–29	Villemain:	*Tableau de littérature française au XVIIIe siècle*
1830	J.-J. Ampère	*Discours sur l'histoire de la poésie*
	Villemain:	*Tableau de la littérature au moyen âge en France, en Espagne et en Angleterre*
1831	Leroux:	"Aux Philosophes. De la poésie de notre époque," in *Revue encyclopédique*
1833	Désiré Nisard:	*Contre la littérature facile*
1834	Gautier:	Preface to *Mademoiselle de Maupin*
	Désiré Nisard:	*Études de mœurs et de critique sur les poètes latin de la décadence*
1836	Gustave Planche:	*Portraits littéraires*
	Victor Cousin:	*Du Vrai, du Beau et du Bien*
	Sainte-Beuve:	*Critiques et portraits littéraires*, 3 vols.

1838	Magnin:	*Les Origines du théâtre moderne*
1839–40	J.-J. Ampère:	*Histoire littéraire de la France avant le douzième siècle*
	Sainte-Beuve:	*Port Royal,* Vol. 1
1841	Ampère:	*Histoire de la littérature française au moyen âge*
1842	Sainte-Beuve:	*Port Royal,* Vol. 2
	Charles Magnin:	*Causeries et méditations*
1843	Saint-Marc Girardin:	*Cours de littérature dramatique* Vol. 1 (5 vols. till 1868)
1844	Désiré Nisard:	*Histoire de littérature française* Vols. 1 and 2
	Gautier:	*Les Grotesques*
	Sainte-Beuve:	*Portraits de femmes* *Portraits littéraires,* 2 vols.
1846	Fauriel:	*Histoire de la poésie provençale*
	Philarète Chasles:	*Etudes sur le XVIIIᵉ siècle en Angleterre*
	Sainte-Beuve:	*Portraits contemporains,* 3 vols.
1847	Chasles:	*Études sur l'Antiquité*
	Alexandre Vinet:	*Études sur Pascal*
1848	Sainte-Beuve:	*Port Royal,* Vol. 3
1849	Alexandre Vinet:	*Études sur la littérature française au XIX siècle,* 3 vols.
	Nisard:	*Histoire de la littérature française,* Vol. 3
1851	Sainte-Beuve:	*Causeries du Lundi,* Vols. 1, 2, 3
1852	Sainte-Beuve:	*Causeries du Lundi,* Vol. 4, 5 *Derniers Portraits littéraires*
1853	Sainte-Beuve:	*Causeries du Lundi,* Vols. 6, 7, 8
	Fauriel:	*Dante,* 2 vols.
	Chasles:	*Études sur l'Allemagne,* 2 vols.
1854	Sainte-Beuve:	*Causeries du Lundi,* Vols. 9, 10
1856	Sainte-Beuve:	*Causeries du Lundi,* Vol. 11
1857	Sainte-Beuve:	*Causeries du Lundi,* Vols. 12, 13 *Études sur Virgile*
1858	Nisard:	*Études de Critiques littéraires*
1859	Sainte-Beuve:	*Port Royal,* Vols. 4, 5
1860	Sainte-Beuve:	*Chateaubriand et son groupe littéraire sous l'Empire,* 2 vols.
1861	Sainte-Beuve:	*Causeries du Lundi,* Vol. 14
1862	Sainte-Beuve:	*Causeries du Lundi,* Vol. 15

1863	Sainte-Beuve:	*Nouveaux Lundis*, Vols. 1, 2
1865	Sainte-Beuve:	*Nouveaux Lundis*, Vols. 3, 4
1866	Sainte-Beuve:	*Nouveaux Lundis*, Vols. 5, 6
1867	Sainte-Beuve:	*Nouveaux Lundis*, Vols. 7, 8, 9
1868	Sainte-Beuve:	*Nouveaux Lundis*, Vols. 10, 11
1870	Sainte-Beuve:	*Nouveaux Lundis*, Vols. 12, 13
		Premiers Lundis, 3 vols.
1872	Gautier:	*Histoire du romantisme*

ITALY

1829	Mazzini:	"D'una letteratura europea"
1831	Scalvini:	*Dei promessi sposi*
1832	Mazzini:	"Pensieri . Ai poeti de secolo XIX"
1836	Mazzini:	"Della fatalità considerata come elemente drammatico"
1837	Mazzini:	"Italian literature since 1830"
1838	Mazzini:	"The Present State of French Literature"
1840	Tommaseo:	*Dizionario estetico*
1841	Gioberti:	*Del Bello*
1843	Gioberti:	*Del Primato morale e civile degli Italiani*
	Mazzini:	"On the Works of Thomas Carlyle"
	Tommaseo:	*Studi critici*
1845	Emiliani Guidici:	*Storia delle belle lettere in Italia*
1846	Tenca:	"Delle condizioni dell'odierna letteratura in Italia"
1852	Tenca:	"A proposito di una storia della letteratura Italiana"
1858	Tommaseo:	*Inspirazione ed Arte*
1860	Scalvini:	*Scritti.* ed. Tommaseo
1861	Mazzini:	*Scritti letterari*, 2 vols.
1866–72	Settembrini:	*Lezioni di letteratura italiana,* 2 vols.
1870–71	De Sanctis:	*Storia della letteratura italiana,* 2 vols.

ENGLAND AND SCOTLAND

| 1820–26 | | *Retrospective Review,* first series, ed. Southern |

1823	De Quincey:	"On the Knocking at the Gate in *Macbeth*"
1824	Richard Price:	Preface to second ed. of Thomas Warton's *History of English Poetry*
1825	Carlyle:	*Life of Schiller*
	Macaulay:	"Milton"
1827	Carlyle:	*German Romance*
		"Jean Paul Friedrich Richter"
		"State of German Literature"
1828	Carlyle	"Burns"
		"Goethe"
	De Quincey:	"Rhetoric"
1829	Carlyle:	"Novalis"
		"Voltaire"
1831	Carlyle:	"William Taylor's *Historic Survey of German Poetry*"
	Macaulay:	"Boswell"
	Collier:	*History of English Dramatic Poetry,* 3 vols.
1832	Carlyle:	"Goethe's Works"
		"Boswell's *Life of Johnson*"
1833	Carlyle:	"Diderot"
	Mill:	"What is Poetry?", "The Two Kinds of Poetry"
1833–34	Carlyle:	"Sartor Resartus" (in *Fraser's Magazine*)
1834–35	De Quincey:	"Samuel Taylor Coleridge"
1836	Robert Chambers:	*History of English Language and Literature*
1837–39	Henry Hallam:	*Literature of Europe*
1837	Mill:	Review of Carlyle's *French Revolution*
1838	Carlyle:	"Sir Walter Scott"
	Mill:	"Alfred de Vigny"
1839	Carlyle:	*Critical and Miscellaneous Essays*
	De Quincey:	"William Wordsworth"
1840	De Quincey:	"Theory of Greek Tragedy"
		"Style"
	Leigh Hunt:	Preface to *Dramatic Works of Wycherley, Congreve, Vanbrugh, Farqhuar, and Sheridan*
	Mill:	Essay on Coleridge

1841	Carlyle:	*On Heroes, Hero-worship and the Heroic in History*
1843	Macaulay:	*Critical and Historical Essays*
	Ruskin:	*Modern Painters*, Vol. 1
1844	Leigh Hunt:	*Imagination and Fancy*
1845	De Quincey:	"On Wordsworth's Poetry"
1846	Leigh Hunt:	*Wit and Humour*
	Ruskin:	*Modern Painters*, Vol. 2
1848	De Quincey:	"The Poetry of Pope"
1851	De Quincey:	"Lord Carlisle on Pope"

THE UNITED STATES

1830	William Ellery Channing:	"The Importance and Means of a National Literature"
1836	Emerson:	*Nature*
1839	Jones Very:	*Essays and Poems*
1841	Emerson:	*Essays*
1842	Poe:	"Hawthorne's Tales" Review of Dickens' *Barnaby Rudge*
1844	Emerson:	*Essays, Second Series*
1845	Margaret Fuller:	*Woman in the Nineteenth Century*
1846	Margaret Fuller:	*Papers on Literature and Art*
	Poe:	"The Philosophy of Composition"
1847	Thoreau:	"Thomas Carlyle and his Works"
1850	Poe:	"The Poetic Principle"
	Emerson:	*Representative Men*
1856	Emerson:	*English Traits*

GERMANY

1822	Uhland:	*Walther von der Vogelweide*
1828	Menzel:	*Die deutsche Literatur*, 2 vols.
1830	Rosenkranz:	*Geschichte der deutschen Poesie im Mittelalter*
1832	Börne:	*Briefe aus Paris*
	Rosenkranz:	*Handbuch einer allgemeinen Geschichte der Poesie*, 3 vols.
1833	Heine:	*Die romantische Schule*
1834	Wienbarg:	*Aesthetische Feldzüge*
1836	Gutzkow:	*Götter, Helden, Don Quixote* *Über Goethe am Wendepunkte zweier Jahrhunderte*

1837–42	Rötscher:	*Abhandlungen zur Philosophie der Kunst*
1835–42	Gervinus:	*Geschichte der poetischen National-litteratur der Deutschen,* 5 vols.
1839	Ulrici:	*Über Shakespeares dramatische Kunst*
1840	Heine:	*Über Ludwig Börne*
1842	Mundt:	*Geschichte der Literatur der Gegenwart*
1843	Carus:	*Goethe, zu dessen näheren Verständnis*
1844	Vischer:	*Kritische Gänge,* Vol. 1
	Hebbel:	Vorwort zu *Maria Magdalena*
	Danzel:	*Über die Aesthetik der Hegelschen Philosophie*
1846–57	Vischer:	*Aesthetik,* 5 vols.
1846	Ruge:	*Gesammelte Schriften,* 10 vols.
1847	Rosenkranz:	*Göthe und seine Werke*
1849	Gervinus:	*Shakespeare,* 4 vols.
1850	Danzel:	*Lessing,* "Shakespeare und noch immer kein Ende"
1853	Rosenkranz:	*Aesthetik des Hässlichen*
1854	Heine:	*Lutezia*
1857	Eichendorff:	*Geschichte der poetischen Literatur Deutschlands*
1859	Lassalle:	*Franz von Sickingen*
1866	Rosenkranz:	*Diderot,* 2 vols.
1886	Vischer:	"Das Symbol"

RUSSIA

1823	Vyazemsky:	Preface to Pushkin's *Prisoner from the Caucasus (Kavkazsky plennik)*
1825	Pushkin:	"On classical and romantic poetry" ("O poezii klassicheskoy i roman-ticheskoy")
1834	Belinsky:	"Literary Reveries" ("Literaturnye mechtaniya")
1835	Belinsky:	"On the Russian short story and the stories of Gogol" ("O russkoy povesti i povestyakh Gogolya")
1836	Pushkin:	"Alexander Radischev"

1838	Belinsky:	"Hamlet"
1840	Belinsky:	"Menzel, as a critic of Goethe" ("Menzel, kritik Gëte")
		"Wit from Woe" ("Gore ot uma")
		"The Hero of Our Time" ("Geroy nashego vremeni")
1841	Belinsky:	"The Poems of M. Lermontov" ("Stikhotvoreniya M. Lermontova")
1842	Belinsky:	"The Division of Poetry into Kinds and Modes" ("Razdelenie poezii na rody i vidy")
		"The Idea of Art" ("Ideya iskusstva," printed in 1862)
		"A General View of Popular Poetry" ("Obschiy vzglyad na narodnuyu poeziyu," printed in 1862)
		"Russian Literature in 1841" ("Russkaya literatura v 1841 godu")
1842	Belinsky:	"Chichikov's Journeys or The Dead Souls" ("Pokhozheniya Chichikova ili Mertvye Dushi")
		"A Speech on Criticism" ("Rech o kritike")
1843	Belinsky:	"Russian Literature in 1842" ("Russkaya literatura v 1842 godu")
1843–46	Belinsky:	"The Works of Alexander Pushkin" ("Sochineniya Aleksandra Push-kina"), 11 articles
1844	Belinsky:	"Russian Literature in 1843" ("Russkaya literatura v 1843 godu")
1845	Belinsky	"Russian Literature in 1844" ("Russkaya literatura v 1844 godu")
1846	Belinsky:	"Russian Literature in 1845" ("Russkaya literatura v 1845 godu")
		"Reflections and remarks on Russian literature" ("Mysli i zametki o russkoy literature")
		"The Petersburg Miscellany" ("Peterburgsky sbornik")
1847	Belinsky:	"A Look at Russian Literature in 1846" ("Vzglyad na russkoyu literaturu 1846 goda")

"Selected Passages from a Corre-
spondence with Friends by Nikolay
Gogol" ("Vybrannye mesta iz pere-
piski s druzyami Nikolaya Gogolya")
Letter to Gogol ("Pismo k
Gogolyu," printed in 1855)

1848   Belinsky: "A Look at Russian literature in
1847" ("Vzglyad na russkoyu
literaturu 1847 goda")

INDEX OF TOPICS AND TERMS